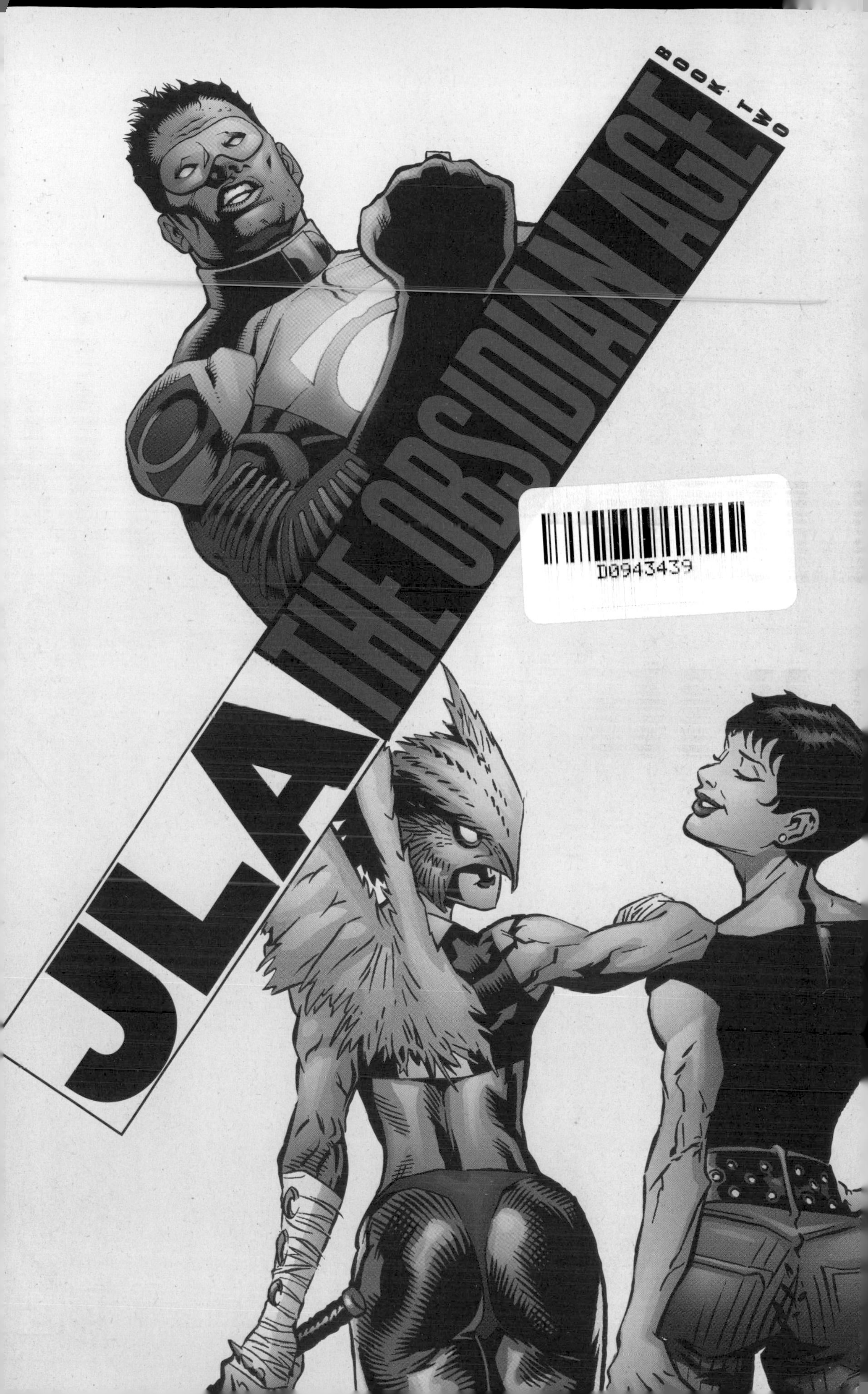
BOOK TWO
JLA
THE OBSIDIAN AGE

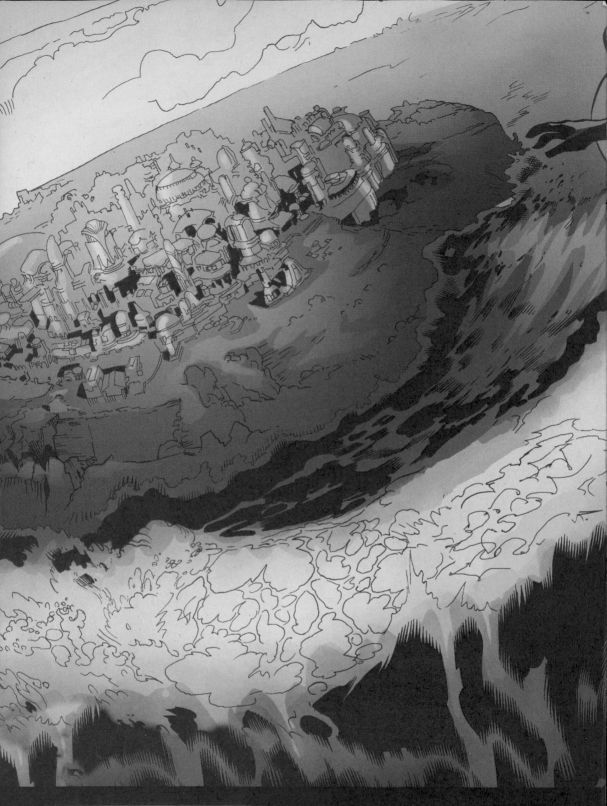

JLA THE OBSIDIAN AGE

Dan DiDio VP-Editorial Dan Raspler Editor-original series Bob Greenberger Senior Editor-Collected Edition Robbin Brosterman Senior Art Director
Paul Levitz President & Publisher Georg Brewer VP-Design & Retail Product Development Richard Bruning VP-Creative Director
Patrick Caldon Senior VP-Finance & Operations Chris Caramalis VP-Finance Terri Cunningham VP-Managing Editor Allison Gill VP-Manufacturing
Lillian Laserson Senior VP & General Counsel David McKillips VP-Advertising John Nee VP-Business Development
Cheryl Rubin VP-Licensing & Merchandising Bob Wayne VP-Sales & Marketing

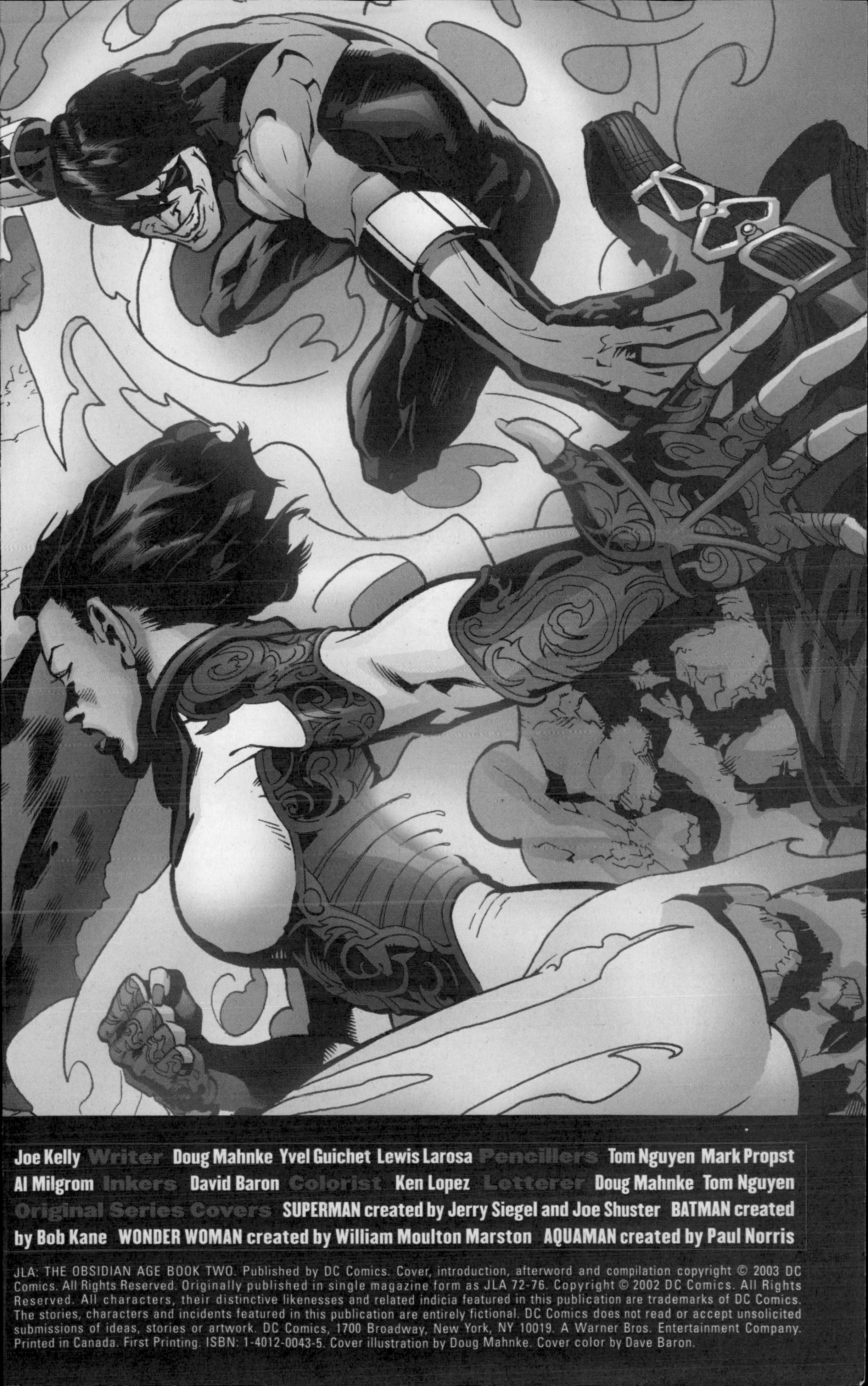

Joe Kelly Writer **Doug Mahnke Yvel Guichet Lewis Larosa** Pencillers **Tom Nguyen Mark Propst Al Milgrom** Inkers **David Baron** Colorist **Ken Lopez** Letterer **Doug Mahnke Tom Nguyen** Original Series Covers **SUPERMAN created by Jerry Siegel and Joe Shuster BATMAN created by Bob Kane WONDER WOMAN created by William Moulton Marston AQUAMAN created by Paul Norris**

WHAT HAS

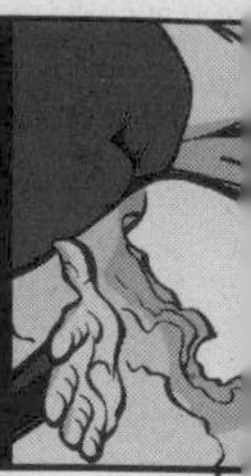

Aquaman and the underwater nation of Atlantis had gone missing during the Imperiex War, and the JLA (after picking up the pieces of the team) created a holographic memorial to their fallen teammate and the lost city.

The next few months were uneventful. Then two warriors from the past, a Native American shaman named *Manitou Raven* and a mechanical monstrosity called *Tezumak* attacked the JLA, without warning, believing the League to be the fabled Destroyers who would seek to eradicate their civilization 3000 years in the past. Mysteriously, Green Lantern recognized Manitou from his recurring dreams of a dying JLA.

The JLA thwarted the pair, but not before they escaped back into the past using an unknown magic. However, when the smoke from battle cleared, there was Atlantis: returned, above water and in ruins. With the help of some of the greatest mages in the DC Universe, the League determined that a change in Atlantis's history had caused it to rise from the depths of the Atlantic Ocean 3000 years in the past, the same era from which Manitou Raven and Tezumak hailed.

After finding the letters "JLA" carved into the bottom of an Atlantean pool, the League determined this was a message from Aquaman who was alive and trapped in the past. Somehow he and Atlantis had been protected from destruction but transported back to a dark, uncharted era. Back to the Obsidian Age.

Led by the Atlantean-born mage Tempest (who has also been Aquaman's partner), the world's most powerful magicians helped the JLA open a portal to the past and charge into the unknown to save their lost teammate.

But the magic was impure; the spell was tainted. Green Lantern's dreams of death grew stronger as the JLA traveled through the portal. The stench of death was everywhere. Batman whispered a command under his breath as suddenly a fiery, chaotic explosion took the lives of the World's Greatest Super-Heroes.

One month passed and signs of trouble began emerging as slowly, almost unnoticeably, the world's oceans and lakes began losing water. And on the above-water Atlantis a demonic presence revealed itself to Zatanna and proceeded to take over and finally consume her body, leaving the mysterious demon hungry for more.

Then from the dark halls of the JLA Watchtower on the moon, probes were launched and sent to eight who were ready to answer the call to duty: former JLAers The Atom, Green Arrow, Firestorm and Major Disaster; the Justice Society's Hawkgirl, the demonic Jason Blood, an enigma named Faith, and their leader, Batman's former partner, Nightwing. These heroes were enlisted by the Dark Knight to accept the solemn honor of following the heroes who served as the greatest heroes of all time. This was the new JLA.

The new League's first mission sent them back to Atlantis for a surprising discovery. The waters of the Earth were being drawn there, to a reservoir under the surface. As they checked their video monitors they made a gruesome discovery: Superman! At least it *was* Superman, his fleshless skeleton covered in the rags of his costume and a trident plunged through his chest on which was etched one word: "Come."

Meanwhile, 3000 years ago, several warriors of different races from all over the Earth had been

GONE BEFORE...

called together by an Atlantean witch called *Gamemnae*. Their duty: to help defend Atlantis against a seven-headed hydra from the future that she had predicted would destroy Atlantis. In this ancient time, she had raised Atlantis from the depths of the sea in hopes of returning it to glory, and fulfilling the nation's destiny of becoming the greatest, most powerful civilization on the planet, a mix of science and sorcery never to be equaled.

Two of her warriors returned from the future where they had battled this hydra, but now one of them, Manitou Raven, began to have doubts about the mission's sanctity. The hydra had seemed honorable, like heroes to him. Could this Gamemnae be trusted to be truthful? What if he was on the wrong side? As he struggled with his doubt he caught a whiff of something in the air… the Destroyers… The Justice League… was here!

The JLA had been weakened by their trip but they had survived. As they investigated an Atlantis that was supposed to be underwater, Green Lantern's dire dreams continued and the League covertly searched for the place in which they had discovered the inscription "JLA."

Then they found what they were looking for as Aquaman rose mightily from the pool. At least it *looked* liked Aquaman, an Aquaman made entirely of… water?

Welcome to the Obsidian Age. The future ends now.

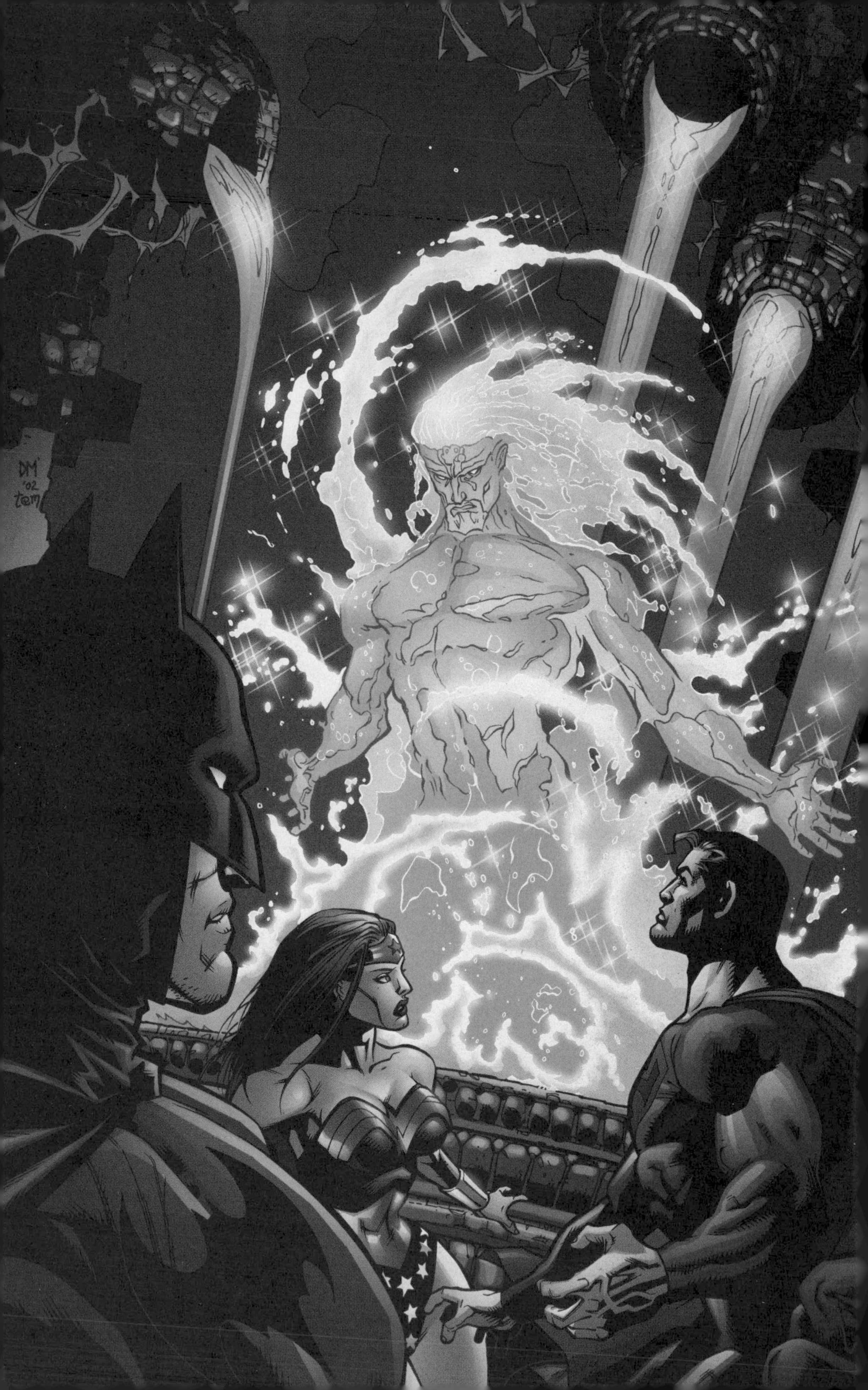
DM '02
tem

IT BEGAN WITH A DREAM.

A NIGHTMARE. FLAMES. *DEATH.* JARHANPUR, MY *BELOVED* HOME IN *RUINS.* MY BELOVED PEOPLE... *BROKEN.*

THEN CAME THE *WORDS,* LIKE A GOD WEEPING, AND I KNEW... IT WAS PROPHECY.

"*A HYDRA* COMES, RIDING TOMORROW'S DAWN TO RAIN HELL ON PARADISE."

"SEVEN RAVENOUS HEADS THAT MUST BE *SEVERED,* LEST THEY DEVOUR THE VERY EARTH AND DRINK HER BLOOD. HER *LIFE.*"

"GATHER FORCES WHILE YE MAY, KINDRED SONS AND DAUGHTERS OF THE EARTH WHO WALK AS GODS, TO *FIGHT* AS GODS DO... *A LEAGUE OF WARRIORS.*"

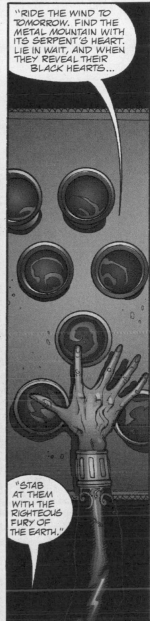

"RIDE THE WIND TO TOMORROW. FIND THE METAL MOUNTAIN WITH ITS SERPENT'S HEART. LIE IN WAIT, AND WHEN THEY REVEAL THEIR BLACK HEARTS..."

"STAB AT THEM WITH THE RIGHTEOUS FURY OF THE EARTH."

THE *DESTROYERS* ARE *HERE,* IN *ATLANTIS.* THE PROPHECY HAS COME *TRUE.*

THE FUTURE *BELONGS* TO THE *DESTROYERS...*

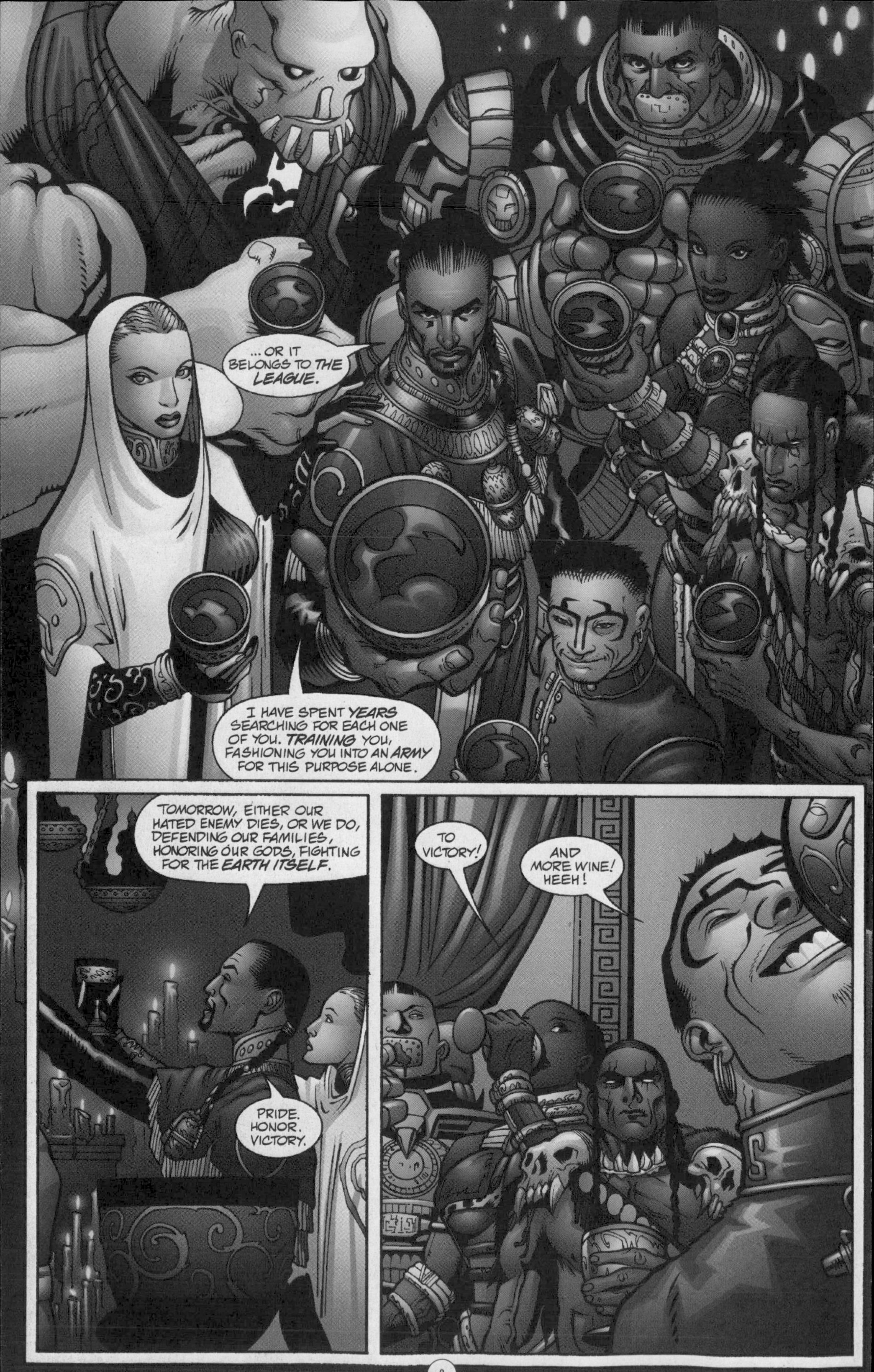
...OR IT BELONGS TO THE LEAGUE.
I HAVE SPENT YEARS SEARCHING FOR EACH ONE OF YOU. TRAINING YOU, FASHIONING YOU INTO AN ARMY FOR THIS PURPOSE ALONE.
TOMORROW, EITHER OUR HATED ENEMY DIES, OR WE DO, DEFENDING OUR FAMILIES, HONORING OUR GODS, FIGHTING FOR THE EARTH ITSELF.
PRIDE. HONOR. VICTORY.
TO VICTORY!
AND MORE WINE! HEEH!

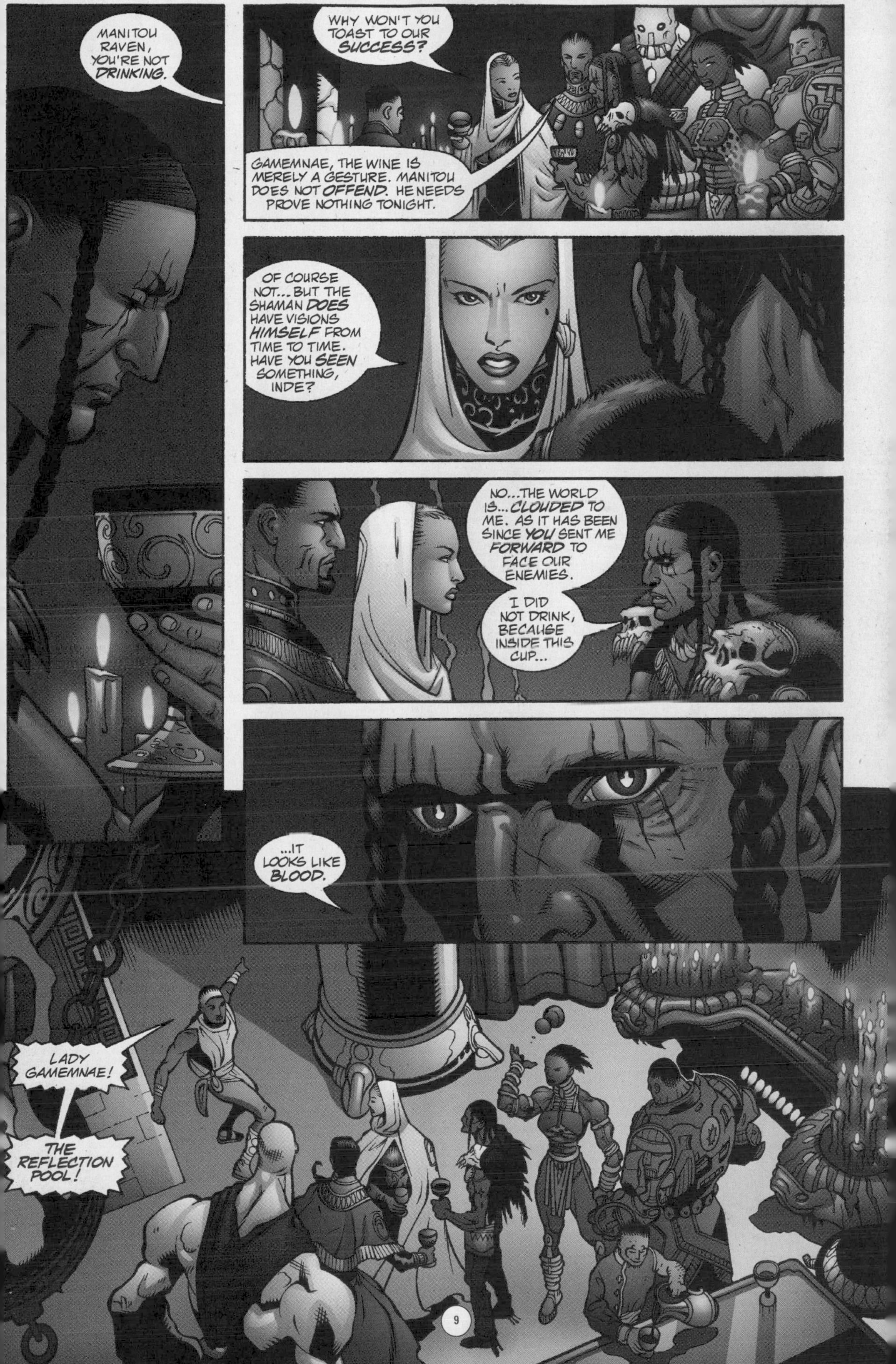
MANITOU RAVEN, YOU'RE NOT DRINKING.
WHY WON'T YOU TOAST TO OUR SUCCESS?
GAMEMNAE, THE WINE IS MERELY A GESTURE. MANITOU DOES NOT OFFEND. HE NEEDS PROVE NOTHING TONIGHT.
OF COURSE NOT... BUT THE SHAMAN DOES HAVE VISIONS HIMSELF FROM TIME TO TIME. HAVE YOU SEEN SOMETHING, INDE?
NO... THE WORLD IS... CLOUDED TO ME. AS IT HAS BEEN SINCE YOU SENT ME FORWARD TO FACE OUR ENEMIES.
I DID NOT DRINK, BECAUSE INSIDE THIS CUP...
...IT LOOKS LIKE BLOOD.
LADY GAMEMNAE!
THE REFLECTION POOL!

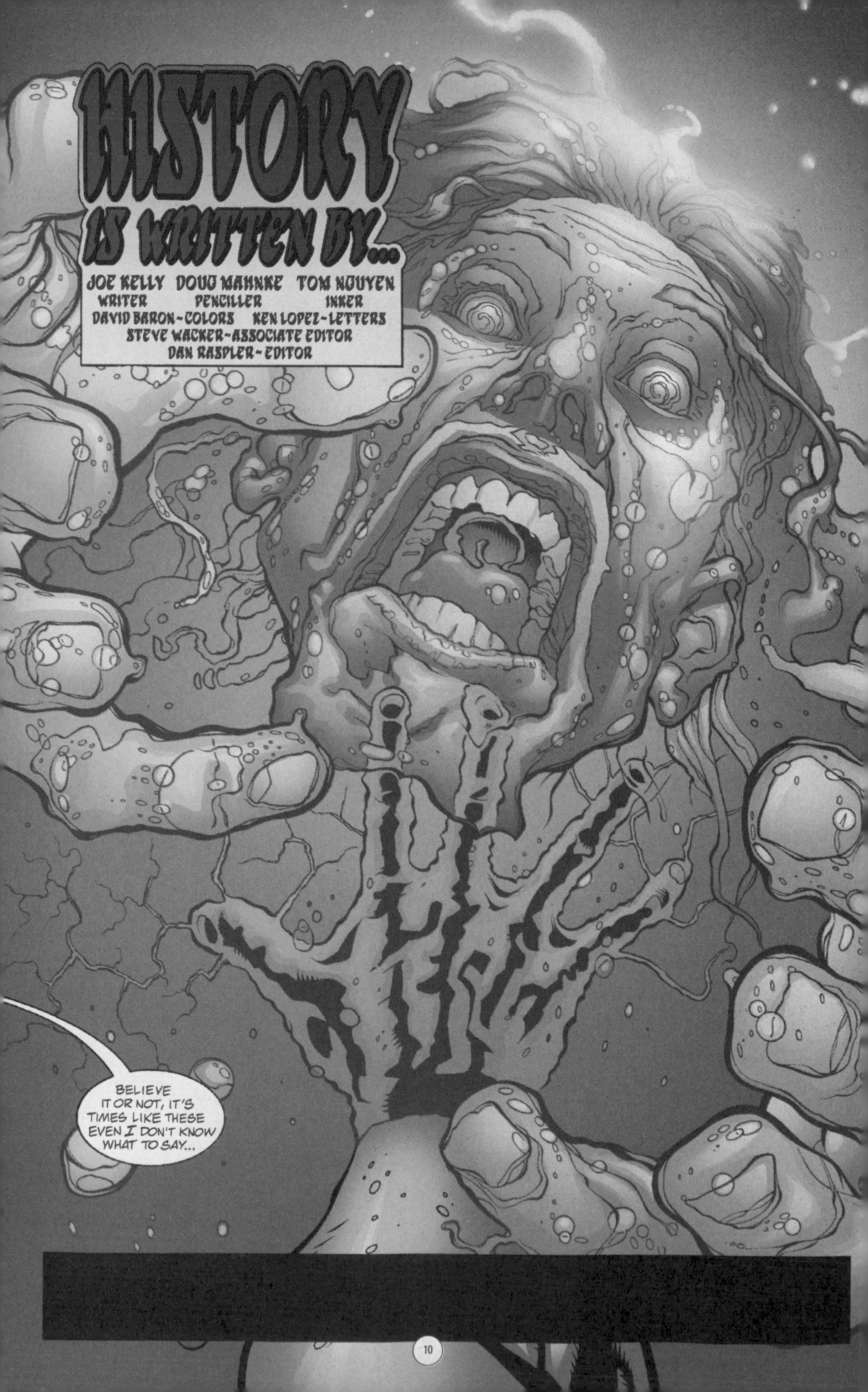
HISTORY IS WRITTEN BY...
JOE KELLY WRITER
DOUG MAHNKE PENCILLER
TOM NGUYEN INKER
DAVID BARON~COLORS
KEN LOPEZ~LETTERS
STEVE WACKER~ASSOCIATE EDITOR
DAN RASPLER~EDITOR
BELIEVE IT OR NOT, IT'S TIMES LIKE THESE EVEN I DON'T KNOW WHAT TO SAY...

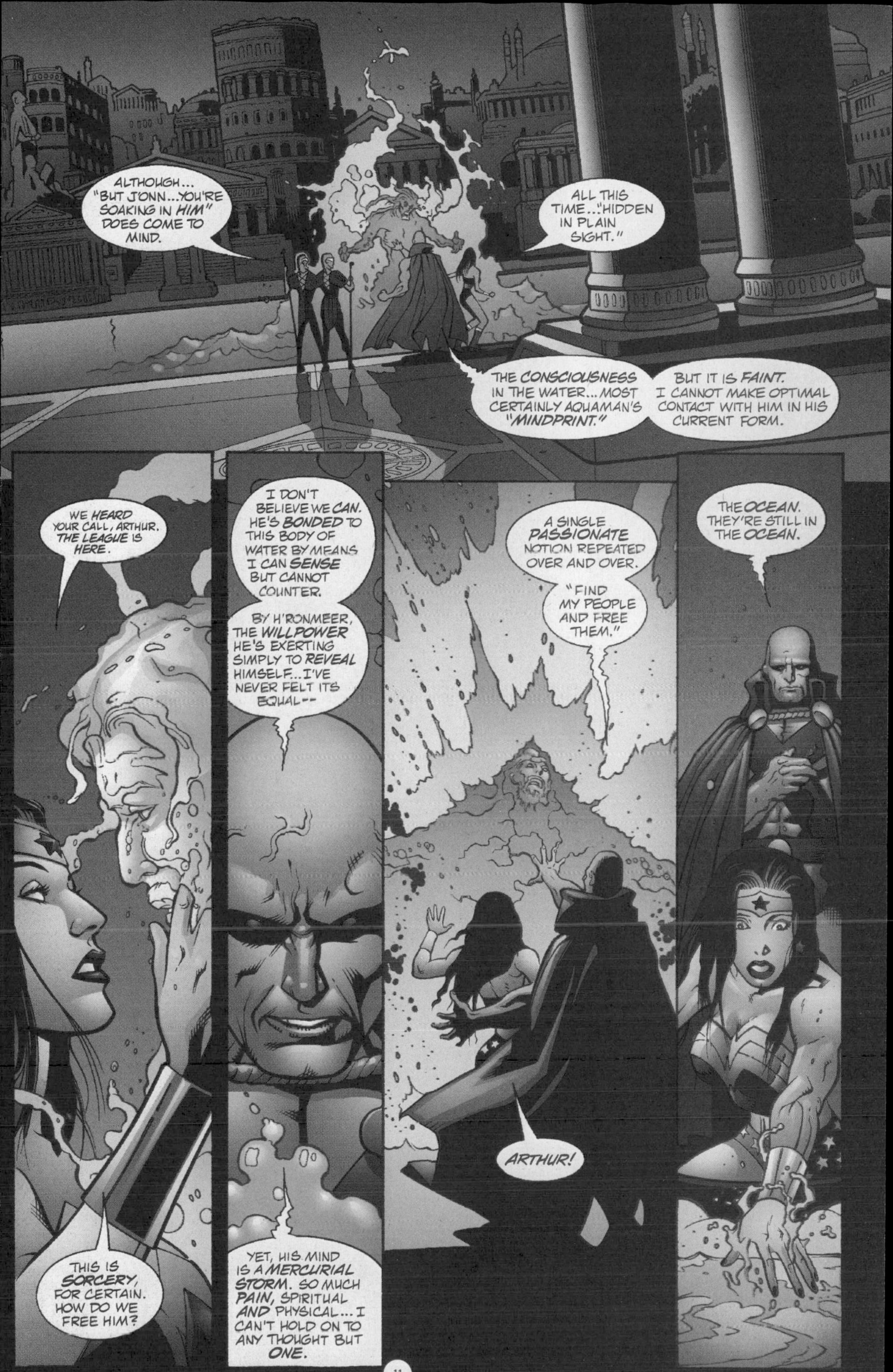
ALTHOUGH... "BUT J'ONN...YOU'RE SOAKING IN *HIM*" DOES COME TO MIND.
ALL THIS TIME..."HIDDEN IN PLAIN SIGHT."
THE *CONSCIOUSNESS* IN THE WATER... MOST CERTAINLY AQUAMAN'S "*MINDPRINT.*"
BUT IT IS *FAINT.* I CANNOT MAKE OPTIMAL CONTACT WITH HIM IN HIS CURRENT FORM.
WE *HEARD* YOUR CALL, ARTHUR. *THE LEAGUE* IS *HERE*.
THIS IS *SORCERY*, FOR CERTAIN. HOW DO WE FREE HIM?
I DON'T BELIEVE WE *CAN*. HE'S *BONDED* TO THIS BODY OF WATER BY MEANS I CAN *SENSE* BUT CANNOT COUNTER.
BY H'RONMEER, THE *WILLPOWER* HE'S EXERTING SIMPLY TO *REVEAL* HIMSELF... I'VE NEVER FELT ITS EQUAL--
YET, HIS MIND IS A *MERCURIAL STORM*. SO MUCH *PAIN*, SPIRITUAL *AND* PHYSICAL... I CAN'T HOLD ON TO ANY THOUGHT BUT *ONE*.
A SINGLE *PASSIONATE* NOTION REPEATED OVER AND OVER.
"FIND MY PEOPLE AND FREE THEM."
ARTHUR!
THE *OCEAN*. THEY'RE STILL IN THE *OCEAN*.

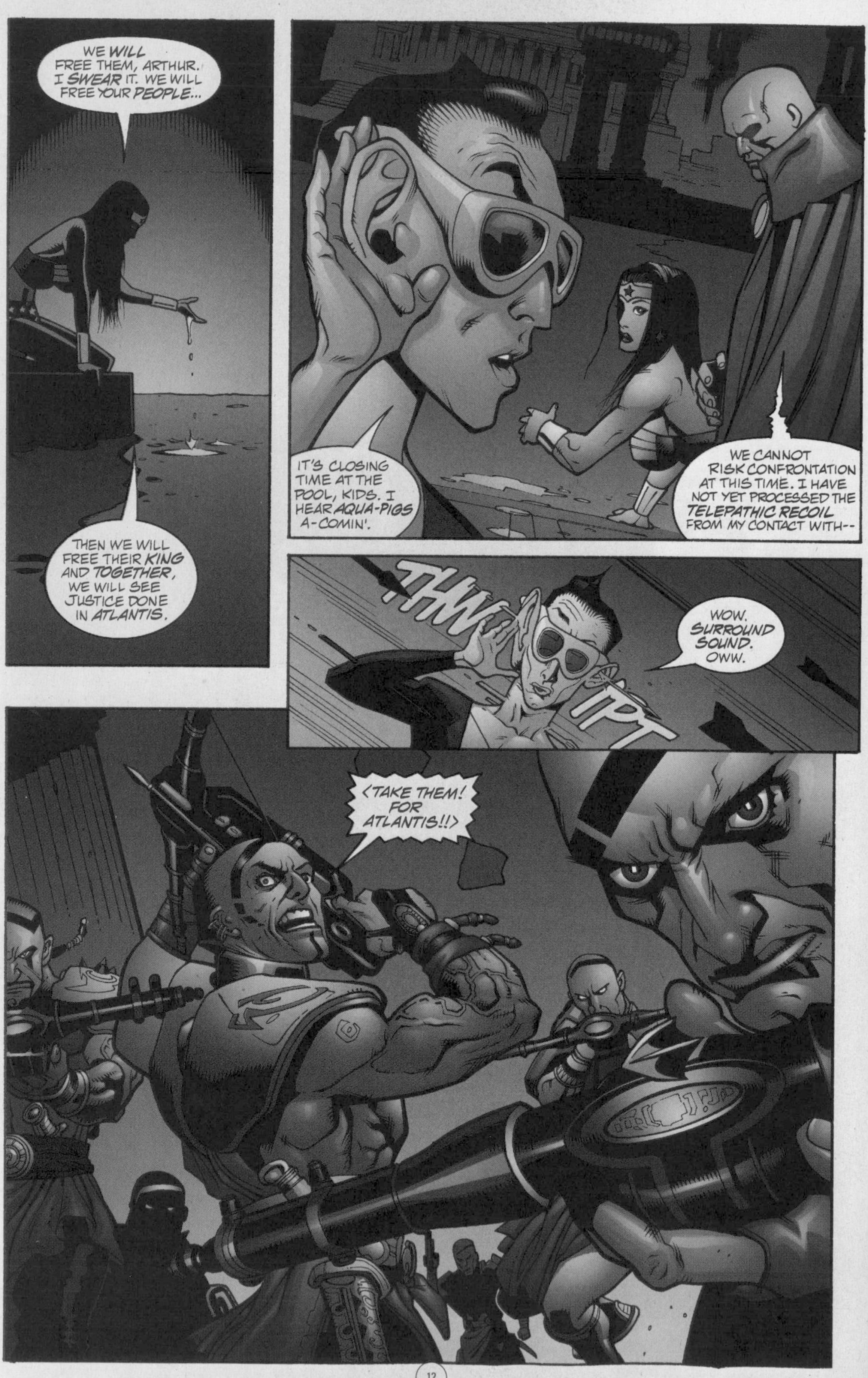
WE WILL FREE THEM, ARTHUR. I SWEAR IT. WE WILL FREE YOUR PEOPLE...
THEN WE WILL FREE THEIR KING AND TOGETHER, WE WILL SEE JUSTICE DONE IN ATLANTIS.
IT'S CLOSING TIME AT THE POOL, KIDS. I HEAR AQUA-PIGS A-COMIN'.
WE CANNOT RISK CONFRONTATION AT THIS TIME. I HAVE NOT YET PROCESSED THE TELEPATHIC RECOIL FROM MY CONTACT WITH--
THWIPT
WOW. SURROUND SOUND. OWW.
<TAKE THEM! FOR ATLANTIS!!>

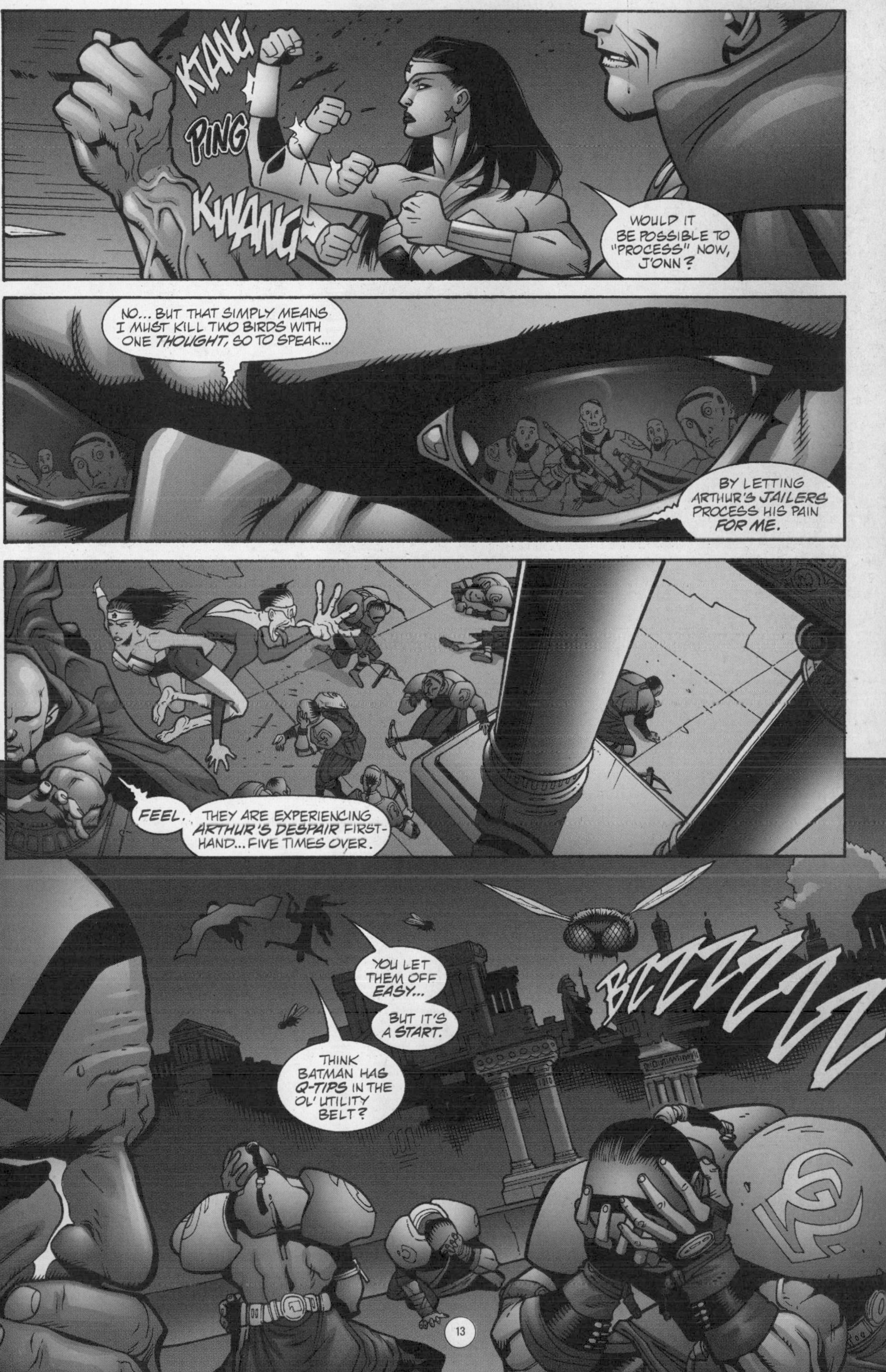
KTANG
PING
KWANG
WOULD IT BE POSSIBLE TO "PROCESS" NOW, J'ONN?
NO... BUT THAT SIMPLY MEANS I MUST KILL TWO BIRDS WITH ONE THOUGHT, SO TO SPEAK...
BY LETTING ARTHUR'S JAILERS PROCESS HIS PAIN FOR ME.
FEEL.
THEY ARE EXPERIENCING ARTHUR'S DESPAIR FIRST-HAND... FIVE TIMES OVER.
YOU LET THEM OFF EASY...
BUT IT'S A START.
THINK BATMAN HAS Q-TIPS IN THE OL' UTILITY BELT?
BZZZZZZ

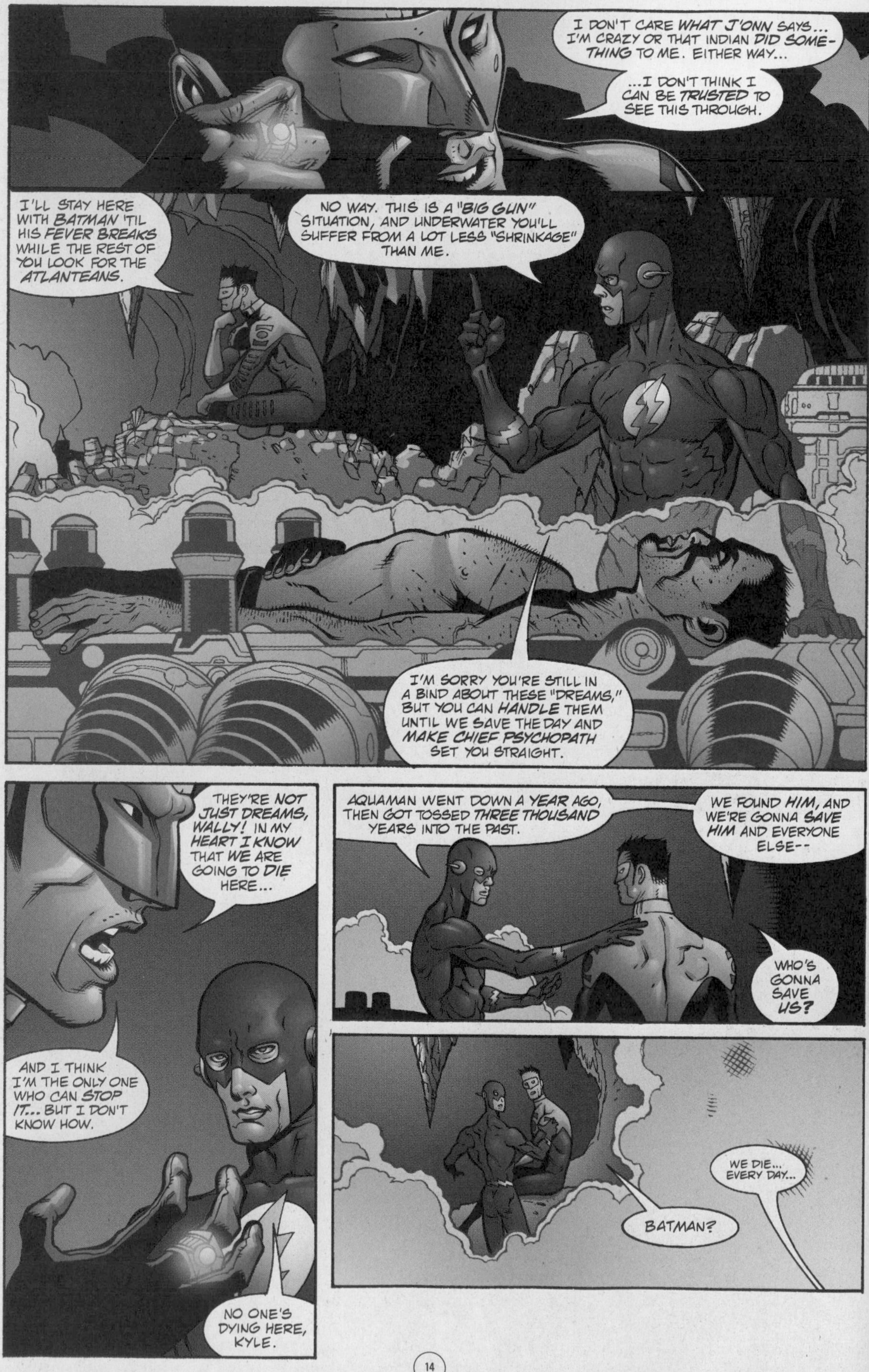
I DON'T CARE WHAT J'ONN SAYS... I'M CRAZY OR THAT INDIAN DID SOMETHING TO ME. EITHER WAY...
...I DON'T THINK I CAN BE TRUSTED TO SEE THIS THROUGH.
I'LL STAY HERE WITH BATMAN 'TIL HIS FEVER BREAKS WHILE THE REST OF YOU LOOK FOR THE ATLANTEANS.
NO WAY. THIS IS A "BIG GUN" SITUATION, AND UNDERWATER YOU'LL SUFFER FROM A LOT LESS "SHRINKAGE" THAN ME.
I'M SORRY YOU'RE STILL IN A BIND ABOUT THESE "DREAMS," BUT YOU CAN HANDLE THEM UNTIL WE SAVE THE DAY AND MAKE CHIEF PSYCHOPATH SET YOU STRAIGHT.
THEY'RE NOT JUST DREAMS, WALLY! IN MY HEART I KNOW THAT WE ARE GOING TO DIE HERE...
AND I THINK I'M THE ONLY ONE WHO CAN STOP IT... BUT I DON'T KNOW HOW.
NO ONE'S DYING HERE, KYLE.
AQUAMAN WENT DOWN A YEAR AGO, THEN GOT TOSSED THREE THOUSAND YEARS INTO THE PAST.
WE FOUND HIM, AND WE'RE GONNA SAVE HIM AND EVERYONE ELSE--
WHO'S GONNA SAVE US?
WE DIE... EVERY DAY...
BATMAN?

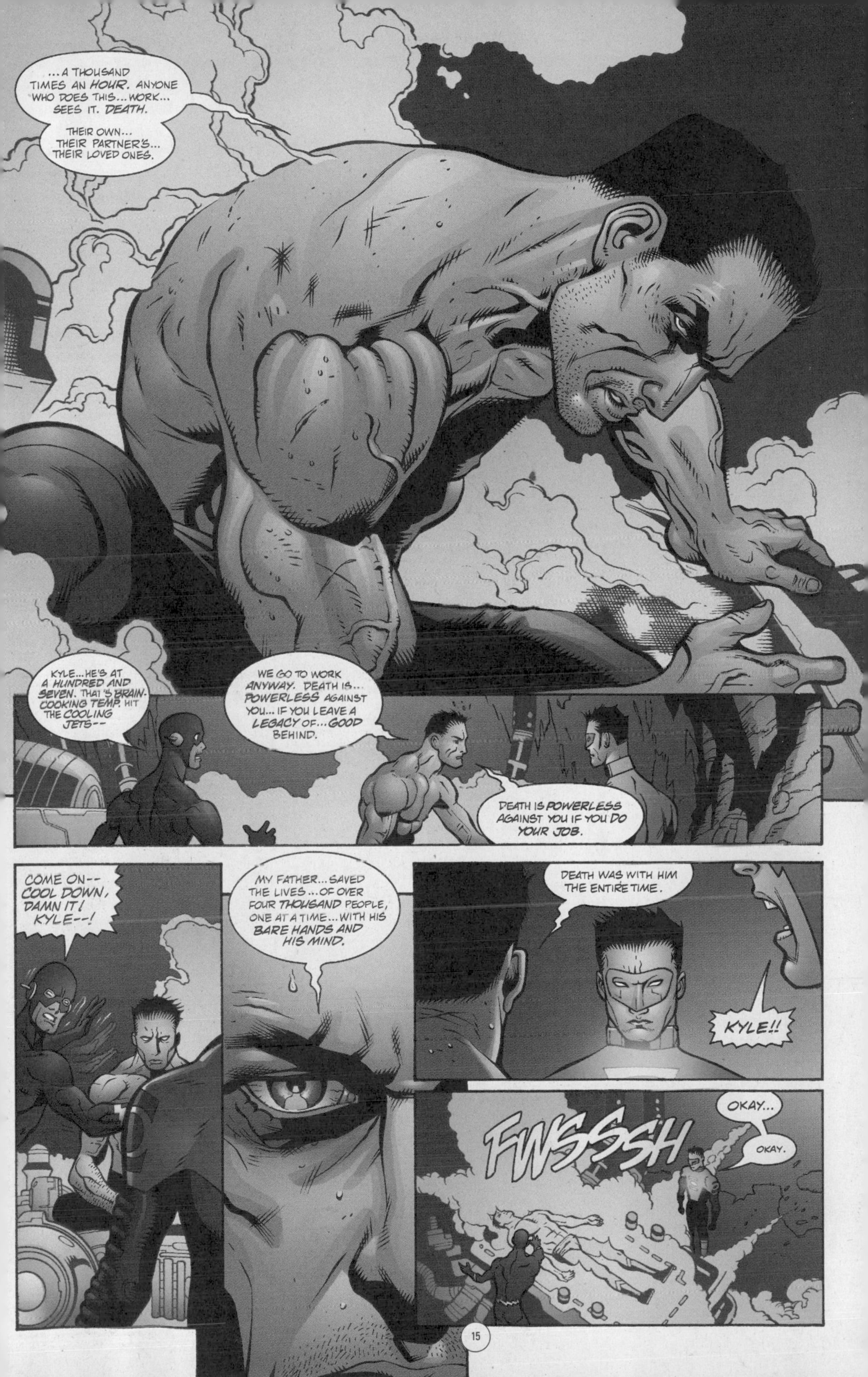
...A THOUSAND TIMES AN HOUR. ANYONE WHO DOES THIS... WORK... SEES IT. DEATH.
THEIR OWN... THEIR PARTNER'S... THEIR LOVED ONES.
KYLE... HE'S AT A HUNDRED AND SEVEN. THAT'S BRAIN-COOKING TEMP. HIT THE COOLING JETS--
WE GO TO WORK ANYWAY. DEATH IS... POWERLESS AGAINST YOU... IF YOU LEAVE A LEGACY OF... GOOD BEHIND.
DEATH IS POWERLESS AGAINST YOU IF YOU DO YOUR JOB.
COME ON-- COOL DOWN, DAMN IT! KYLE--!
MY FATHER... SAVED THE LIVES... OF OVER FOUR THOUSAND PEOPLE, ONE AT A TIME... WITH HIS BARE HANDS AND HIS MIND.
DEATH WAS WITH HIM THE ENTIRE TIME.
KYLE!!
FWSSSH
OKAY...
OKAY.

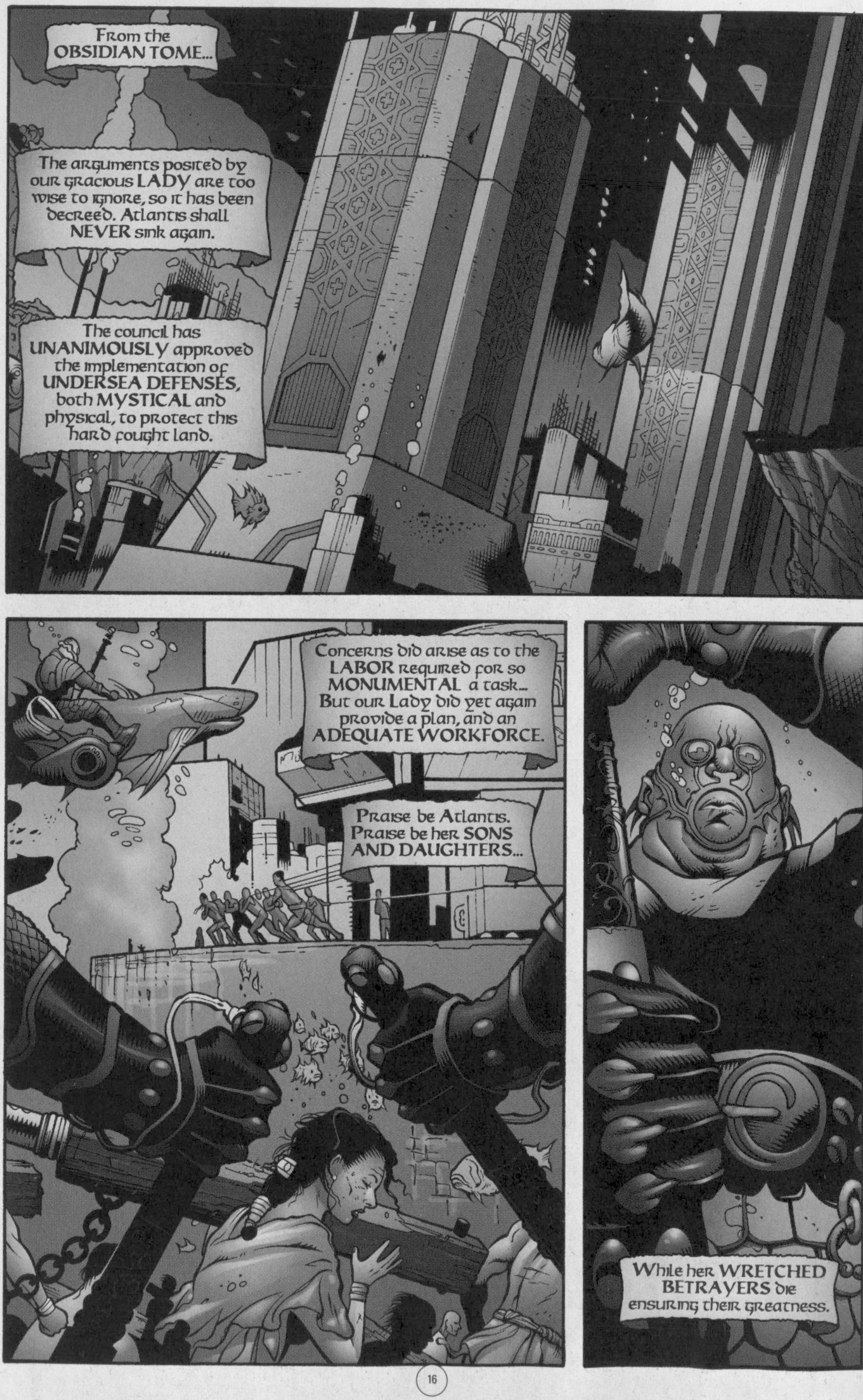
From the OBSIDIAN TOME...
The arguments posited by our gracious LADY are too wise to ignore, so it has been decreed. Atlantis shall NEVER sink again.
The council has UNANIMOUSLY approved the implementation of UNDERSEA DEFENSES, both MYSTICAL and physical, to protect this hard fought land.
Concerns did arise as to the LABOR required for so MONUMENTAL a task... But our Lady did yet again provide a plan, and an ADEQUATE WORKFORCE.
Praise be Atlantis. Praise be her SONS AND DAUGHTERS...
While her WRETCHED BETRAYERS die ensuring their greatness.

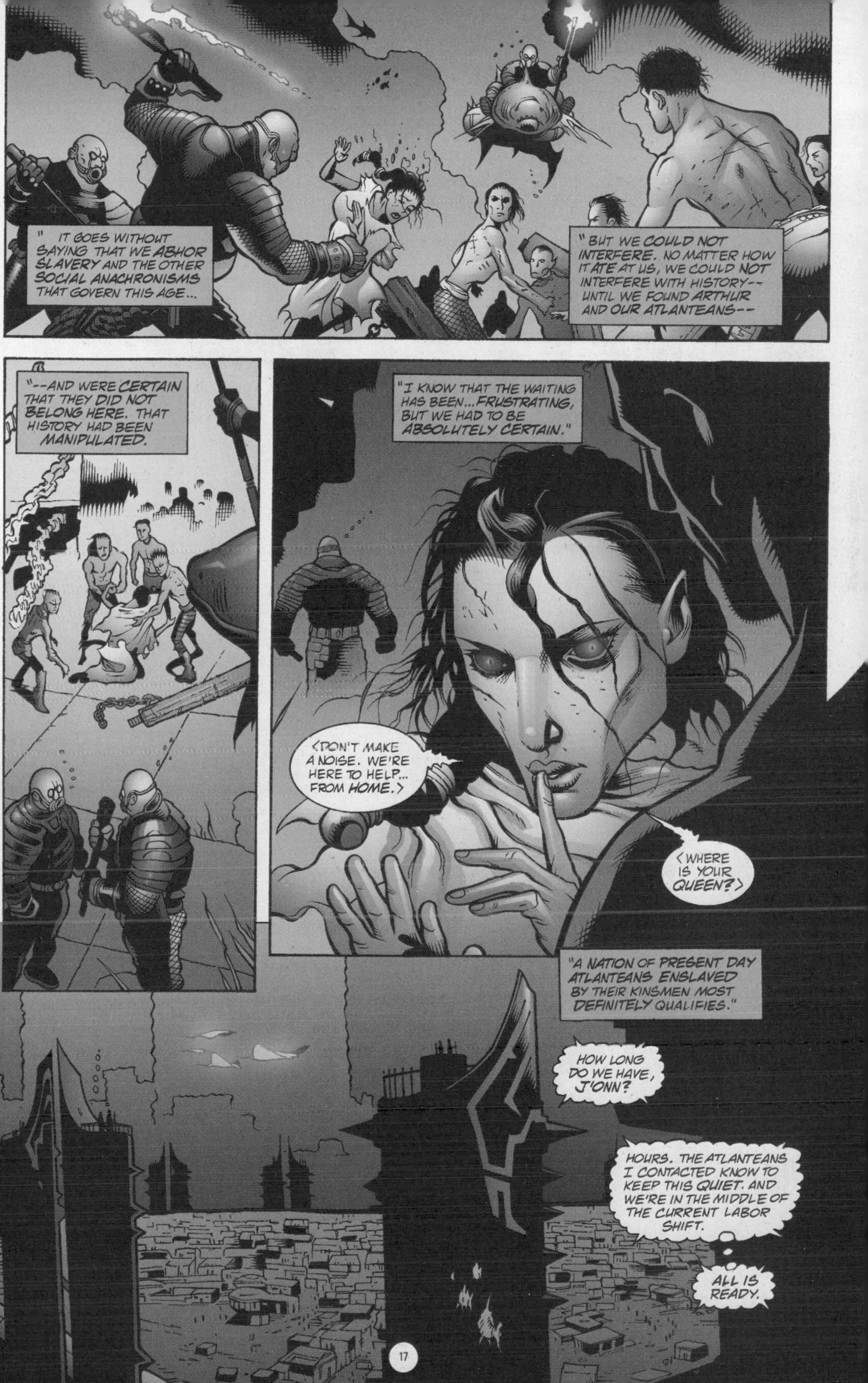
"IT GOES WITHOUT SAYING THAT WE ABHOR SLAVERY AND THE OTHER SOCIAL ANACHRONISMS THAT GOVERN THIS AGE...
"BUT WE COULD NOT INTERFERE. NO MATTER HOW IT ATE AT US, WE COULD NOT INTERFERE WITH HISTORY--UNTIL WE FOUND ARTHUR AND OUR ATLANTEANS--
"--AND WERE CERTAIN THAT THEY DID NOT BELONG HERE. THAT HISTORY HAD BEEN MANIPULATED.
"I KNOW THAT THE WAITING HAS BEEN...FRUSTRATING, BUT WE HAD TO BE ABSOLUTELY CERTAIN."
<DON'T MAKE A NOISE. WE'RE HERE TO HELP... FROM HOME.>
<WHERE IS YOUR QUEEN?>
"A NATION OF PRESENT DAY ATLANTEANS ENSLAVED BY THEIR KINSMEN MOST DEFINITELY QUALIFIES."
HOW LONG DO WE HAVE, J'ONN?
HOURS. THE ATLANTEANS I CONTACTED KNOW TO KEEP THIS QUIET. AND WE'RE IN THE MIDDLE OF THE CURRENT LABOR SHIFT.
ALL IS READY.

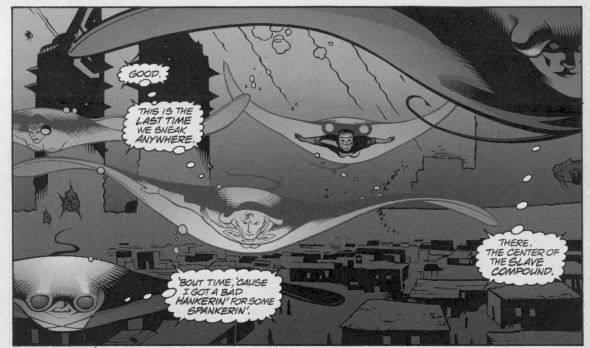

GOOD.

THIS IS THE LAST TIME WE SNEAK ANYWHERE.

'BOUT TIME, 'CAUSE I GOT A BAD HANKERIN' FOR SOME SPANKERIN'.

THERE. THE CENTER OF THE SLAVE COMPOUND.

STAY ON GUARD.

SUPERMAN!

POSEIDON BE PRAISED—IT *IS* YOU! I KNEW YOU WOULD COME... I KNEW YOU WOULDN'T LEAVE US!

LORI? LORI LEMARIS?

HEH... YOU LOOK SURPRISED. WHAT DID YOU EXPECT ME TO LOOK LIKE AFTER *FIFTEEN YEARS* OF HARD LABOR?

FIFTEEN?

COME. THE QUEEN WAITS. SHE'LL EXPLAIN EVERYTHING.

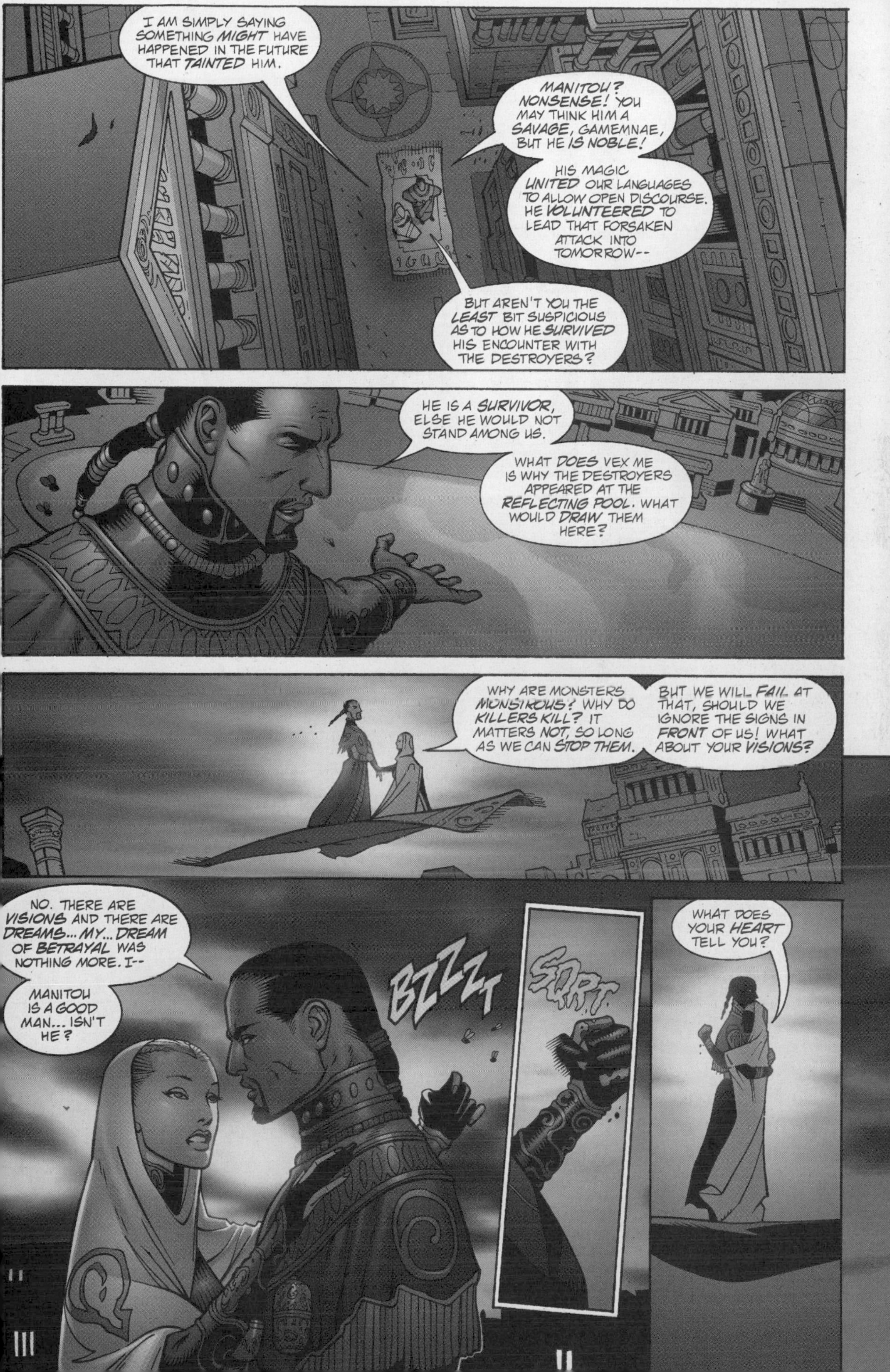
I AM SIMPLY SAYING SOMETHING MIGHT HAVE HAPPENED IN THE FUTURE THAT TAINTED HIM.
MANITOU? NONSENSE! YOU MAY THINK HIM A SAVAGE, GAMEMNAE, BUT HE IS NOBLE!
HIS MAGIC UNITED OUR LANGUAGES TO ALLOW OPEN DISCOURSE. HE VOLUNTEERED TO LEAD THAT FORSAKEN ATTACK INTO TOMORROW--
BUT AREN'T YOU THE LEAST BIT SUSPICIOUS AS TO HOW HE SURVIVED HIS ENCOUNTER WITH THE DESTROYERS?
HE IS A SURVIVOR, ELSE HE WOULD NOT STAND AMONG US.
WHAT DOES VEX ME IS WHY THE DESTROYERS APPEARED AT THE REFLECTING POOL. WHAT WOULD DRAW THEM HERE?
WHY ARE MONSTERS MONSTROUS? WHY DO KILLERS KILL? IT MATTERS NOT, SO LONG AS WE CAN STOP THEM.
BUT WE WILL FAIL AT THAT, SHOULD WE IGNORE THE SIGNS IN FRONT OF US! WHAT ABOUT YOUR VISIONS?
NO. THERE ARE VISIONS AND THERE ARE DREAMS... MY... DREAM OF BETRAYAL WAS NOTHING MORE. I--
MANITOU IS A GOOD MAN... ISN'T HE?
BZZZT
SQRT
WHAT DOES YOUR HEART TELL YOU?

YOU *HEARD* SOMETHING. WHAT IS IT?

NO, I *DIDN'T.* WHY?

YOUR BREATH STOPPED.

YOU ARE VERY PERCEPTIVE.

I HAVE TO BE, MAGICIAN. SO WHAT WAS IT?

A *FLY.*

SOME BELIEVE THAT FLIES ARE EARTHLY PRISONS FOR *FALLEN ANGELS.* SPIES FOR *SATAN.*

THEY SAY THAT THEIR VOICES CARRY *LIES,* HISSING BUZZING *UNTRUTHS.*

HMMM. THAT THEY DO.

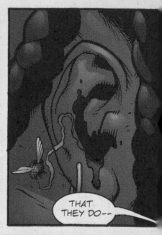

THAT THEY DO--

NO MORE TALK OF THE DEVILS WE *CANNOT* SEE.

LET US *HUNT.*

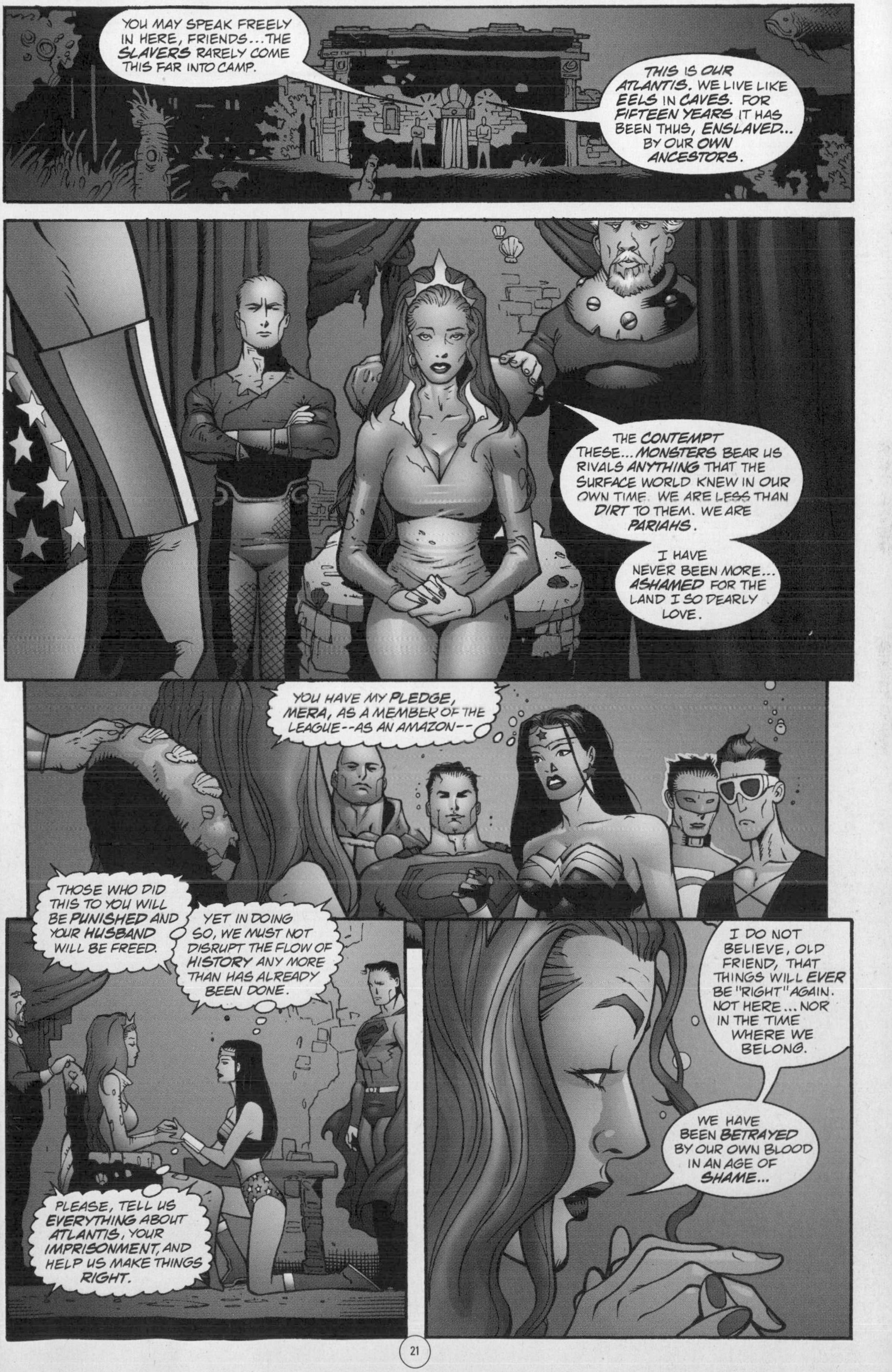
YOU MAY SPEAK FREELY IN HERE, FRIENDS... THE SLAVERS RARELY COME THIS FAR INTO CAMP.
THIS IS OUR ATLANTIS. WE LIVE LIKE EELS IN CAVES. FOR FIFTEEN YEARS IT HAS BEEN THUS, ENSLAVED... BY OUR OWN ANCESTORS.
THE CONTEMPT THESE... MONSTERS BEAR US RIVALS ANYTHING THAT THE SURFACE WORLD KNEW IN OUR OWN TIME. WE ARE LESS THAN DIRT TO THEM. WE ARE PARIAHS.
I HAVE NEVER BEEN MORE... ASHAMED FOR THE LAND I SO DEARLY LOVE.
YOU HAVE MY PLEDGE, MERA, AS A MEMBER OF THE LEAGUE--AS AN AMAZON--
THOSE WHO DID THIS TO YOU WILL BE PUNISHED AND YOUR HUSBAND WILL BE FREED.
YET IN DOING SO, WE MUST NOT DISRUPT THE FLOW OF HISTORY ANY MORE THAN HAS ALREADY BEEN DONE.
PLEASE, TELL US EVERYTHING ABOUT ATLANTIS, YOUR IMPRISONMENT, AND HELP US MAKE THINGS RIGHT.
I DO NOT BELIEVE, OLD FRIEND, THAT THINGS WILL EVER BE "RIGHT" AGAIN. NOT HERE... NOR IN THE TIME WHERE WE BELONG.
WE HAVE BEEN BETRAYED BY OUR OWN BLOOD IN AN AGE OF SHAME...

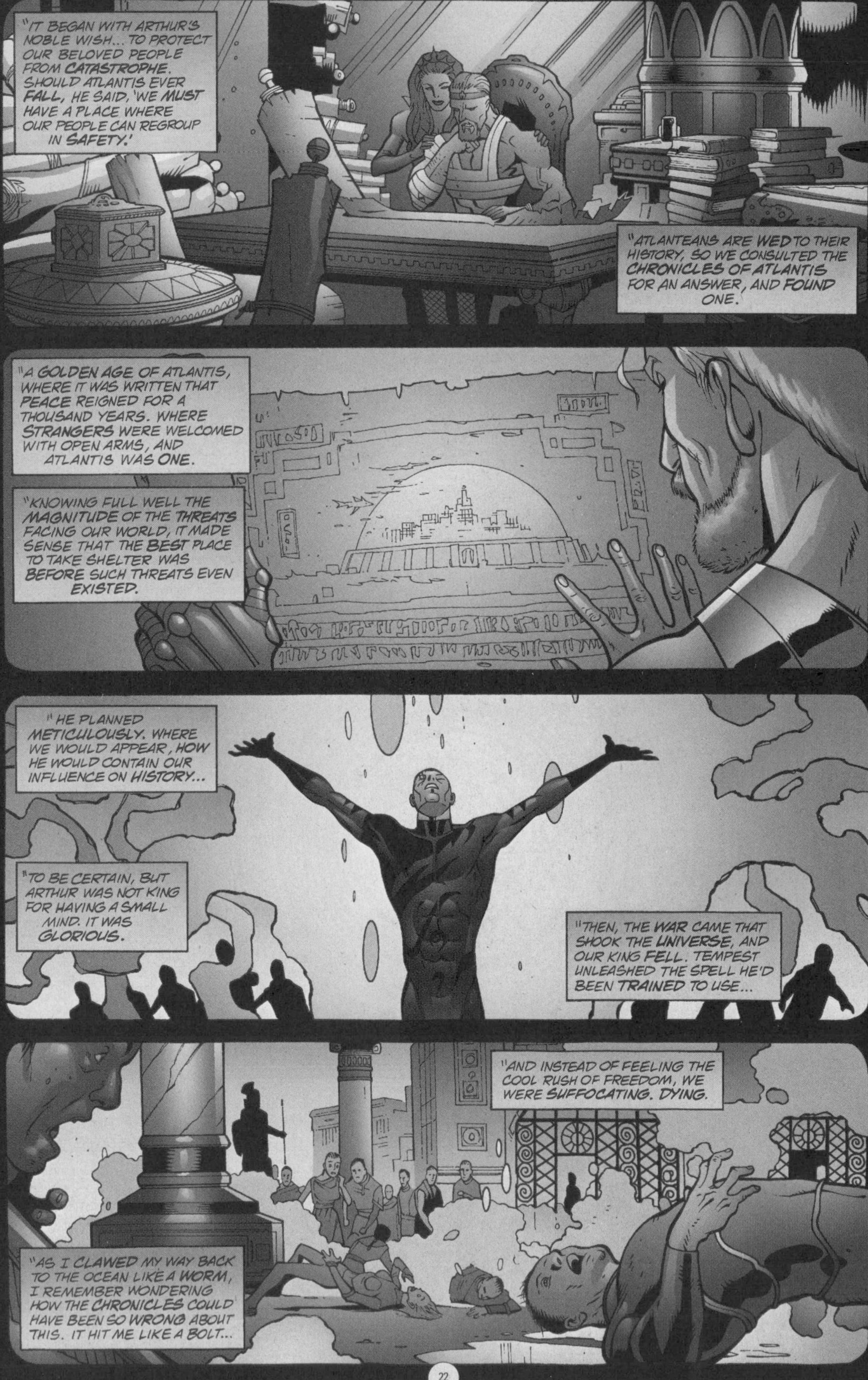
"IT BEGAN WITH ARTHUR'S NOBLE WISH... TO PROTECT OUR BELOVED PEOPLE FROM CATASTROPHE. SHOULD ATLANTIS EVER FALL, HE SAID, 'WE MUST HAVE A PLACE WHERE OUR PEOPLE CAN REGROUP IN SAFETY.'
"ATLANTEANS ARE WED TO THEIR HISTORY, SO WE CONSULTED THE CHRONICLES OF ATLANTIS FOR AN ANSWER, AND FOUND ONE.
"A GOLDEN AGE OF ATLANTIS, WHERE IT WAS WRITTEN THAT PEACE REIGNED FOR A THOUSAND YEARS. WHERE STRANGERS WERE WELCOMED WITH OPEN ARMS, AND ATLANTIS WAS ONE.
"KNOWING FULL WELL THE MAGNITUDE OF THE THREATS FACING OUR WORLD, IT MADE SENSE THAT THE BEST PLACE TO TAKE SHELTER WAS BEFORE SUCH THREATS EVEN EXISTED.
"HE PLANNED METICULOUSLY. WHERE WE WOULD APPEAR, HOW HE WOULD CONTAIN OUR INFLUENCE ON HISTORY...
"TO BE CERTAIN, BUT ARTHUR WAS NOT KING FOR HAVING A SMALL MIND. IT WAS GLORIOUS.
"THEN, THE WAR CAME THAT SHOOK THE UNIVERSE, AND OUR KING FELL. TEMPEST UNLEASHED THE SPELL HE'D BEEN TRAINED TO USE...
"AND INSTEAD OF FEELING THE COOL RUSH OF FREEDOM, WE WERE SUFFOCATING. DYING.
"AS I CLAWED MY WAY BACK TO THE OCEAN LIKE A WORM, I REMEMBER WONDERING HOW THE CHRONICLES COULD HAVE BEEN SO WRONG ABOUT THIS. IT HIT ME LIKE A BOLT...

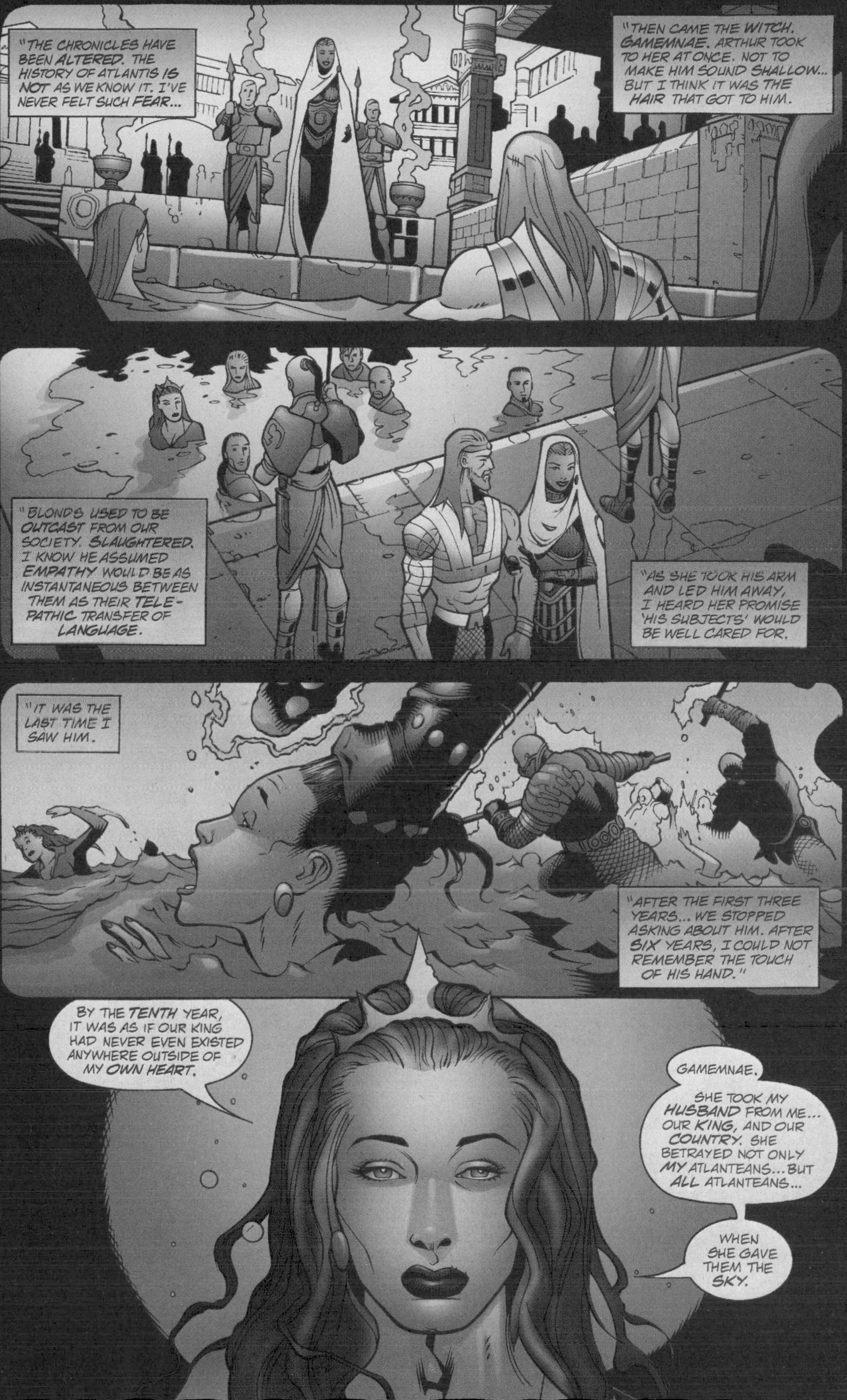
"THE CHRONICLES HAVE BEEN ALTERED. THE HISTORY OF ATLANTIS IS NOT AS WE KNOW IT. I'VE NEVER FELT SUCH FEAR...
"THEN CAME THE WITCH, GAMEMNAE. ARTHUR TOOK TO HER AT ONCE. NOT TO MAKE HIM SOUND SHALLOW... BUT I THINK IT WAS THE HAIR THAT GOT TO HIM.
"BLONDS USED TO BE OUTCAST FROM OUR SOCIETY. SLAUGHTERED. I KNOW HE ASSUMED EMPATHY WOULD BE AS INSTANTANEOUS BETWEEN THEM AS THEIR TELE-PATHIC TRANSFER OF LANGUAGE.
"AS SHE TOOK HIS ARM AND LED HIM AWAY, I HEARD HER PROMISE 'HIS SUBJECTS' WOULD BE WELL CARED FOR.
"IT WAS THE LAST TIME I SAW HIM.
"AFTER THE FIRST THREE YEARS... WE STOPPED ASKING ABOUT HIM. AFTER SIX YEARS, I COULD NOT REMEMBER THE TOUCH OF HIS HAND."
BY THE TENTH YEAR, IT WAS AS IF OUR KING HAD NEVER EVEN EXISTED ANYWHERE OUTSIDE OF MY OWN HEART.
GAMEMNAE.
SHE TOOK MY HUSBAND FROM ME... OUR KING, AND OUR COUNTRY. SHE BETRAYED NOT ONLY MY ATLANTEANS... BUT ALL ATLANTEANS...
WHEN SHE GAVE THEM THE SKY.

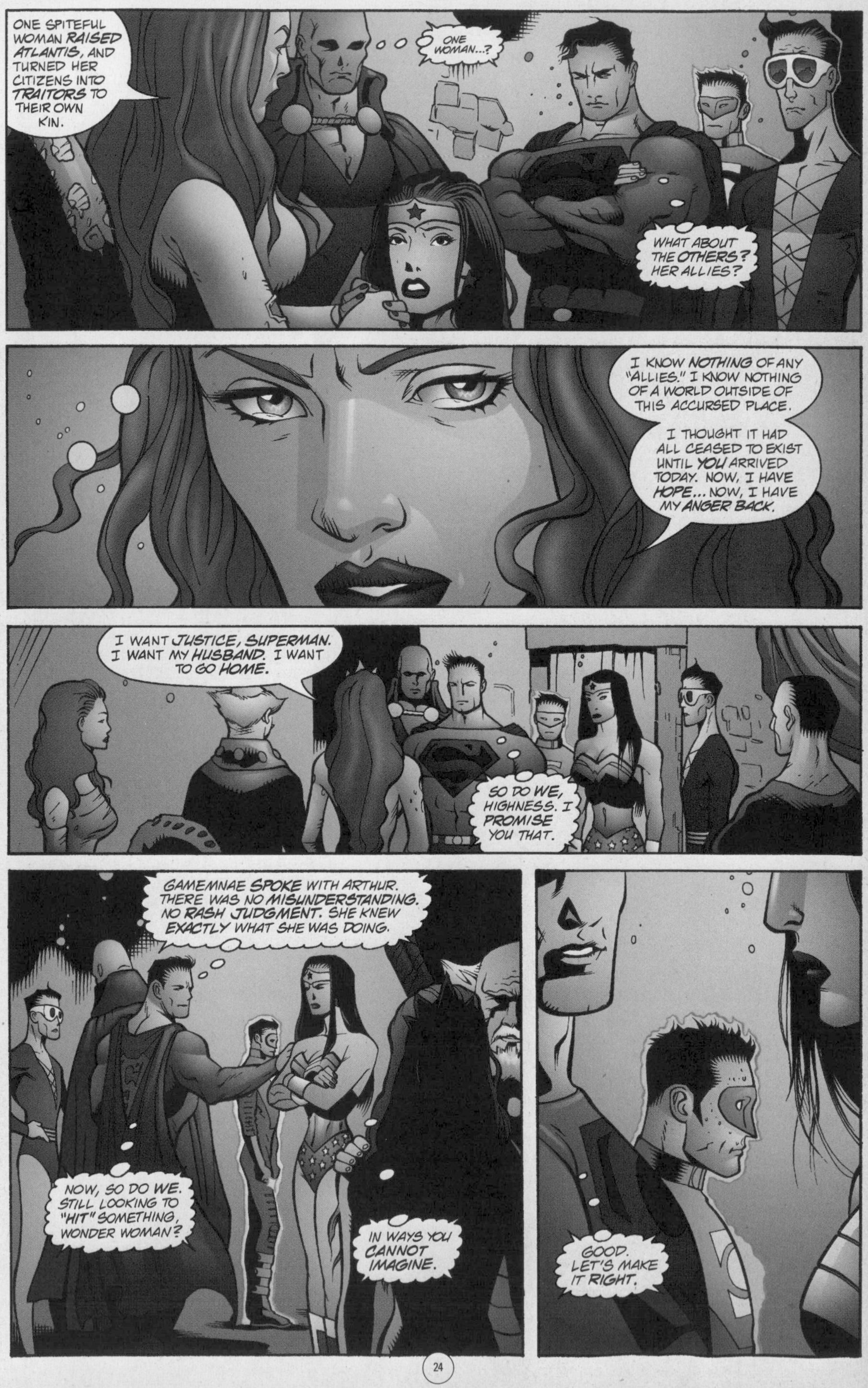
ONE SPITEFUL WOMAN RAISED ATLANTIS, AND TURNED HER CITIZENS INTO TRAITORS TO THEIR OWN KIN.
ONE WOMAN...?
WHAT ABOUT THE OTHERS? HER ALLIES?
I KNOW NOTHING OF ANY "ALLIES." I KNOW NOTHING OF A WORLD OUTSIDE OF THIS ACCURSED PLACE.
I THOUGHT IT HAD ALL CEASED TO EXIST UNTIL YOU ARRIVED TODAY. NOW, I HAVE HOPE... NOW, I HAVE MY ANGER BACK.
I WANT JUSTICE, SUPERMAN. I WANT MY HUSBAND. I WANT TO GO HOME.
SO DO WE, HIGHNESS. I PROMISE YOU THAT.
GAMEMNAE SPOKE WITH ARTHUR. THERE WAS NO MISUNDERSTANDING. NO RASH JUDGMENT. SHE KNEW EXACTLY WHAT SHE WAS DOING.
NOW, SO DO WE. STILL LOOKING TO "HIT" SOMETHING, WONDER WOMAN?
IN WAYS YOU CANNOT IMAGINE.
GOOD. LET'S MAKE IT RIGHT.

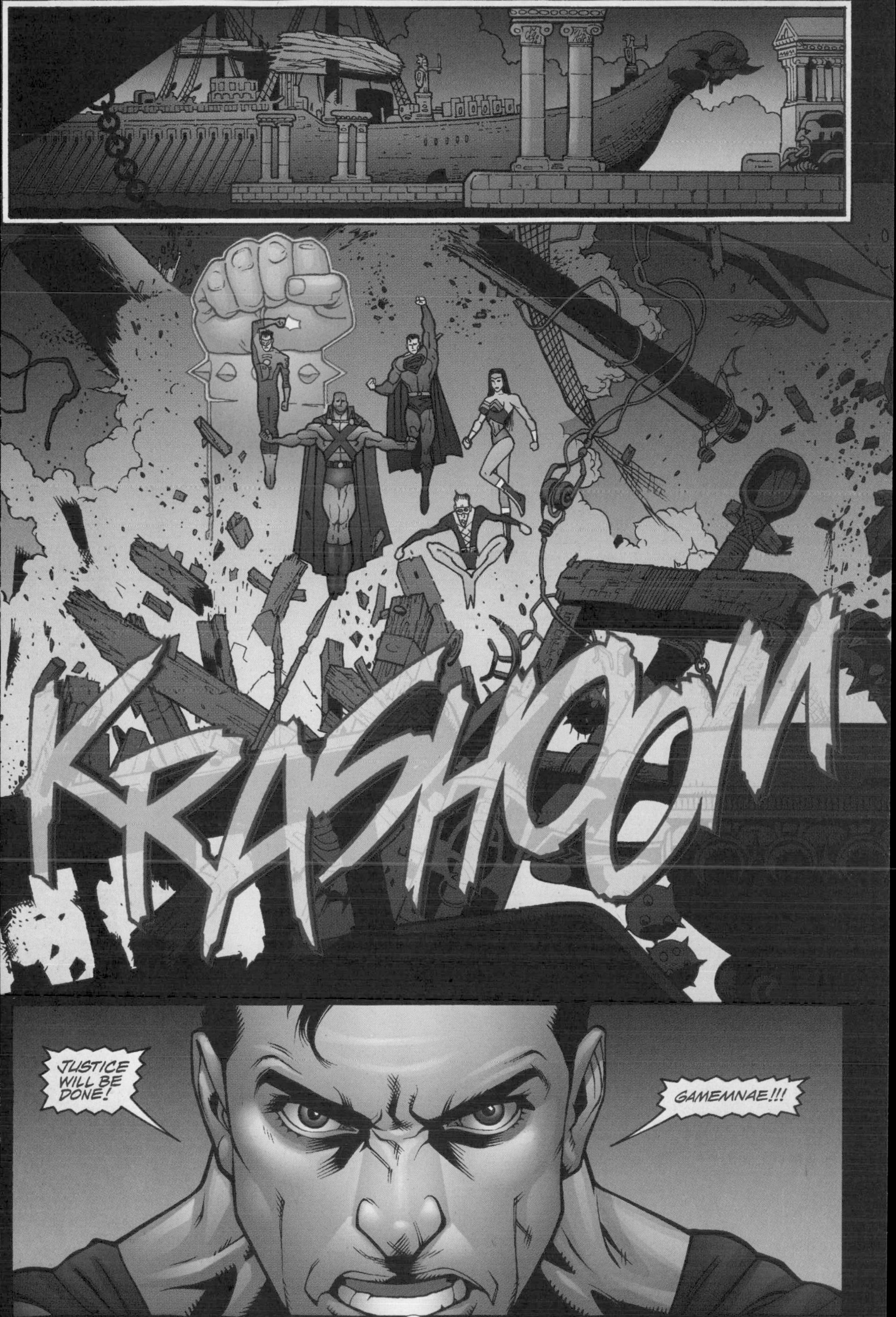
KRASHOOM
JUSTICE WILL BE DONE!
GAMEMNAE!!!

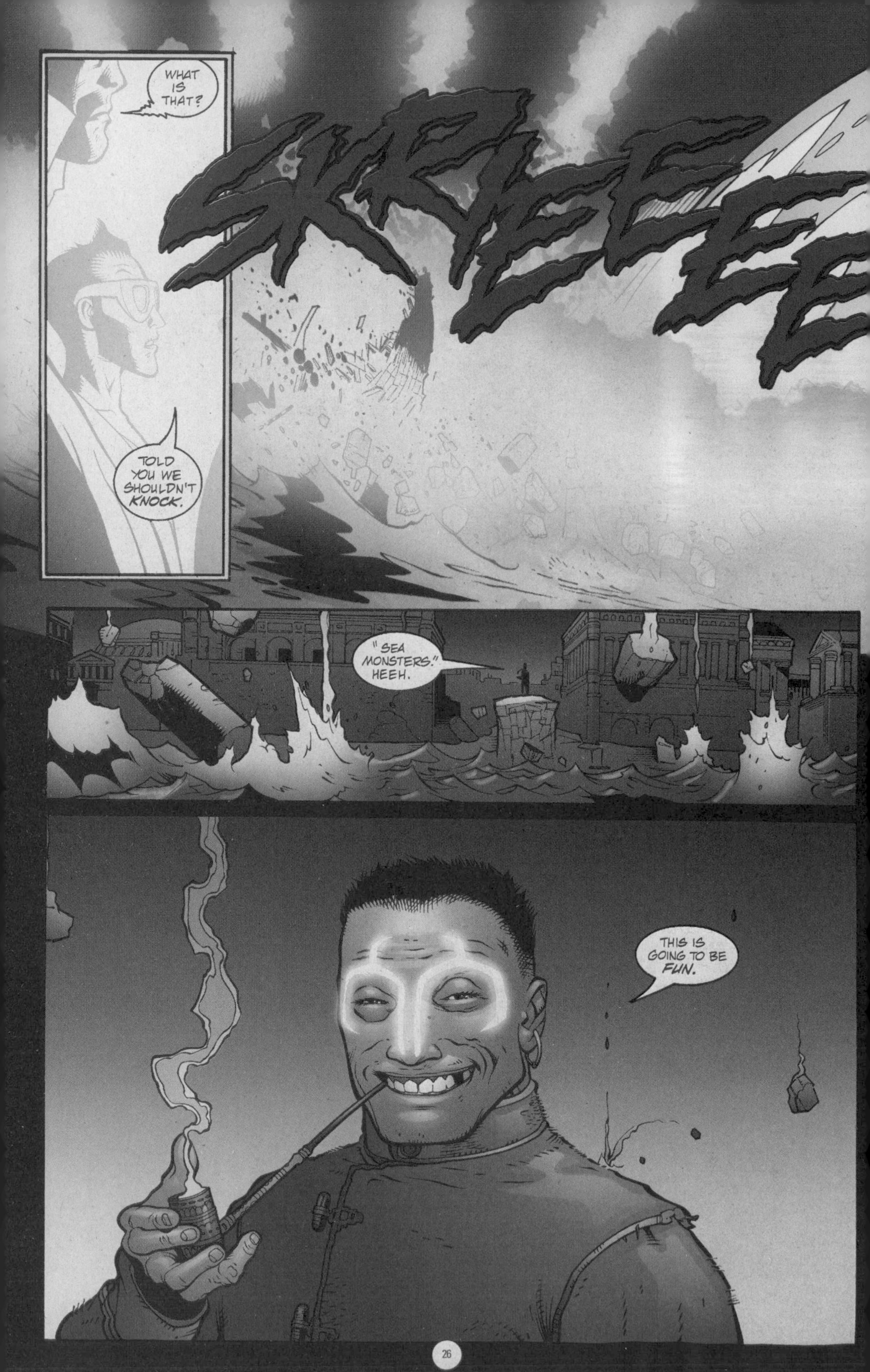
WHAT IS THAT?
SKREEEEE
TOLD YOU WE SHOULDN'T KNOCK.
"SEA MONSTERS." HEEH.
THIS IS GOING TO BE FUN.

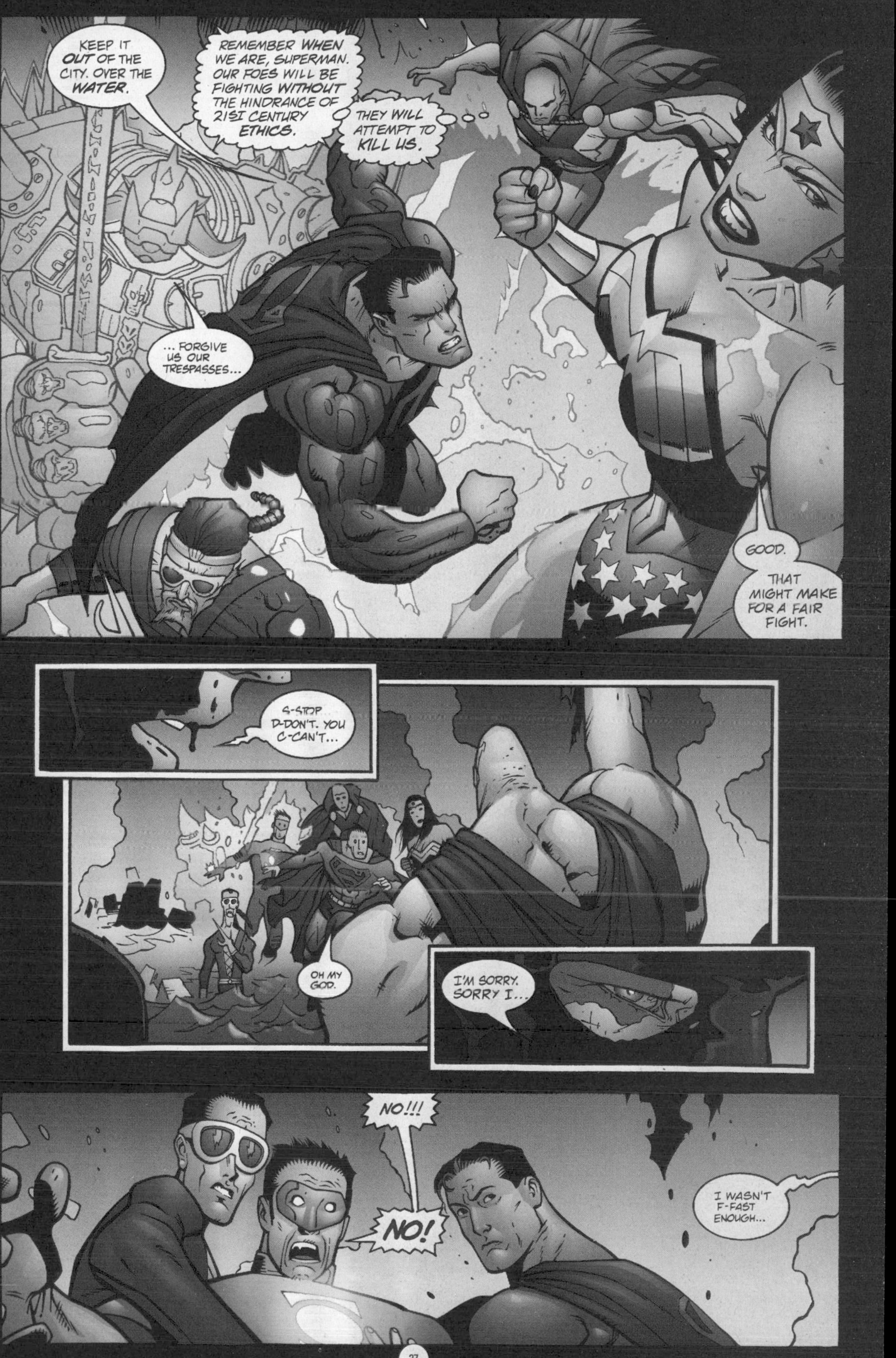
KEEP IT OUT OF THE CITY. OVER THE WATER.
REMEMBER WHEN WE ARE, SUPERMAN. OUR FOES WILL BE FIGHTING WITHOUT THE HINDRANCE OF 21ST CENTURY ETHICS.
THEY WILL ATTEMPT TO KILL US.
... FORGIVE US OUR TRESPASSES...
GOOD.
THAT MIGHT MAKE FOR A FAIR FIGHT.
S-STOP... D-DON'T. YOU C-CAN'T...
OH MY GOD.
I'M SORRY. SORRY I...
NO!!!
NO!
I WASN'T F-FAST ENOUGH...

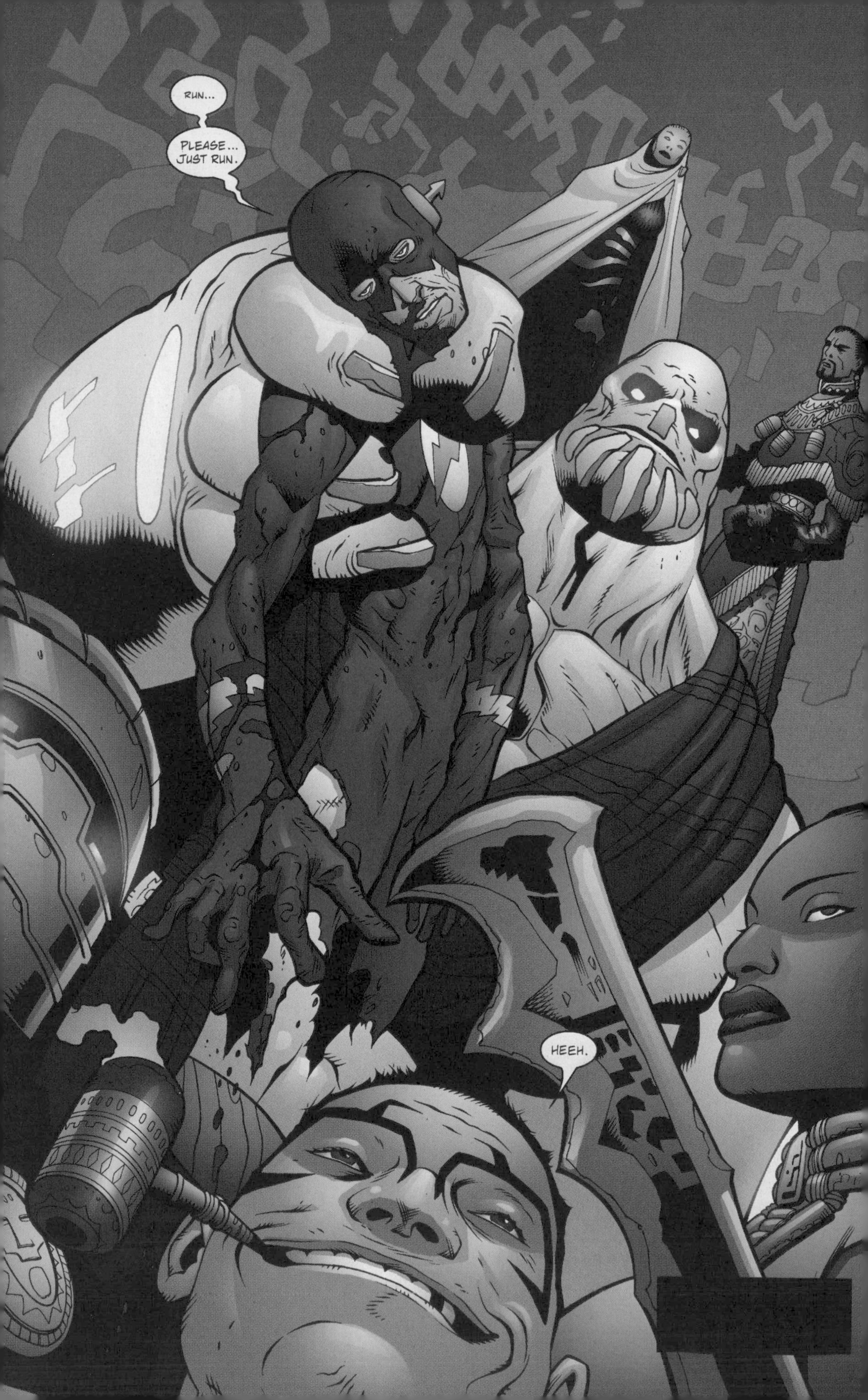
RUN...
PLEASE... JUST RUN.
HEEH.
[redacted]

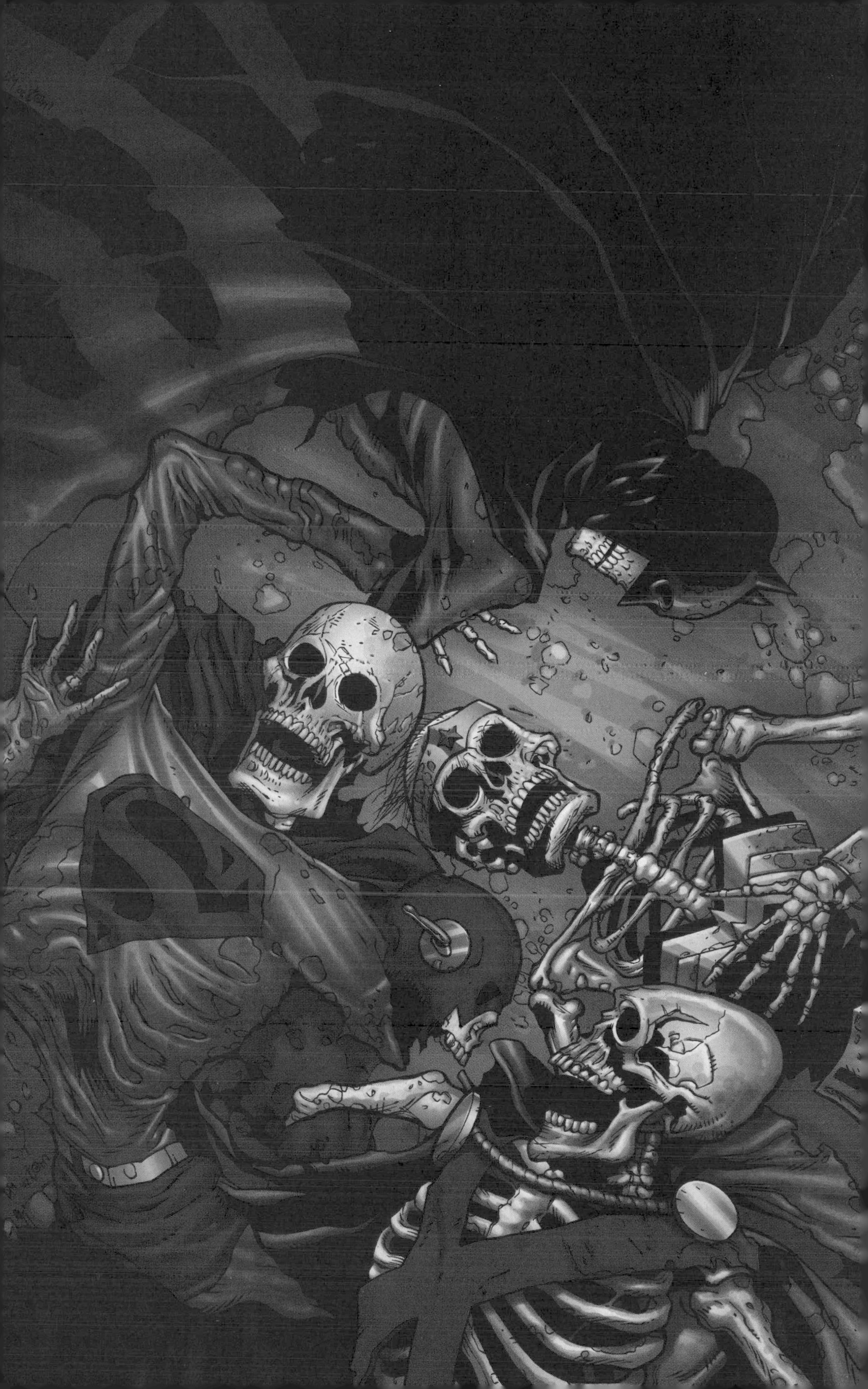

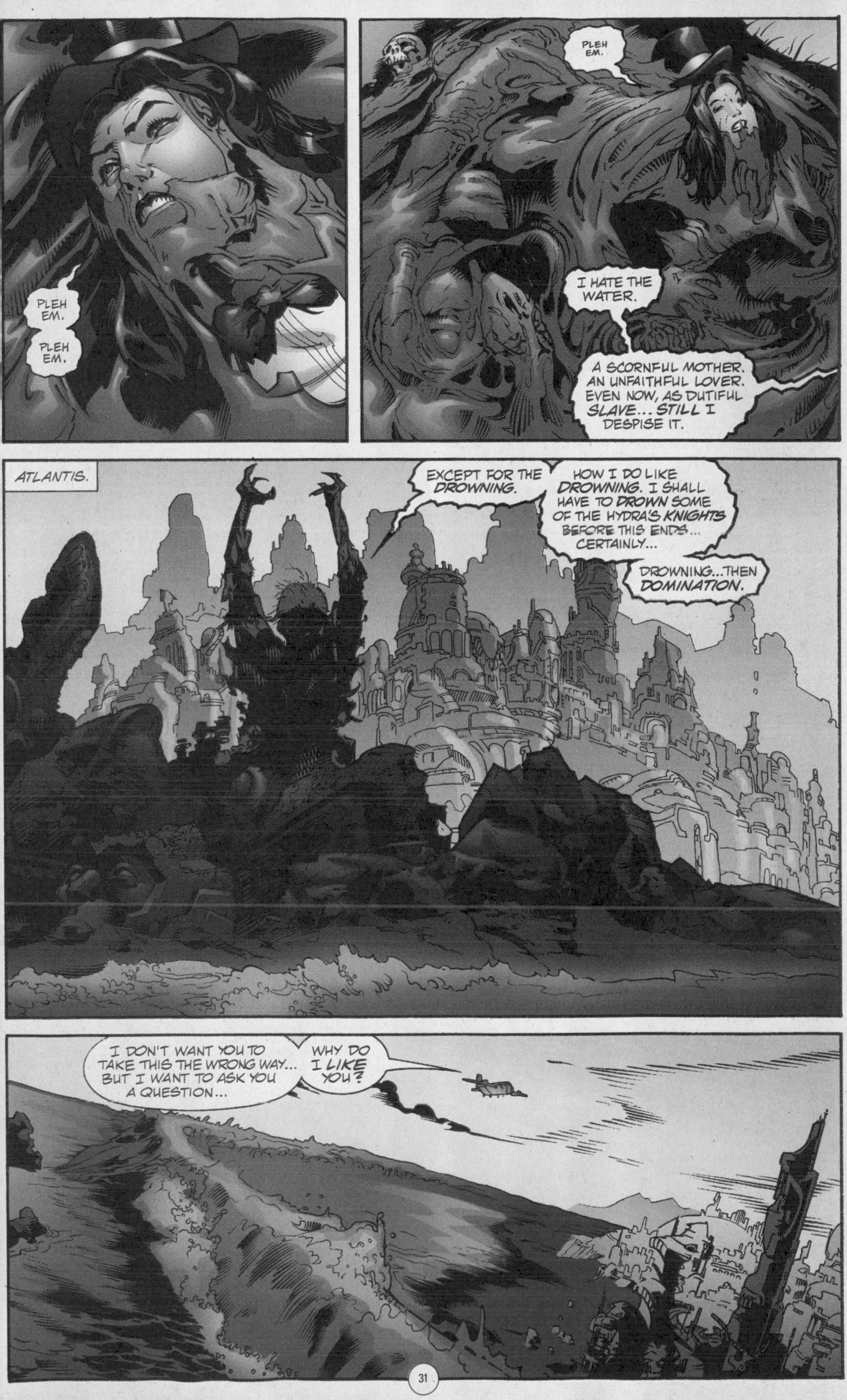
PLEH EM.
PLEH EM.
PLEH EM.
I HATE THE WATER.
A SCORNFUL MOTHER. AN UNFAITHFUL LOVER. EVEN NOW, AS DUTIFUL SLAVE... STILL I DESPISE IT.
ATLANTIS.
EXCEPT FOR THE DROWNING.
HOW I DO LIKE DROWNING. I SHALL HAVE TO DROWN SOME OF THE HYDRA'S KNIGHTS BEFORE THIS ENDS... CERTAINLY...
DROWNING...THEN DOMINATION.
I DON'T WANT YOU TO TAKE THIS THE WRONG WAY... BUT I WANT TO ASK YOU A QUESTION...
WHY DO I LIKE YOU?

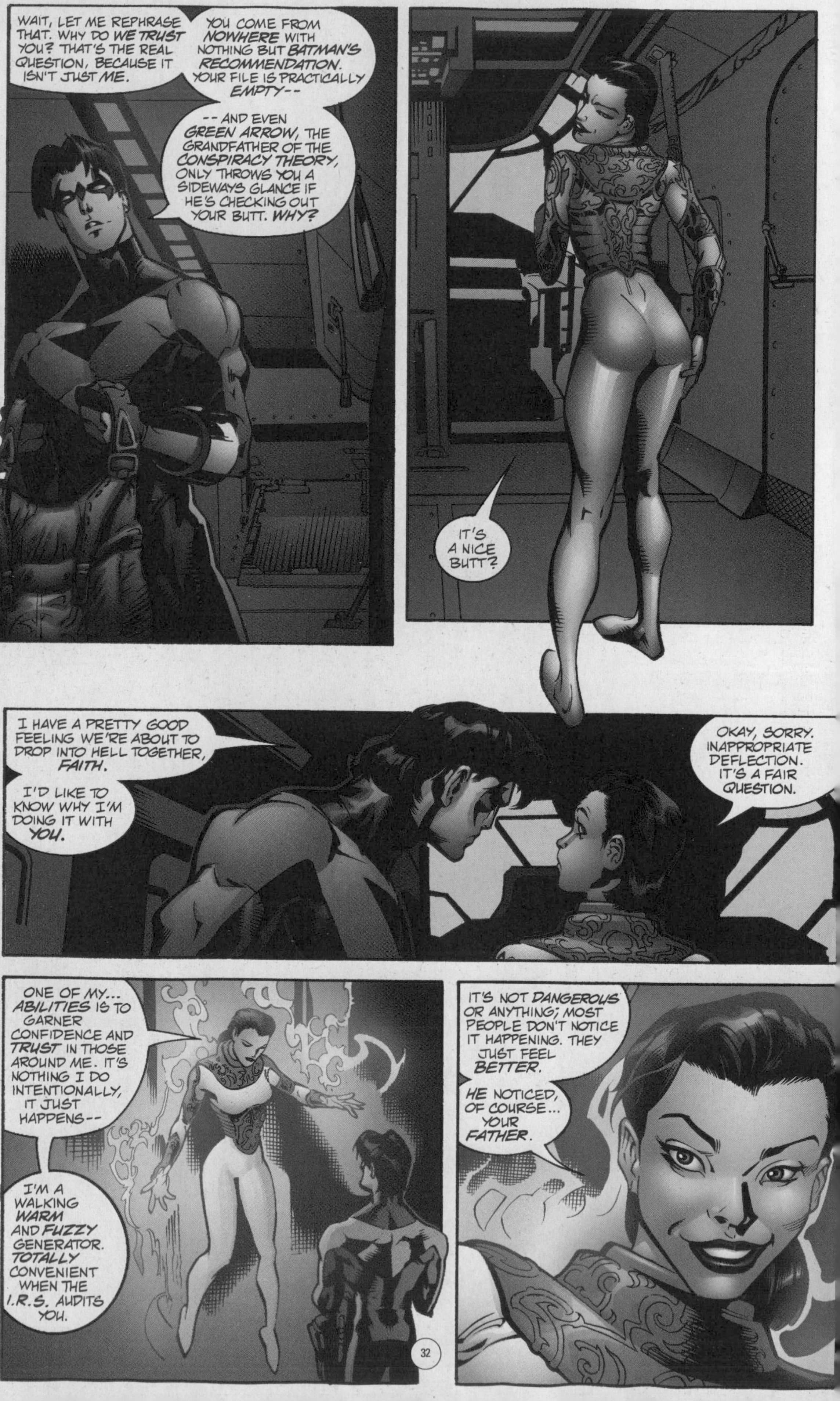
WAIT, LET ME REPHRASE THAT. WHY DO WE TRUST YOU? THAT'S THE REAL QUESTION, BECAUSE IT ISN'T JUST ME.
YOU COME FROM NOWHERE WITH NOTHING BUT BATMAN'S RECOMMENDATION. YOUR FILE IS PRACTICALLY EMPTY--
--AND EVEN GREEN ARROW, THE GRANDFATHER OF THE CONSPIRACY THEORY, ONLY THROWS YOU A SIDEWAYS GLANCE IF HE'S CHECKING OUT YOUR BUTT. WHY?
IT'S A NICE BUTT?
I HAVE A PRETTY GOOD FEELING WE'RE ABOUT TO DROP INTO HELL TOGETHER, FAITH.
I'D LIKE TO KNOW WHY I'M DOING IT WITH YOU.
OKAY, SORRY. INAPPROPRIATE DEFLECTION. IT'S A FAIR QUESTION.
ONE OF MY... ABILITIES IS TO GARNER CONFIDENCE AND TRUST IN THOSE AROUND ME. IT'S NOTHING I DO INTENTIONALLY, IT JUST HAPPENS--
I'M A WALKING WARM AND FUZZY GENERATOR. TOTALLY CONVENIENT WHEN THE I.R.S. AUDITS YOU.
IT'S NOT DANGEROUS OR ANYTHING; MOST PEOPLE DON'T NOTICE IT HAPPENING. THEY JUST FEEL BETTER.
HE NOTICED, OF COURSE... YOUR FATHER.

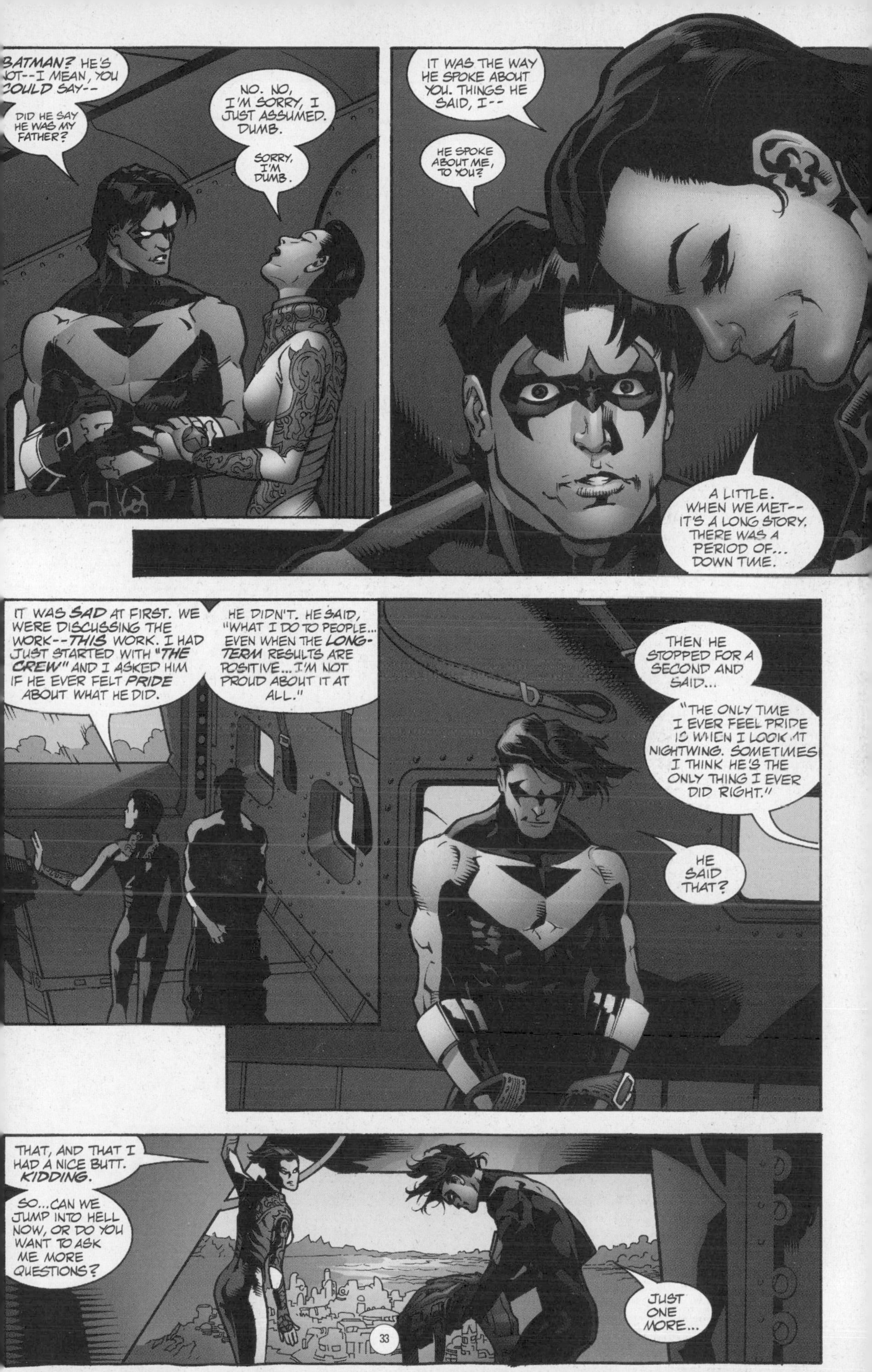
BATMAN? HE'S NOT--I MEAN, YOU COULD SAY--
DID HE SAY HE WAS MY FATHER?
NO. NO, I'M SORRY, I JUST ASSUMED. DUMB.
SORRY, I'M DUMB.
IT WAS THE WAY HE SPOKE ABOUT YOU. THINGS HE SAID, I--
HE SPOKE ABOUT ME, TO YOU?
A LITTLE. WHEN WE MET--IT'S A LONG STORY. THERE WAS A PERIOD OF... DOWN TIME.
IT WAS SAD AT FIRST. WE WERE DISCUSSING THE WORK--THIS WORK. I HAD JUST STARTED WITH "THE CREW" AND I ASKED HIM IF HE EVER FELT PRIDE ABOUT WHAT HE DID.
HE DIDN'T. HE SAID, "WHAT I DO TO PEOPLE... EVEN WHEN THE LONG-TERM RESULTS ARE POSITIVE... I'M NOT PROUD ABOUT IT AT ALL."
THEN HE STOPPED FOR A SECOND AND SAID...
"THE ONLY TIME I EVER FEEL PRIDE IS WHEN I LOOK AT NIGHTWING. SOMETIMES I THINK HE'S THE ONLY THING I EVER DID RIGHT."
HE SAID THAT?
THAT, AND THAT I HAD A NICE BUTT. KIDDING.
SO...CAN WE JUMP INTO HELL NOW, OR DO YOU WANT TO ASK ME MORE QUESTIONS?
JUST ONE MORE...

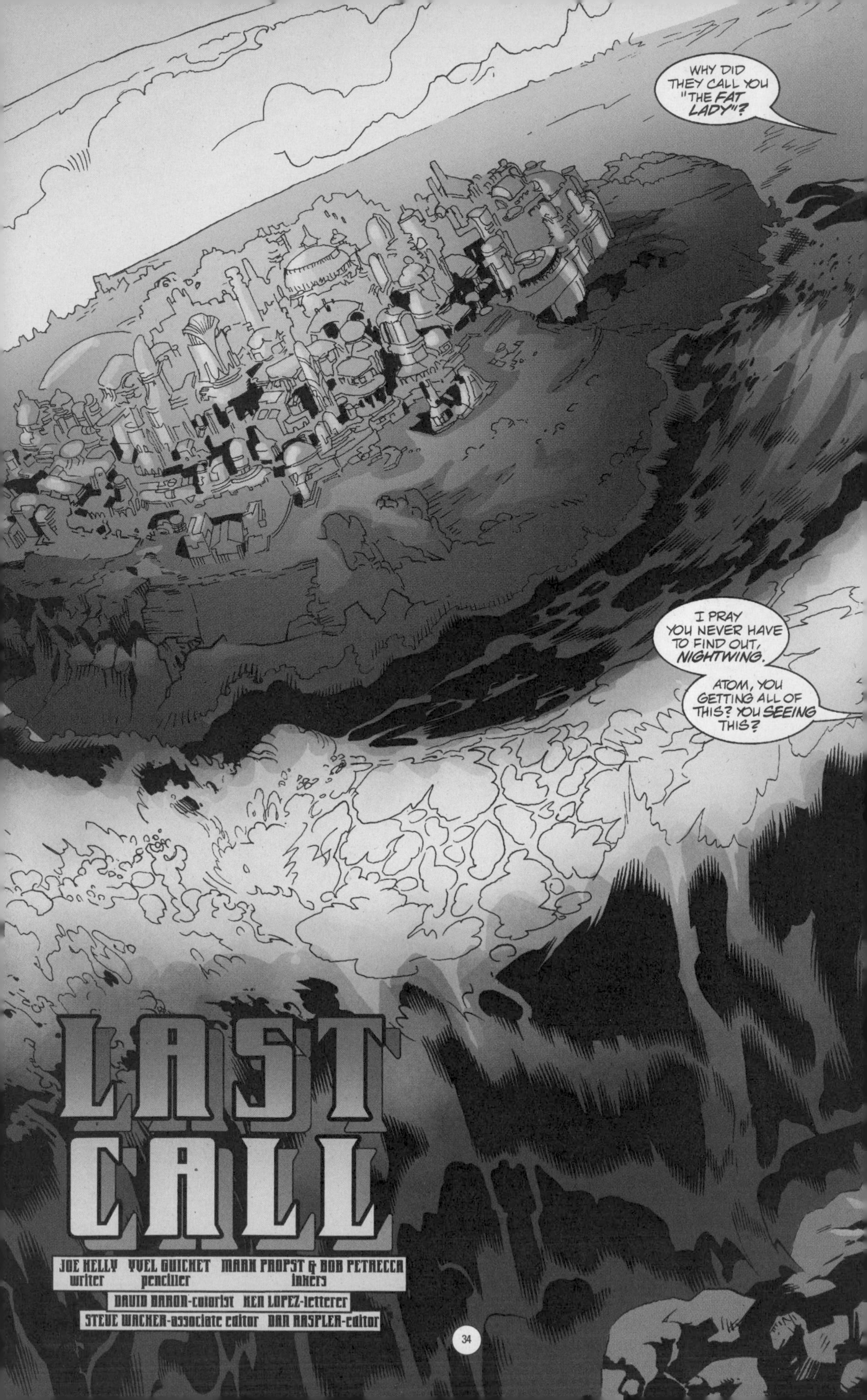
WHY DID THEY CALL YOU "THE FAT LADY"?
I PRAY YOU NEVER HAVE TO FIND OUT, NIGHTWING.
ATOM, YOU GETTING ALL OF THIS? YOU SEEING THIS?
LAST CALL
JOE KELLY writer YVEL GUICHET penciller MARK PROPST & BOB PETRECCA inkers
DAVID BARON-colorist KEN LOPEZ-letterer
STEVE WACKER-associate editor DAN RASPLER-editor

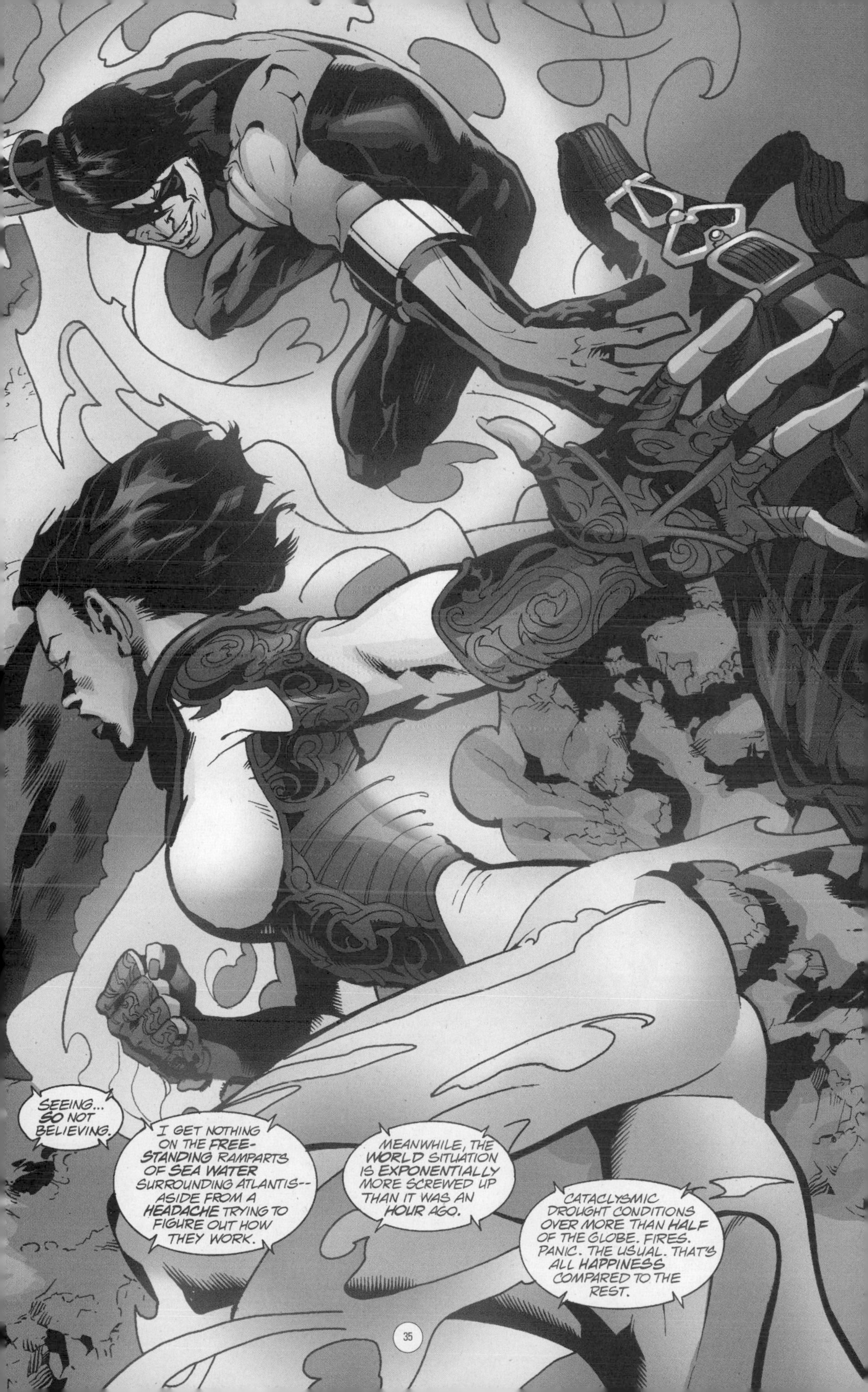

SEEING... SO NOT BELIEVING.
I GET NOTHING ON THE FREE-STANDING RAMPARTS OF SEA WATER SURROUNDING ATLANTIS-- ASIDE FROM A HEADACHE TRYING TO FIGURE OUT HOW THEY WORK.
MEANWHILE, THE WORLD SITUATION IS EXPONENTIALLY MORE SCREWED UP THAN IT WAS AN HOUR AGO.
CATACLYSMIC DROUGHT CONDITIONS OVER MORE THAN HALF OF THE GLOBE. FIRES. PANIC. THE USUAL. THAT'S ALL HAPPINESS COMPARED TO THE REST.

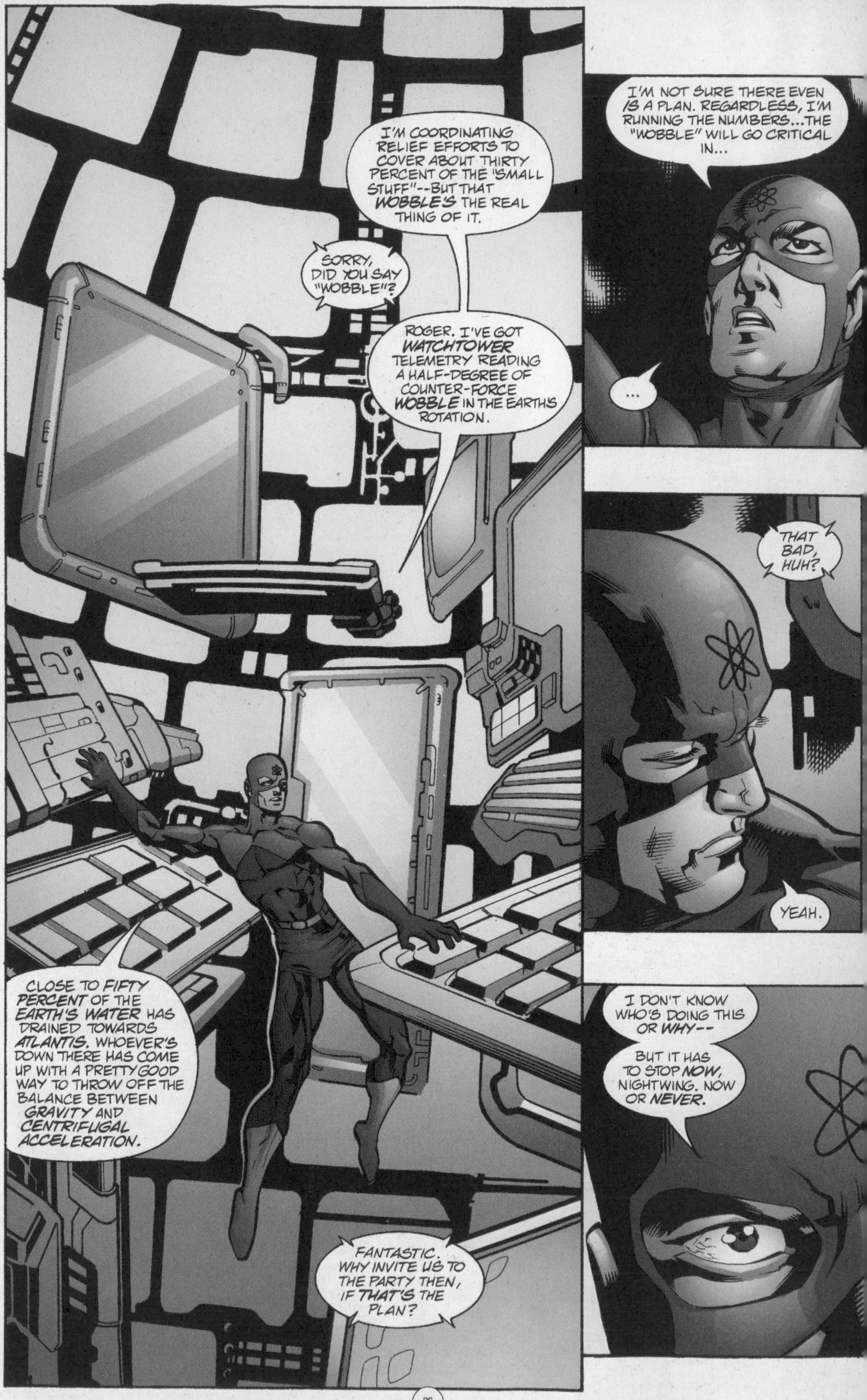
I'M COORDINATING RELIEF EFFORTS TO COVER ABOUT THIRTY PERCENT OF THE "SMALL STUFF"--BUT THAT WOBBLE'S THE REAL THING OF IT.
SORRY, DID YOU SAY "WOBBLE"?
ROGER. I'VE GOT WATCHTOWER TELEMETRY READING A HALF-DEGREE OF COUNTER-FORCE WOBBLE IN THE EARTH'S ROTATION.
CLOSE TO FIFTY PERCENT OF THE EARTH'S WATER HAS DRAINED TOWARDS ATLANTIS. WHOEVER'S DOWN THERE HAS COME UP WITH A PRETTY GOOD WAY TO THROW OFF THE BALANCE BETWEEN GRAVITY AND CENTRIFUGAL ACCELERATION.
FANTASTIC. WHY INVITE US TO THE PARTY THEN, IF THAT'S THE PLAN?
I'M NOT SURE THERE EVEN IS A PLAN. REGARDLESS, I'M RUNNING THE NUMBERS...THE "WOBBLE" WILL GO CRITICAL IN...
...
THAT BAD, HUH?
YEAH.
I DON'T KNOW WHO'S DOING THIS OR WHY--
BUT IT HAS TO STOP NOW, NIGHTWING. NOW OR NEVER.

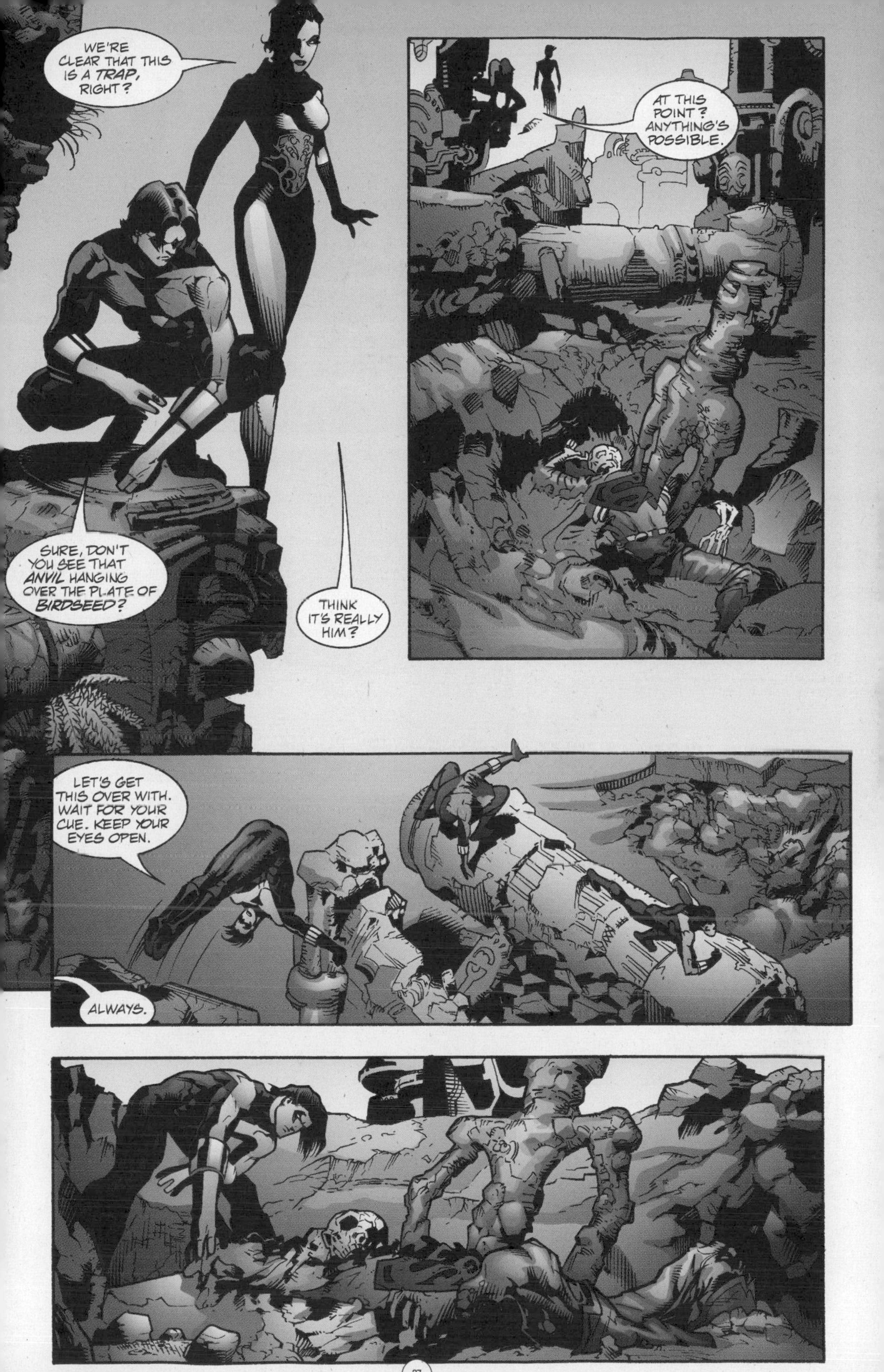
WE'RE CLEAR THAT THIS IS A *TRAP*, RIGHT?
SURE, DON'T YOU SEE THAT *ANVIL* HANGING OVER THE PLATE OF *BIRDSEED*?
THINK IT'S REALLY HIM?
AT THIS POINT? ANYTHING'S POSSIBLE.
LET'S GET THIS OVER WITH. WAIT FOR YOUR CUE. KEEP YOUR EYES OPEN.
ALWAYS.

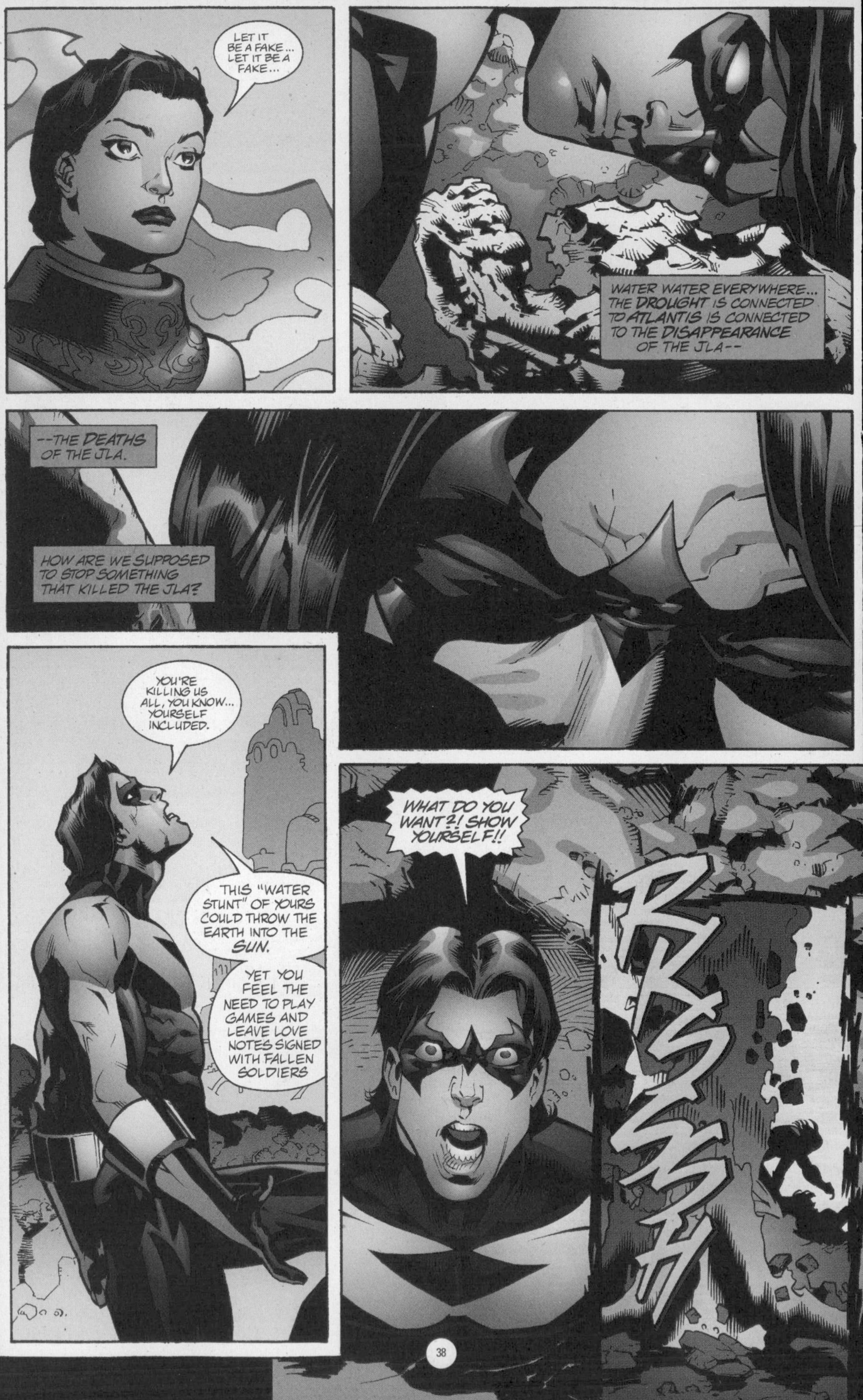
LET IT BE A FAKE... LET IT BE A FAKE...
WATER WATER EVERYWHERE... THE DROUGHT IS CONNECTED TO ATLANTIS IS CONNECTED TO THE DISAPPEARANCE OF THE JLA--
--THE DEATHS OF THE JLA.
HOW ARE WE SUPPOSED TO STOP SOMETHING THAT KILLED THE JLA?
YOU'RE KILLING US ALL, YOU KNOW... YOURSELF INCLUDED.
THIS "WATER STUNT" OF YOURS COULD THROW THE EARTH INTO THE SUN.
YET YOU FEEL THE NEED TO PLAY GAMES AND LEAVE LOVE NOTES SIGNED WITH FALLEN SOLDIERS
WHAT DO YOU WANT?! SHOW YOURSELF!!
RRSMMH

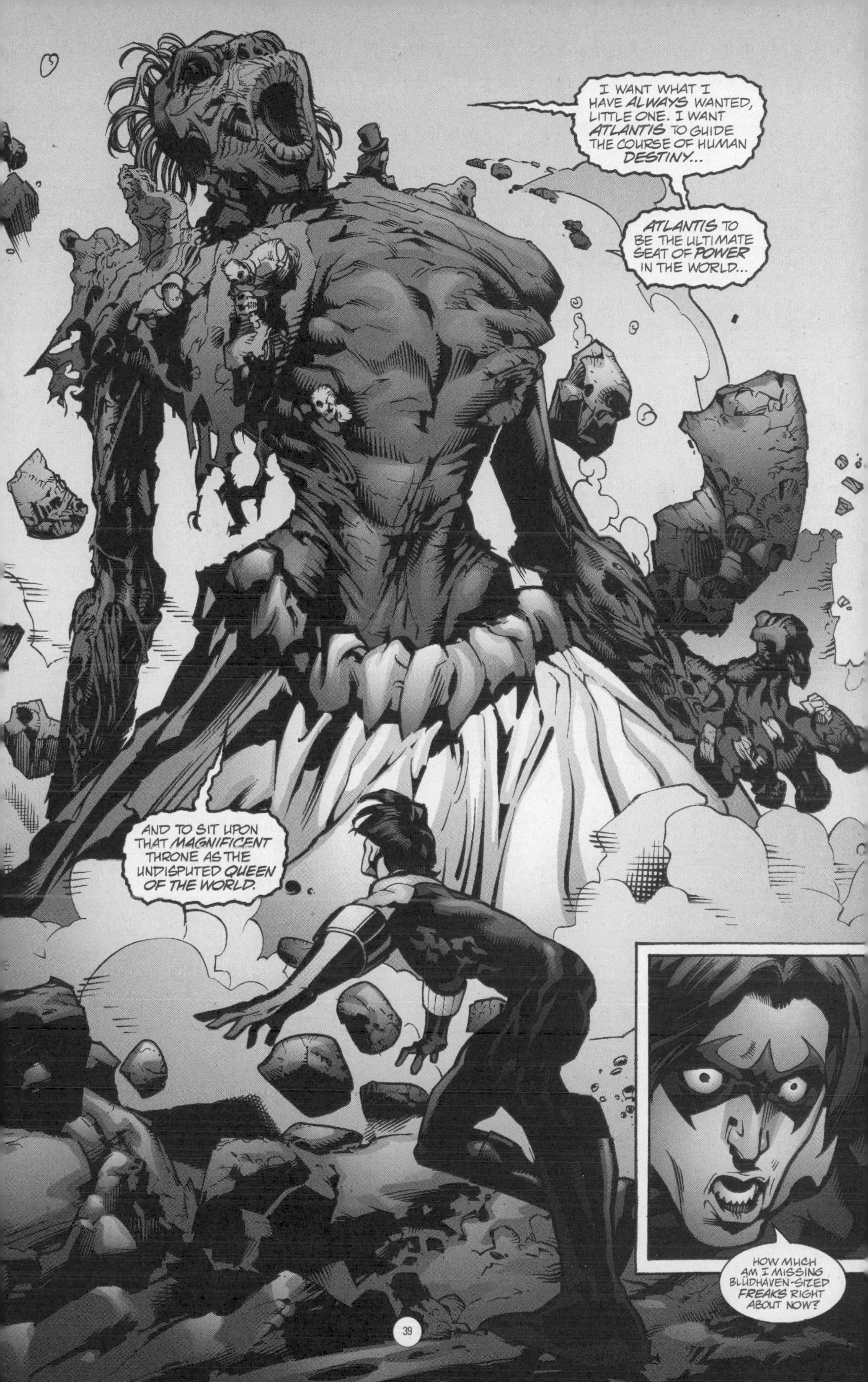
I WANT WHAT I HAVE ALWAYS WANTED, LITTLE ONE. I WANT ATLANTIS TO GUIDE THE COURSE OF HUMAN DESTINY...
ATLANTIS TO BE THE ULTIMATE SEAT OF POWER IN THE WORLD...
AND TO SIT UPON THAT MAGNIFICENT THRONE AS THE UNDISPUTED QUEEN OF THE WORLD.
HOW MUCH AM I MISSING BLÜDHAVEN-SIZED FREAKS RIGHT ABOUT NOW?

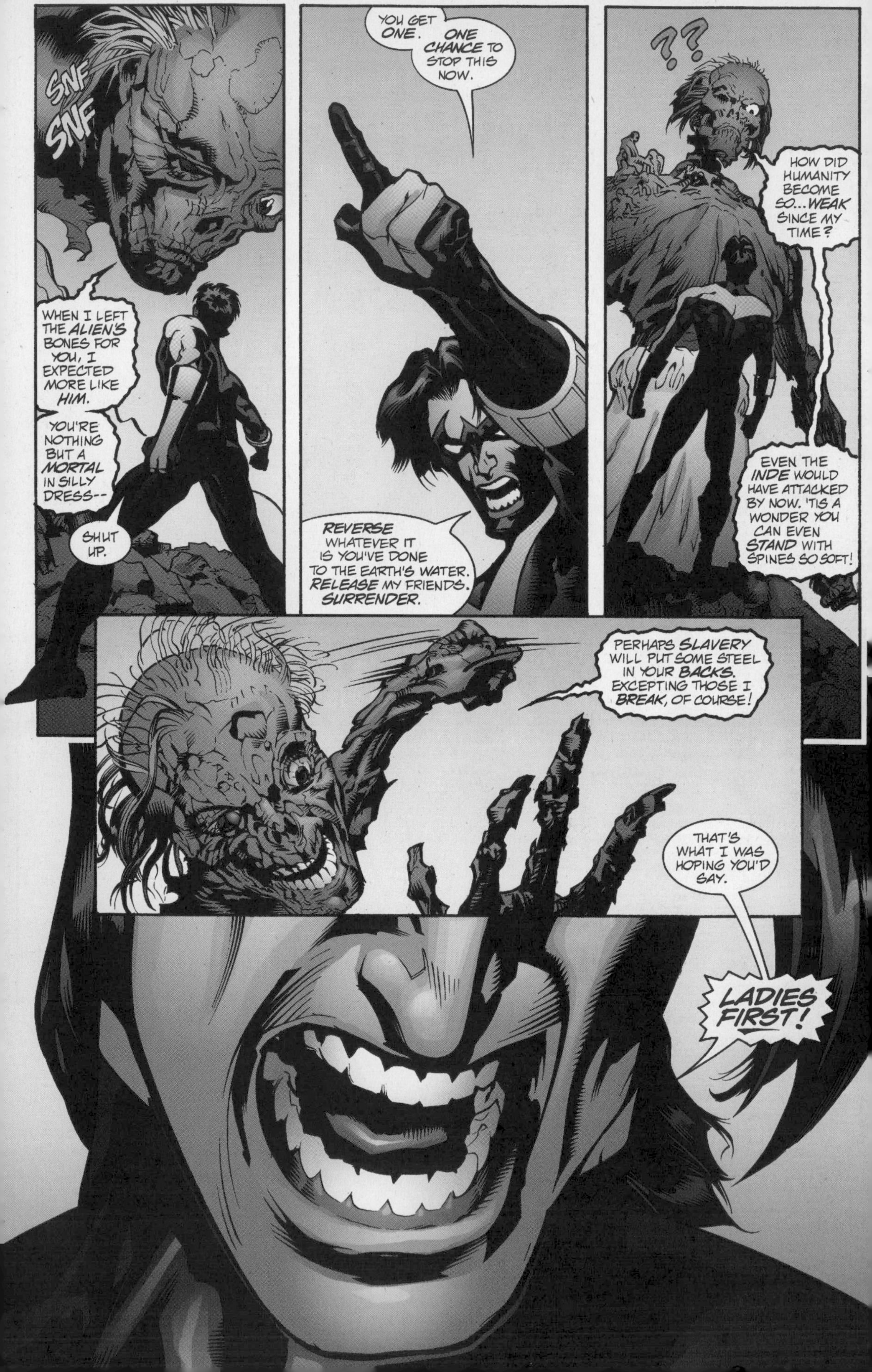

SNF SNF
WHEN I LEFT THE ALIEN'S BONES FOR YOU, I EXPECTED MORE LIKE HIM.
YOU'RE NOTHING BUT A MORTAL IN SILLY DRESS--
SHUT UP.
YOU GET ONE. ONE CHANCE TO STOP THIS NOW.
REVERSE WHATEVER IT IS YOU'VE DONE TO THE EARTH'S WATER. RELEASE MY FRIENDS. SURRENDER.
??
HOW DID HUMANITY BECOME SO...WEAK SINCE MY TIME?
EVEN THE INDE WOULD HAVE ATTACKED BY NOW. 'TIS A WONDER YOU CAN EVEN STAND WITH SPINES SO SOFT!
PERHAPS SLAVERY WILL PUT SOME STEEL IN YOUR BACKS. EXCEPTING THOSE I BREAK, OF COURSE!
THAT'S WHAT I WAS HOPING YOU'D SAY.
LADIES FIRST!

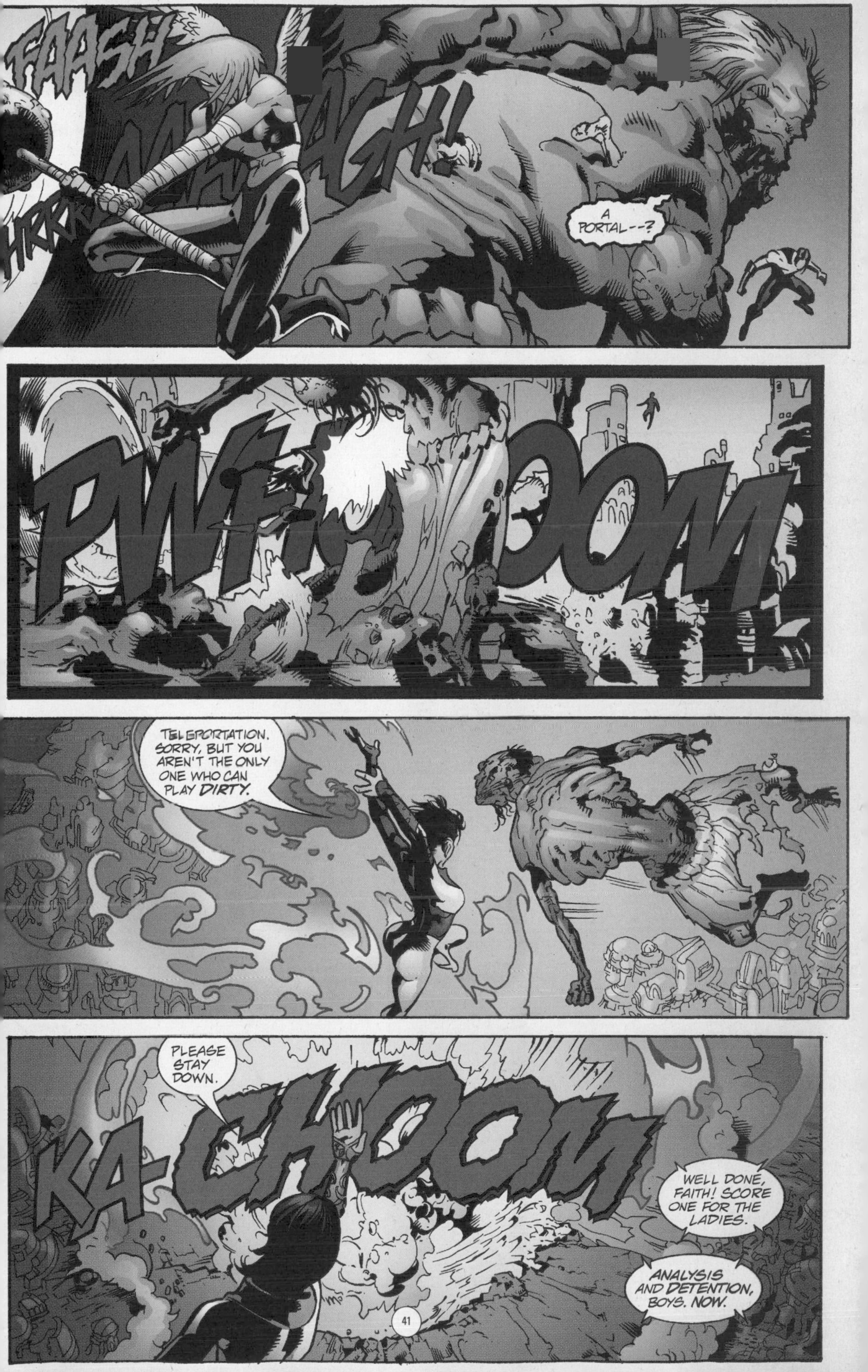
FAASH
A PORTAL--?
TELEPORTATION. SORRY, BUT YOU AREN'T THE ONLY ONE WHO CAN PLAY DIRTY.
PLEASE STAY DOWN.
KA-CHOOM
WELL DONE, FAITH! SCORE ONE FOR THE LADIES.
ANALYSIS AND DETENTION, BOYS. NOW.

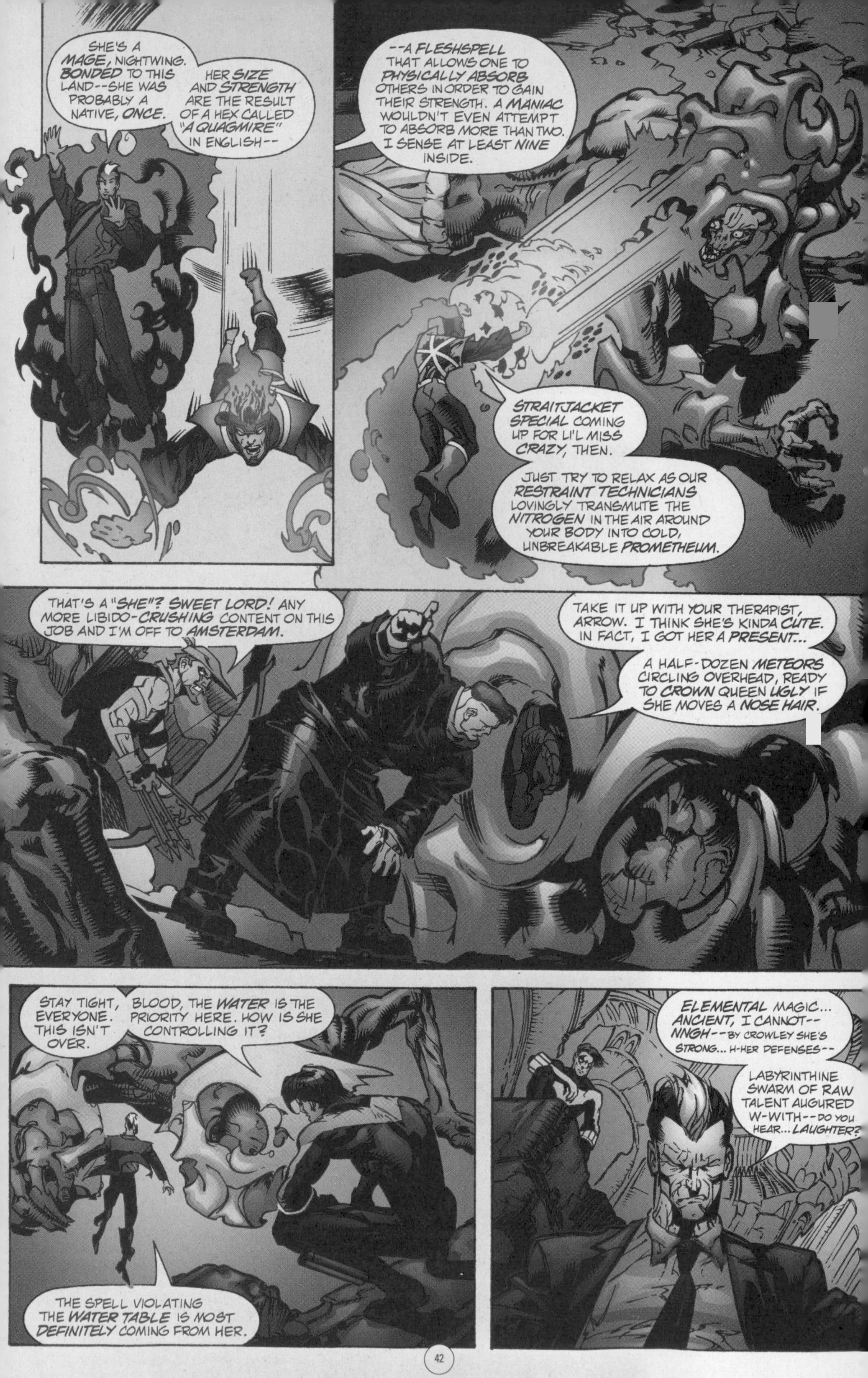
SHE'S A MAGE, NIGHTWING. BONDED TO THIS LAND--SHE WAS PROBABLY A NATIVE, ONCE.
HER SIZE AND STRENGTH ARE THE RESULT OF A HEX CALLED "A QUAGMIRE" IN ENGLISH--
--A FLESHSPELL THAT ALLOWS ONE TO PHYSICALLY ABSORB OTHERS IN ORDER TO GAIN THEIR STRENGTH. A MANIAC WOULDN'T EVEN ATTEMPT TO ABSORB MORE THAN TWO. I SENSE AT LEAST NINE INSIDE.
STRAITJACKET SPECIAL COMING UP FOR LI'L MISS CRAZY, THEN.
JUST TRY TO RELAX AS OUR RESTRAINT TECHNICIANS LOVINGLY TRANSMUTE THE NITROGEN IN THE AIR AROUND YOUR BODY INTO COLD, UNBREAKABLE PROMETHEUM.
THAT'S A "SHE"? SWEET LORD! ANY MORE LIBIDO-CRUSHING CONTENT ON THIS JOB AND I'M OFF TO AMSTERDAM.
TAKE IT UP WITH YOUR THERAPIST, ARROW. I THINK SHE'S KINDA CUTE. IN FACT, I GOT HER A PRESENT...
A HALF-DOZEN METEORS CIRCLING OVERHEAD, READY TO CROWN QUEEN UGLY IF SHE MOVES A NOSE HAIR.
STAY TIGHT, EVERYONE. THIS ISN'T OVER.
BLOOD, THE WATER IS THE PRIORITY HERE. HOW IS SHE CONTROLLING IT?
THE SPELL VIOLATING THE WATER TABLE IS MOST DEFINITELY COMING FROM HER.
ELEMENTAL MAGIC... ANCIENT, I CANNOT--NNGH--BY CROWLEY SHE'S STRONG... H-HER DEFENSES--
LABYRINTHINE SWARM OF RAW TALENT AUGURED W-WITH--DO YOU HEAR... LAUGHTER?

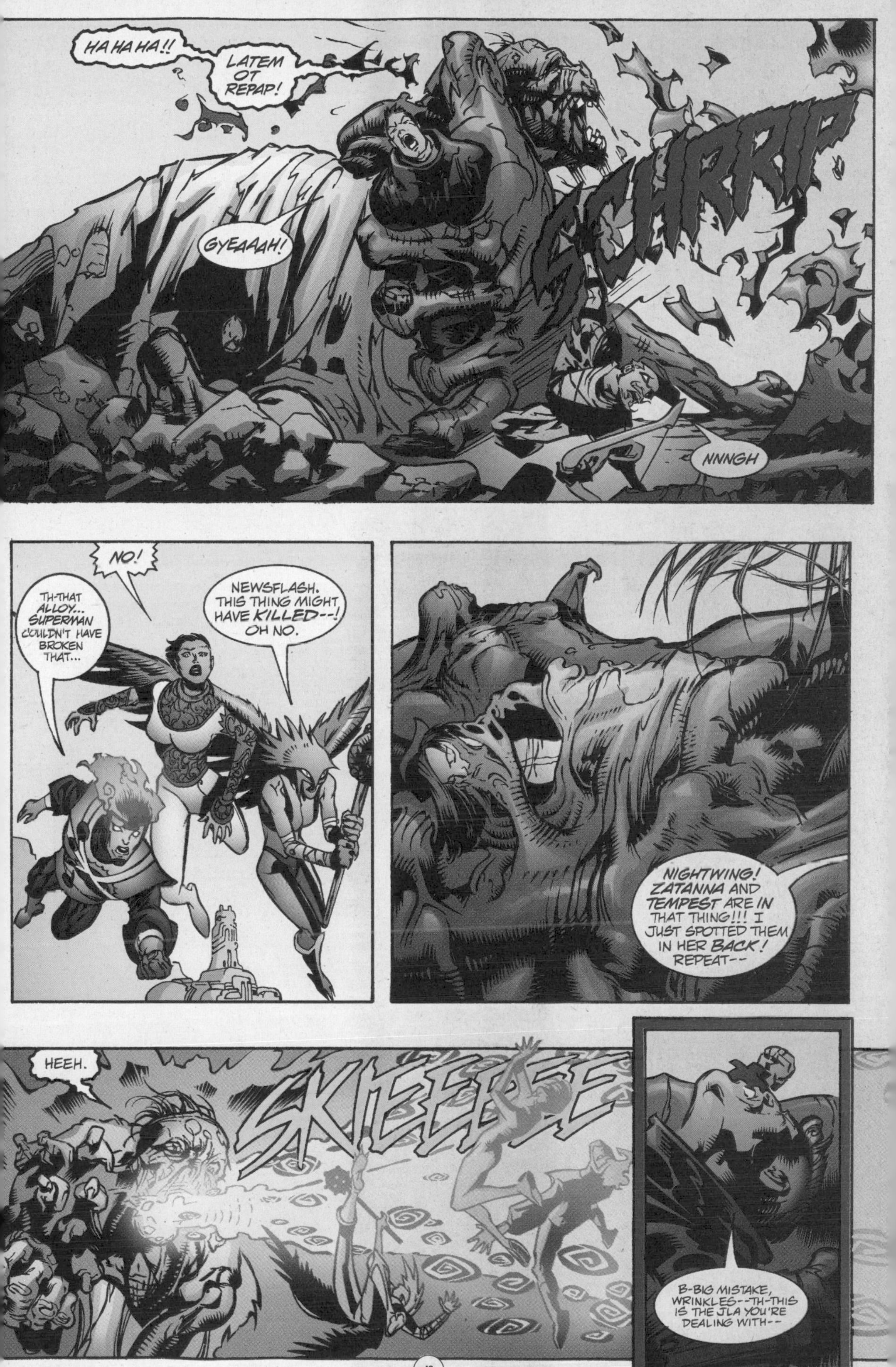
HA HA HA!!
LATEM OT REPAP!
SCHRRIP
GYEAAAH!
NNNGH
NO!
TH-THAT ALLOY... SUPERMAN COULDN'T HAVE BROKEN THAT...
NEWSFLASH. THIS THING MIGHT HAVE KILLED--! OH NO.
NIGHTWING! ZATANNA AND TEMPEST ARE IN THAT THING!!! I JUST SPOTTED THEM IN HER BACK! REPEAT--
HEEH.
B-BIG MISTAKE, WRINKLES--TH-THIS IS THE JLA YOU'RE DEALING WITH--

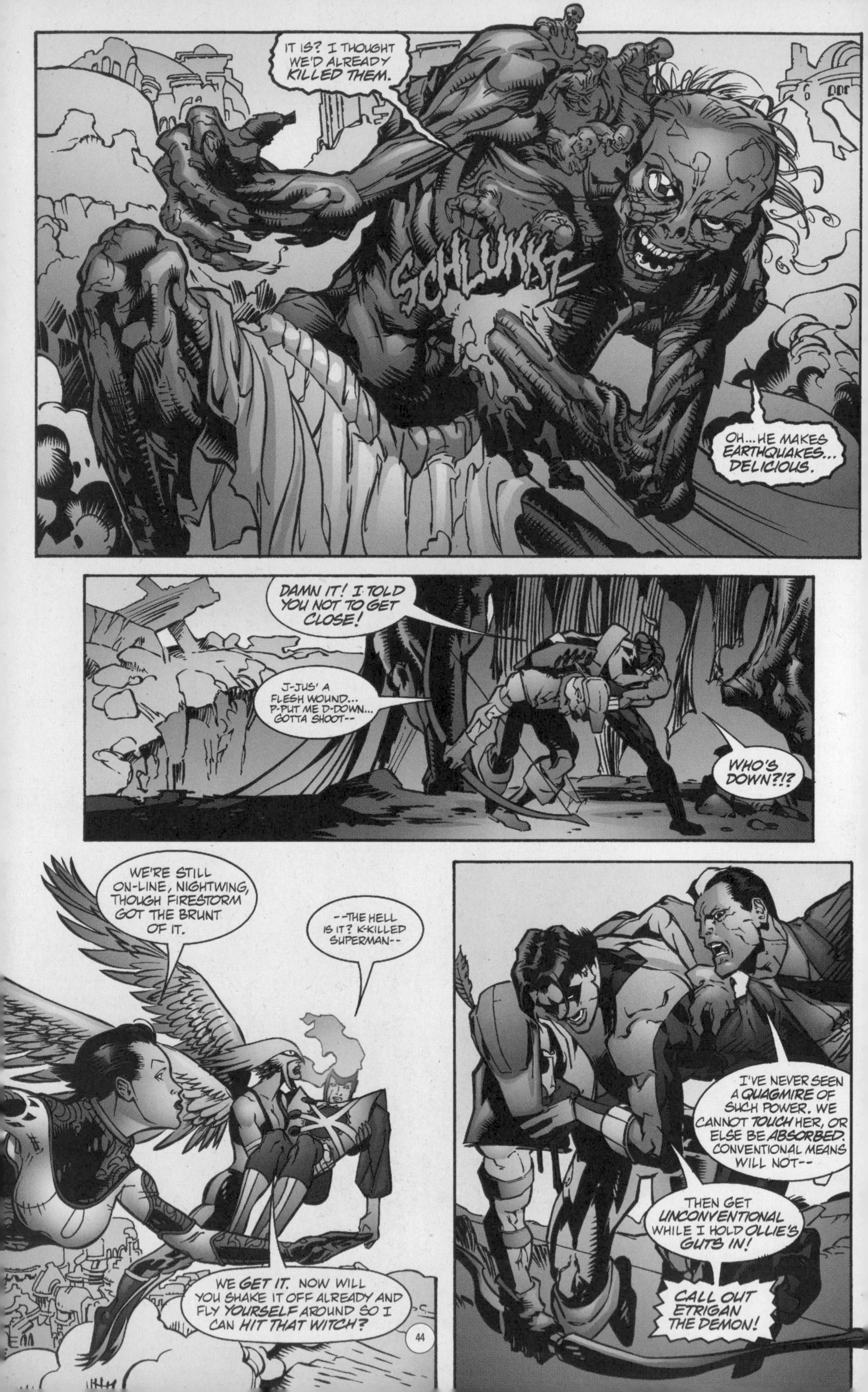
IT IS? I THOUGHT WE'D ALREADY KILLED THEM.
SCHLUKKT
OH...HE MAKES EARTHQUAKES... DELICIOUS.
DAMN IT! I TOLD YOU NOT TO GET CLOSE!
J-JUS' A FLESH WOUND... P-PUT ME D-DOWN... GOTTA SHOOT--
WHO'S DOWN?!?
WE'RE STILL ON-LINE, NIGHTWING, THOUGH FIRESTORM GOT THE BRUNT OF IT.
--THE HELL IS IT? K-KILLED SUPERMAN--
WE GET IT. NOW WILL YOU SHAKE IT OFF ALREADY AND FLY YOURSELF AROUND SO I CAN HIT THAT WITCH?
I'VE NEVER SEEN A QUAGMIRE OF SUCH POWER. WE CANNOT TOUCH HER, OR ELSE BE ABSORBED. CONVENTIONAL MEANS WILL NOT--
THEN GET UNCONVENTIONAL WHILE I HOLD OLLIE'S GUTS IN!
CALL OUT ETRIGAN THE DEMON!

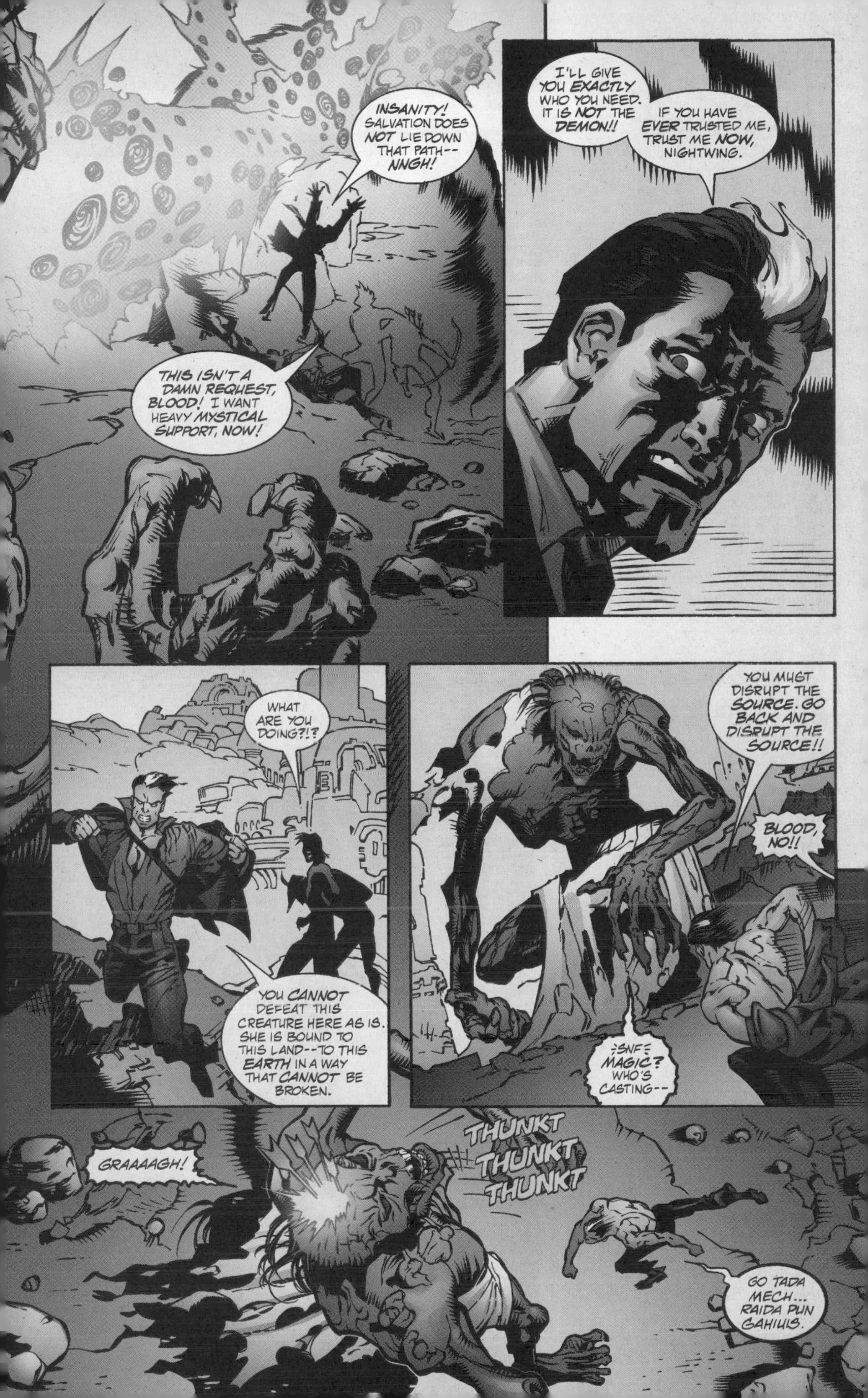
INSANITY! SALVATION DOES NOT LIE DOWN THAT PATH-- NNGH!
THIS ISN'T A DAMN REQUEST, BLOOD! I WANT HEAVY MYSTICAL SUPPORT, NOW!
I'LL GIVE YOU EXACTLY WHO YOU NEED. IT IS NOT THE DEMON!!
IF YOU HAVE EVER TRUSTED ME, TRUST ME NOW, NIGHTWING.
WHAT ARE YOU DOING?!?
YOU CANNOT DEFEAT THIS CREATURE HERE AS IS. SHE IS BOUND TO THIS LAND--TO THIS EARTH IN A WAY THAT CANNOT BE BROKEN.
YOU MUST DISRUPT THE SOURCE. GO BACK AND DISRUPT THE SOURCE!!
BLOOD, NO!!
SNF MAGIC? WHO'S CASTING--
GRAAAAGH!
THUNKT THUNKT THUNKT
GO TADA MECH... RAIDA PUN GAHIUIS.

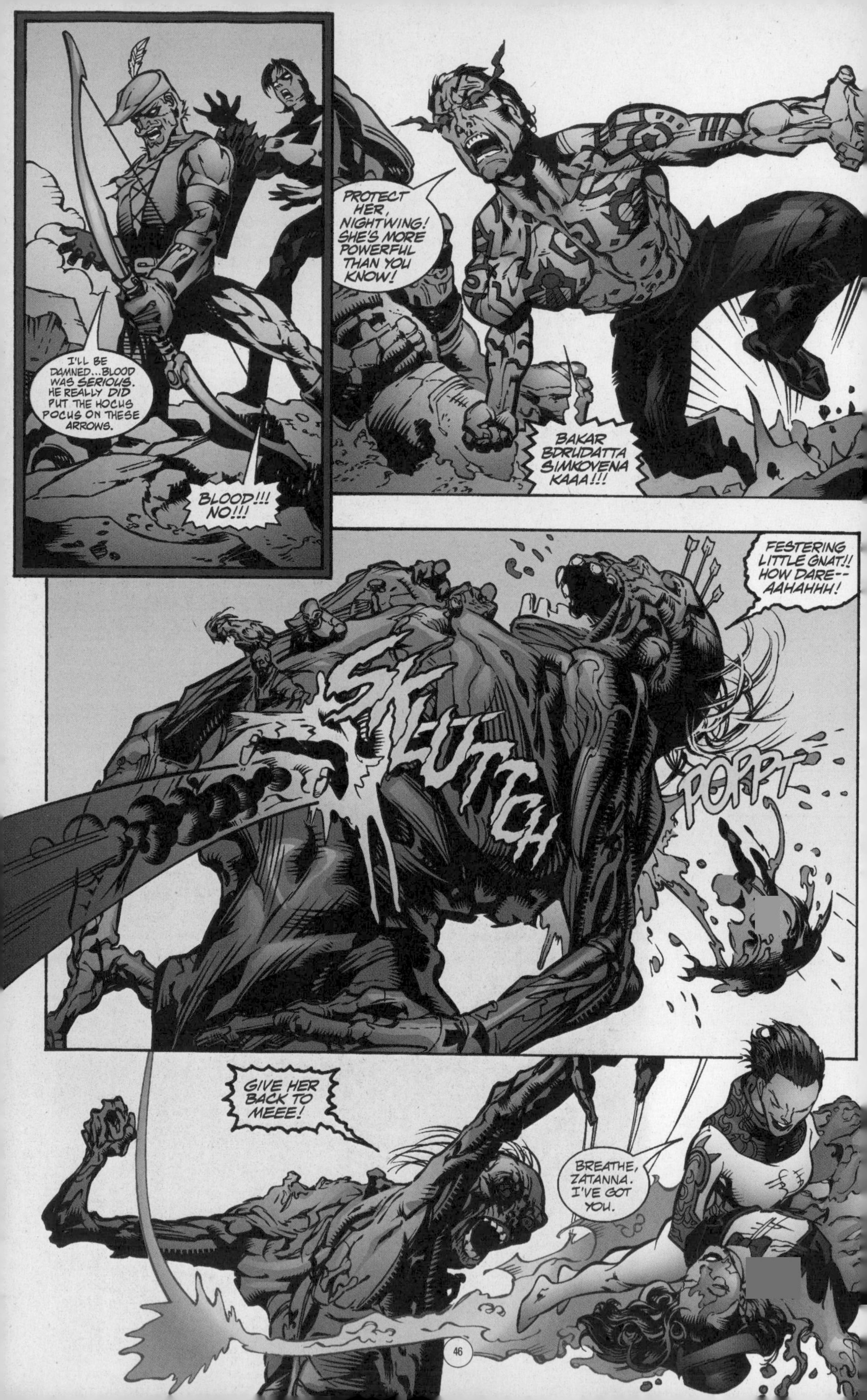
I'LL BE DAMNED...BLOOD WAS SERIOUS. HE REALLY DID PUT THE HOCUS POCUS ON THESE ARROWS.
BLOOD!!! NO!!!
PROTECT HER, NIGHTWING! SHE'S MORE POWERFUL THAN YOU KNOW!
BAKAR BDRUDATTA SIMKOVENA KAAA!!!
FESTERING LITTLE GNAT!! HOW DARE-- AAHAHHH!
SKLUTTCH
POPPT
GIVE HER BACK TO MEEE!
BREATHE, ZATANNA. I'VE GOT YOU.

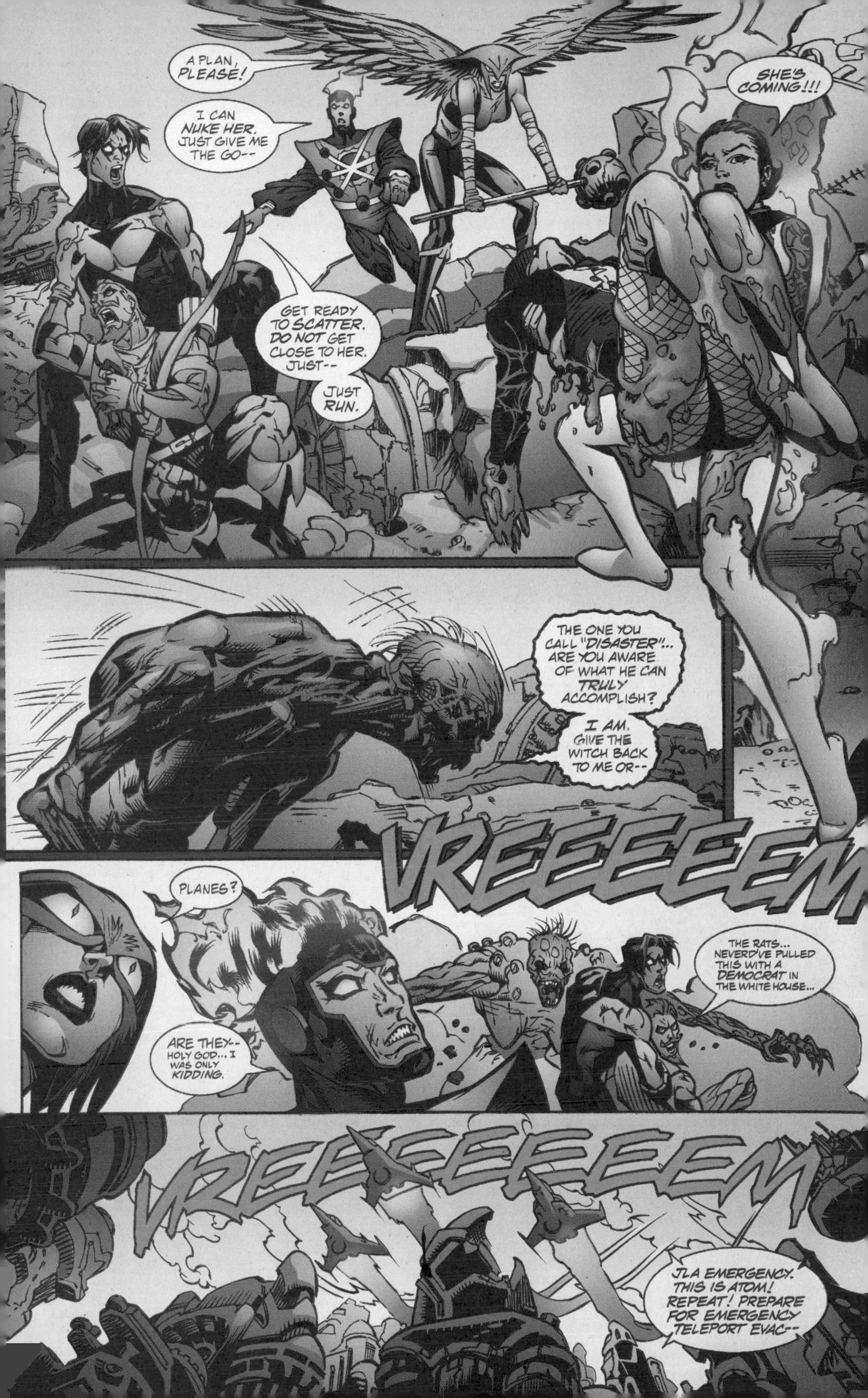
A PLAN, PLEASE!
I CAN NUKE HER. JUST GIVE ME THE GO--
SHE'S COMING!!!
GET READY TO SCATTER. DO NOT GET CLOSE TO HER. JUST--
JUST RUN.
THE ONE YOU CALL "DISASTER"... ARE YOU AWARE OF WHAT HE CAN TRULY ACCOMPLISH?
I AM. GIVE THE WITCH BACK TO ME OR--
VREEEEEM
PLANES?
THE RATS... NEVER'D'VE PULLED THIS WITH A DEMOCRAT IN THE WHITE HOUSE...
ARE THEY-- HOLY GOD... I WAS ONLY KIDDING.
VREEEEEEEM
JLA EMERGENCY. THIS IS ATOM! REPEAT! PREPARE FOR EMERGENCY TELEPORT EVAC--

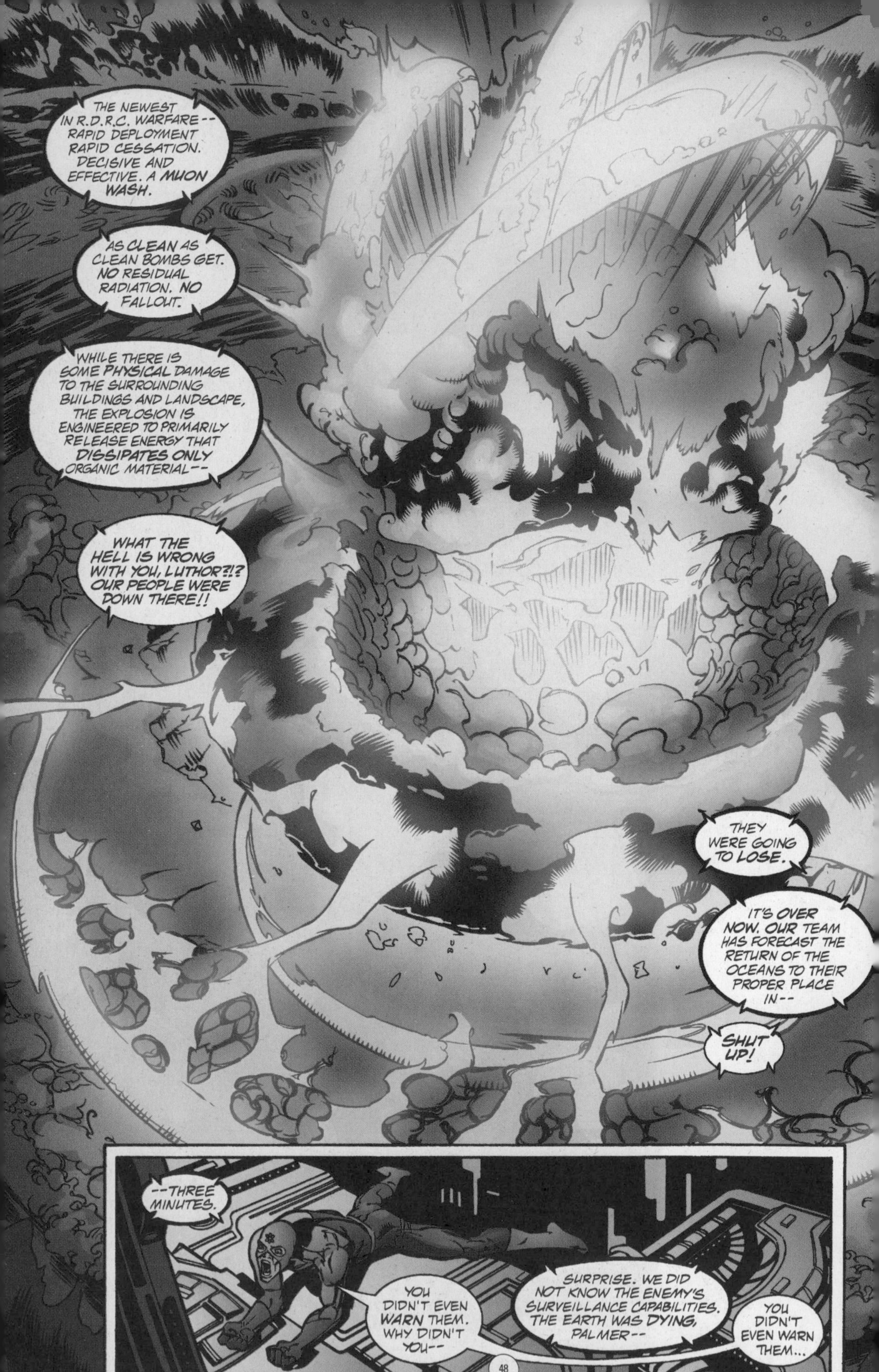
THE NEWEST IN R.D.R.C. WARFARE-- RAPID DEPLOYMENT RAPID CESSATION. DECISIVE AND EFFECTIVE. A MUON WASH.
AS CLEAN AS CLEAN BOMBS GET. NO RESIDUAL RADIATION. NO FALLOUT.
WHILE THERE IS SOME PHYSICAL DAMAGE TO THE SURROUNDING BUILDINGS AND LANDSCAPE, THE EXPLOSION IS ENGINEERED TO PRIMARILY RELEASE ENERGY THAT DISSIPATES ONLY ORGANIC MATERIAL--
WHAT THE HELL IS WRONG WITH YOU, LUTHOR?!? OUR PEOPLE WERE DOWN THERE!!
THEY WERE GOING TO LOSE.
IT'S OVER NOW. OUR TEAM HAS FORECAST THE RETURN OF THE OCEANS TO THEIR PROPER PLACE IN--
SHUT UP!
--THREE MINUTES.
YOU DIDN'T EVEN WARN THEM. WHY DIDN'T YOU--
SURPRISE. WE DID NOT KNOW THE ENEMY'S SURVEILLANCE CAPABILITIES. THE EARTH WAS DYING, PALMER--
YOU DIDN'T EVEN WARN THEM...

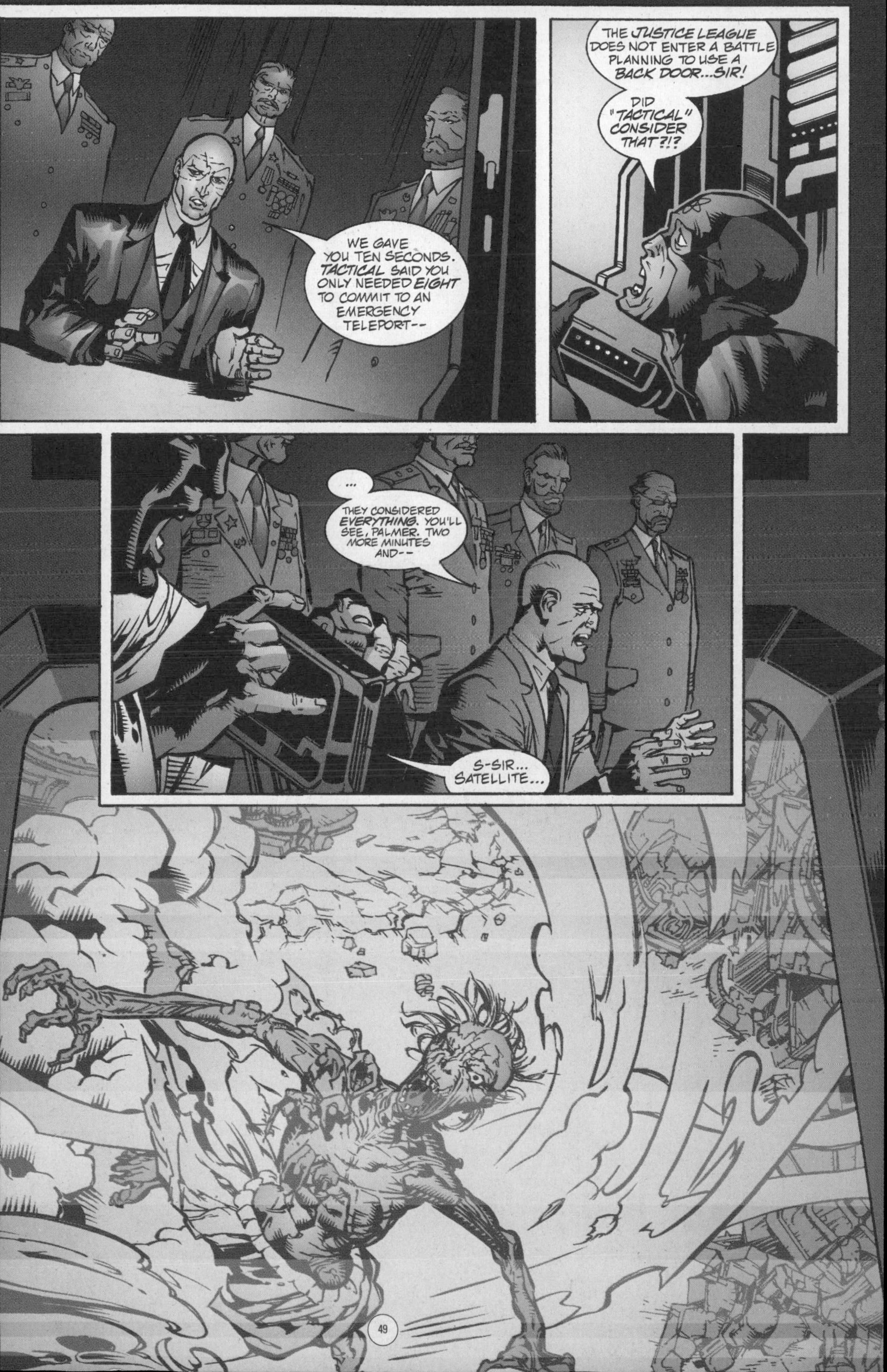
WE GAVE YOU TEN SECONDS. TACTICAL SAID YOU ONLY NEEDED EIGHT TO COMMIT TO AN EMERGENCY TELEPORT--
THE JUSTICE LEAGUE DOES NOT ENTER A BATTLE PLANNING TO USE A BACK DOOR...SIR!
DID "TACTICAL" CONSIDER THAT?!?
...
THEY CONSIDERED EVERYTHING. YOU'LL SEE, PALMER. TWO MORE MINUTES AND--
S-SIR... SATELLITE...

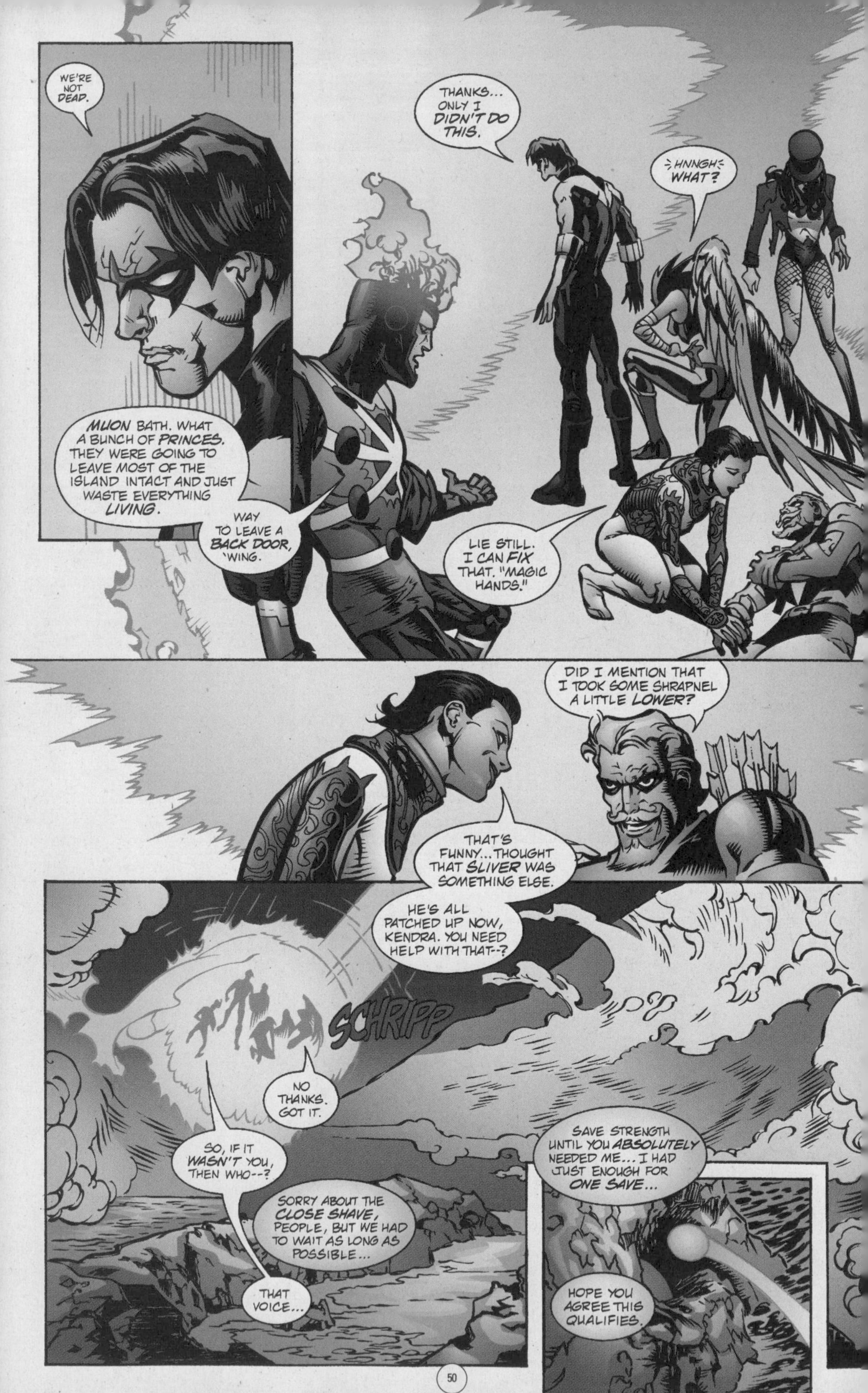
WE'RE NOT DEAD.
THANKS... ONLY I DIDN'T DO THIS.
HNNGH WHAT?
MUON BATH. WHAT A BUNCH OF PRINCES. THEY WERE GOING TO LEAVE MOST OF THE ISLAND INTACT AND JUST WASTE EVERYTHING LIVING.
WAY TO LEAVE A BACK DOOR, 'WING.
LIE STILL. I CAN FIX THAT. "MAGIC HANDS."
DID I MENTION THAT I TOOK SOME SHRAPNEL A LITTLE LOWER?
THAT'S FUNNY... THOUGHT THAT SLIVER WAS SOMETHING ELSE.
HE'S ALL PATCHED UP NOW, KENDRA. YOU NEED HELP WITH THAT--?
SCHRIPP
NO THANKS. GOT IT.
SO, IF IT WASN'T YOU, THEN WHO--?
SORRY ABOUT THE CLOSE SHAVE, PEOPLE, BUT WE HAD TO WAIT AS LONG AS POSSIBLE...
THAT VOICE...
SAVE STRENGTH UNTIL YOU ABSOLUTELY NEEDED ME... I HAD JUST ENOUGH FOR ONE SAVE...
HOPE YOU AGREE THIS QUALIFIES.

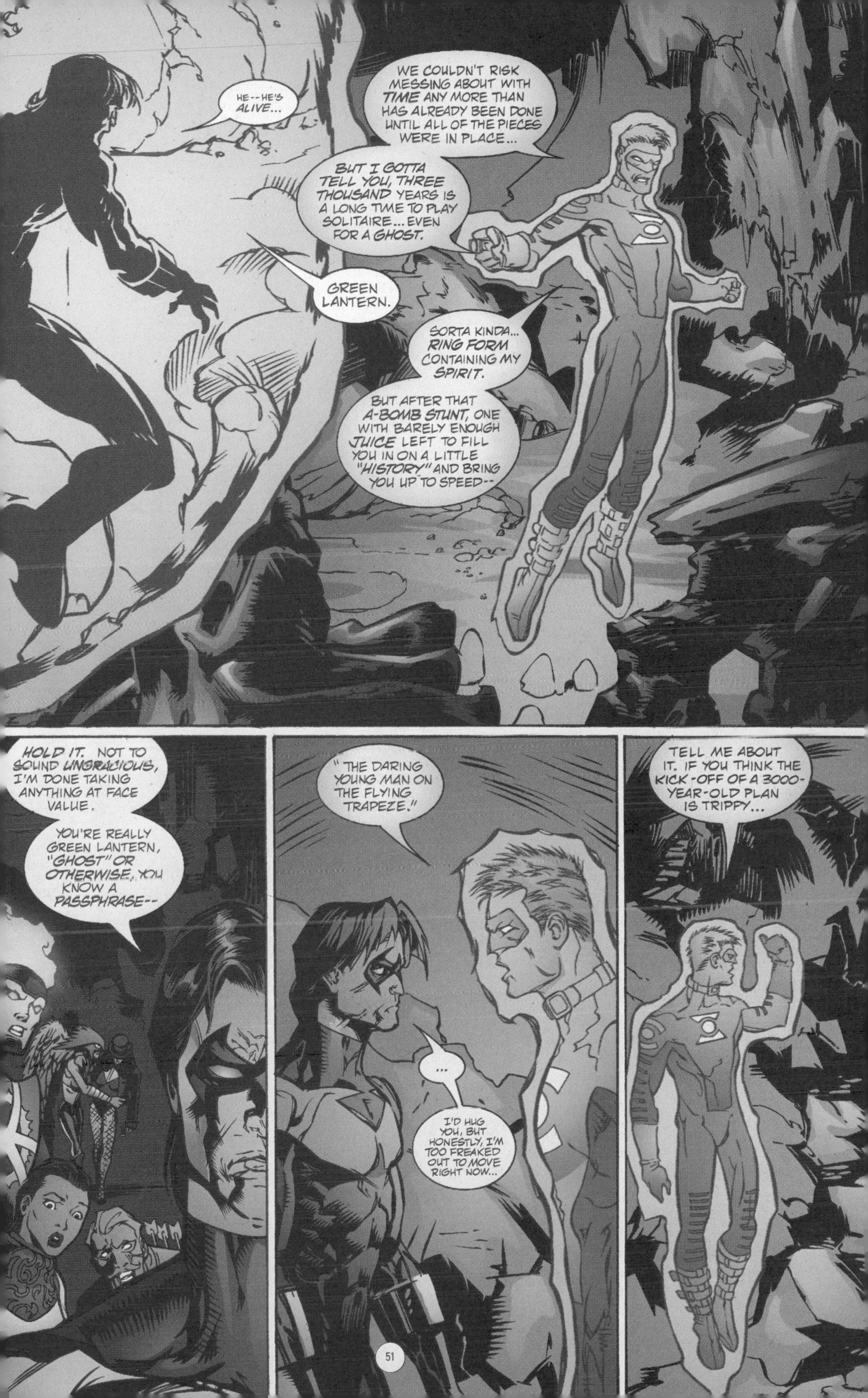
HE--HE'S ALIVE...
WE COULDN'T RISK MESSING ABOUT WITH TIME ANY MORE THAN HAS ALREADY BEEN DONE UNTIL ALL OF THE PIECES WERE IN PLACE...
BUT I GOTTA TELL YOU, THREE THOUSAND YEARS IS A LONG TIME TO PLAY SOLITAIRE... EVEN FOR A GHOST.
GREEN LANTERN.
SORTA KINDA... RING FORM CONTAINING MY SPIRIT.
BUT AFTER THAT A-BOMB STUNT, ONE WITH BARELY ENOUGH JUICE LEFT TO FILL YOU IN ON A LITTLE "HISTORY" AND BRING YOU UP TO SPEED--
HOLD IT. NOT TO SOUND UNGRACIOUS, I'M DONE TAKING ANYTHING AT FACE VALUE.
YOU'RE REALLY GREEN LANTERN, "GHOST" OR OTHERWISE, YOU KNOW A PASSPHRASE--
"THE DARING YOUNG MAN ON THE FLYING TRAPEZE."
...
I'D HUG YOU, BUT HONESTLY, I'M TOO FREAKED OUT TO MOVE RIGHT NOW...
TELL ME ABOUT IT. IF YOU THINK THE KICK-OFF OF A 3000-YEAR-OLD PLAN IS TRIPPY...

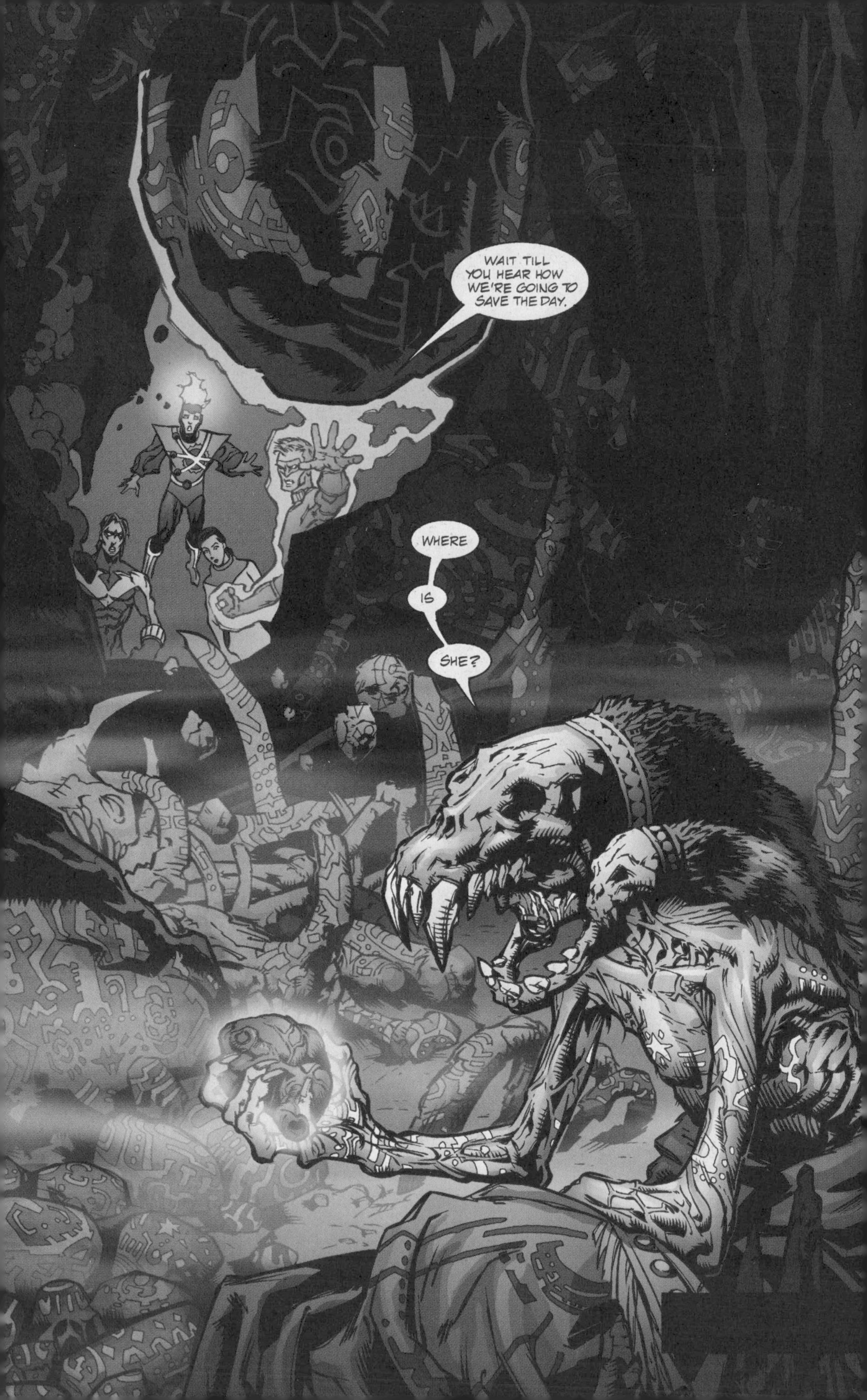
WAIT TILL YOU HEAR HOW WE'RE GOING TO SAVE THE DAY.
WHERE
IS
SHE?

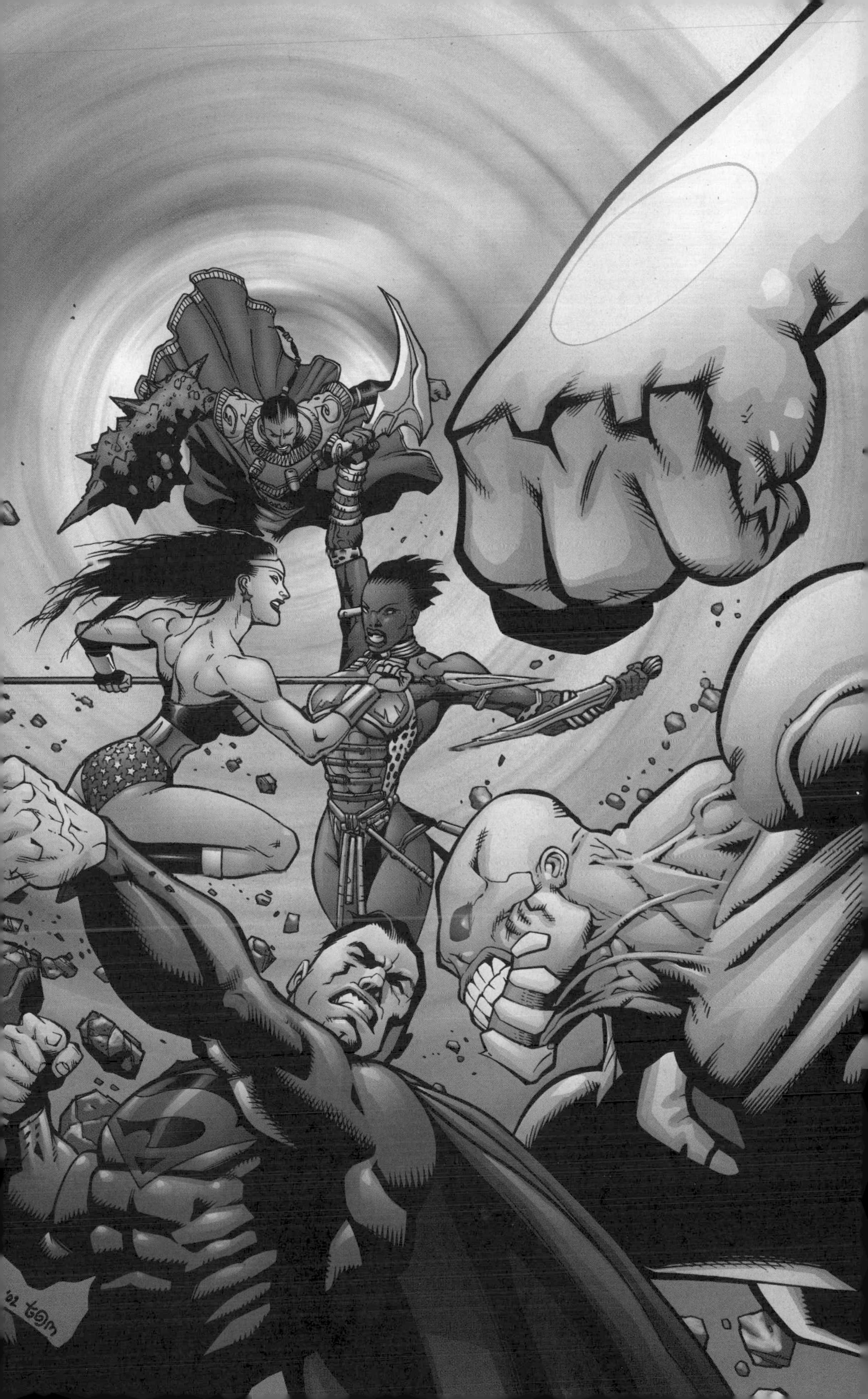

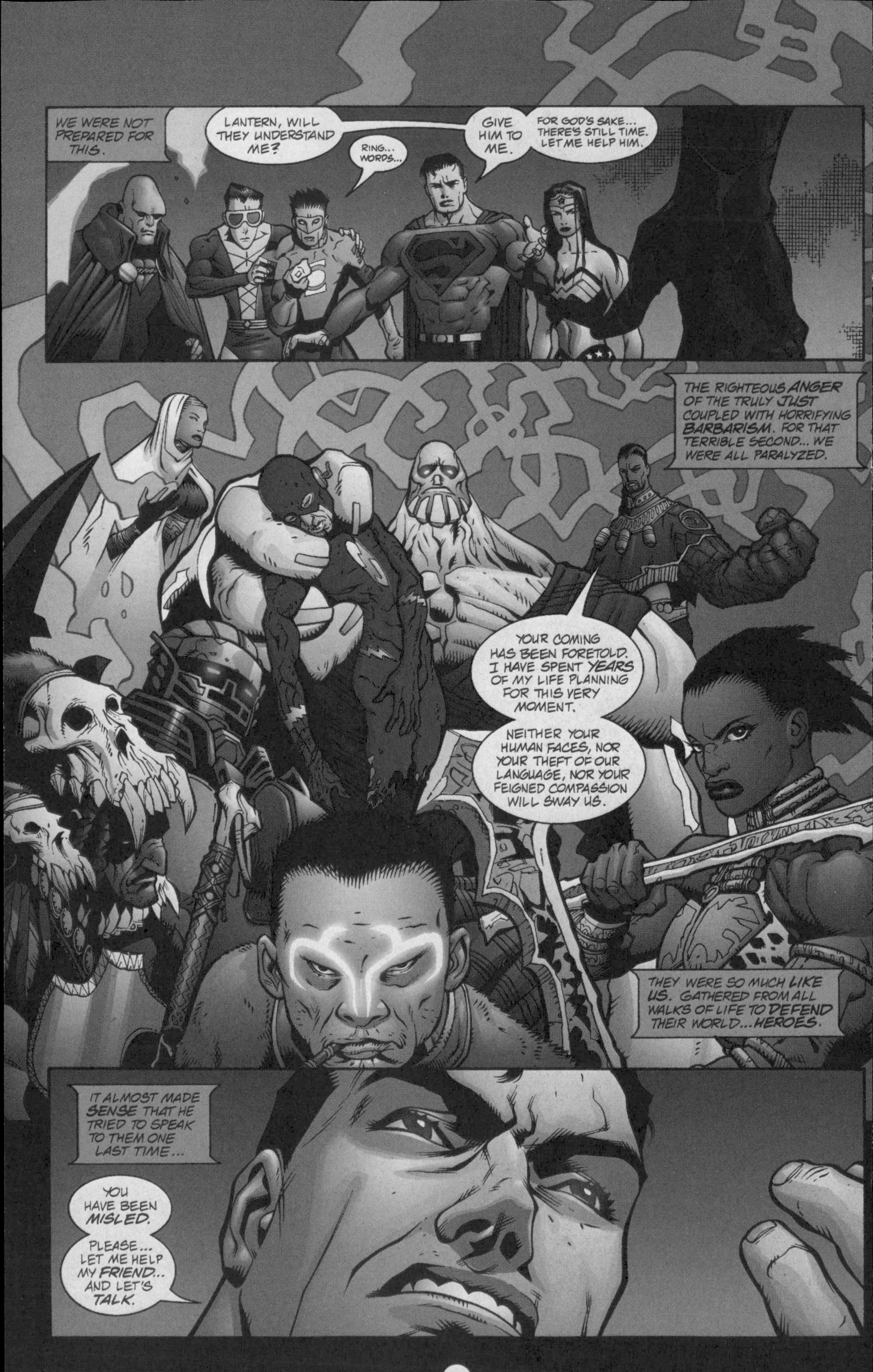
WE WERE NOT PREPARED FOR THIS.
LANTERN, WILL THEY UNDERSTAND ME?
RING... WORDS...
GIVE HIM TO ME.
FOR GOD'S SAKE... THERE'S STILL TIME. LET ME HELP HIM.
THE RIGHTEOUS ANGER OF THE TRULY JUST COUPLED WITH HORRIFYING BARBARISM. FOR THAT TERRIBLE SECOND... WE WERE ALL PARALYZED.
YOUR COMING HAS BEEN FORETOLD. I HAVE SPENT YEARS OF MY LIFE PLANNING FOR THIS VERY MOMENT.
NEITHER YOUR HUMAN FACES, NOR YOUR THEFT OF OUR LANGUAGE, NOR YOUR FEIGNED COMPASSION WILL SWAY US.
THEY WERE SO MUCH LIKE US. GATHERED FROM ALL WALKS OF LIFE TO DEFEND THEIR WORLD... HEROES.
IT ALMOST MADE SENSE THAT HE TRIED TO SPEAK TO THEM ONE LAST TIME...
YOU HAVE BEEN MISLED.
PLEASE... LET ME HELP MY FRIEND... AND LET'S TALK.

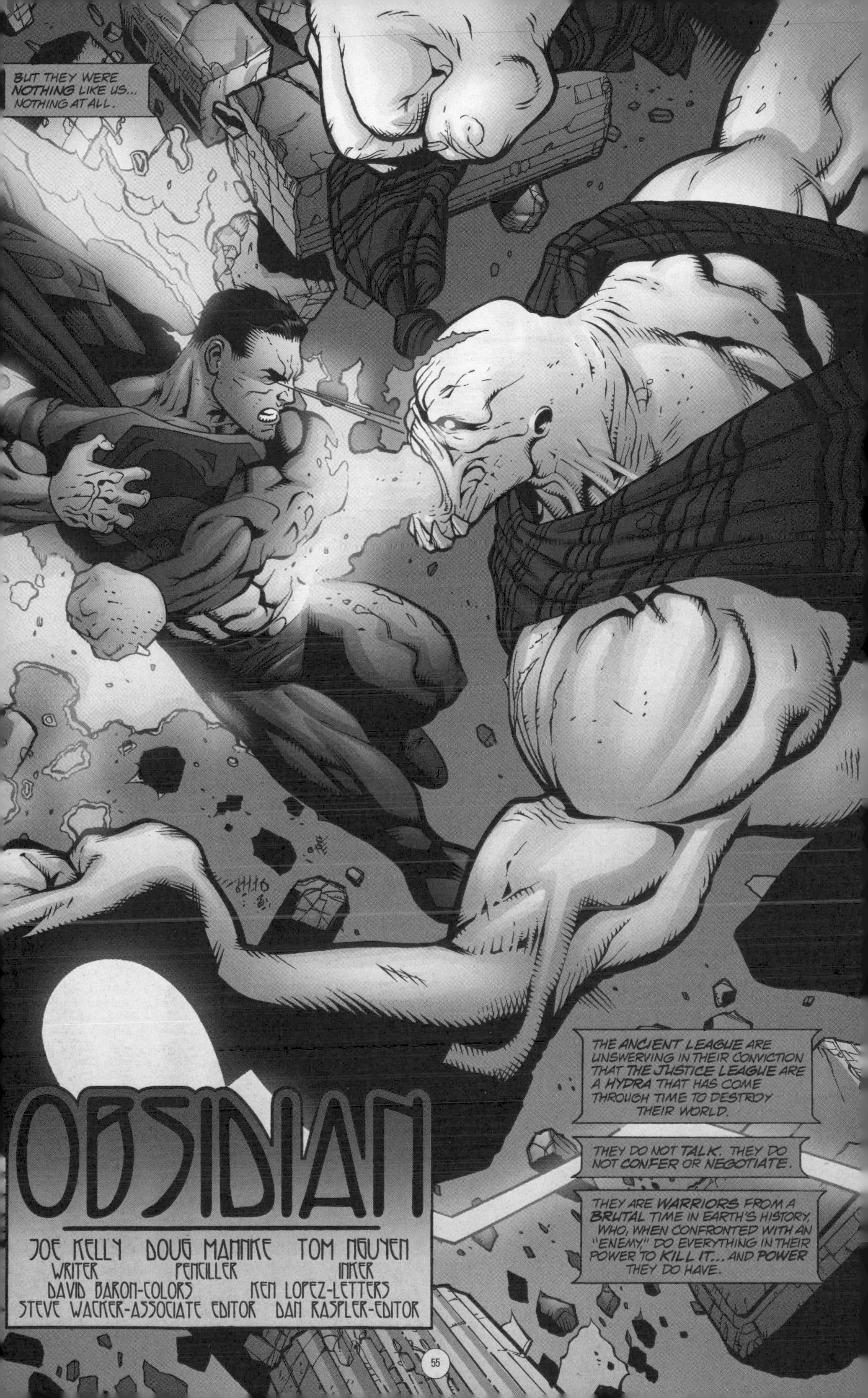

BUT THEY WERE NOTHING LIKE US... NOTHING AT ALL.
THE ANCIENT LEAGUE ARE UNSWERVING IN THEIR CONVICTION THAT THE JUSTICE LEAGUE ARE A HYDRA THAT HAS COME THROUGH TIME TO DESTROY THEIR WORLD.
THEY DO NOT TALK. THEY DO NOT CONFER OR NEGOTIATE.
THEY ARE WARRIORS FROM A BRUTAL TIME IN EARTH'S HISTORY, WHO, WHEN CONFRONTED WITH AN "ENEMY," DO EVERYTHING IN THEIR POWER TO KILL IT... AND POWER THEY DO HAVE.
OBSIDIAN
JOE KELLY WRITER
DOUG MAHNKE PENCILLER
TOM NGUYEN INKER
DAVID BARON-COLORS
KEN LOPEZ-LETTERS
STEVE WACKER-ASSOCIATE EDITOR
DAN RASPLER-EDITOR

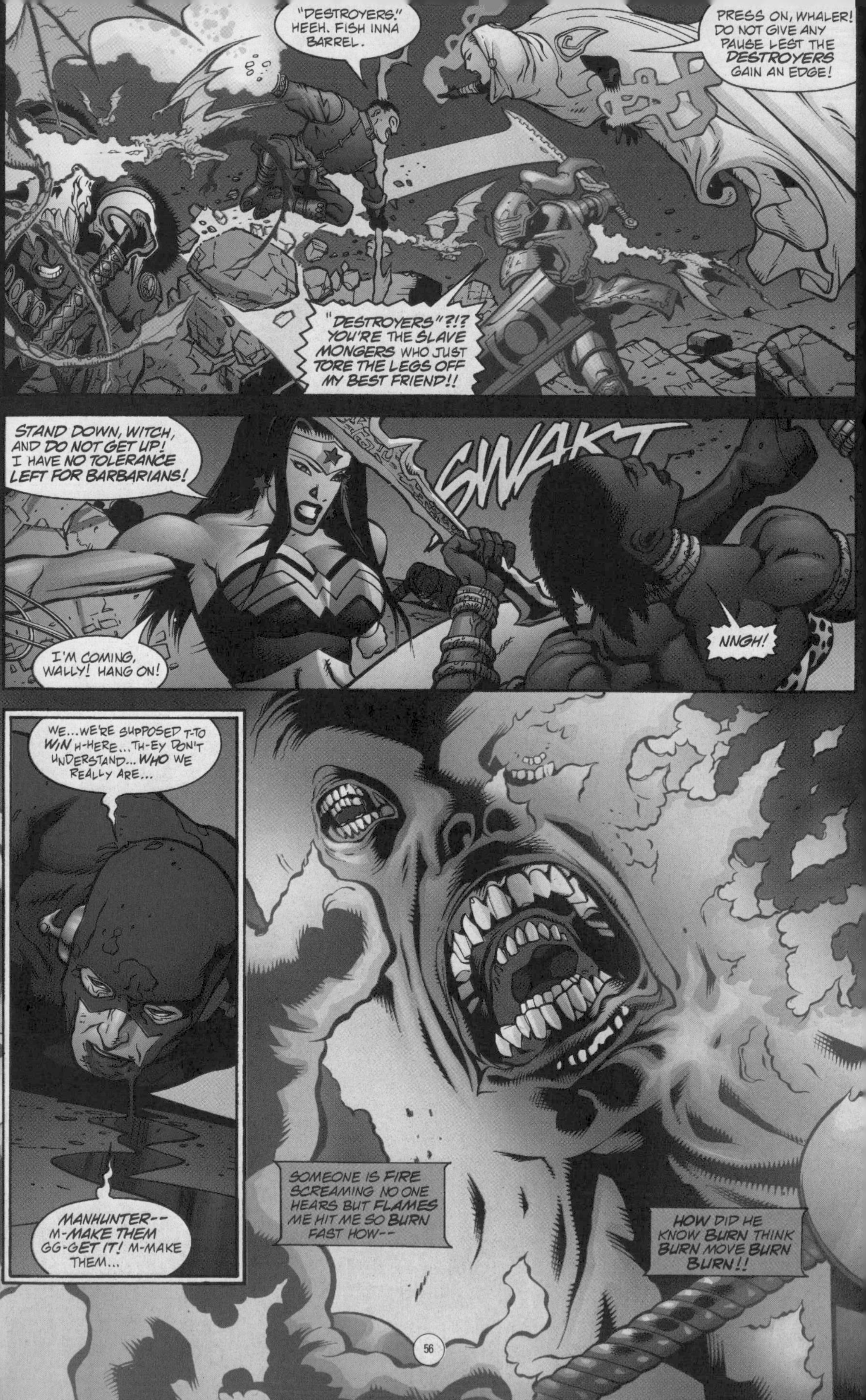
"DESTROYERS." HEEH. FISH INNA BARREL.
PRESS ON, WHALER! DO NOT GIVE ANY PAUSE LEST THE DESTROYERS GAIN AN EDGE!
"DESTROYERS"?!? YOU'RE THE SLAVE MONGERS WHO JUST TORE THE LEGS OFF MY BEST FRIEND!!
STAND DOWN, WITCH, AND DO NOT GET UP! I HAVE NO TOLERANCE LEFT FOR BARBARIANS!
SWAK!
NNGH!
I'M COMING, WALLY! HANG ON!
WE...WE'RE SUPPOSED T-TO WIN H-HERE...TH-EY DON'T UNDERSTAND...WHO WE REALLY ARE...
MANHUNTER-- M-MAKE THEM GG-GET IT! M-MAKE THEM...
SOMEONE IS FIRE SCREAMING NO ONE HEARS BUT FLAMES ME HIT ME SO BURN FAST HOW--
HOW DID HE KNOW BURN THINK BURN MOVE BURN BURN!!

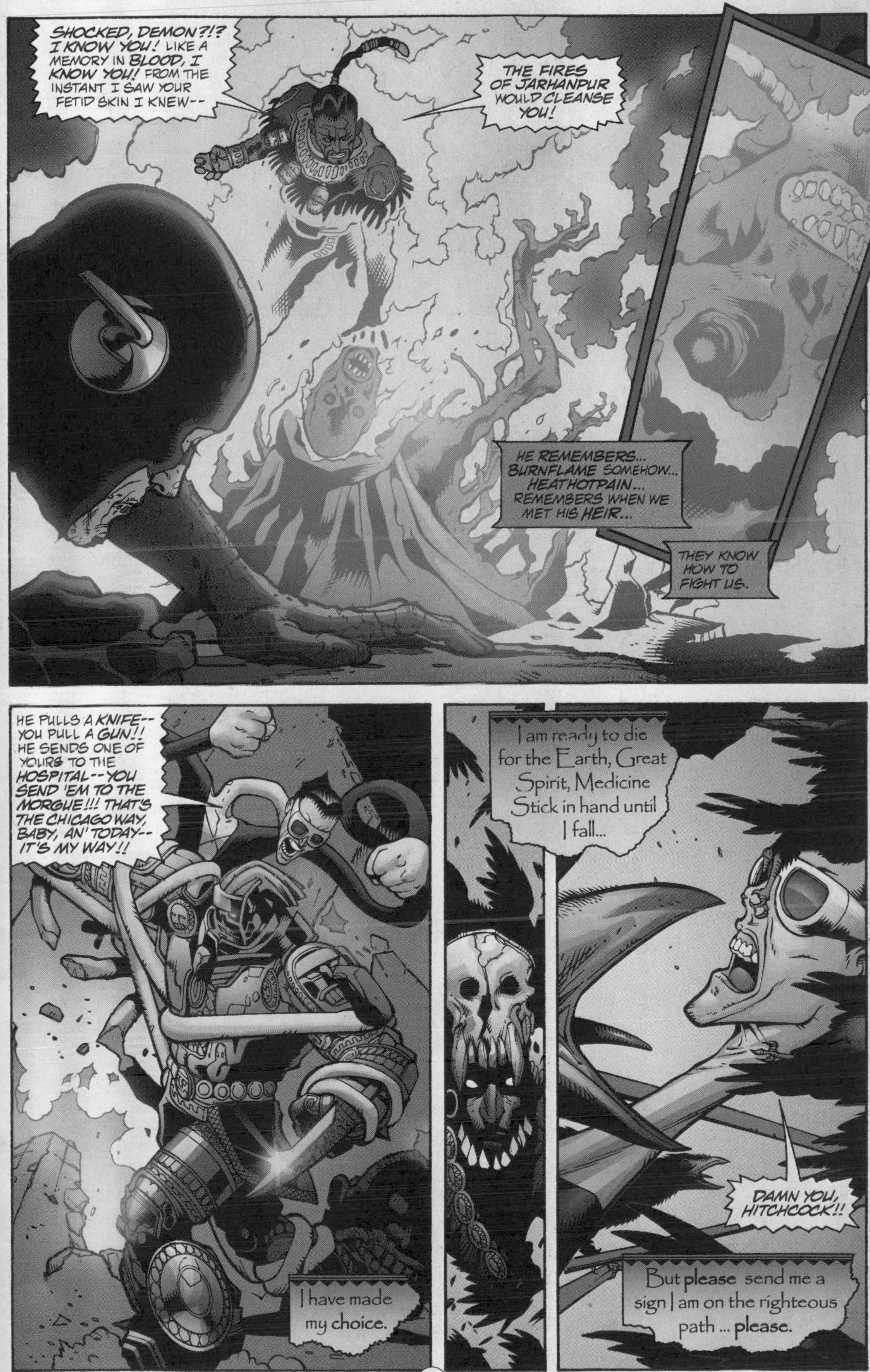
SHOCKED, DEMON?!? I KNOW YOU! LIKE A MEMORY IN BLOOD, I KNOW YOU! FROM THE INSTANT I SAW YOUR FETID SKIN I KNEW--
THE FIRES OF JARHANPUR WOULD CLEANSE YOU!
HE REMEMBERS... BURNFLAME SOMEHOW... HEATHOTPAIN... REMEMBERS WHEN WE MET HIS HEIR...
THEY KNOW HOW TO FIGHT US.
HE PULLS A KNIFE-- YOU PULL A GUN!! HE SENDS ONE OF YOURS TO THE HOSPITAL--YOU SEND 'EM TO THE MORGUE!!! THAT'S THE CHICAGO WAY, BABY, AN' TODAY-- IT'S MY WAY!!
I have made my choice.
I am ready to die for the Earth, Great Spirit, Medicine Stick in hand until I fall...
DAMN YOU, HITCHCOCK!!
But please send me a sign I am on the righteous path ... please.

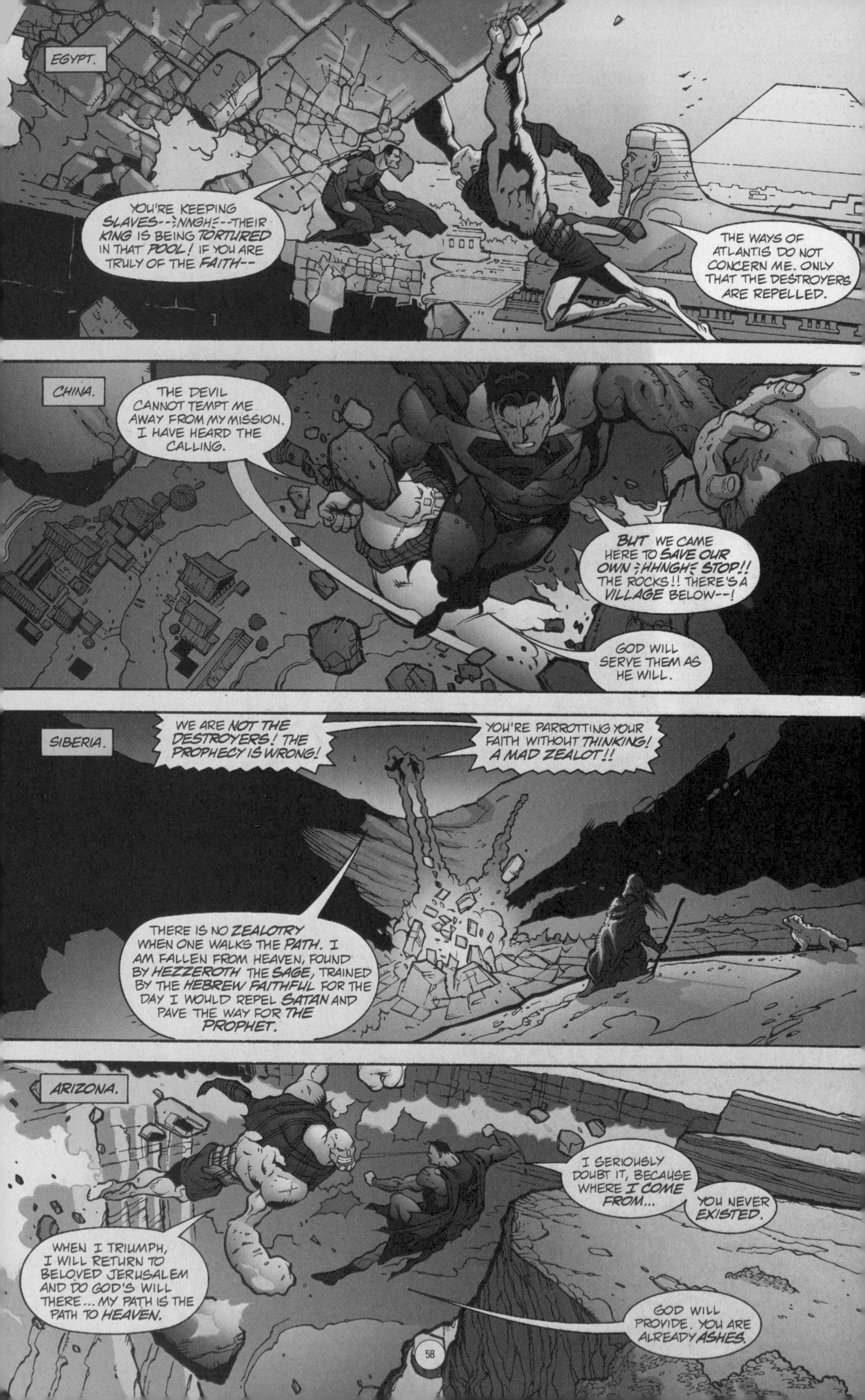
EGYPT.
YOU'RE KEEPING SLAVES--;NNGH;--THEIR KING IS BEING TORTURED IN THAT POOL! IF YOU ARE TRULY OF THE FAITH--
THE WAYS OF ATLANTIS DO NOT CONCERN ME. ONLY THAT THE DESTROYERS ARE REPELLED.
CHINA.
THE DEVIL CANNOT TEMPT ME AWAY FROM MY MISSION. I HAVE HEARD THE CALLING.
BUT WE CAME HERE TO SAVE OUR OWN ;HHNGH; STOP!! THE ROCKS!! THERE'S A VILLAGE BELOW--!
GOD WILL SERVE THEM AS HE WILL.
SIBERIA.
WE ARE NOT THE DESTROYERS! THE PROPHECY IS WRONG!
YOU'RE PARROTTING YOUR FAITH WITHOUT THINKING! A MAD ZEALOT!!
THERE IS NO ZEALOTRY WHEN ONE WALKS THE PATH. I AM FALLEN FROM HEAVEN, FOUND BY HEZZEROTH THE SAGE, TRAINED BY THE HEBREW FAITHFUL FOR THE DAY I WOULD REPEL SATAN AND PAVE THE WAY FOR THE PROPHET.
ARIZONA.
I SERIOUSLY DOUBT IT, BECAUSE WHERE I COME FROM...
YOU NEVER EXISTED.
WHEN I TRIUMPH, I WILL RETURN TO BELOVED JERUSALEM AND DO GOD'S WILL THERE... MY PATH IS THE PATH TO HEAVEN.
GOD WILL PROVIDE. YOU ARE ALREADY ASHES.

NO BLEEDING. THE WOUND IS *SEALED*, BUT YOU'RE IN *SHOCK*. I'LL GET YOU TO SAFETY--

IT PARALYZED ME, SOMEHOW... THE SHAMAN...

B-BATMAN... I DIDN'T SEE... BATMAN. HE--

SKUTCH

AAAAH!

HGSSSSSK

MANHUNTER!!

KHAN...

YEAAAH!

YOU LIKE BURNING?!?

MGLFF!!

HOW ABOUT THE BURNING INSIDE YOUR LUNGS AS THEY CHOKE FOR *AIR*?!? LIKE THAT?!?

GAMEMNAE CAN STOP THE EEL, BUT... SHE WAITS?!?

WHY DO YOU HESITATE, WOMAN?!?

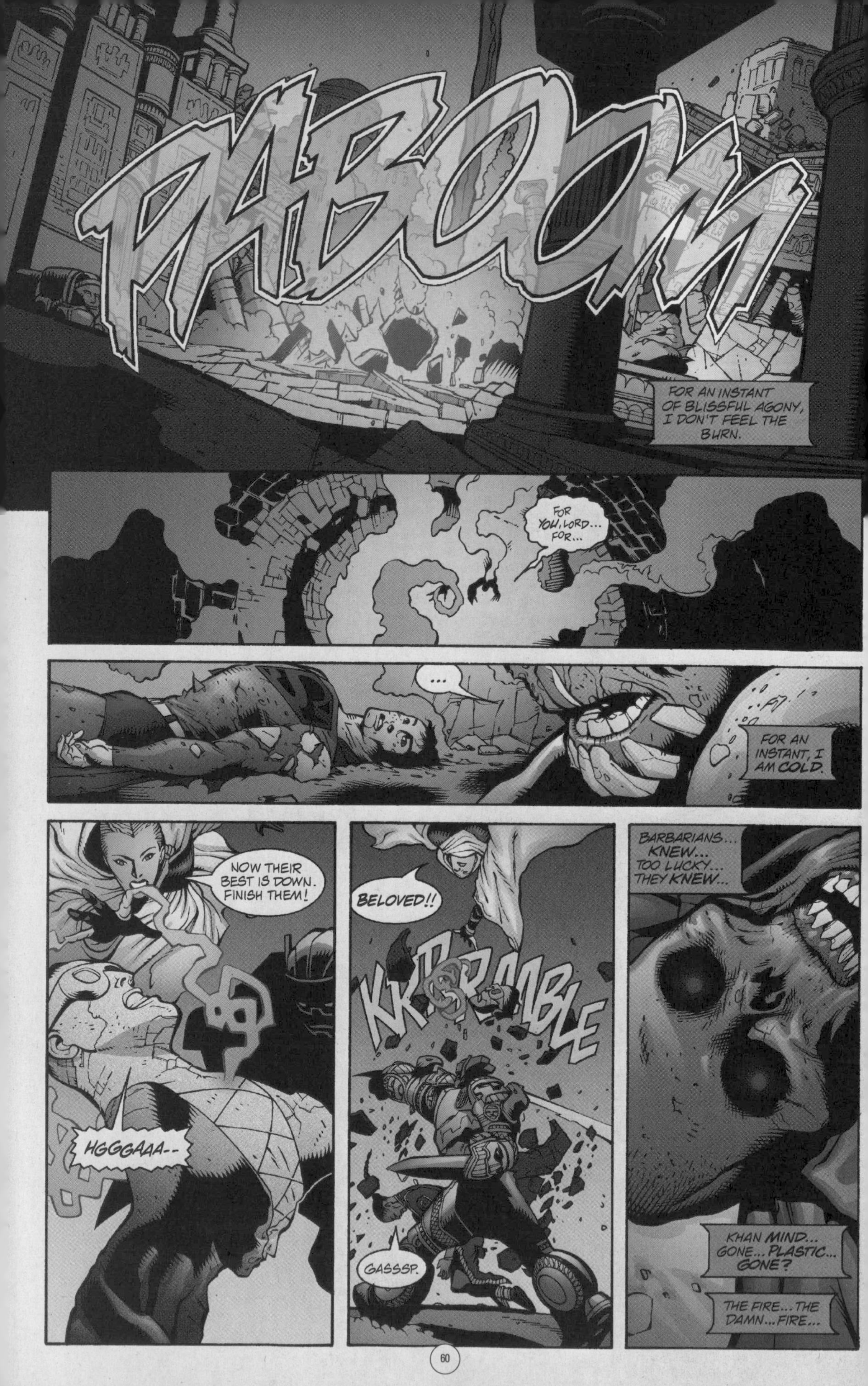

FABOOM
FOR AN INSTANT OF BLISSFUL AGONY, I DON'T FEEL THE BURN.
FOR YOU, LORD... FOR...
...
FOR AN INSTANT, I AM COLD.
NOW THEIR BEST IS DOWN. FINISH THEM!
HGGGAAA--
BELOVED!!
KRRRABBLE
GASSSP.
BARBARIANS... KNEW... TOO LUCKY... THEY KNEW...
KHAN MIND... GONE... PLASTIC... GONE?
THE FIRE... THE DAMN... FIRE...

SOFT.
THAT'S WHAT YOU GET LIVING ON AN ISLAND WITH NO MEN, AMAZ--
SHUNKT
WE WERE SET UP. ALL THIS TIME, PROCEEDING WITH CAUTION...
SHE KNEW ALL ALONG WE WERE COMING, AND EXACTLY WHAT WOULD HAPPEN.
BRUCE...?
DON'T CALL ME THAT. IT ISN'T OVER. IT ISN'T. LISTEN TO ME VERY CLOSELY...
THIS IS NOT HOW IT WORKS!!!
KYLE... HOPE. DESPERATION I WAKE FROM DARKNESS... A MOMENT...
TO SEE A MOMENT UNFOLD WITH A DIFFERENT FIRE...

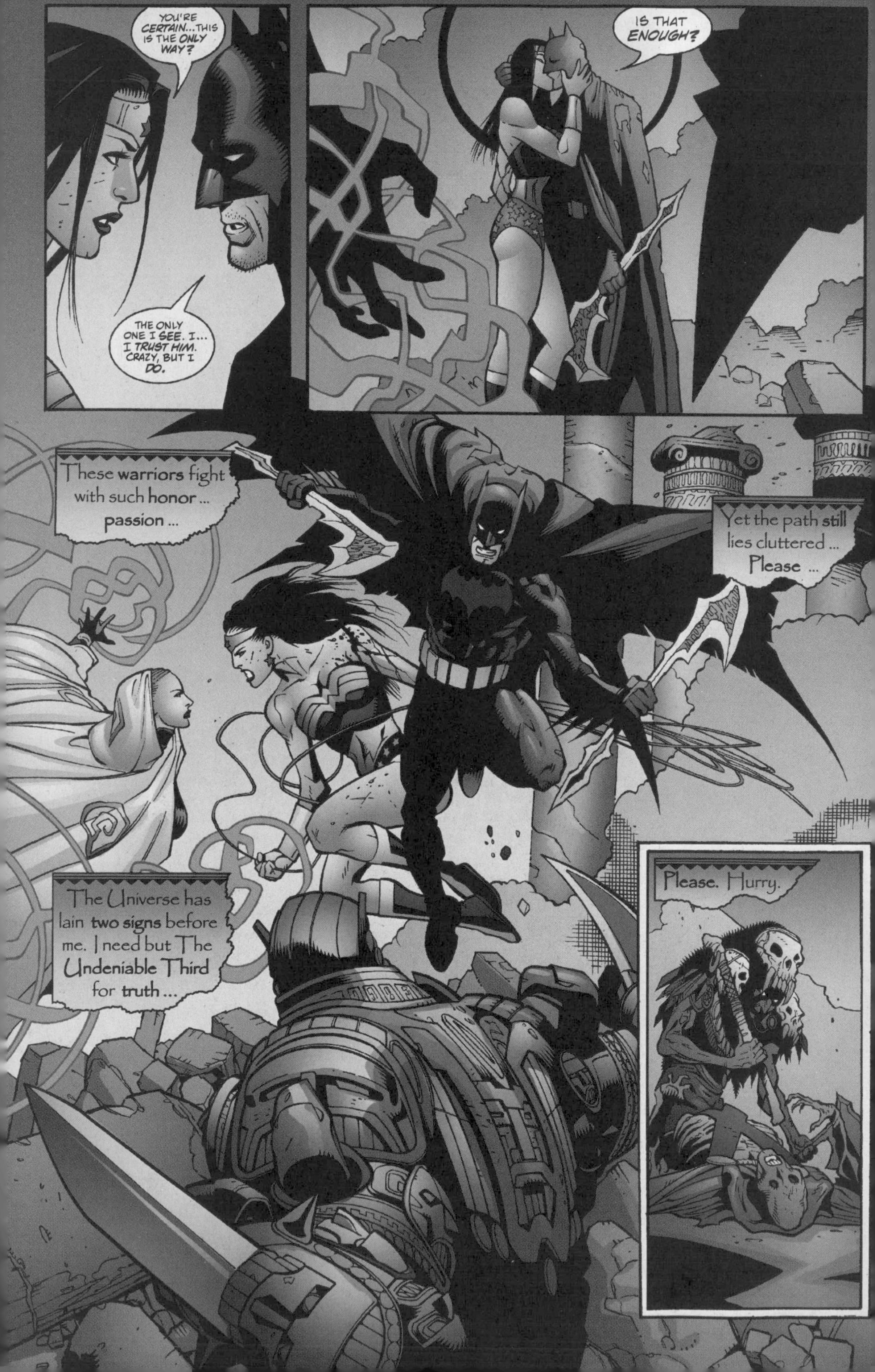
YOU'RE CERTAIN... THIS IS THE ONLY WAY?
THE ONLY ONE I SEE. I... I TRUST HIM. CRAZY, BUT I DO.
IS THAT ENOUGH?
These warriors fight with such honor ... passion ...
Yet the path still lies cluttered ... Please ...
The Universe has lain two signs before me. I need but The Undeniable Third for truth ...
Please. Hurry.

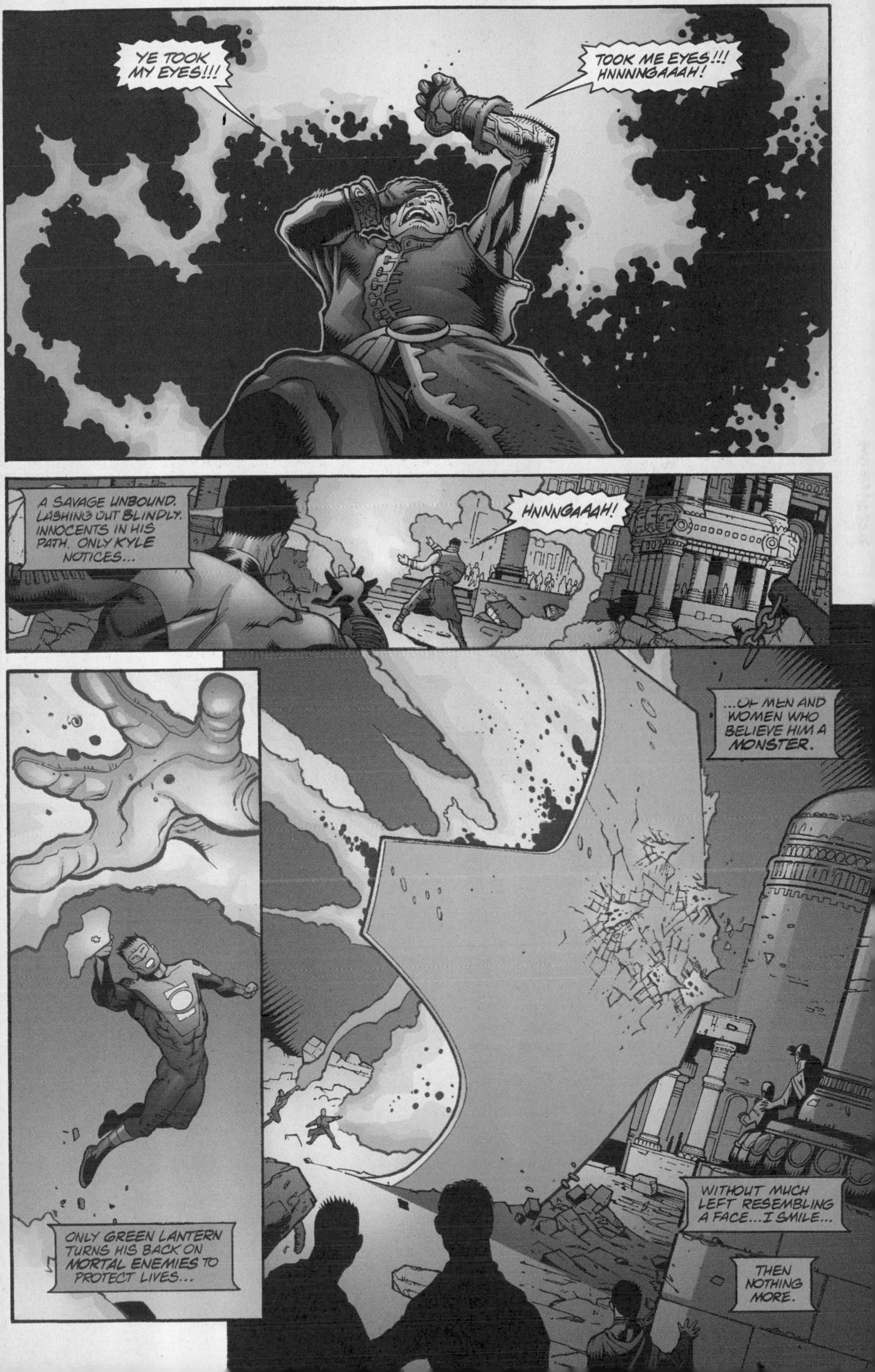
YE TOOK MY EYES!!!
TOOK ME EYES!!! HNNNNGAAAH!
A SAVAGE UNBOUND. LASHING OUT BLINDLY. INNOCENTS IN HIS PATH. ONLY KYLE NOTICES...
HNNNGAAAH!
...OF MEN AND WOMEN WHO BELIEVE HIM A MONSTER.
ONLY GREEN LANTERN TURNS HIS BACK ON MORTAL ENEMIES TO PROTECT LIVES...
WITHOUT MUCH LEFT RESEMBLING A FACE...I SMILE...
THEN NOTHING MORE.

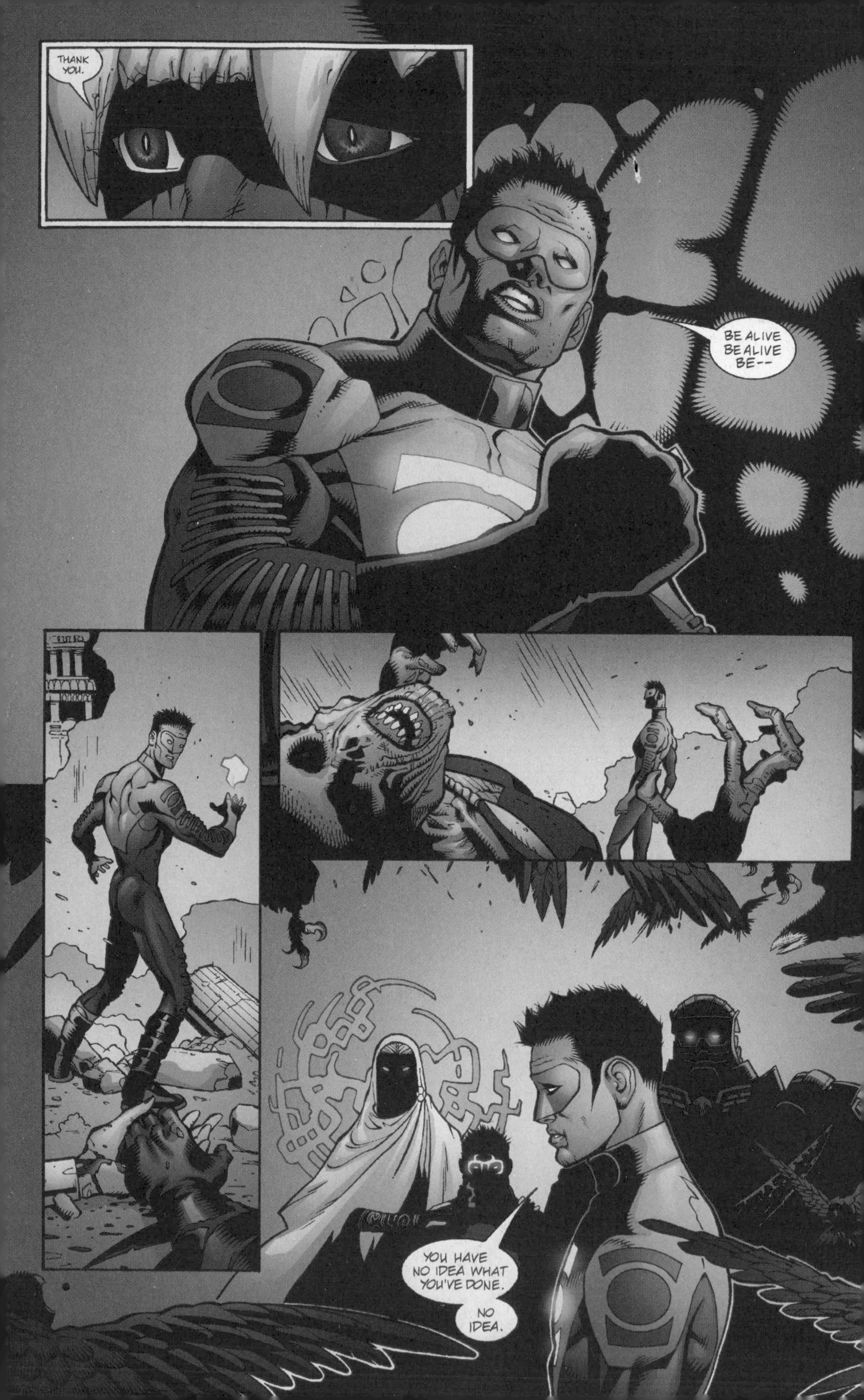
THANK YOU.
BE ALIVE BE ALIVE BE--
YOU HAVE NO IDEA WHAT YOU'VE DONE.
NO IDEA.

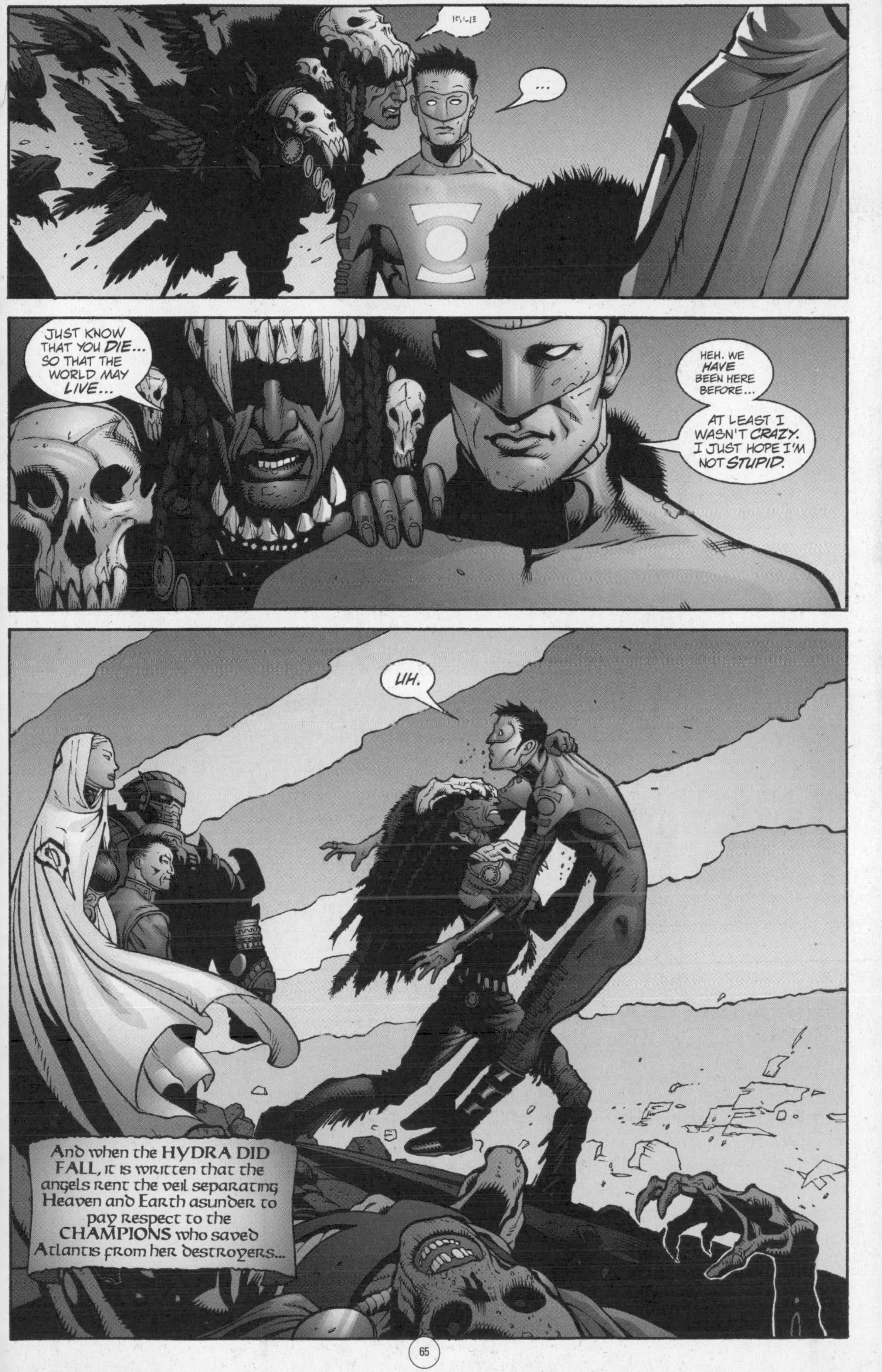
KYLE
...
JUST KNOW THAT YOU DIE... SO THAT THE WORLD MAY LIVE...
HEH. WE HAVE BEEN HERE BEFORE...
AT LEAST I WASN'T CRAZY. I JUST HOPE I'M NOT STUPID.
UH.
And when the HYDRA DID FALL, it is written that the angels rent the veil separating Heaven and Earth asunder to pay respect to the CHAMPIONS who saved Atlantis from her destroyers...

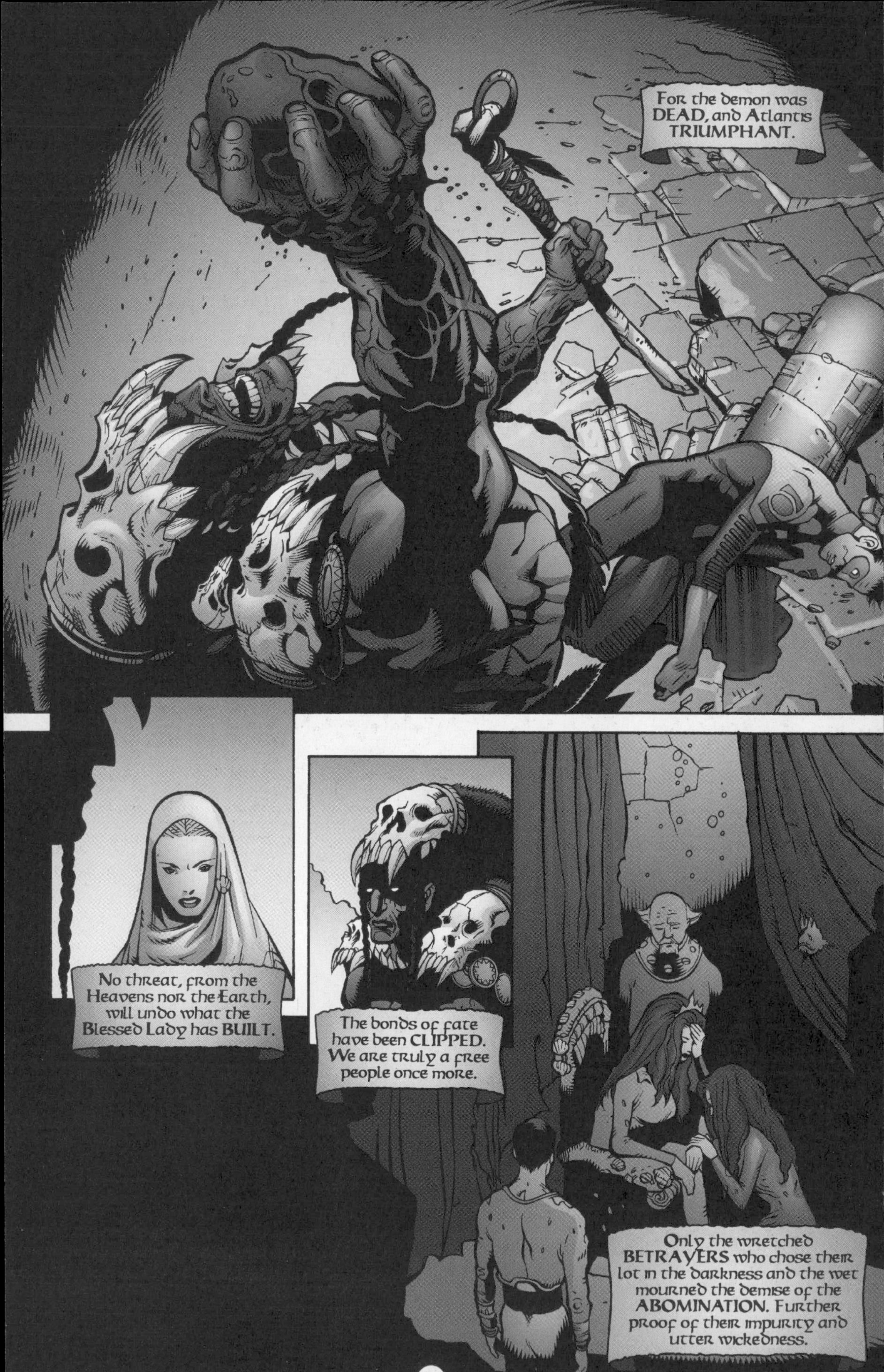
For the demon was DEAD, and Atlantis TRIUMPHANT.
No threat, from the Heavens nor the Earth, will undo what the Blessed Lady has BUILT.
The bonds of fate have been CLIPPED. We are truly a free people once more.
Only the wretched BETRAYERS who chose their lot in the darkness and the wet mourned the demise of the ABOMINATION. Further proof of their impurity and utter wickedness.

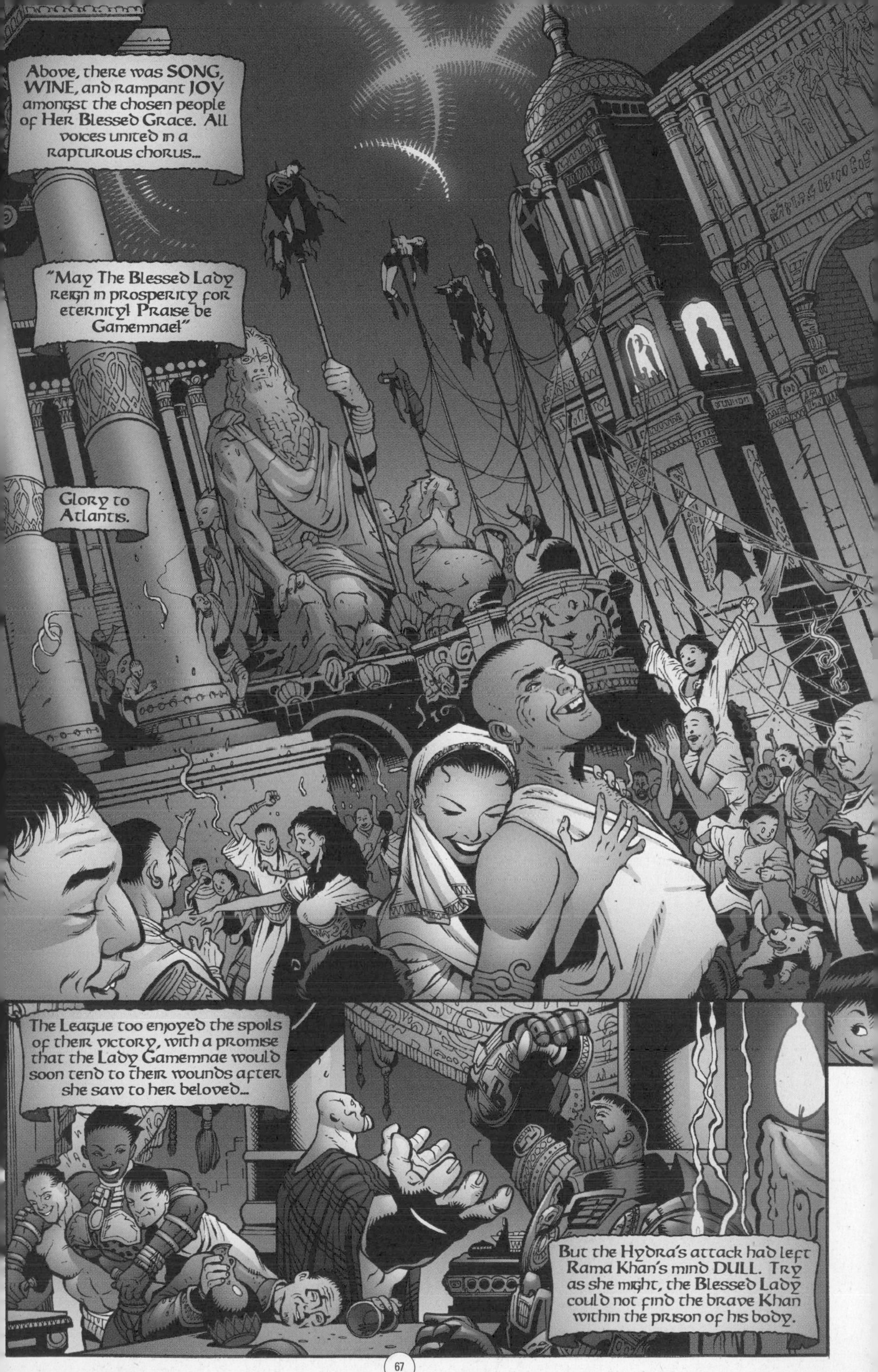
Above, there was SONG, WINE, and rampant JOY amongst the chosen people of Her Blessed Grace. All voices united in a rapturous chorus...
"May The Blessed Lady reign in prosperity for eternity! Praise be Gamemnae!"
Glory to Atlantis.
The League too enjoyed the spoils of their victory, with a promise that the Lady Gamemnae would soon tend to their wounds after she saw to her beloved...
But the Hydra's attack had left Rama Khan's mind DULL. Try as she might, the Blessed Lady could not find the brave Khan within the prison of his body.

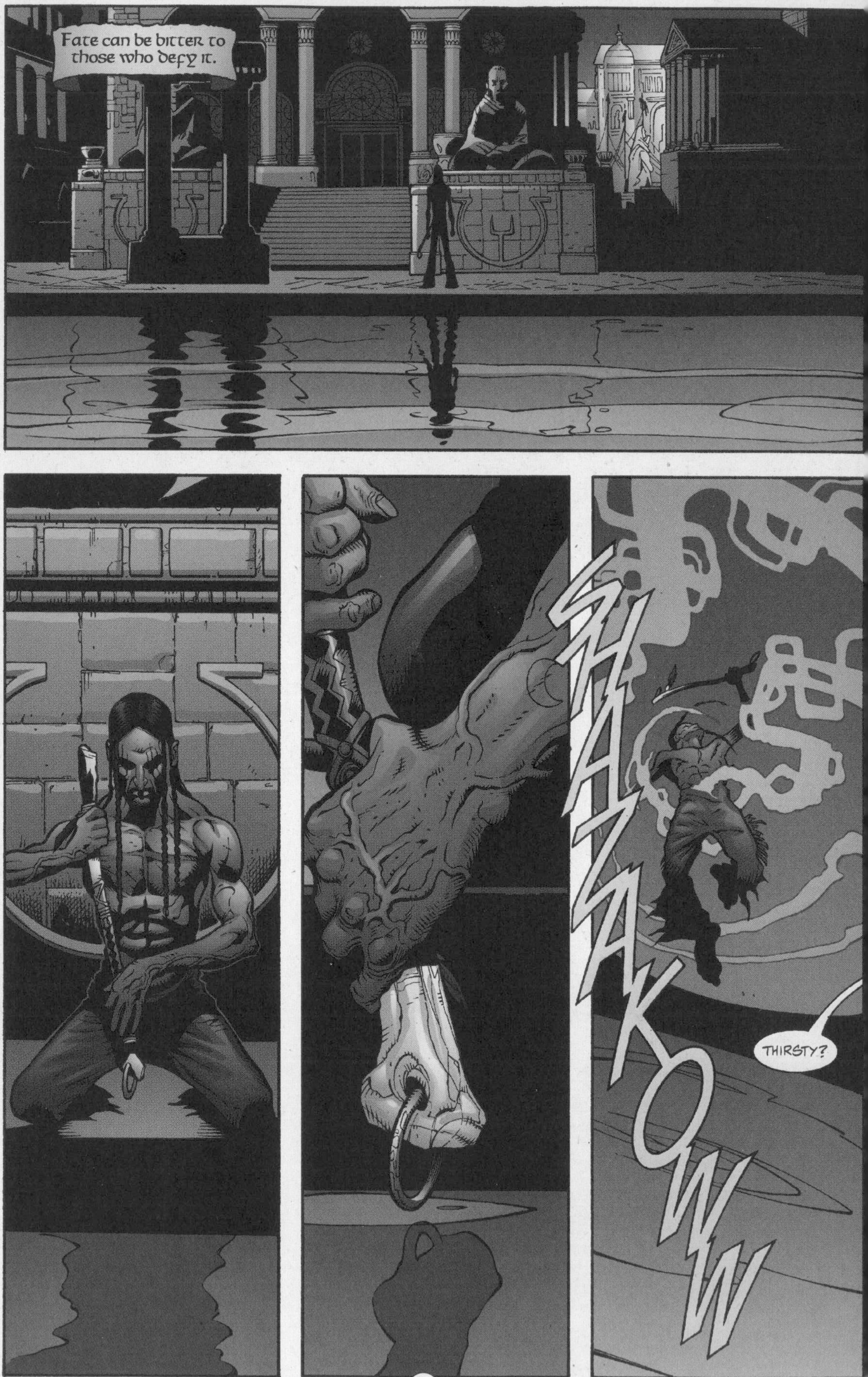
Fate can be bitter to those who defy it.
SHHAKOWW
THIRSTY?

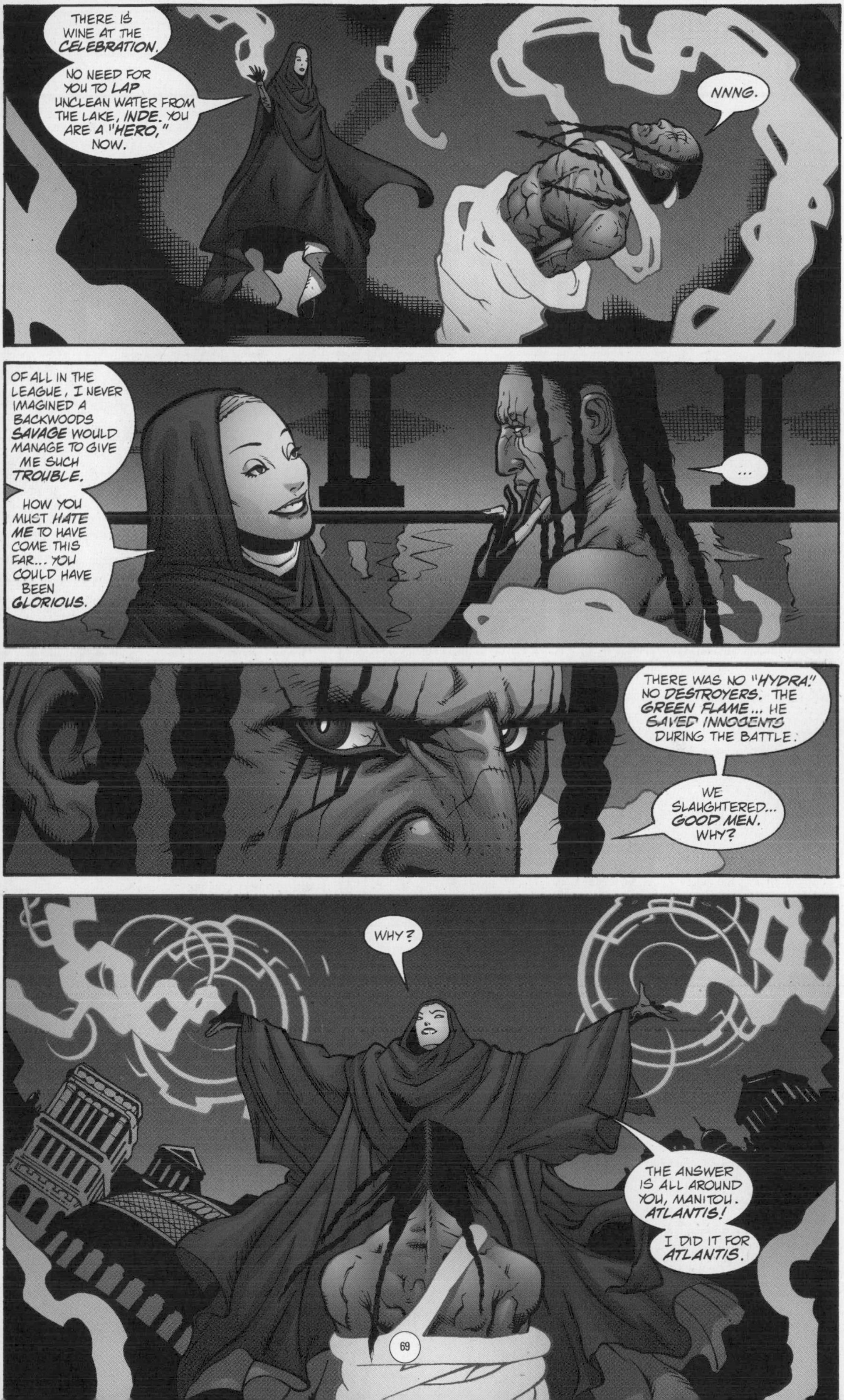
THERE IS WINE AT THE CELEBRATION.
NO NEED FOR YOU TO LAP UNCLEAN WATER FROM THE LAKE, INDE. YOU ARE A "HERO," NOW.
NNNG.
OF ALL IN THE LEAGUE, I NEVER IMAGINED A BACKWOODS SAVAGE WOULD MANAGE TO GIVE ME SUCH TROUBLE.
HOW YOU MUST HATE ME TO HAVE COME THIS FAR... YOU COULD HAVE BEEN GLORIOUS.
...
THERE WAS NO "HYDRA." NO DESTROYERS. THE GREEN FLAME... HE SAVED INNOCENTS DURING THE BATTLE.
WE SLAUGHTERED... GOOD MEN. WHY?
WHY?
THE ANSWER IS ALL AROUND YOU, MANITOU. ATLANTIS!
I DID IT FOR ATLANTIS.

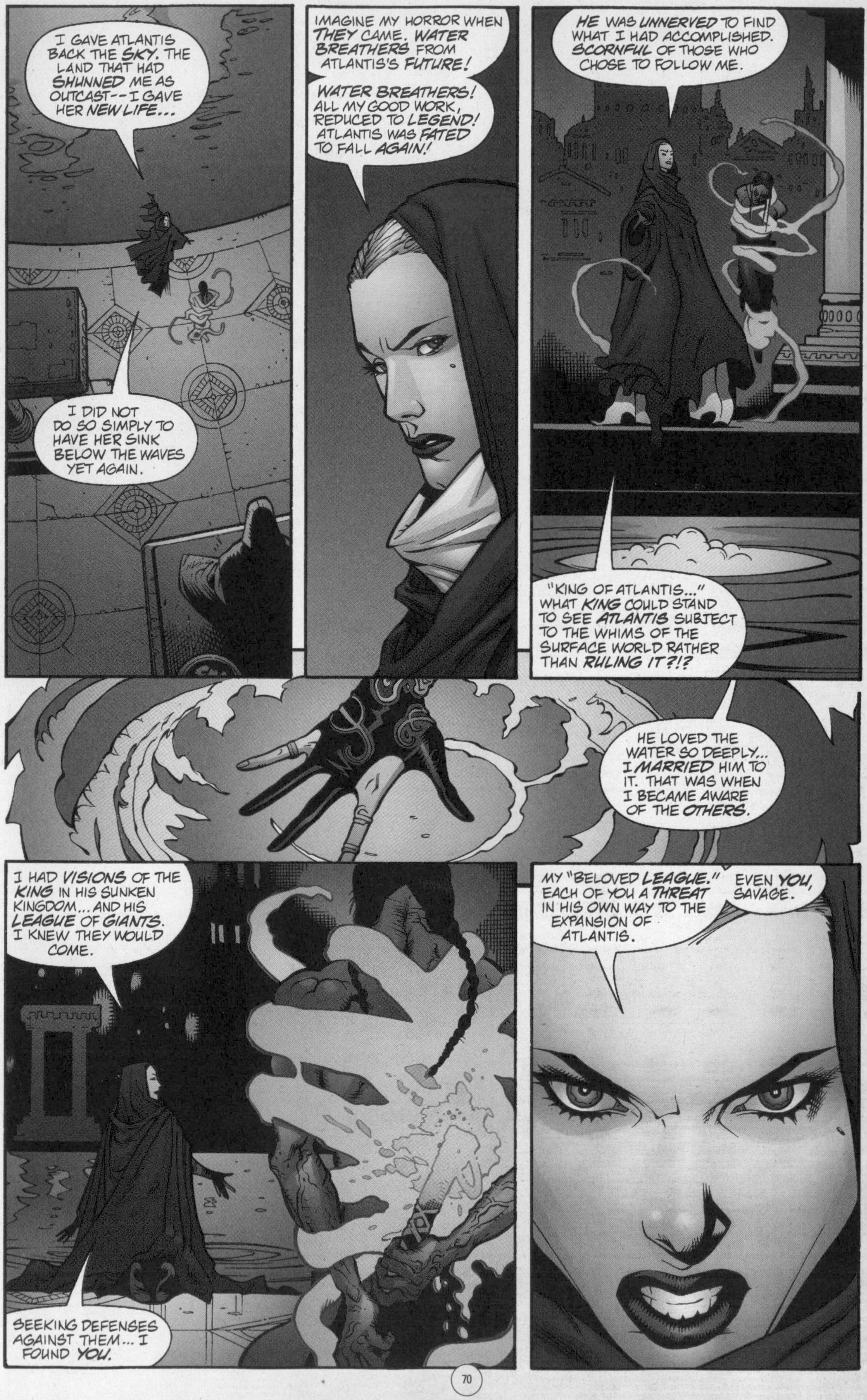

I GAVE ATLANTIS BACK THE SKY. THE LAND THAT HAD SHUNNED ME AS OUTCAST--I GAVE HER NEW LIFE...
I DID NOT DO SO SIMPLY TO HAVE HER SINK BELOW THE WAVES YET AGAIN.
IMAGINE MY HORROR WHEN THEY CAME. WATER BREATHERS FROM ATLANTIS'S FUTURE!
WATER BREATHERS! ALL MY GOOD WORK, REDUCED TO LEGEND! ATLANTIS WAS FATED TO FALL AGAIN!
HE WAS UNNERVED TO FIND WHAT I HAD ACCOMPLISHED. SCORNFUL OF THOSE WHO CHOSE TO FOLLOW ME.
"KING OF ATLANTIS..." WHAT KING COULD STAND TO SEE ATLANTIS SUBJECT TO THE WHIMS OF THE SURFACE WORLD RATHER THAN RULING IT?!?
HE LOVED THE WATER SO DEEPLY... I MARRIED HIM TO IT. THAT WAS WHEN I BECAME AWARE OF THE OTHERS.
I HAD VISIONS OF THE KING IN HIS SUNKEN KINGDOM... AND HIS LEAGUE OF GIANTS. I KNEW THEY WOULD COME.
SEEKING DEFENSES AGAINST THEM... I FOUND YOU.
MY "BELOVED LEAGUE." EACH OF YOU A THREAT IN HIS OWN WAY TO THE EXPANSION OF ATLANTIS.
EVEN YOU, SAVAGE.

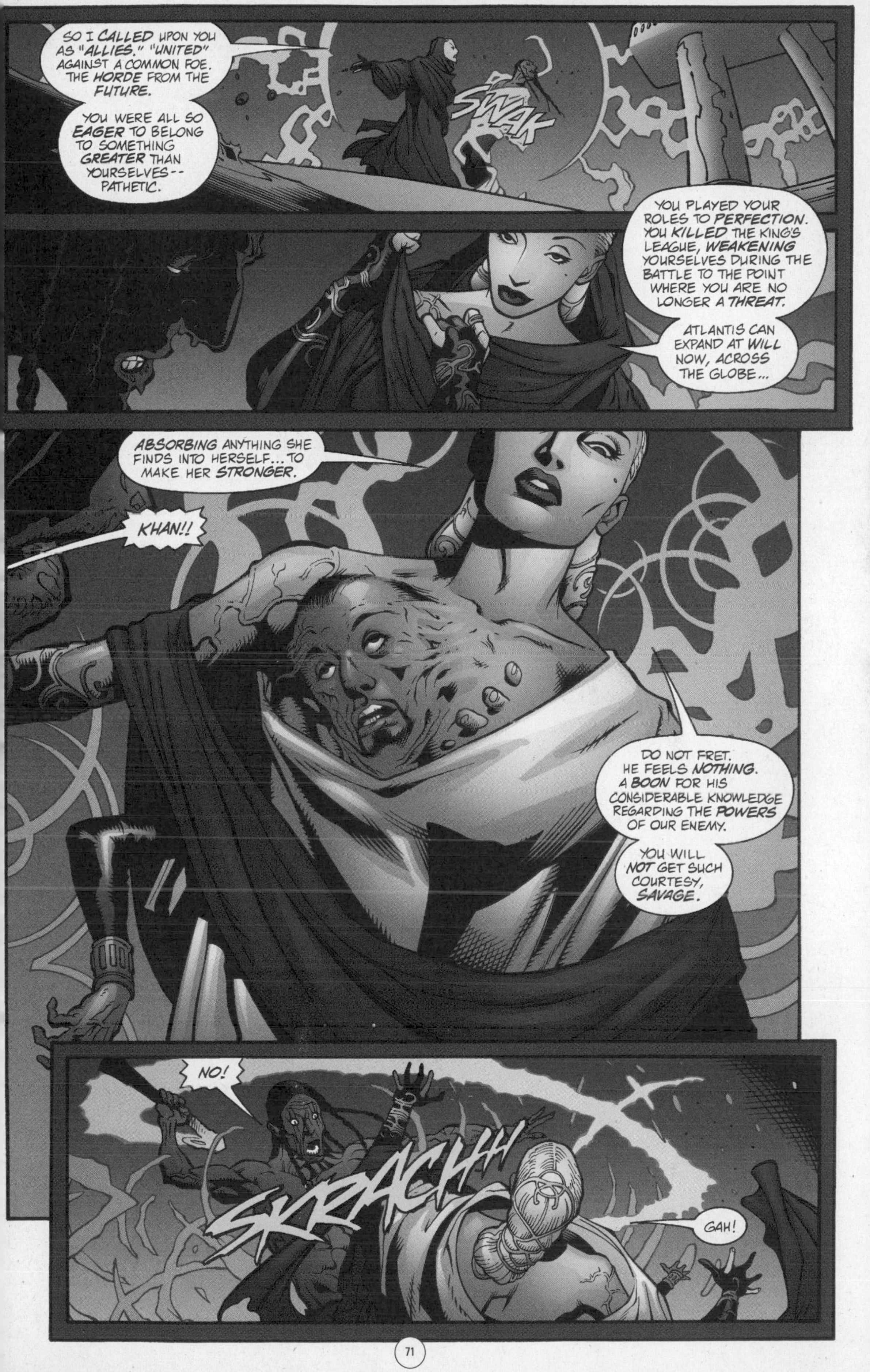

SO I CALLED UPON YOU AS "ALLIES." "UNITED" AGAINST A COMMON FOE. THE HORDE FROM THE FUTURE.
YOU WERE ALL SO EAGER TO BELONG TO SOMETHING GREATER THAN YOURSELVES-- PATHETIC.
SWAK
YOU PLAYED YOUR ROLES TO PERFECTION. YOU KILLED THE KING'S LEAGUE, WEAKENING YOURSELVES DURING THE BATTLE TO THE POINT WHERE YOU ARE NO LONGER A THREAT.
ATLANTIS CAN EXPAND AT WILL NOW, ACROSS THE GLOBE...
ABSORBING ANYTHING SHE FINDS INTO HERSELF... TO MAKE HER STRONGER.
KHAN!!
DO NOT FRET. HE FEELS NOTHING. A BOON FOR HIS CONSIDERABLE KNOWLEDGE REGARDING THE POWERS OF OUR ENEMY.
YOU WILL NOT GET SUCH COURTESY, SAVAGE.
NO!
SKRACHH
GAH!

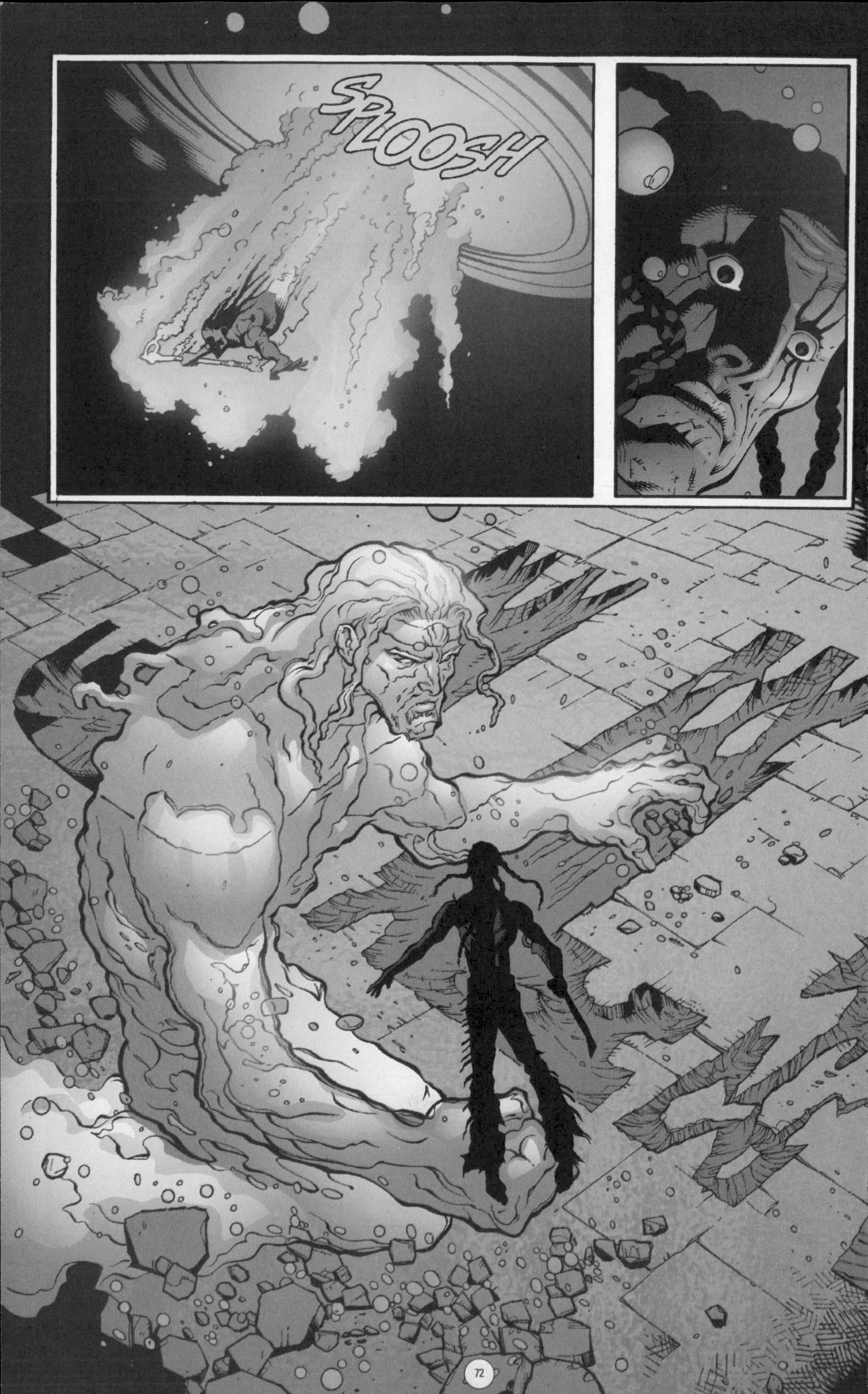
SPLOOSH

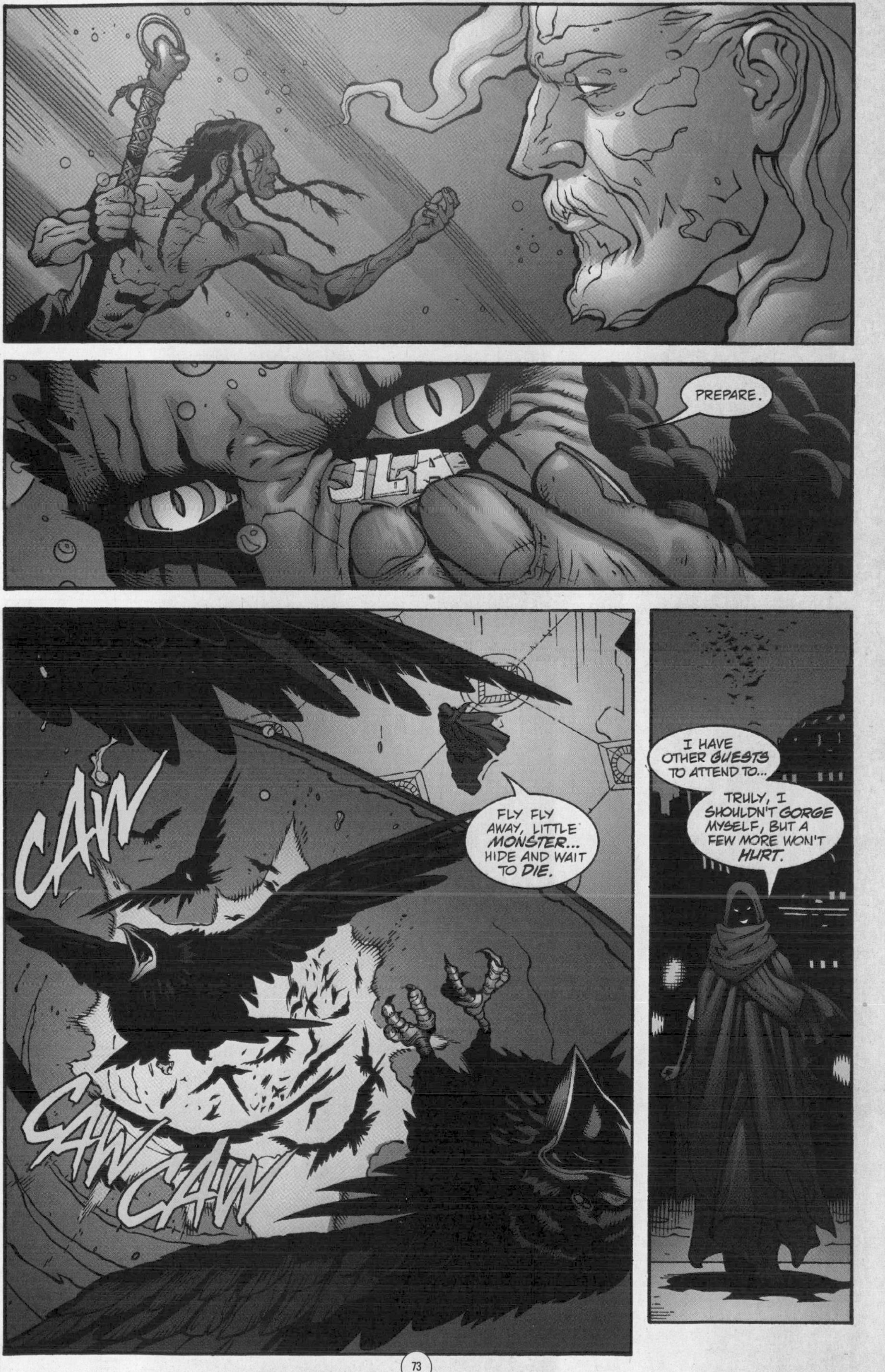
PREPARE.
CAW
FLY FLY AWAY, LITTLE MONSTER... HIDE AND WAIT TO DIE.
CAW CAW
I HAVE OTHER GUESTS TO ATTEND TO...
TRULY, I SHOULDN'T GORGE MYSELF, BUT A FEW MORE WON'T HURT.

‹FATHER. GRANDFATHER. ALL OF THOSE GONE BEFORE... *FORGIVE ME*...›

‹I ALLOWED MYSELF TO BE LED DOWN THE WINDING PATH WHERE THE WIND DOES NOT BLOW... AND I HAVE *FALLEN*.›

I have fallen... But I have found my wings again. You gave me the signs...

I tested the Bat, and he passed. Your tomahawk, father, blessed so it cannot pierce the skin of a good man...

‹THIS *GIFT* OPENED MY EYES.›

‹WATCHING THE "DESTROYERS" IN BATTLE, PROTECTING ONE ANOTHER, AND THE LIVES OF INNOCENTS...›

‹OPENED MY HEART... AND *THEN*...›

KYLE.

DO NOT SPEAK. THE SILENT BREATH WILL LAST ONLY FOR A SECOND.

I KNOW NOW I WAS WRONG.

74

<...THAT FINAL *GENEROUS SACRIFICE*...>

I KNOW NOW YOU ARE NOT THE DESTROYERS. YOU SHOULD NOT DIE. BUT I CANNOT HELP YOU NOR YOUR ALLIES...

UNLESS YOU *TRUST ME*.

TRUST ME NOW... GIVE ME YOUR *FAITH*, AND KNOW...

YOU DIE SO THAT THE WORLD MAY *LIVE*.

<...THAT SACRIFICE OPENED MY *SPIRIT*.>

MMB-BMMP

MMB-BMMP

MMP-BMMP

<SO NOW I BEG YOU TO *SAVE* ME... AS *KYLE* DID HIS KIN BY *ENTRUSTING* ME WITH THE *LAST BEATS* OF HIS HEART...>

<HELP ME TO SET THINGS *RIGHT*...>

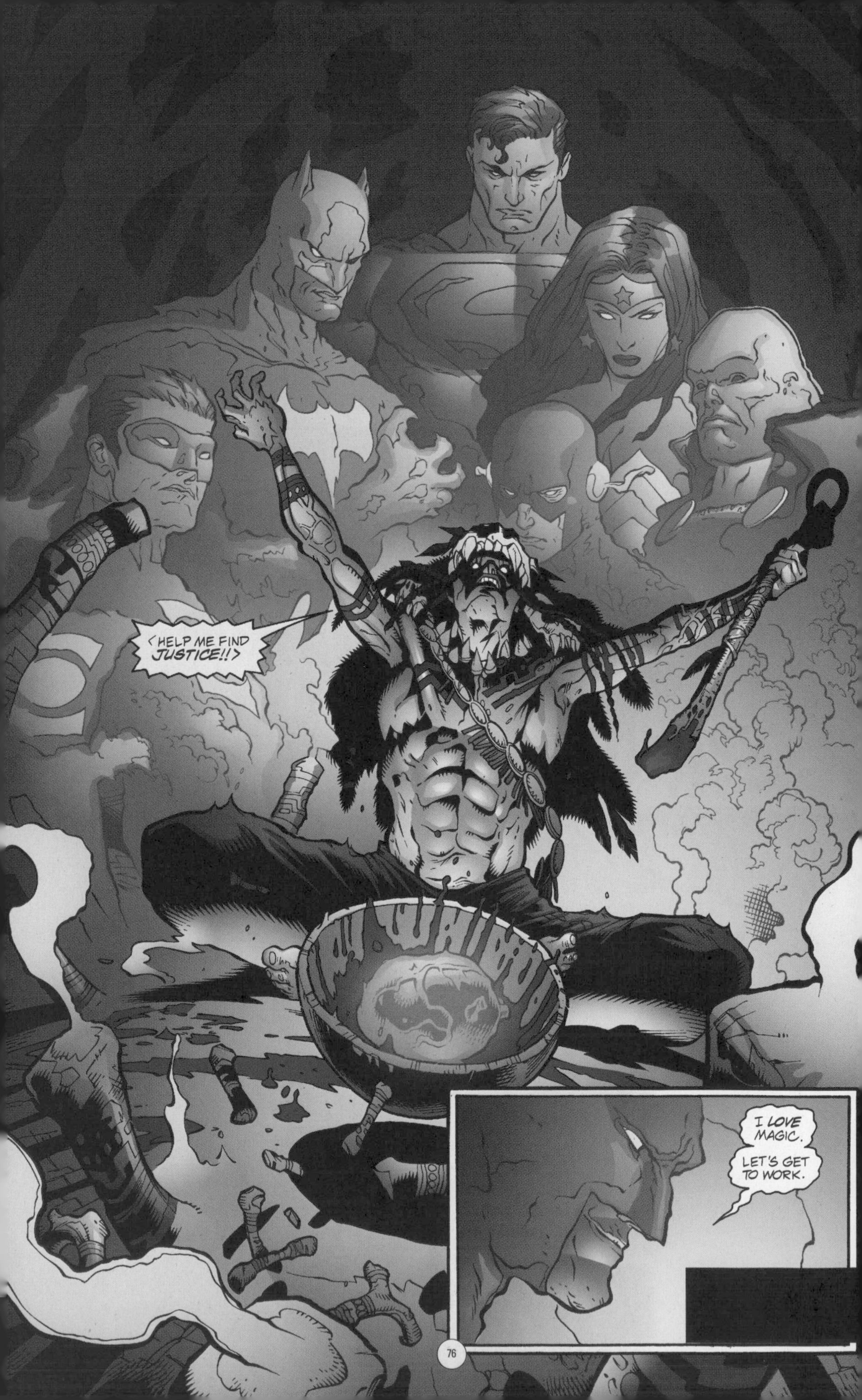
<HELP ME FIND JUSTICE!!>
I LOVE MAGIC.
LET'S GET TO WORK.

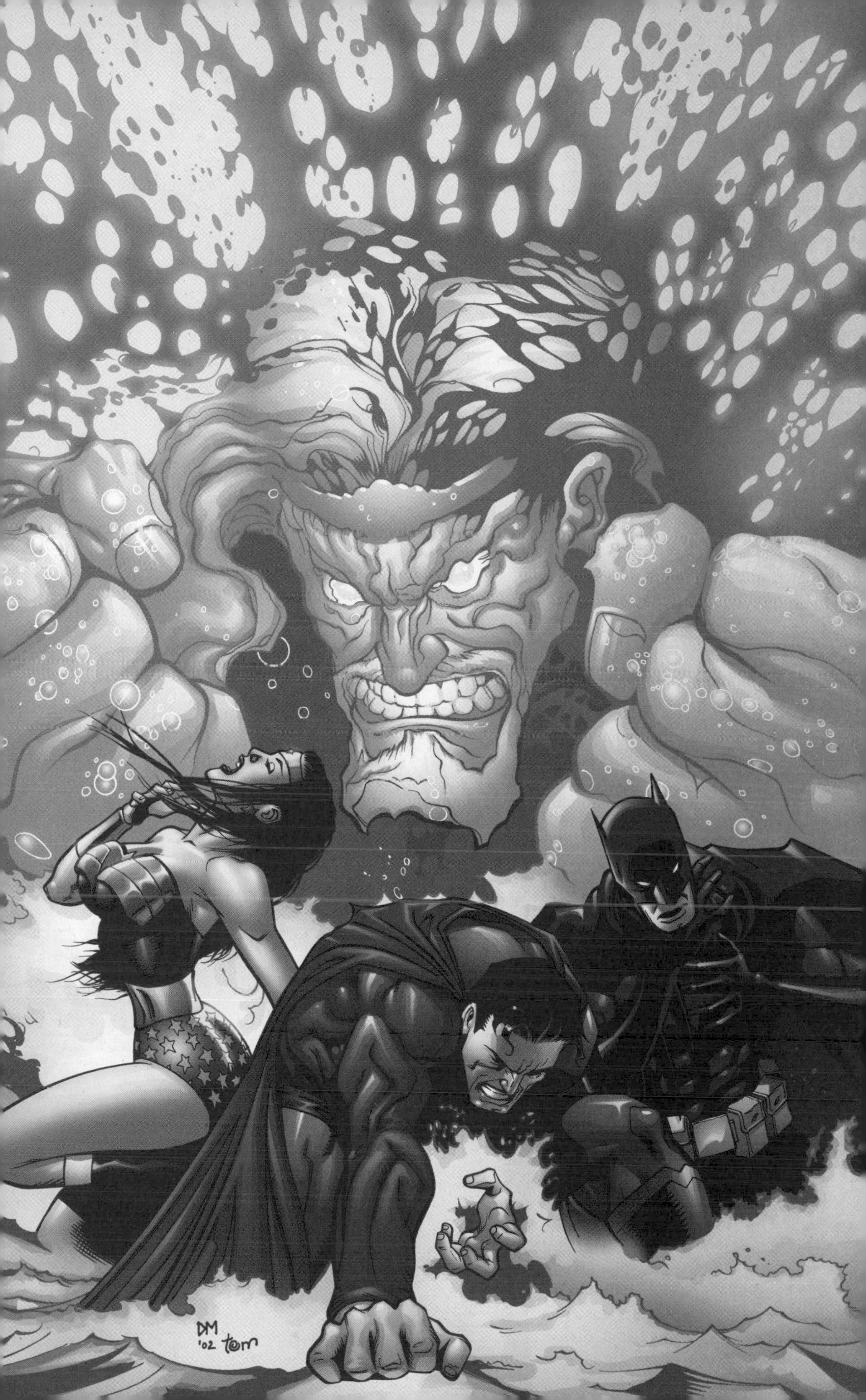
DM
'02 tom

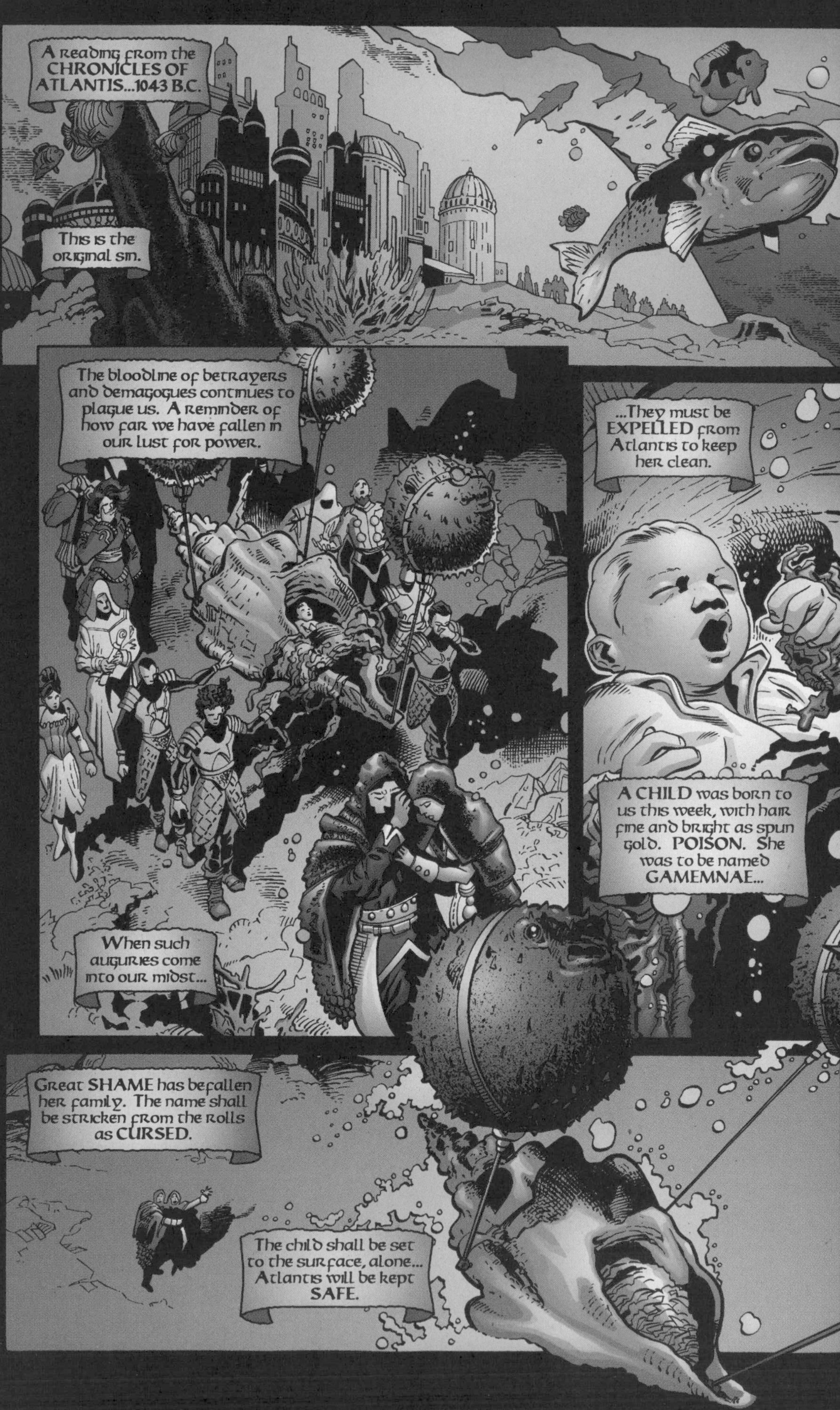

A reading from the CHRONICLES OF ATLANTIS...1043 B.C.
This is the original sin.
The bloodline of betrayers and demagogues continues to plague us. A reminder of how far we have fallen in our lust for power.
When such auguries come into our midst...
...They must be EXPELLED from Atlantis to keep her clean.
A CHILD was born to us this week, with hair fine and bright as spun gold. POISON. She was to be named GAMEMNAE...
Great SHAME has befallen her family. The name shall be stricken from the rolls as CURSED.
The child shall be set to the surface, alone... Atlantis will be kept SAFE.

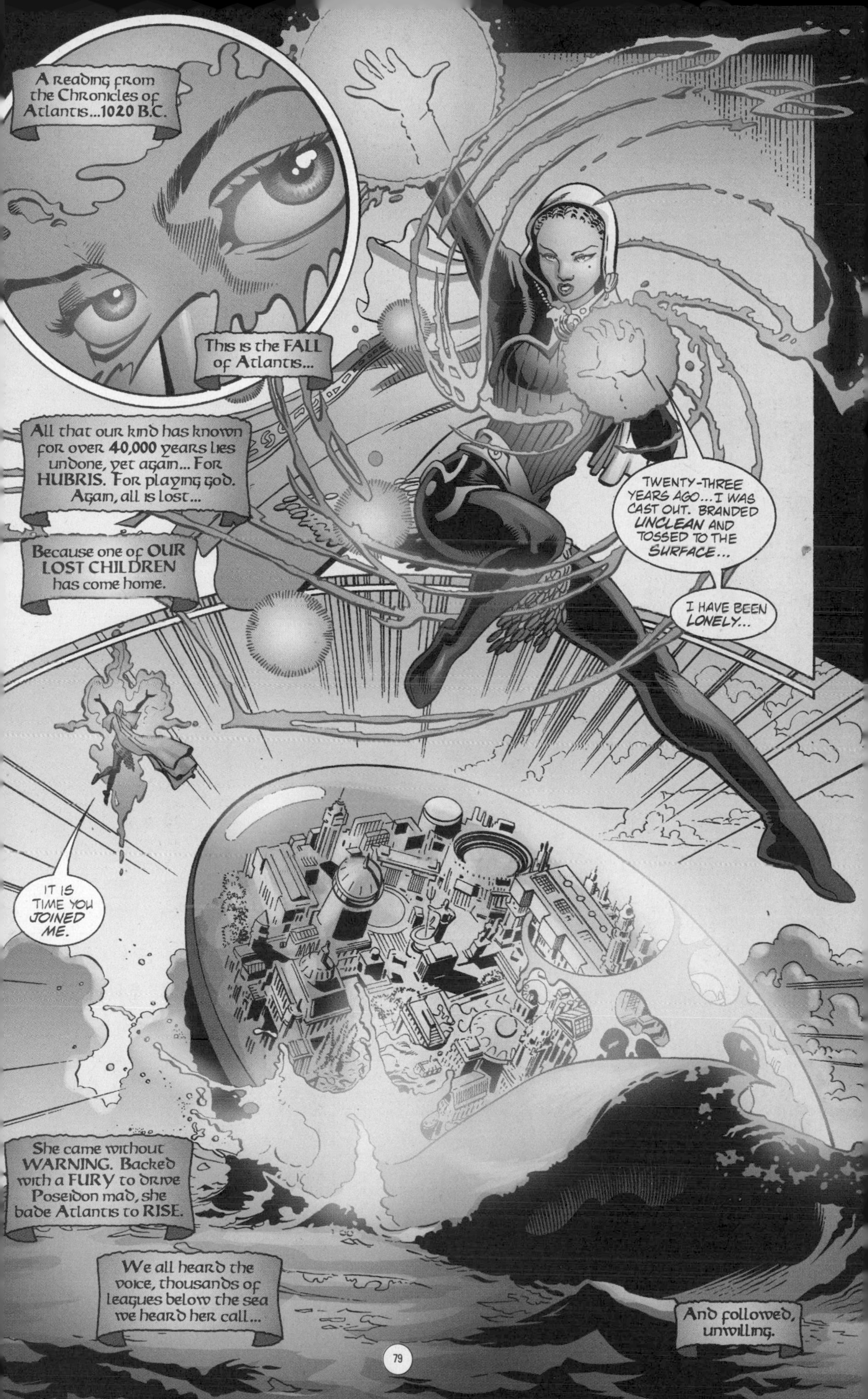

A reading from the Chronicles of Atlantis...1020 B.C.
This is the FALL of Atlantis...
All that our kind has known for over 40,000 years lies undone, yet again... For HUBRIS. For playing god. Again, all is lost...
Because one of OUR LOST CHILDREN has come home.
TWENTY-THREE YEARS AGO... I WAS CAST OUT. BRANDED UNCLEAN AND TOSSED TO THE SURFACE...
I HAVE BEEN LONELY...
IT IS TIME YOU JOINED ME.
She came without WARNING. Backed with a FURY to drive Poseidon mad, she bade Atlantis to RISE.
We all heard the voice, thousands of leagues below the sea we heard her call...
And followed, unwilling.

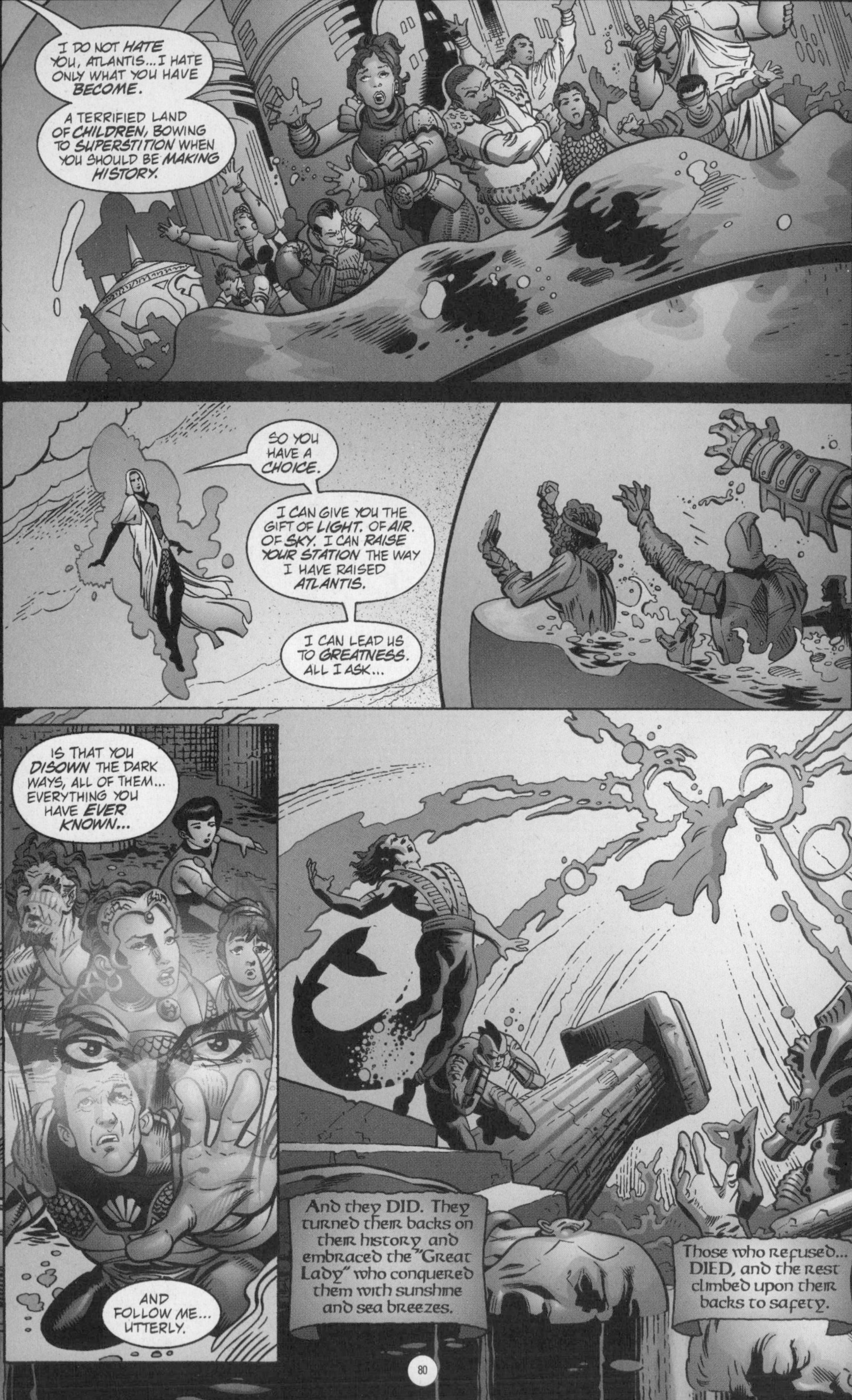
I DO NOT HATE YOU, ATLANTIS... I HATE ONLY WHAT YOU HAVE BECOME.
A TERRIFIED LAND OF CHILDREN, BOWING TO SUPERSTITION WHEN YOU SHOULD BE MAKING HISTORY.
SO YOU HAVE A CHOICE.
I CAN GIVE YOU THE GIFT OF LIGHT. OF AIR. OF SKY. I CAN RAISE YOUR STATION THE WAY I HAVE RAISED ATLANTIS.
I CAN LEAD US TO GREATNESS. ALL I ASK...
IS THAT YOU DISOWN THE DARK WAYS, ALL OF THEM... EVERYTHING YOU HAVE EVER KNOWN...
AND FOLLOW ME... UTTERLY.
And they DID. They turned their backs on their history and embraced the "Great Lady" who conquered them with sunshine and sea breezes.
Those who refused... DIED, and the rest climbed upon their backs to safety.

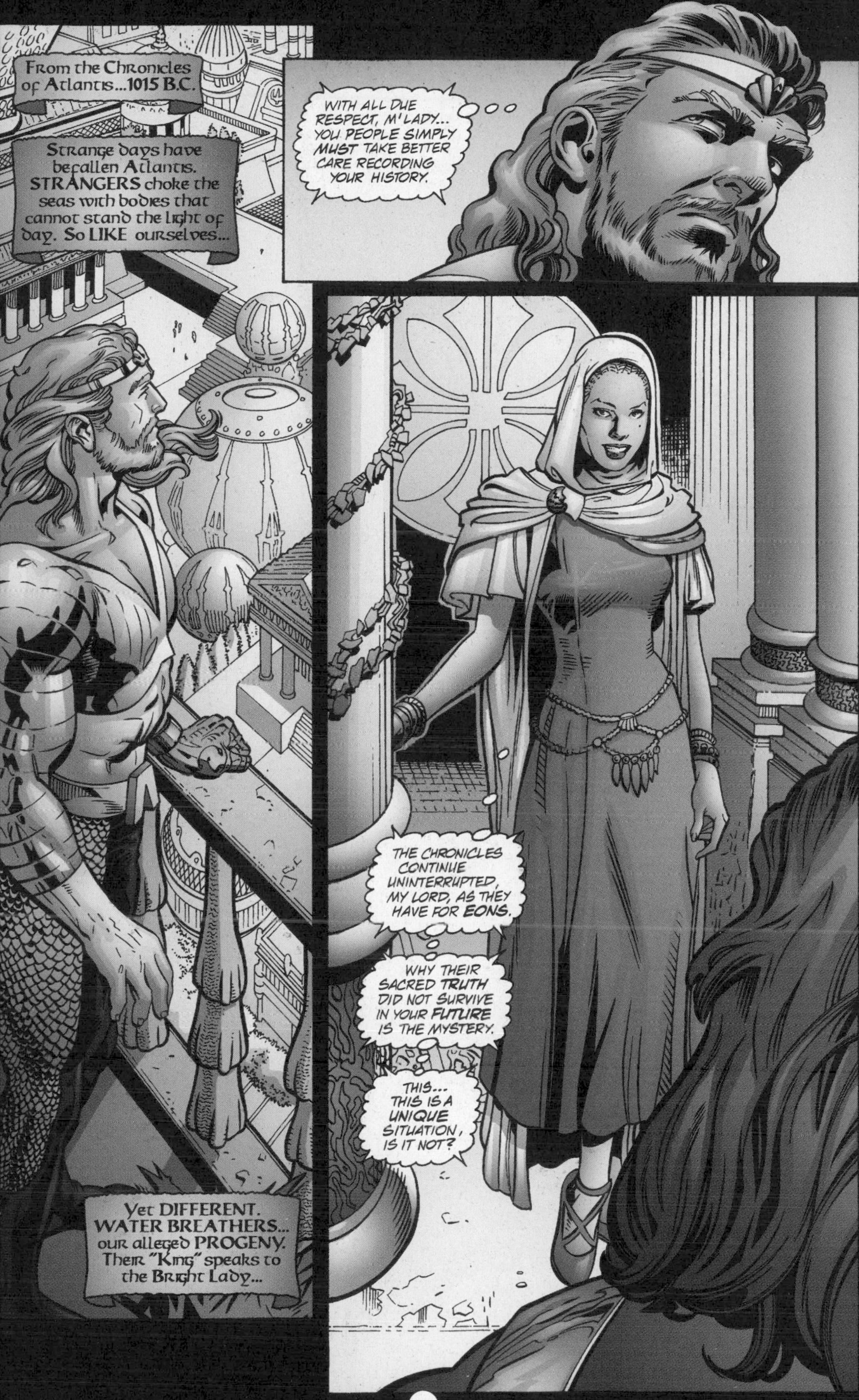
From the Chronicles of Atlantis...1015 B.C.
Strange days have befallen Atlantis. STRANGERS choke the seas with bodies that cannot stand the light of day. So LIKE ourselves...
Yet DIFFERENT. WATER BREATHERS... our alleged PROGENY. Their "King" speaks to the Bright Lady...
WITH ALL DUE RESPECT, M'LADY... YOU PEOPLE SIMPLY MUST TAKE BETTER CARE RECORDING YOUR HISTORY.
THE CHRONICLES CONTINUE UNINTERRUPTED, MY LORD, AS THEY HAVE FOR EONS.
WHY THEIR SACRED TRUTH DID NOT SURVIVE IN YOUR FUTURE IS THE MYSTERY.
THIS... THIS IS A UNIQUE SITUATION, IS IT NOT?

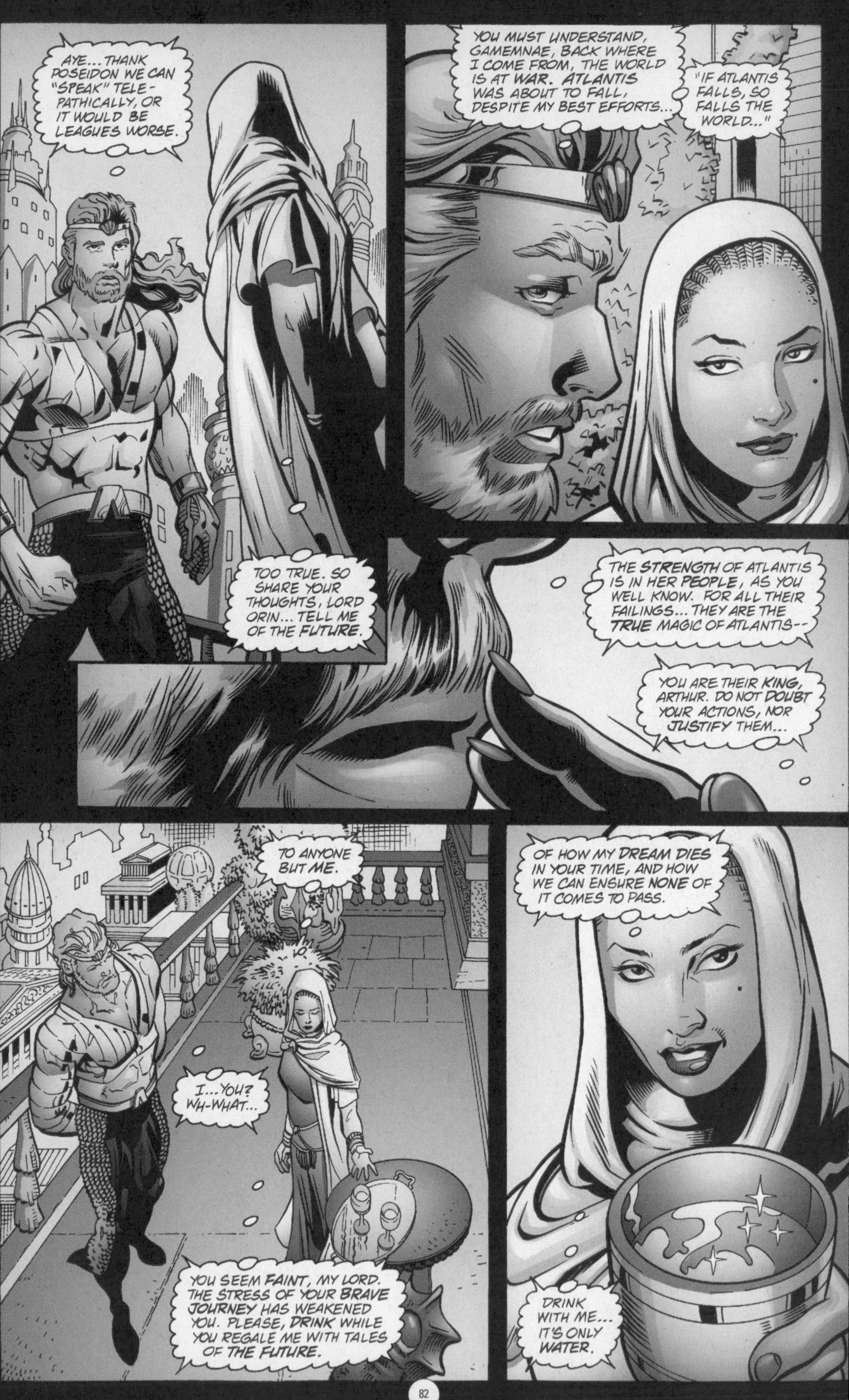
AYE... THANK POSEIDON WE CAN "SPEAK" TELEPATHICALLY, OR IT WOULD BE LEAGUES WORSE.
TOO TRUE. SO SHARE YOUR THOUGHTS, LORD ORIN... TELL ME OF THE FUTURE.
YOU MUST UNDERSTAND, GAMEMNAE, BACK WHERE I COME FROM, THE WORLD IS AT WAR. ATLANTIS WAS ABOUT TO FALL, DESPITE MY BEST EFFORTS...
"IF ATLANTIS FALLS, SO FALLS THE WORLD..."
THE STRENGTH OF ATLANTIS IS IN HER PEOPLE, AS YOU WELL KNOW. FOR ALL THEIR FAILINGS... THEY ARE THE TRUE MAGIC OF ATLANTIS--
YOU ARE THEIR KING, ARTHUR. DO NOT DOUBT YOUR ACTIONS, NOR JUSTIFY THEM...
TO ANYONE BUT ME.
I... YOU? WH-WHAT...
YOU SEEM FAINT, MY LORD. THE STRESS OF YOUR BRAVE JOURNEY HAS WEAKENED YOU. PLEASE, DRINK WHILE YOU REGALE ME WITH TALES OF THE FUTURE.
OF HOW MY DREAM DIES IN YOUR TIME, AND HOW WE CAN ENSURE NONE OF IT COMES TO PASS.
DRINK WITH ME... IT'S ONLY WATER.

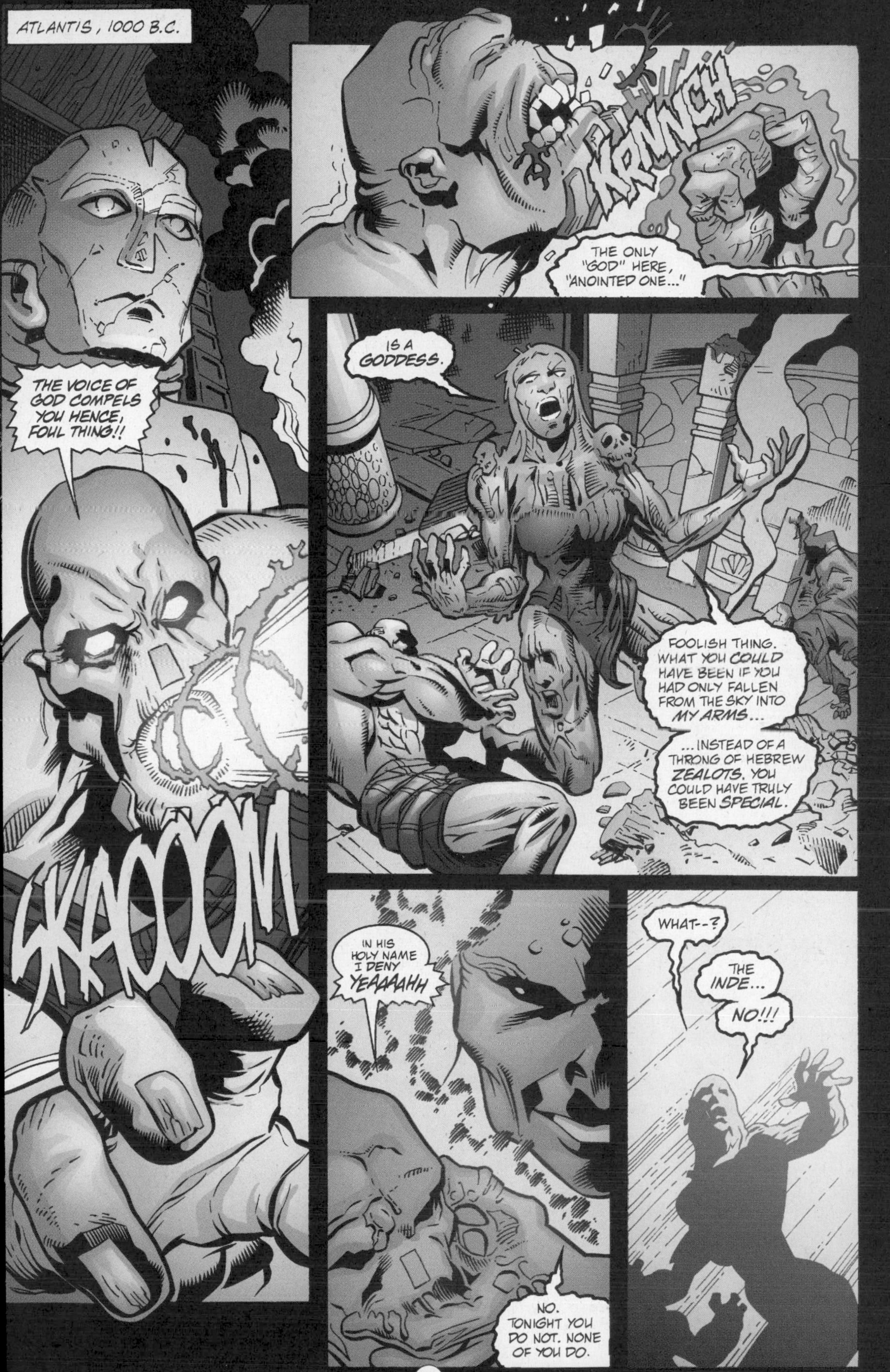
ATLANTIS, 1000 B.C.
THE VOICE OF GOD COMPELS YOU HENCE, FOUL THING!!
SKAOOOM
KRNNCH
THE ONLY "GOD" HERE, "ANOINTED ONE..."
IS A GODDESS.
FOOLISH THING. WHAT YOU COULD HAVE BEEN IF YOU HAD ONLY FALLEN FROM THE SKY INTO MY ARMS...
...INSTEAD OF A THRONG OF HEBREW ZEALOTS. YOU COULD HAVE TRULY BEEN SPECIAL.
IN HIS HOLY NAME I DENY YEAAAAHH
NO. TONIGHT YOU DO NOT. NONE OF YOU DO.
WHAT--?
THE INDE...
NO!!!

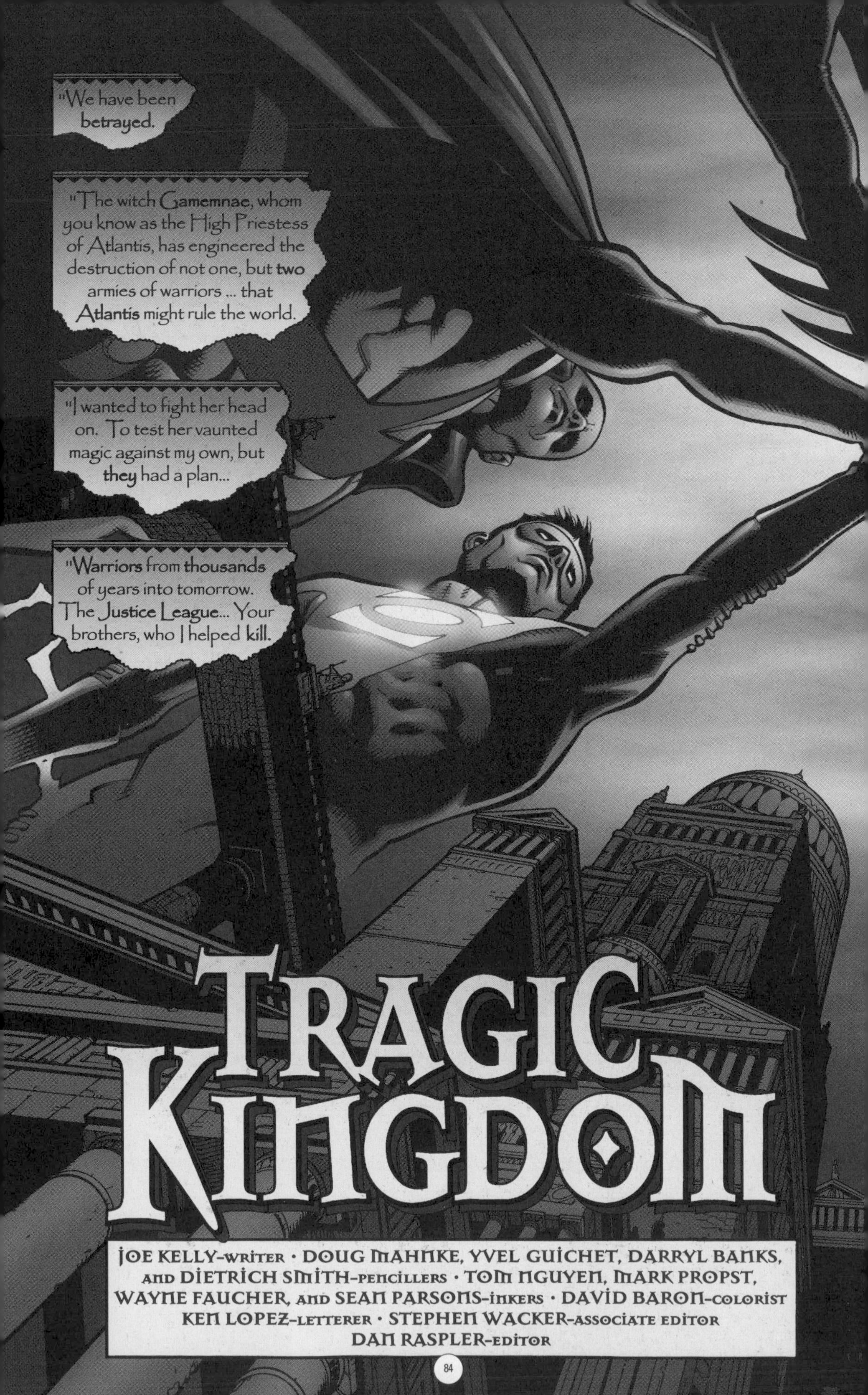
"We have been betrayed.
"The witch Gamemnae, whom you know as the High Priestess of Atlantis, has engineered the destruction of not one, but two armies of warriors ... that Atlantis might rule the world.
"I wanted to fight her head on. To test her vaunted magic against my own, but they had a plan...
"Warriors from thousands of years into tomorrow. The Justice League... Your brothers, who I helped kill.
TRAGIC KINGDOM
JOE KELLY-WRITER • DOUG MAHNKE, YVEL GUICHET, DARRYL BANKS, AND DIETRICH SMITH-PENCILLERS • TOM NGUYEN, MARK PROPST, WAYNE FAUCHER, AND SEAN PARSONS-INKERS • DAVID BARON-COLORIST
KEN LOPEZ-LETTERER • STEPHEN WACKER-ASSOCIATE EDITOR
DAN RASPLER-EDITOR

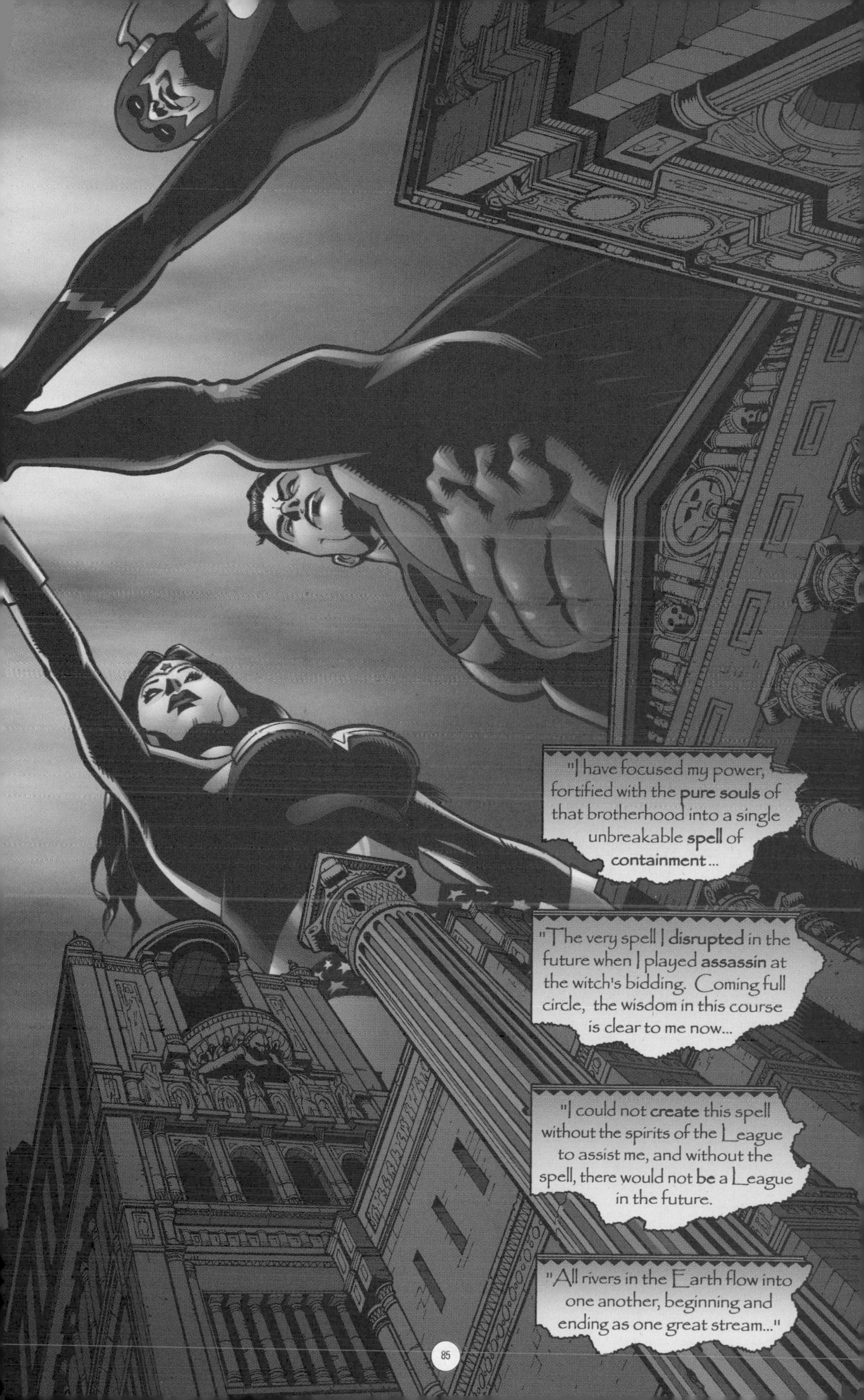
"I have focused my power, fortified with the pure souls of that brotherhood into a single unbreakable spell of containment...
"The very spell I disrupted in the future when I played assassin at the witch's bidding. Coming full circle, the wisdom in this course is clear to me now...
"I could not create this spell without the spirits of the League to assist me, and without the spell, there would not be a League in the future.
"All rivers in the Earth flow into one another, beginning and ending as one great stream..."

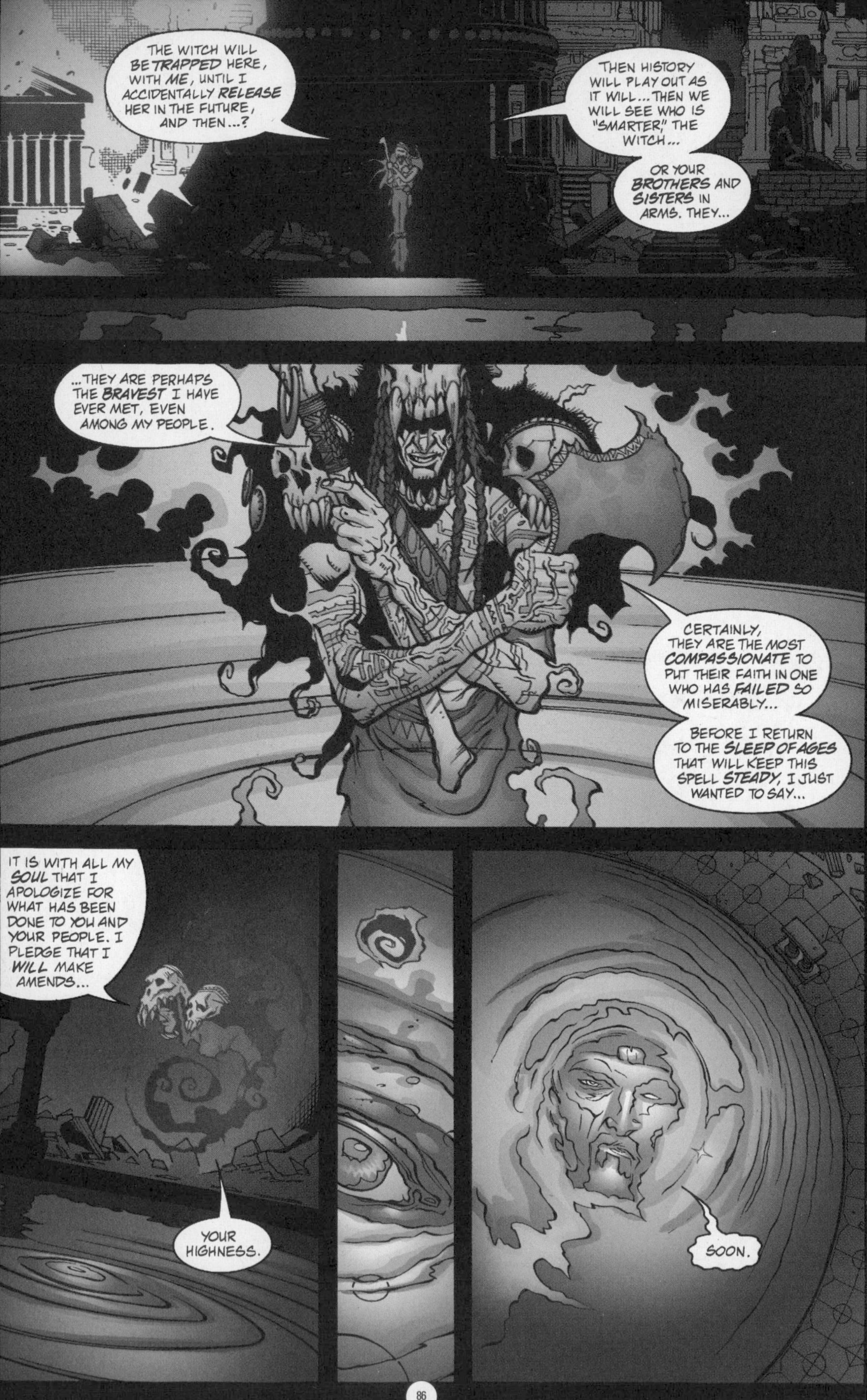
THE WITCH WILL BE TRAPPED HERE, WITH ME, UNTIL I ACCIDENTALLY RELEASE HER IN THE FUTURE, AND THEN...?
THEN HISTORY WILL PLAY OUT AS IT WILL... THEN WE WILL SEE WHO IS "SMARTER," THE WITCH...
OR YOUR BROTHERS AND SISTERS IN ARMS. THEY...
...THEY ARE PERHAPS THE BRAVEST I HAVE EVER MET, EVEN AMONG MY PEOPLE.
CERTAINLY, THEY ARE THE MOST COMPASSIONATE TO PUT THEIR FAITH IN ONE WHO HAS FAILED SO MISERABLY...
BEFORE I RETURN TO THE SLEEP OF AGES THAT WILL KEEP THIS SPELL STEADY, I JUST WANTED TO SAY...
IT IS WITH ALL MY SOUL THAT I APOLOGIZE FOR WHAT HAS BEEN DONE TO YOU AND YOUR PEOPLE. I PLEDGE THAT I WILL MAKE AMENDS...
YOUR HIGHNESS.
SOON.

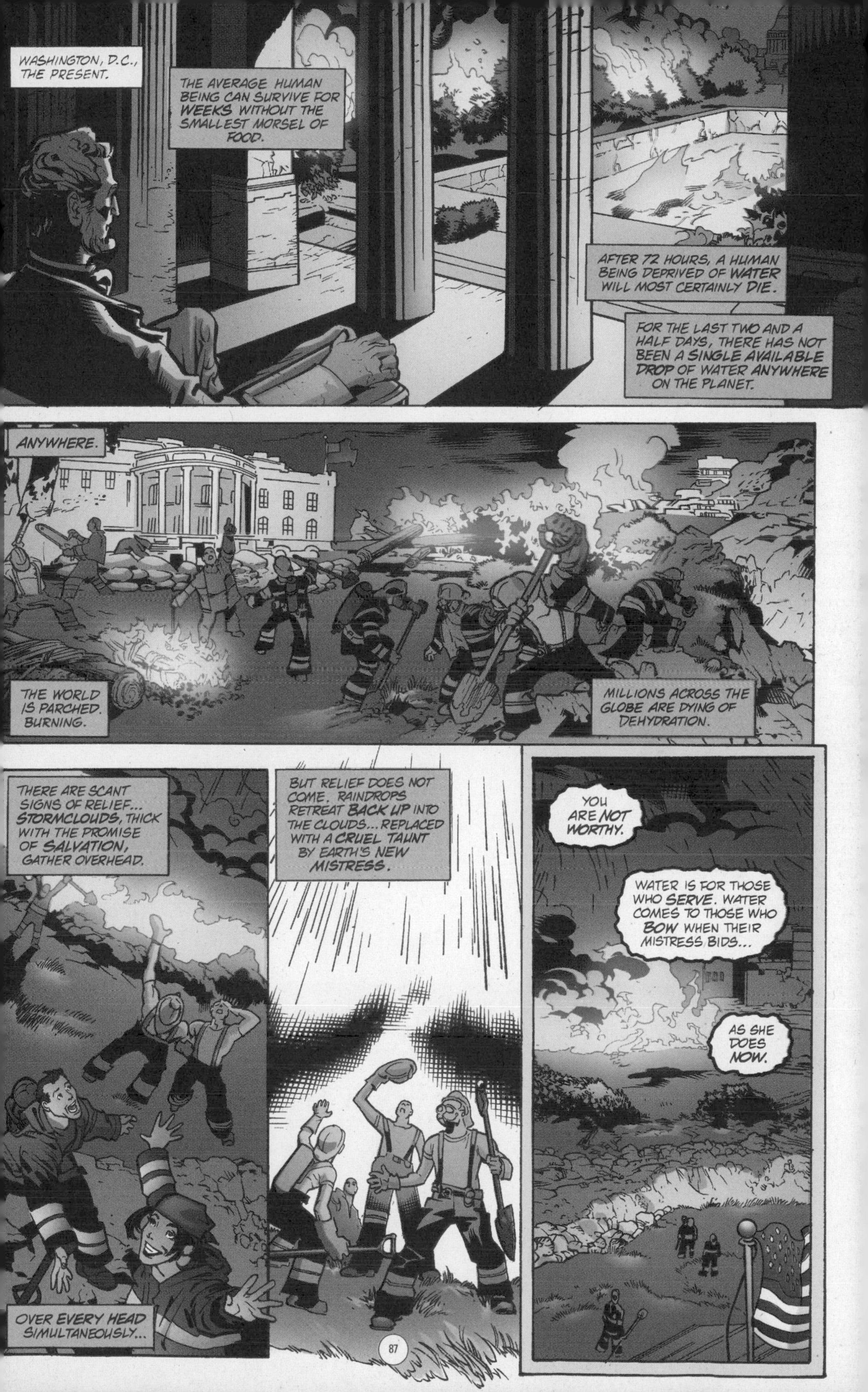
WASHINGTON, D.C., THE PRESENT.
THE AVERAGE HUMAN BEING CAN SURVIVE FOR WEEKS WITHOUT THE SMALLEST MORSEL OF FOOD.
AFTER 72 HOURS, A HUMAN BEING DEPRIVED OF WATER WILL MOST CERTAINLY DIE.
FOR THE LAST TWO AND A HALF DAYS, THERE HAS NOT BEEN A SINGLE AVAILABLE DROP OF WATER ANYWHERE ON THE PLANET.
ANYWHERE.
THE WORLD IS PARCHED. BURNING.
MILLIONS ACROSS THE GLOBE ARE DYING OF DEHYDRATION.
THERE ARE SCANT SIGNS OF RELIEF... STORMCLOUDS, THICK WITH THE PROMISE OF SALVATION, GATHER OVERHEAD.
OVER EVERY HEAD SIMULTANEOUSLY...
BUT RELIEF DOES NOT COME. RAINDROPS RETREAT BACK UP INTO THE CLOUDS... REPLACED WITH A CRUEL TAUNT BY EARTH'S NEW MISTRESS.
YOU ARE NOT WORTHY.
WATER IS FOR THOSE WHO SERVE. WATER COMES TO THOSE WHO BOW WHEN THEIR MISTRESS BIDS...
AS SHE DOES NOW.

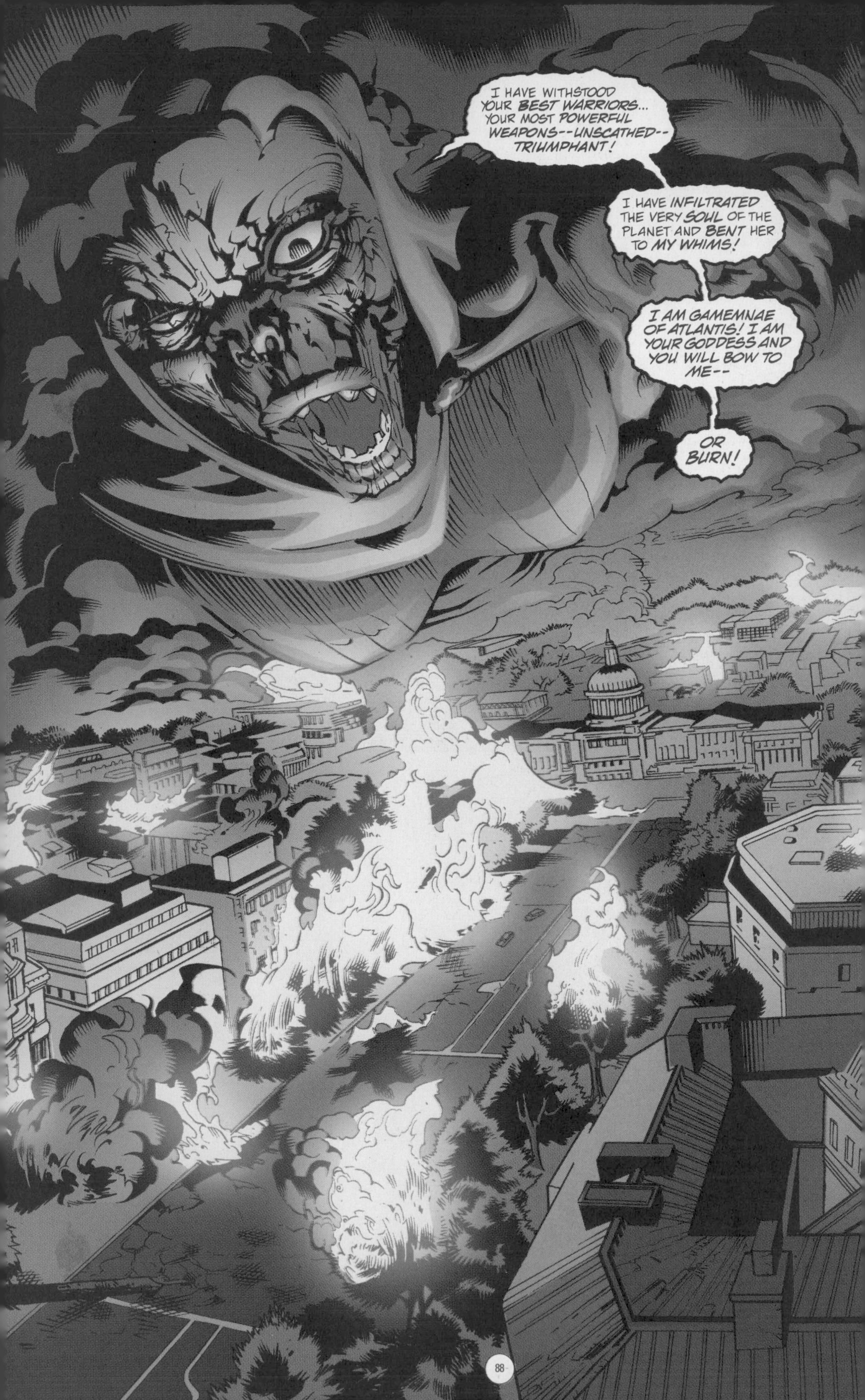
I HAVE WITHSTOOD YOUR BEST WARRIORS... YOUR MOST POWERFUL WEAPONS--UNSCATHED--TRIUMPHANT!
I HAVE INFILTRATED THE VERY SOUL OF THE PLANET AND BENT HER TO MY WHIMS!
I AM GAMEMNAE OF ATLANTIS! I AM YOUR GODDESS AND YOU WILL BOW TO ME--
OR BURN!

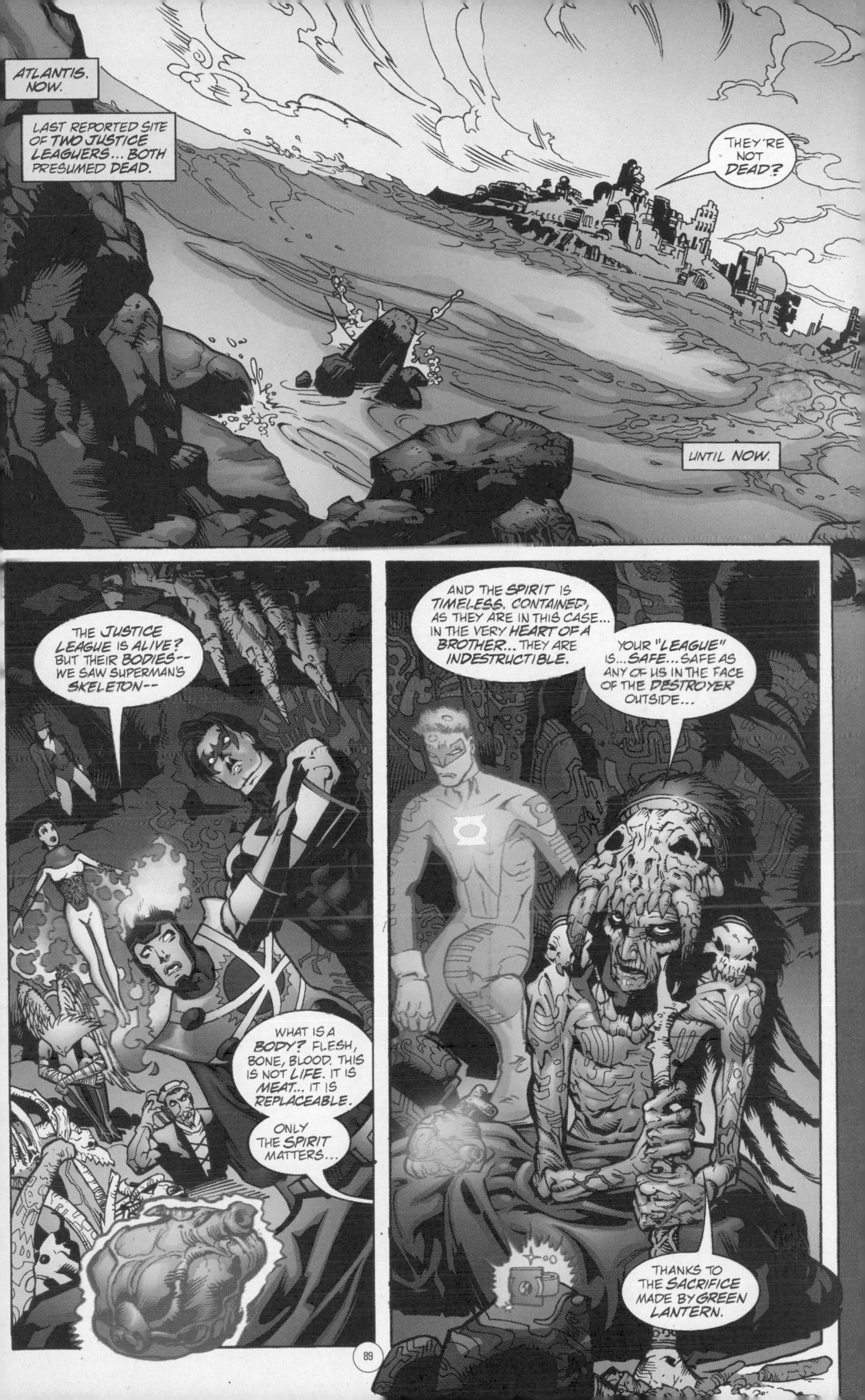
ATLANTIS. NOW.
LAST REPORTED SITE OF TWO JUSTICE LEAGUERS... BOTH PRESUMED DEAD.
THEY'RE NOT DEAD?
UNTIL NOW.
THE JUSTICE LEAGUE IS ALIVE? BUT THEIR BODIES-- WE SAW SUPERMAN'S SKELETON--
WHAT IS A BODY? FLESH, BONE, BLOOD. THIS IS NOT LIFE. IT IS MEAT... IT IS REPLACEABLE.
ONLY THE SPIRIT MATTERS...
AND THE SPIRIT IS TIMELESS. CONTAINED, AS THEY ARE IN THIS CASE... IN THE VERY HEART OF A BROTHER... THEY ARE INDESTRUCTIBLE.
YOUR "LEAGUE" IS... SAFE... SAFE AS ANY OF US IN THE FACE OF THE DESTROYER OUTSIDE...
THANKS TO THE SACRIFICE MADE BY GREEN LANTERN.

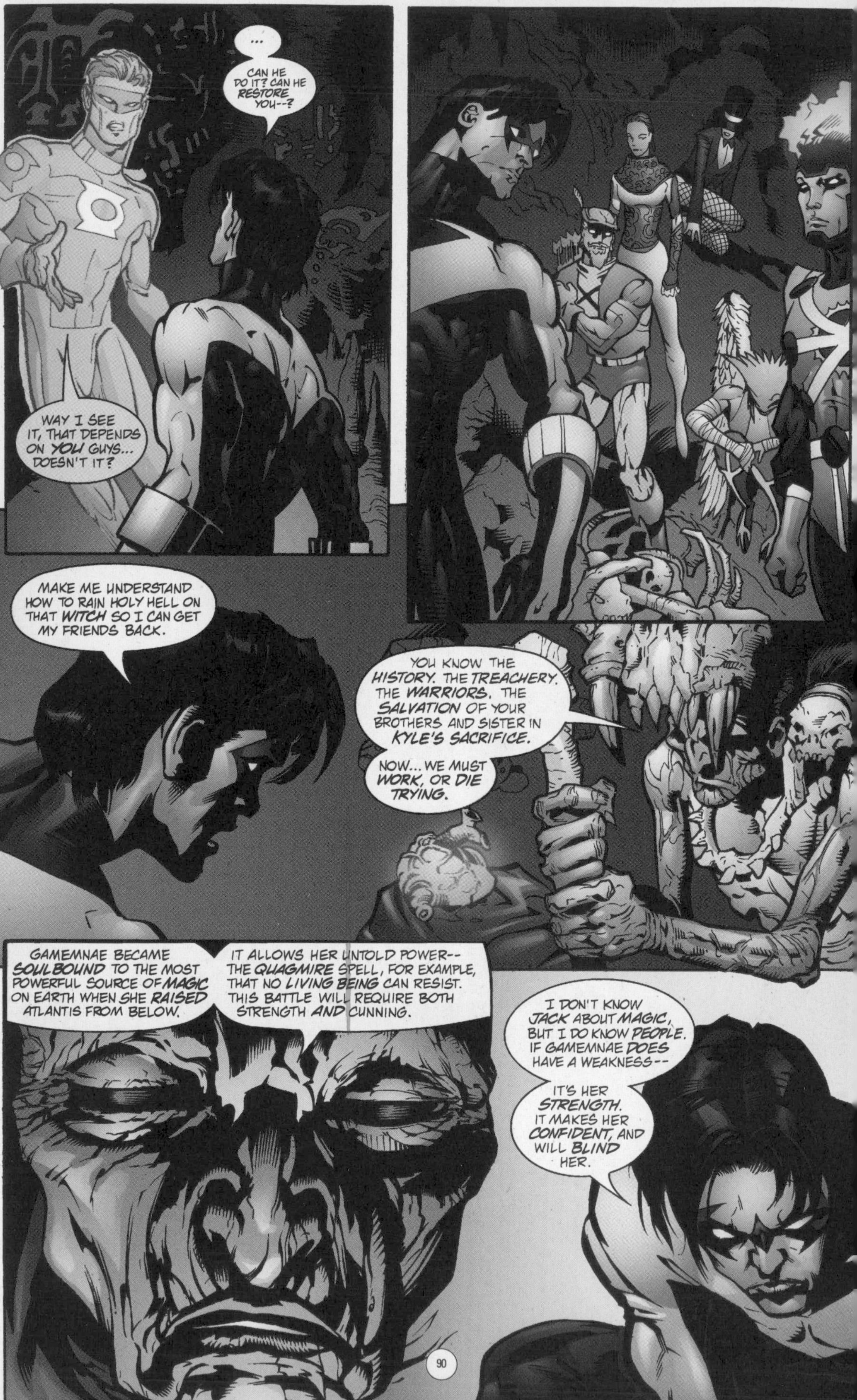
...
CAN HE DO IT? CAN HE RESTORE YOU--?
WAY I SEE IT, THAT DEPENDS ON YOU GUYS... DOESN'T IT?
MAKE ME UNDERSTAND HOW TO RAIN HOLY HELL ON THAT WITCH SO I CAN GET MY FRIENDS BACK.
YOU KNOW THE HISTORY. THE TREACHERY. THE WARRIORS. THE SALVATION OF YOUR BROTHERS AND SISTER IN KYLE'S SACRIFICE.
NOW... WE MUST WORK, OR DIE TRYING.
GAMEMNAE BECAME SOULBOUND TO THE MOST POWERFUL SOURCE OF MAGIC ON EARTH WHEN SHE RAISED ATLANTIS FROM BELOW.
IT ALLOWS HER UNTOLD POWER-- THE QUAGMIRE SPELL, FOR EXAMPLE, THAT NO LIVING BEING CAN RESIST. THIS BATTLE WILL REQUIRE BOTH STRENGTH AND CUNNING.
I DON'T KNOW JACK ABOUT MAGIC, BUT I DO KNOW PEOPLE. IF GAMEMNAE DOES HAVE A WEAKNESS--
IT'S HER STRENGTH. IT MAKES HER CONFIDENT, AND WILL BLIND HER.

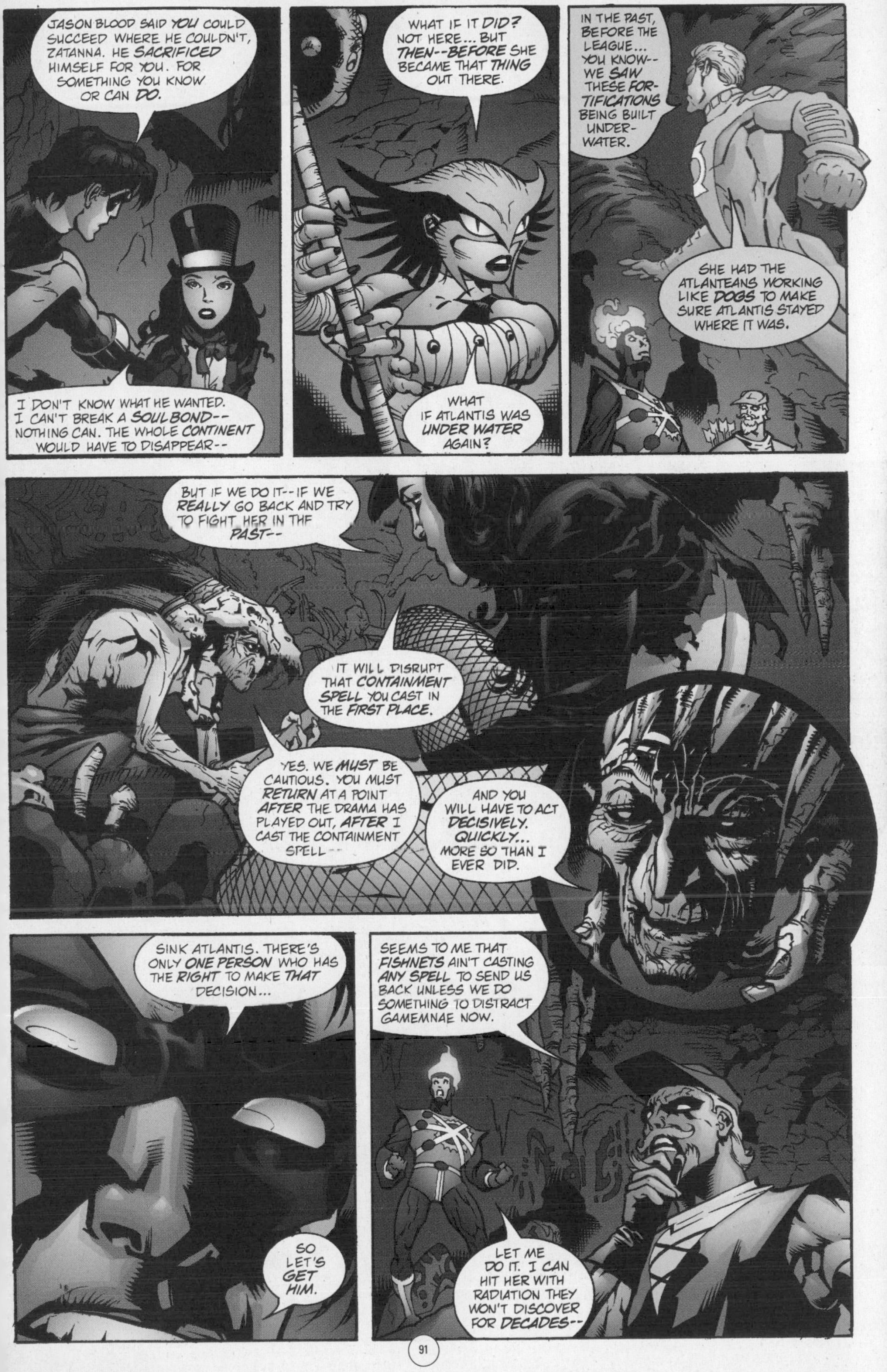
JASON BLOOD SAID YOU COULD SUCCEED WHERE HE COULDN'T, ZATANNA. HE SACRIFICED HIMSELF FOR YOU. FOR SOMETHING YOU KNOW OR CAN DO.
I DON'T KNOW WHAT HE WANTED. I CAN'T BREAK A SOULBOND-- NOTHING CAN. THE WHOLE CONTINENT WOULD HAVE TO DISAPPEAR--
WHAT IF IT DID? NOT HERE... BUT THEN--BEFORE SHE BECAME THAT THING OUT THERE.
WHAT IF ATLANTIS WAS UNDER WATER AGAIN?
IN THE PAST, BEFORE THE LEAGUE... YOU KNOW-- WE SAW THESE FORTIFICATIONS BEING BUILT UNDERWATER.
SHE HAD THE ATLANTEANS WORKING LIKE DOGS TO MAKE SURE ATLANTIS STAYED WHERE IT WAS.
BUT IF WE DO IT--IF WE REALLY GO BACK AND TRY TO FIGHT HER IN THE PAST--
IT WILL DISRUPT THAT CONTAINMENT SPELL YOU CAST IN THE FIRST PLACE.
YES. WE MUST BE CAUTIOUS. YOU MUST RETURN AT A POINT AFTER THE DRAMA HAS PLAYED OUT, AFTER I CAST THE CONTAINMENT SPELL--
AND YOU WILL HAVE TO ACT DECISIVELY. QUICKLY... MORE SO THAN I EVER DID.
SINK ATLANTIS. THERE'S ONLY ONE PERSON WHO HAS THE RIGHT TO MAKE THAT DECISION...
SO LET'S GET HIM.
SEEMS TO ME THAT FISHNETS AIN'T CASTING ANY SPELL TO SEND US BACK UNLESS WE DO SOMETHING TO DISTRACT GAMEMNAE NOW.
LET ME DO IT. I CAN HIT HER WITH RADIATION THEY WON'T DISCOVER FOR DECADES--

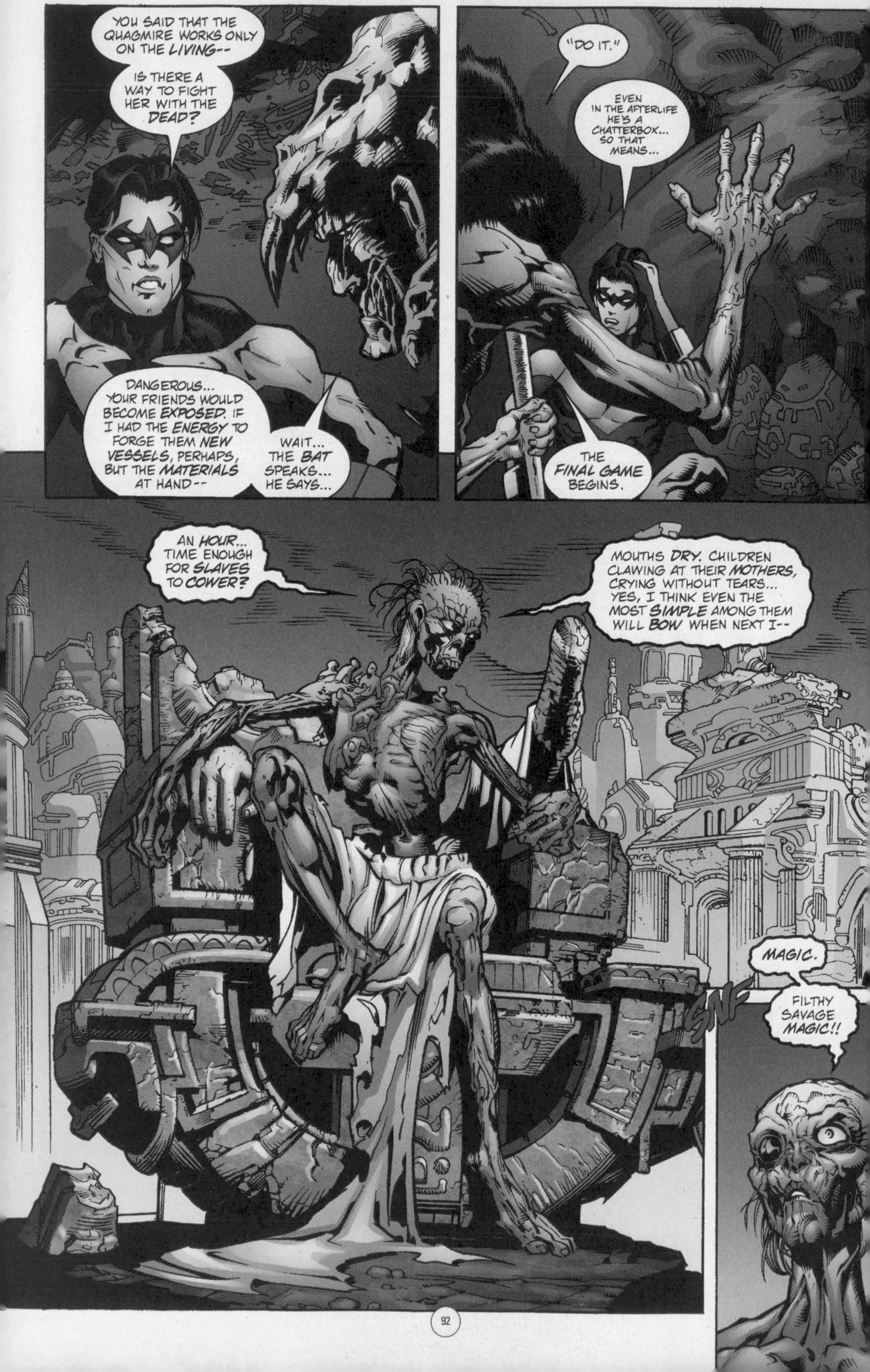
YOU SAID THAT THE QUAGMIRE WORKS ONLY ON THE LIVING--
IS THERE A WAY TO FIGHT HER WITH THE DEAD?
DANGEROUS... YOUR FRIENDS WOULD BECOME EXPOSED. IF I HAD THE ENERGY TO FORGE THEM NEW VESSELS, PERHAPS, BUT THE MATERIALS AT HAND--
WAIT... THE BAT SPEAKS... HE SAYS...
"DO IT."
EVEN IN THE AFTERLIFE HE'S A CHATTERBOX... SO THAT MEANS...
THE FINAL GAME BEGINS.
AN HOUR... TIME ENOUGH FOR SLAVES TO COWER?
MOUTHS DRY. CHILDREN CLAWING AT THEIR MOTHERS, CRYING WITHOUT TEARS... YES, I THINK EVEN THE MOST SIMPLE AMONG THEM WILL BOW WHEN NEXT I--
SNF
MAGIC.
FILTHY SAVAGE MAGIC!!

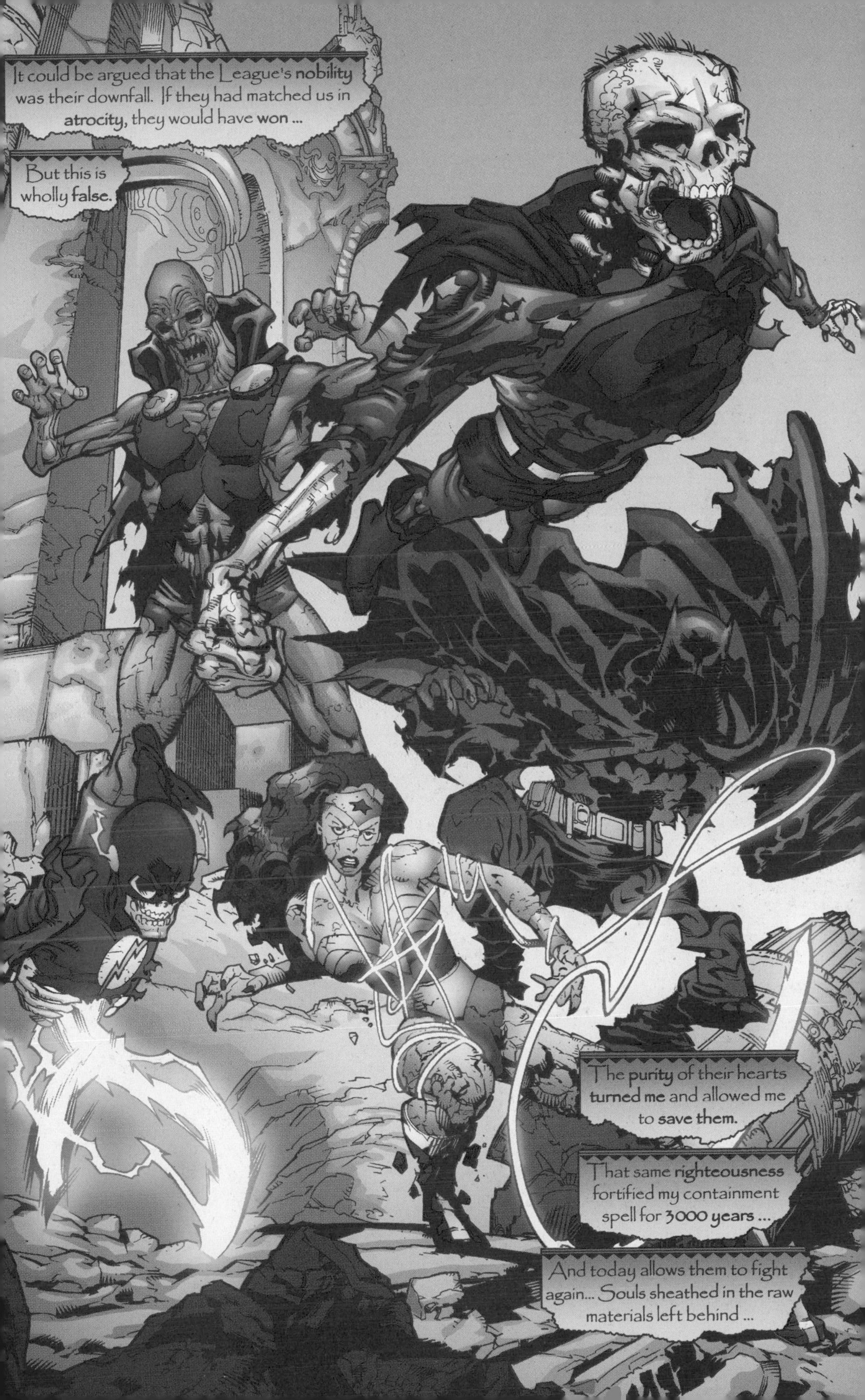
It could be argued that the League's nobility was their downfall. If they had matched us in atrocity, they would have won ...
But this is wholly false.
The purity of their hearts turned me and allowed me to save them.
That same righteousness fortified my containment spell for 3000 years ...
And today allows them to fight again... Souls sheathed in the raw materials left behind ...

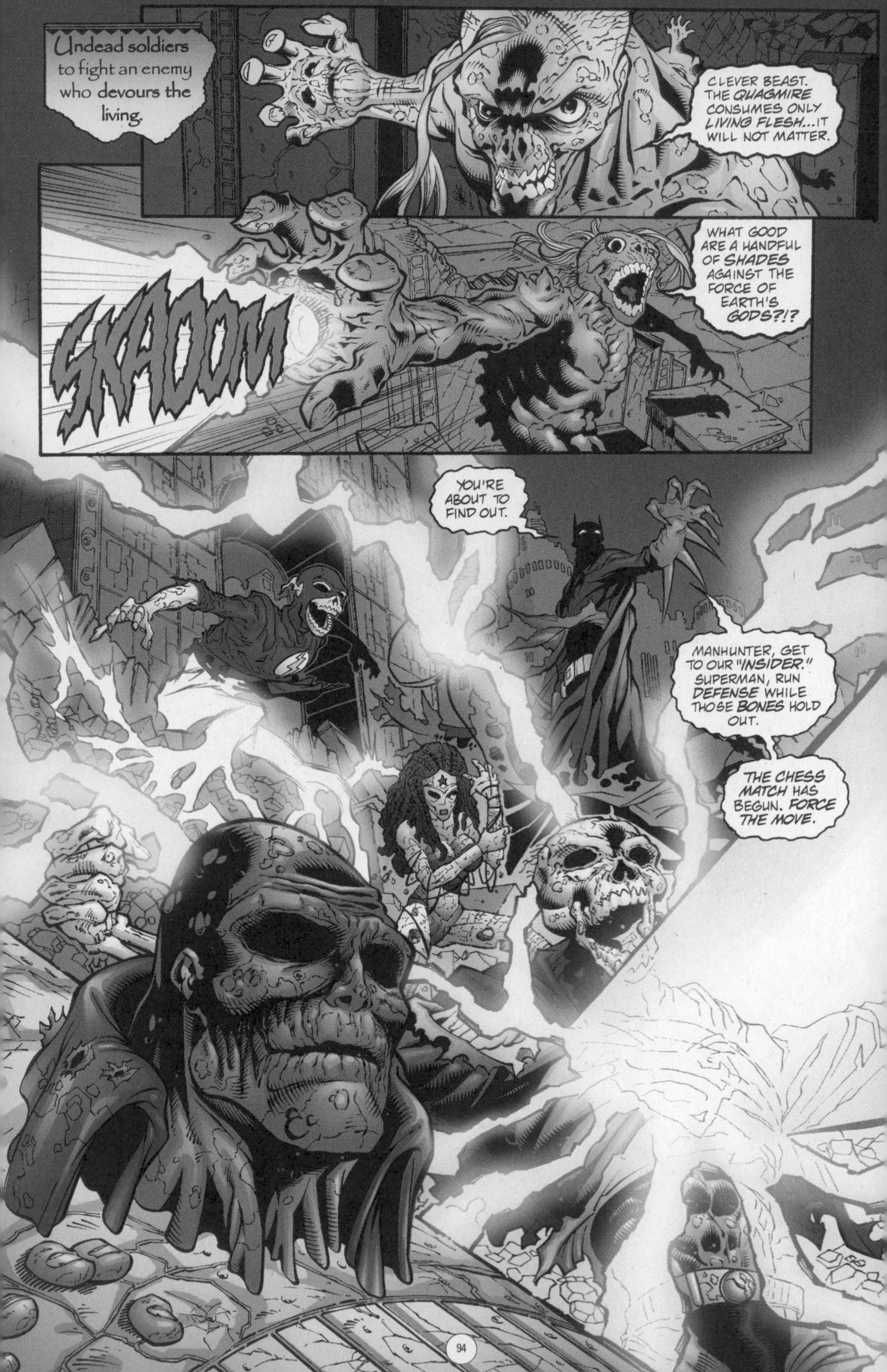

Undead soldiers to fight an enemy who devours the living.
CLEVER BEAST. THE QUAGMIRE CONSUMES ONLY LIVING FLESH...IT WILL NOT MATTER.
SKAOOM
WHAT GOOD ARE A HANDFUL OF SHADES AGAINST THE FORCE OF EARTH'S GODS?!?
YOU'RE ABOUT TO FIND OUT.
MANHUNTER, GET TO OUR "INSIDER." SUPERMAN, RUN DEFENSE WHILE THOSE BONES HOLD OUT.
THE CHESS MATCH HAS BEGUN. FORCE THE MOVE.

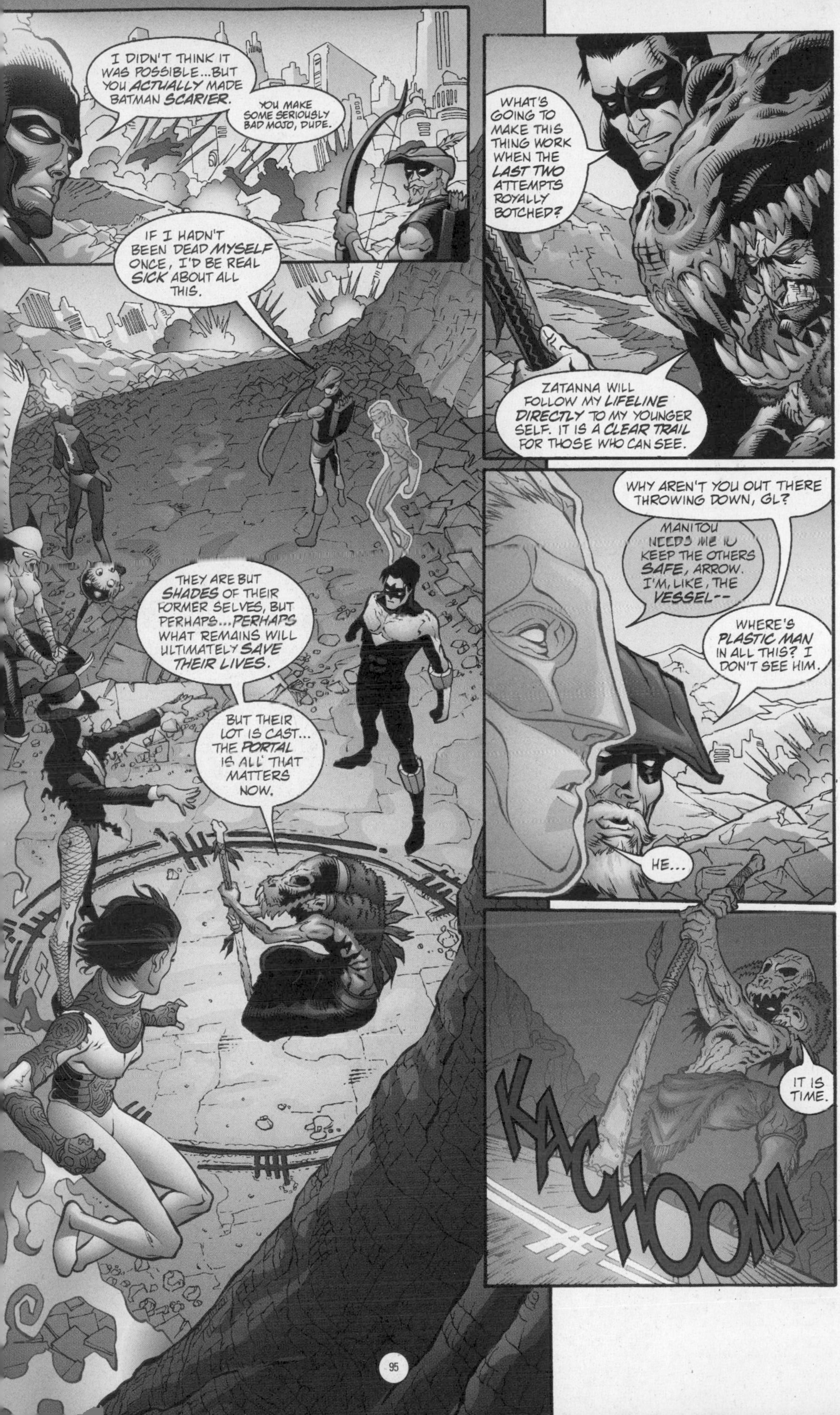

I DIDN'T THINK IT WAS POSSIBLE...BUT YOU ACTUALLY MADE BATMAN SCARIER.
YOU MAKE SOME SERIOUSLY BAD MOJO, DUDE.
IF I HADN'T BEEN DEAD MYSELF ONCE, I'D BE REAL SICK ABOUT ALL THIS.
THEY ARE BUT SHADES OF THEIR FORMER SELVES, BUT PERHAPS...PERHAPS WHAT REMAINS WILL ULTIMATELY SAVE THEIR LIVES.
BUT THEIR LOT IS CAST... THE PORTAL IS ALL THAT MATTERS NOW.
WHAT'S GOING TO MAKE THIS THING WORK WHEN THE LAST TWO ATTEMPTS ROYALLY BOTCHED?
ZATANNA WILL FOLLOW MY LIFELINE DIRECTLY TO MY YOUNGER SELF. IT IS A CLEAR TRAIL FOR THOSE WHO CAN SEE.
WHY AREN'T YOU OUT THERE THROWING DOWN, GL?
MANITOU NEEDS ME TO KEEP THE OTHERS SAFE, ARROW. I'M, LIKE, THE VESSEL--
WHERE'S PLASTIC MAN IN ALL THIS? I DON'T SEE HIM.
HE...
IT IS TIME.
KACHOOM

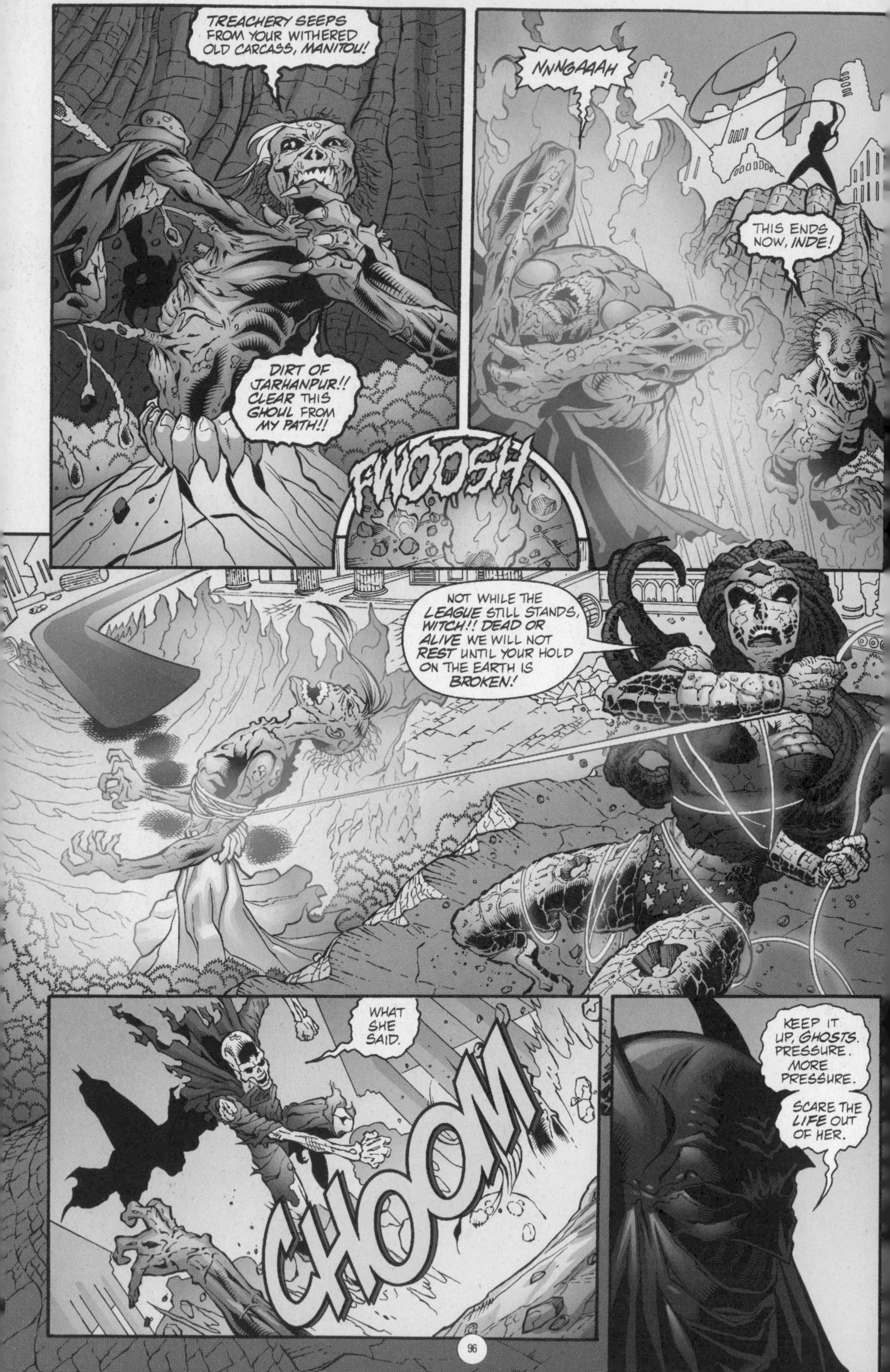
TREACHERY SEEPS FROM YOUR WITHERED OLD CARCASS, MANITOU!
DIRT OF JARHANPUR!! CLEAR THIS GHOUL FROM MY PATH!!
NNNGAAAH
THIS ENDS NOW, INDE!
FWOOSH
NOT WHILE THE LEAGUE STILL STANDS, WITCH!! DEAD OR ALIVE WE WILL NOT REST UNTIL YOUR HOLD ON THE EARTH IS BROKEN!
WHAT SHE SAID.
CHOOM
KEEP IT UP, GHOSTS. PRESSURE. MORE PRESSURE.
SCARE THE LIFE OUT OF HER.

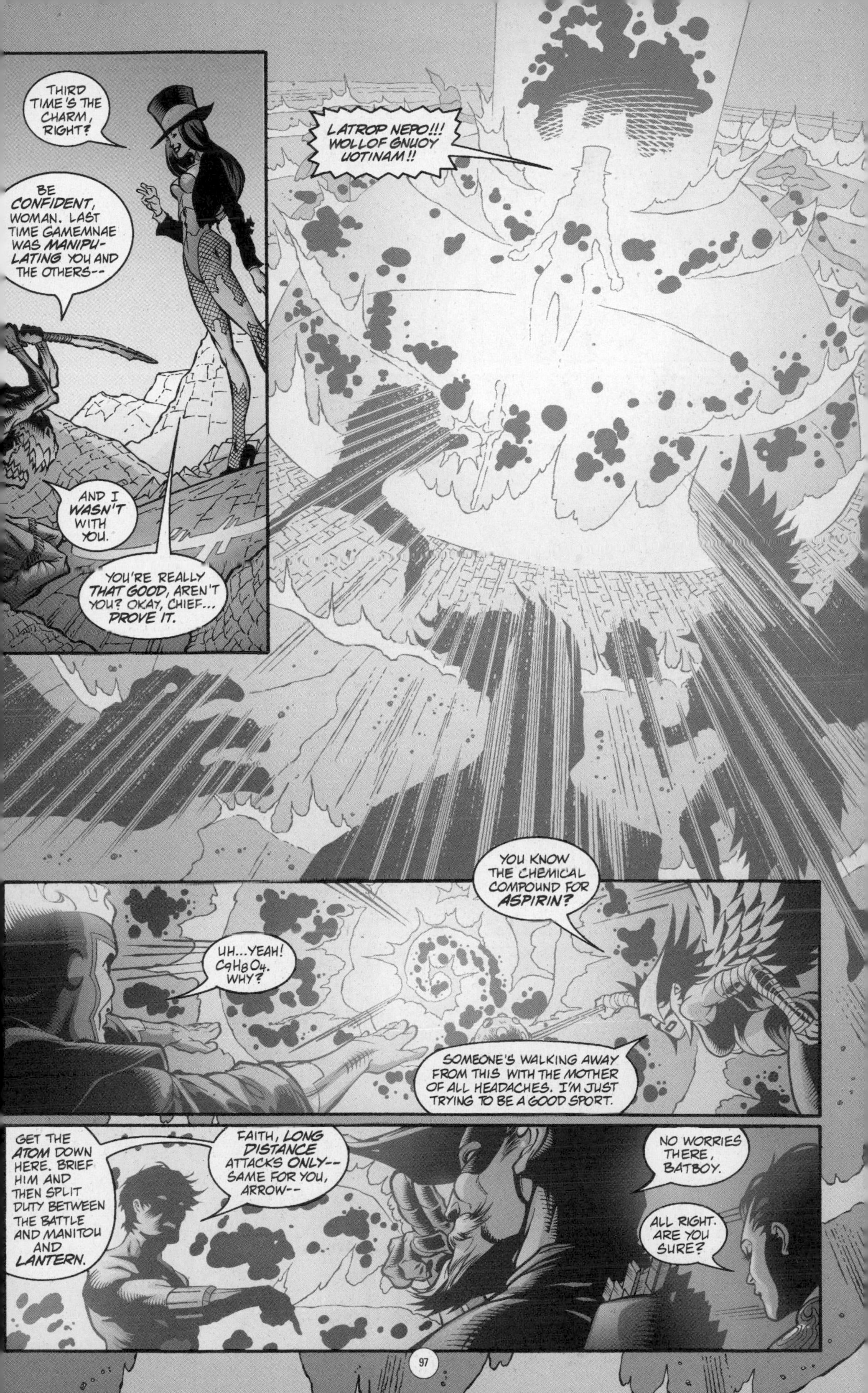
THIRD TIME'S THE CHARM, RIGHT?
BE CONFIDENT, WOMAN. LAST TIME GAMEMNAE WAS MANIPULATING YOU AND THE OTHERS--
AND I WASN'T WITH YOU.
YOU'RE REALLY THAT GOOD, AREN'T YOU? OKAY, CHIEF... PROVE IT.
LATROP NEPO!!! WOLLOF GNUOY UOTINAM!!
YOU KNOW THE CHEMICAL COMPOUND FOR ASPIRIN?
UH...YEAH! C9H8O4. WHY?
SOMEONE'S WALKING AWAY FROM THIS WITH THE MOTHER OF ALL HEADACHES. I'M JUST TRYING TO BE A GOOD SPORT.
GET THE ATOM DOWN HERE. BRIEF HIM AND THEN SPLIT DUTY BETWEEN THE BATTLE AND MANITOU AND LANTERN.
FAITH, LONG DISTANCE ATTACKS ONLY-- SAME FOR YOU, ARROW--
NO WORRIES THERE, BATBOY.
ALL RIGHT. ARE YOU SURE?

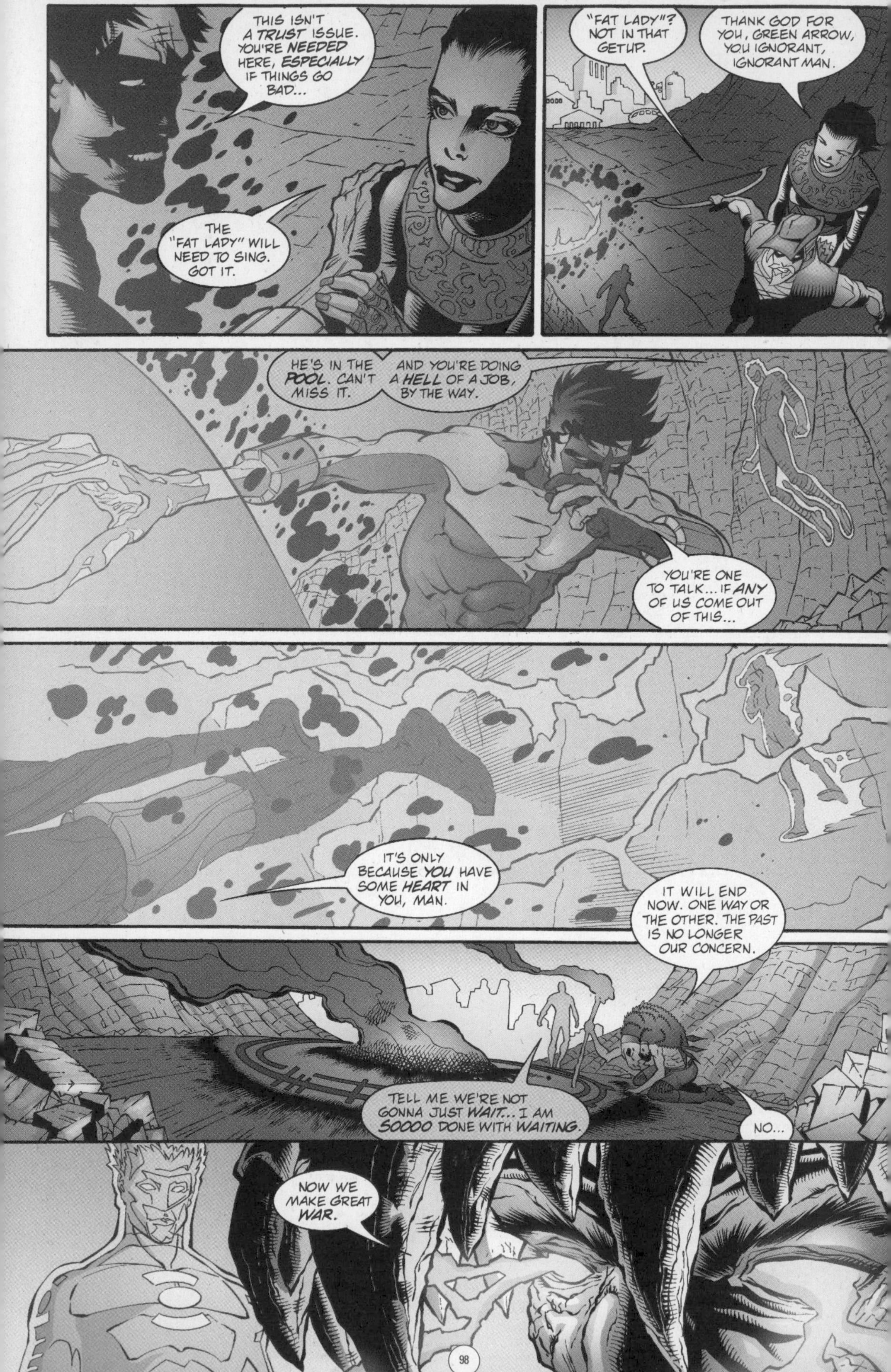

THIS ISN'T A TRUST ISSUE. YOU'RE NEEDED HERE, ESPECIALLY IF THINGS GO BAD...
THE "FAT LADY" WILL NEED TO SING. GOT IT.
"FAT LADY"? NOT IN THAT GETUP.
THANK GOD FOR YOU, GREEN ARROW, YOU IGNORANT, IGNORANT MAN.
HE'S IN THE POOL. CAN'T MISS IT.
AND YOU'RE DOING A HELL OF A JOB, BY THE WAY.
YOU'RE ONE TO TALK... IF ANY OF US COME OUT OF THIS...
IT'S ONLY BECAUSE YOU HAVE SOME HEART IN YOU, MAN.
IT WILL END NOW. ONE WAY OR THE OTHER. THE PAST IS NO LONGER OUR CONCERN.
TELL ME WE'RE NOT GONNA JUST WAIT... I AM SOOOO DONE WITH WAITING.
NO...
NOW WE MAKE GREAT WAR.

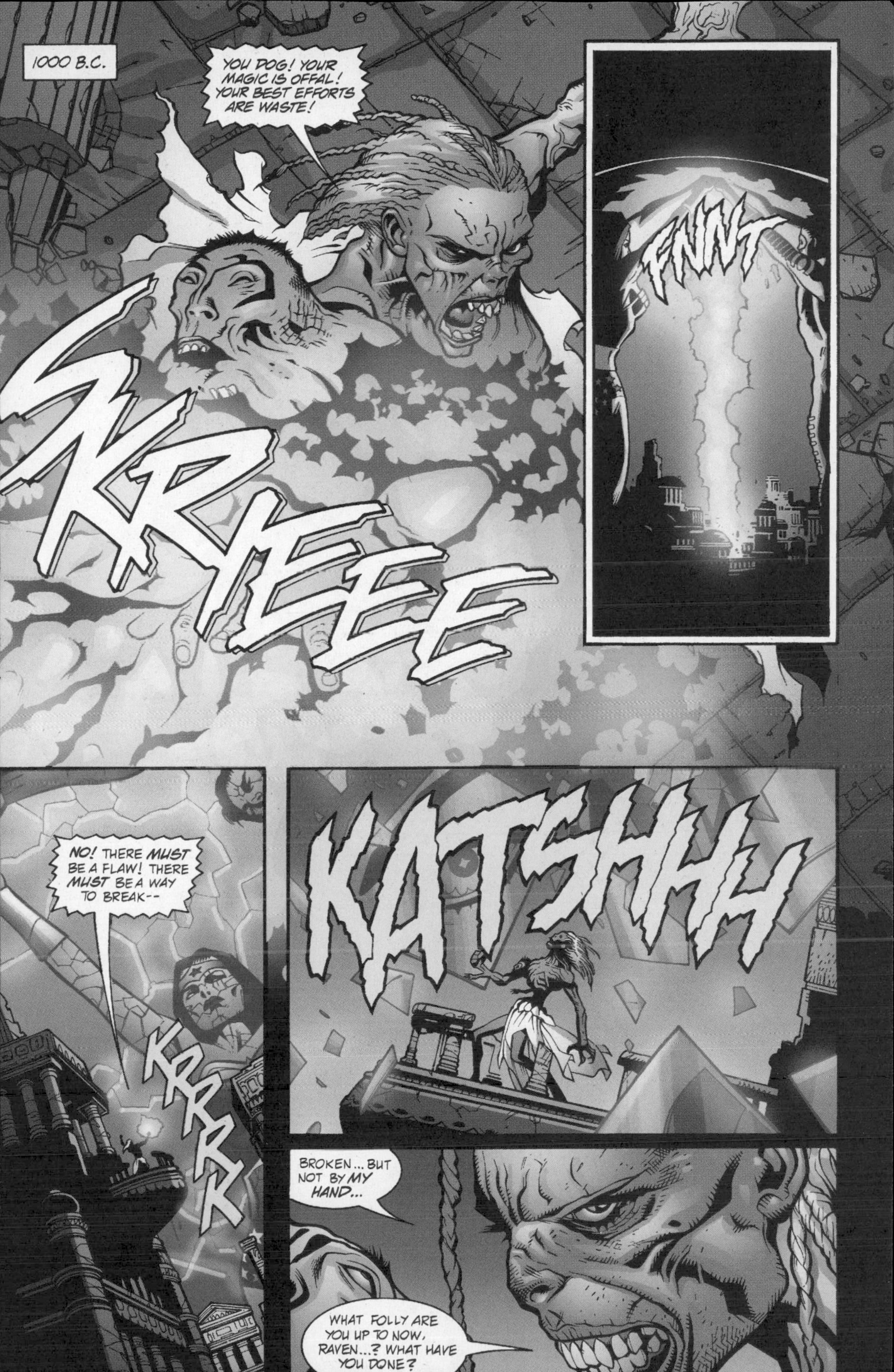
1000 B.C.
YOU DOG! YOUR MAGIC IS OFFAL! YOUR BEST EFFORTS ARE WASTE!
KRYEEE
FNNT
NO! THERE MUST BE A FLAW! THERE MUST BE A WAY TO BREAK--
KRRRR
KATSHH
BROKEN... BUT NOT BY MY HAND...
WHAT FOLLY ARE YOU UP TO NOW, RAVEN...? WHAT HAVE YOU DONE?

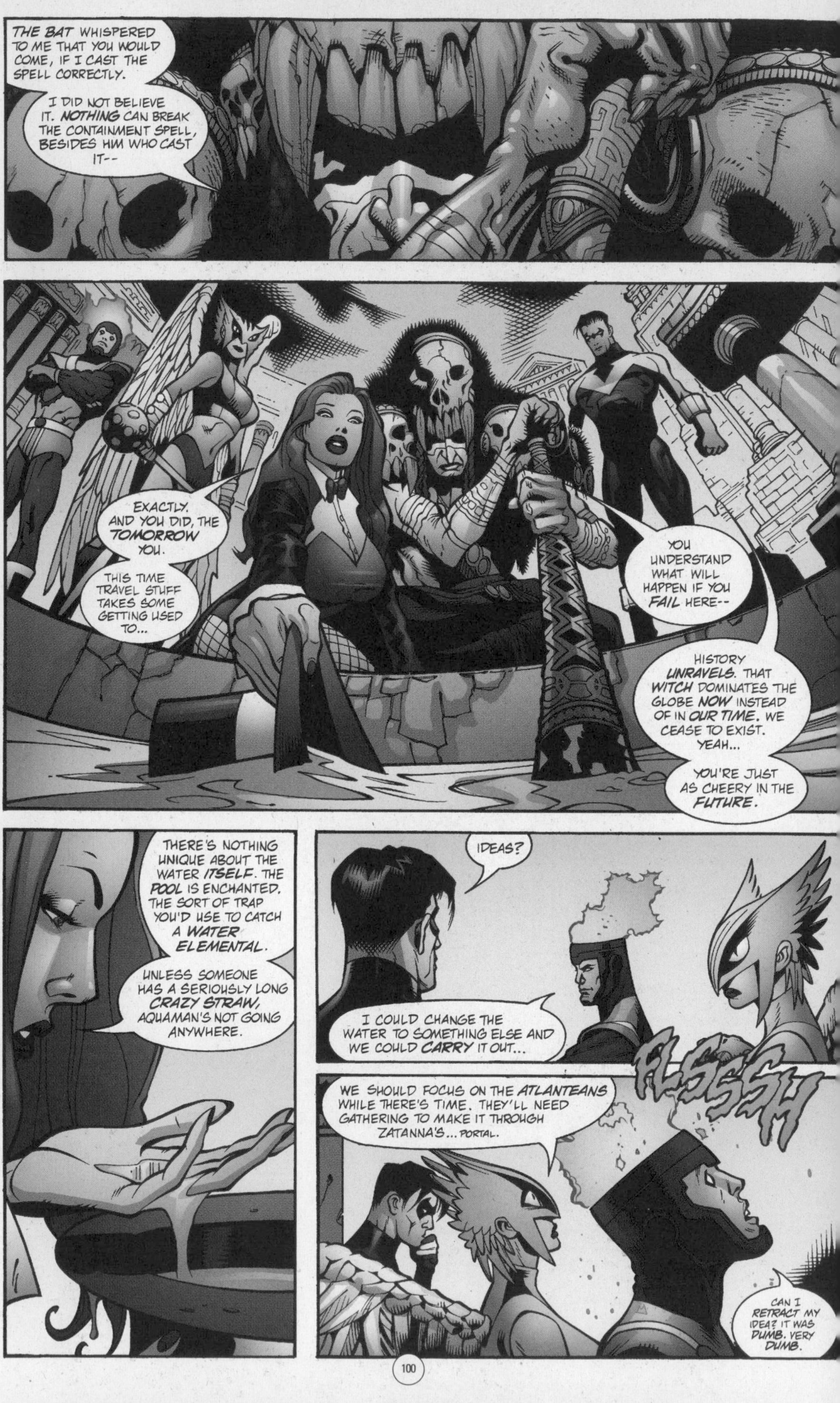
THE BAT WHISPERED TO ME THAT YOU WOULD COME, IF I CAST THE SPELL CORRECTLY.
I DID NOT BELIEVE IT. NOTHING CAN BREAK THE CONTAINMENT SPELL, BESIDES HIM WHO CAST IT--
EXACTLY. AND YOU DID, THE TOMORROW YOU.
THIS TIME TRAVEL STUFF TAKES SOME GETTING USED TO...
YOU UNDERSTAND WHAT WILL HAPPEN IF YOU FAIL HERE--
HISTORY UNRAVELS. THAT WITCH DOMINATES THE GLOBE NOW INSTEAD OF IN OUR TIME. WE CEASE TO EXIST.
YEAH...
YOU'RE JUST AS CHEERY IN THE FUTURE.
THERE'S NOTHING UNIQUE ABOUT THE WATER ITSELF. THE POOL IS ENCHANTED. THE SORT OF TRAP YOU'D USE TO CATCH A WATER ELEMENTAL.
UNLESS SOMEONE HAS A SERIOUSLY LONG CRAZY STRAW, AQUAMAN'S NOT GOING ANYWHERE.
IDEAS?
I COULD CHANGE THE WATER TO SOMETHING ELSE AND WE COULD CARRY IT OUT...
FLSSSH
WE SHOULD FOCUS ON THE ATLANTEANS WHILE THERE'S TIME. THEY'LL NEED GATHERING TO MAKE IT THROUGH ZATANNA'S... PORTAL.
CAN I RETRACT MY IDEA? IT WAS DUMB. VERY DUMB.

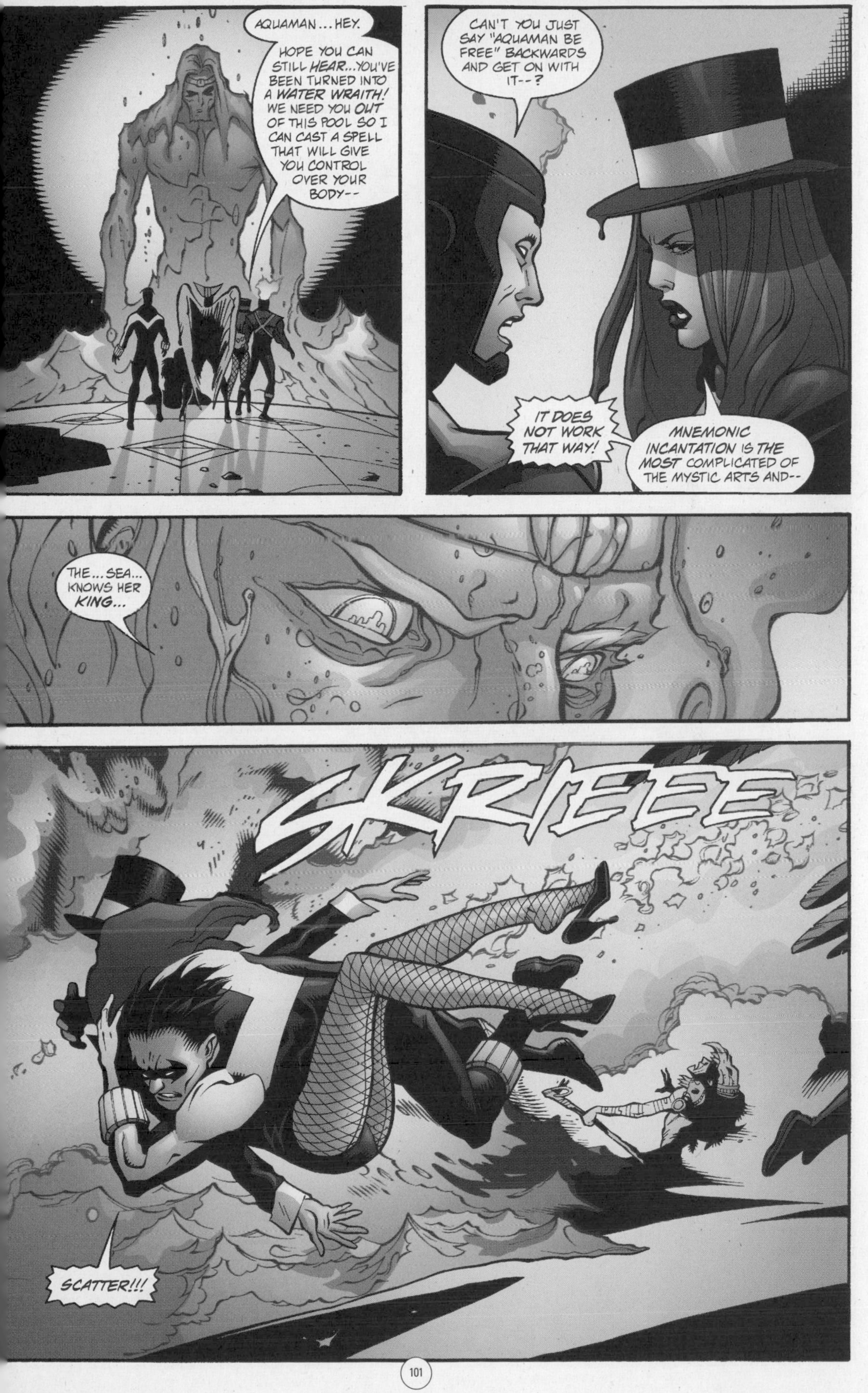
AQUAMAN... HEY.
HOPE YOU CAN STILL HEAR...YOU'VE BEEN TURNED INTO A WATER WRAITH! WE NEED YOU OUT OF THIS POOL SO I CAN CAST A SPELL THAT WILL GIVE YOU CONTROL OVER YOUR BODY--
CAN'T YOU JUST SAY "AQUAMAN BE FREE" BACKWARDS AND GET ON WITH IT--?
IT DOES NOT WORK THAT WAY!
MNEMONIC INCANTATION IS THE MOST COMPLICATED OF THE MYSTIC ARTS AND--
THE... SEA... KNOWS HER KING...
SKRIEEE
SCATTER!!!

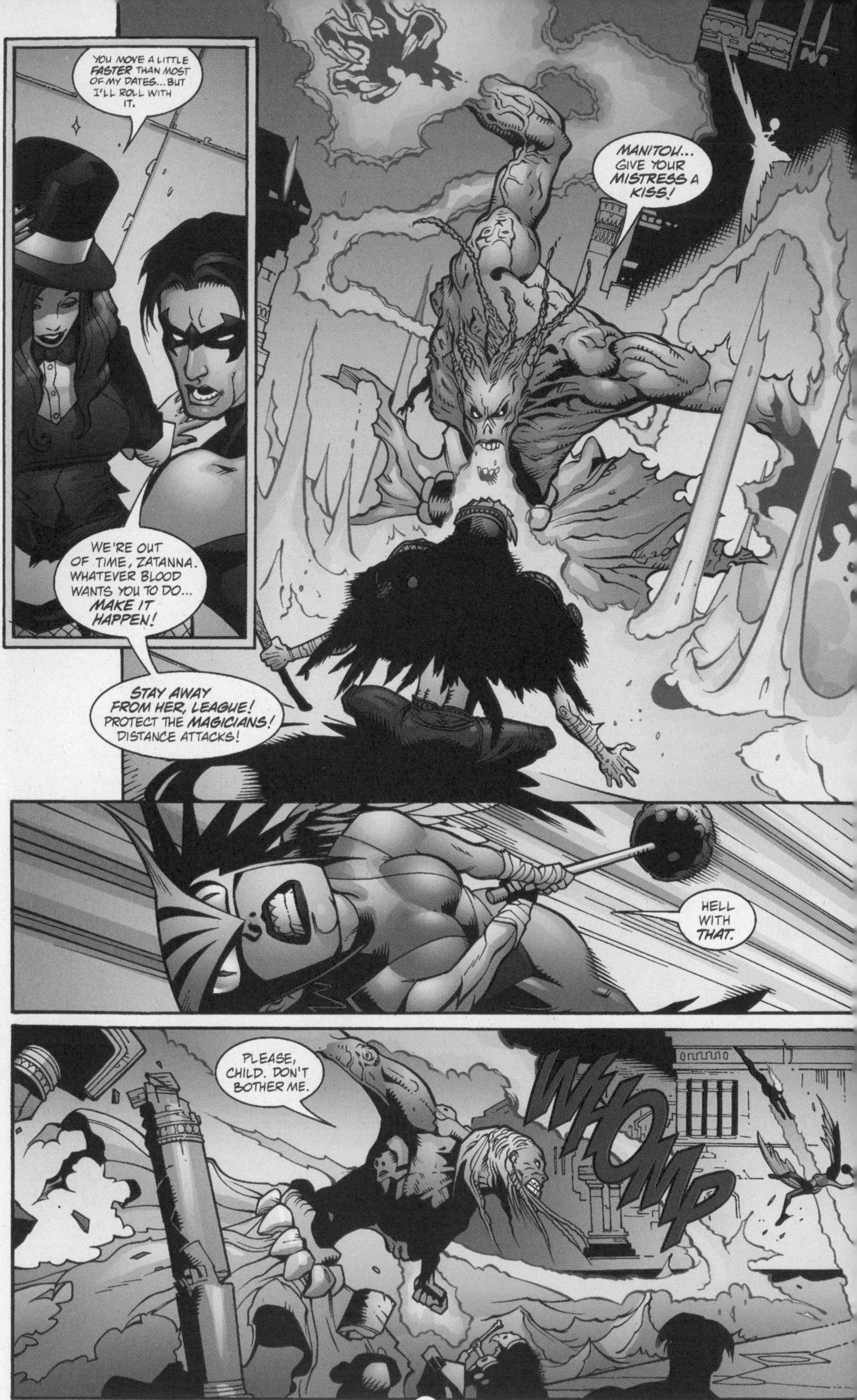
YOU MOVE A LITTLE FASTER THAN MOST OF MY DATES... BUT I'LL ROLL WITH IT.
MANITOU... GIVE YOUR MISTRESS A KISS!
WE'RE OUT OF TIME, ZATANNA. WHATEVER BLOOD WANTS YOU TO DO... MAKE IT HAPPEN!
STAY AWAY FROM HER, LEAGUE! PROTECT THE MAGICIANS! DISTANCE ATTACKS!
HELL WITH THAT.
PLEASE, CHILD. DON'T BOTHER ME.
WHOMP

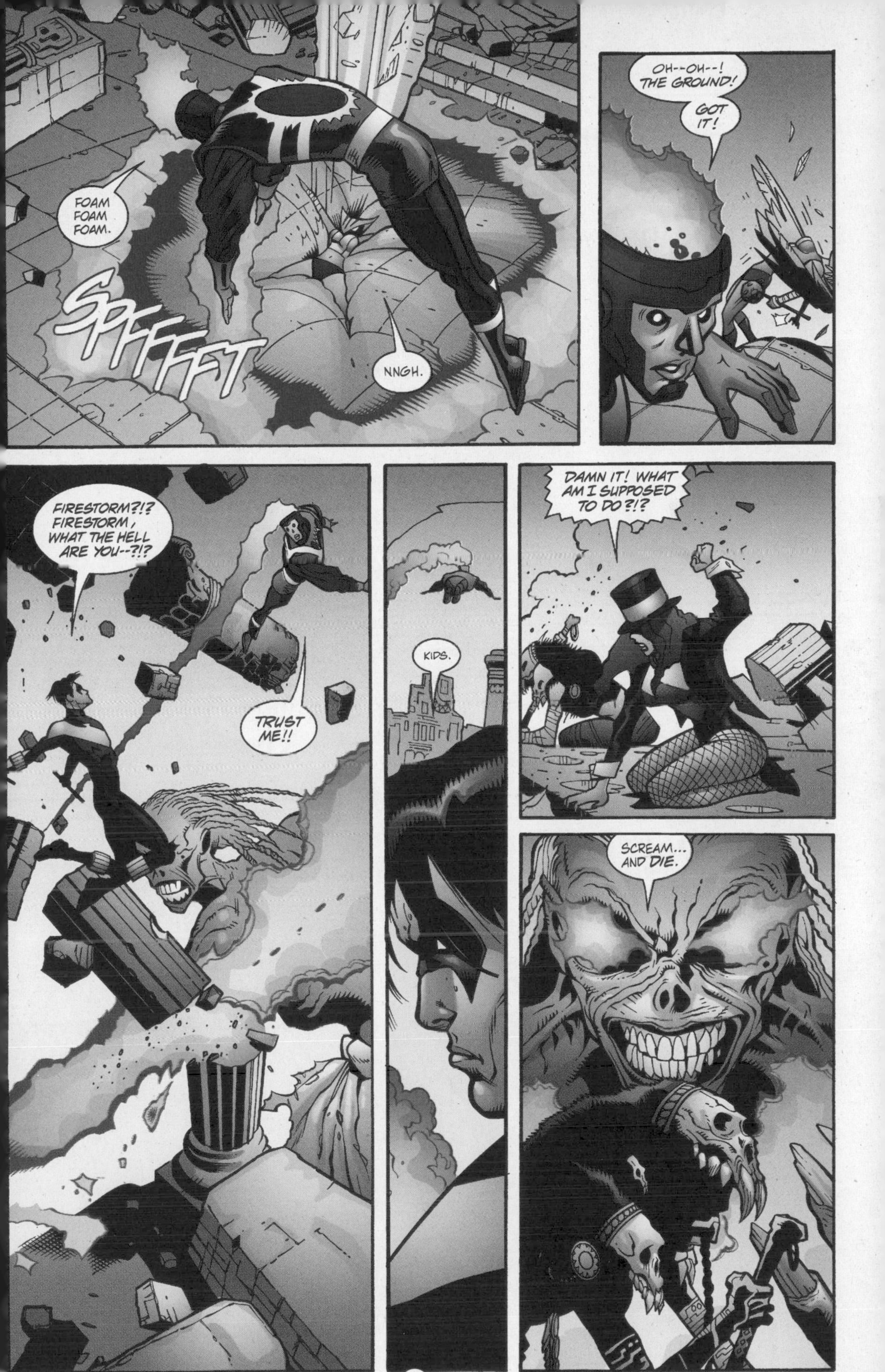
FOAM
FOAM
FOAM.
SPFFFFFT
NNGH.
OH--OH--! THE GROUND!
GOT IT!
FIRESTORM?!? FIRESTORM, WHAT THE HELL ARE YOU--?!?
TRUST ME!!
KIDS.
DAMN IT! WHAT AM I SUPPOSED TO DO?!?
SCREAM... AND DIE.

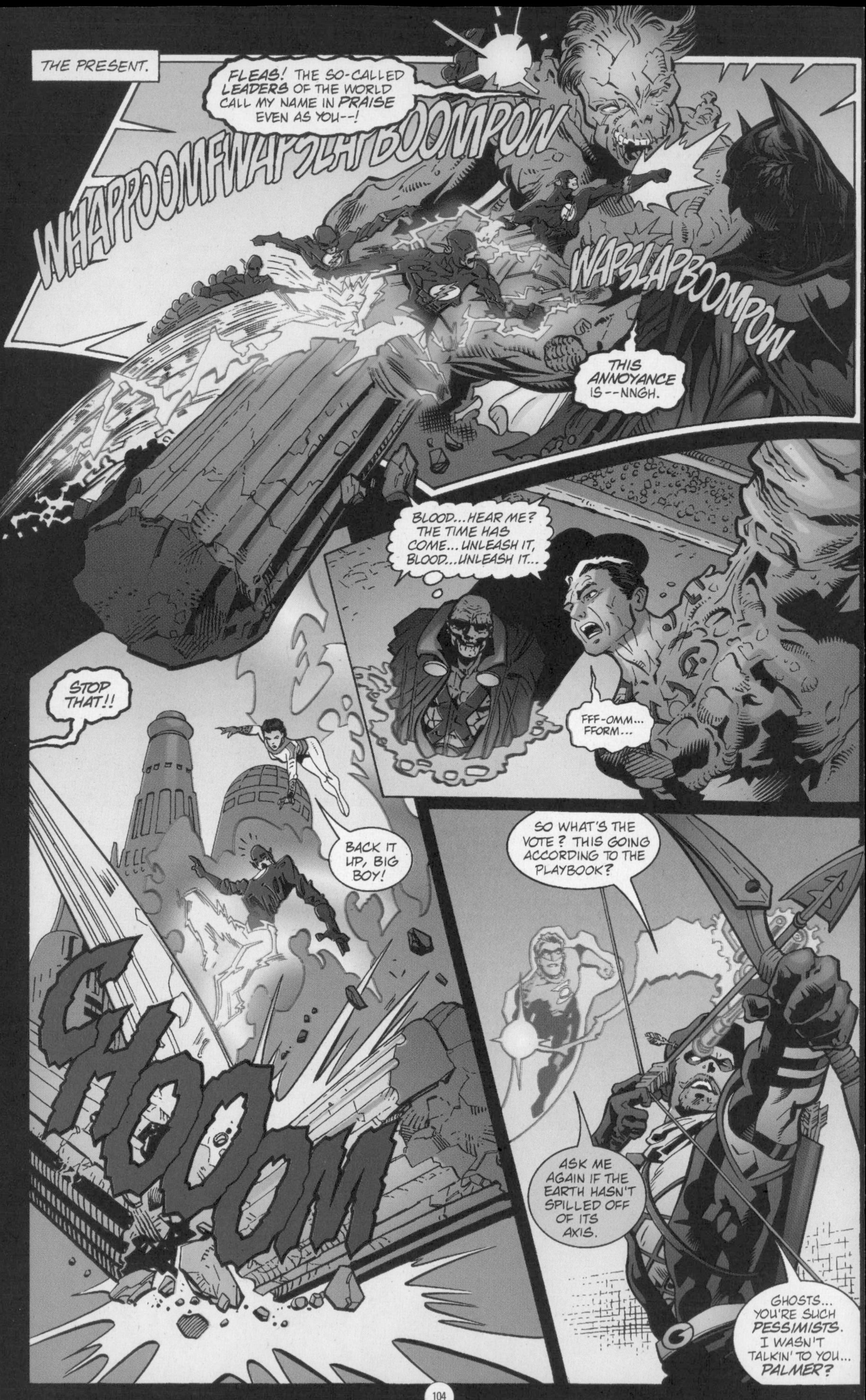
THE PRESENT.
FLEAS! THE SO-CALLED LEADERS OF THE WORLD CALL MY NAME IN PRAISE EVEN AS YOU--!
WHAPPOOMFWAPSLAPBOOMPOW
WAPSLAPBOOMPOW
THIS ANNOYANCE IS--NNGH.
BLOOD...HEAR ME? THE TIME HAS COME...UNLEASH IT, BLOOD...UNLEASH IT...
FFF-OMM... FFORM...
STOP THAT!!
BACK IT UP, BIG BOY!
CHOOOM
SO WHAT'S THE VOTE? THIS GOING ACCORDING TO THE PLAYBOOK?
ASK ME AGAIN IF THE EARTH HASN'T SPILLED OFF OF ITS AXIS.
GHOSTS... YOU'RE SUCH PESSIMISTS. I WASN'T TALKIN' TO YOU... PALMER?

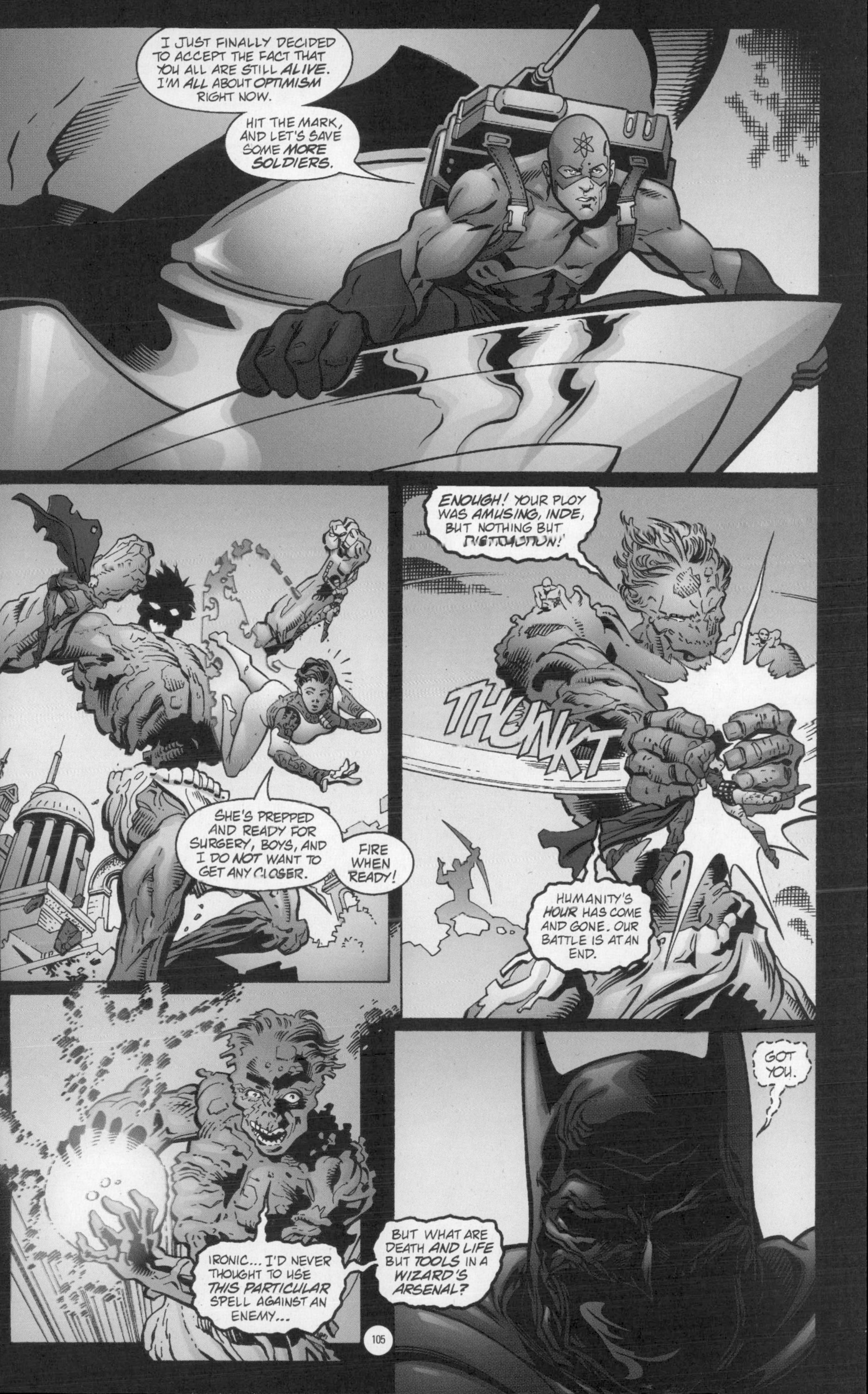
I JUST FINALLY DECIDED TO ACCEPT THE FACT THAT YOU ALL ARE STILL ALIVE. I'M ALL ABOUT OPTIMISM RIGHT NOW.
HIT THE MARK, AND LET'S SAVE SOME MORE SOLDIERS.
SHE'S PREPPED AND READY FOR SURGERY, BOYS, AND I DO NOT WANT TO GET ANY CLOSER.
FIRE WHEN READY!
ENOUGH! YOUR PLOY WAS AMUSING, INDE, BUT NOTHING BUT
THUNKT
HUMANITY'S HOUR HAS COME AND GONE. OUR BATTLE IS AT AN END.
IRONIC... I'D NEVER THOUGHT TO USE THIS PARTICULAR SPELL AGAINST AN ENEMY...
BUT WHAT ARE DEATH AND LIFE BUT TOOLS IN A WIZARD'S ARSENAL?
GOT YOU.

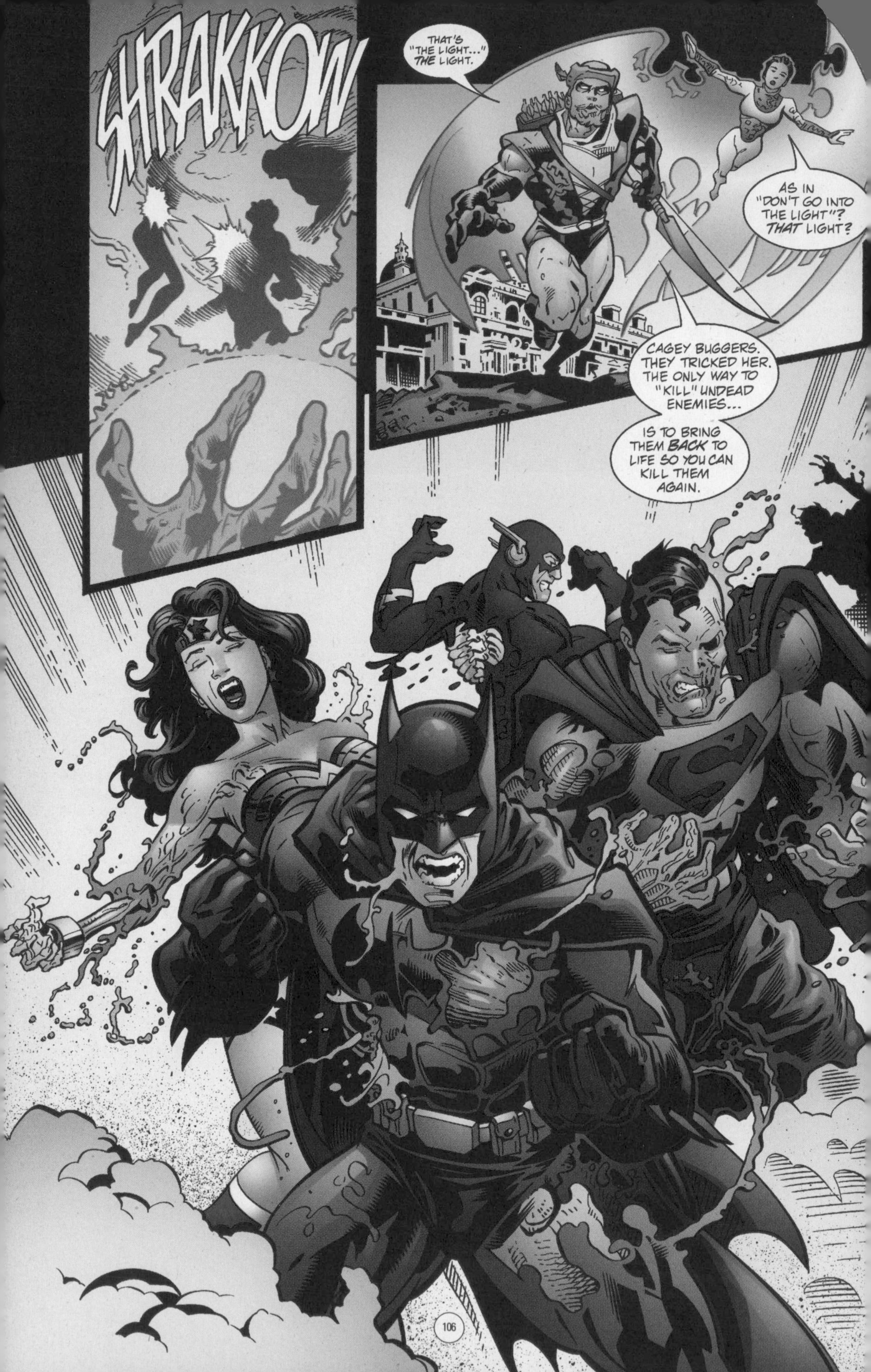

SHRAKKOW
THAT'S "THE LIGHT..." *THE* LIGHT.
AS IN "DON'T GO INTO THE LIGHT"? *THAT* LIGHT?
CAGEY BUGGERS. THEY TRICKED HER. THE ONLY WAY TO "KILL" UNDEAD ENEMIES...
IS TO BRING THEM *BACK* TO LIFE SO YOU CAN KILL THEM AGAIN.

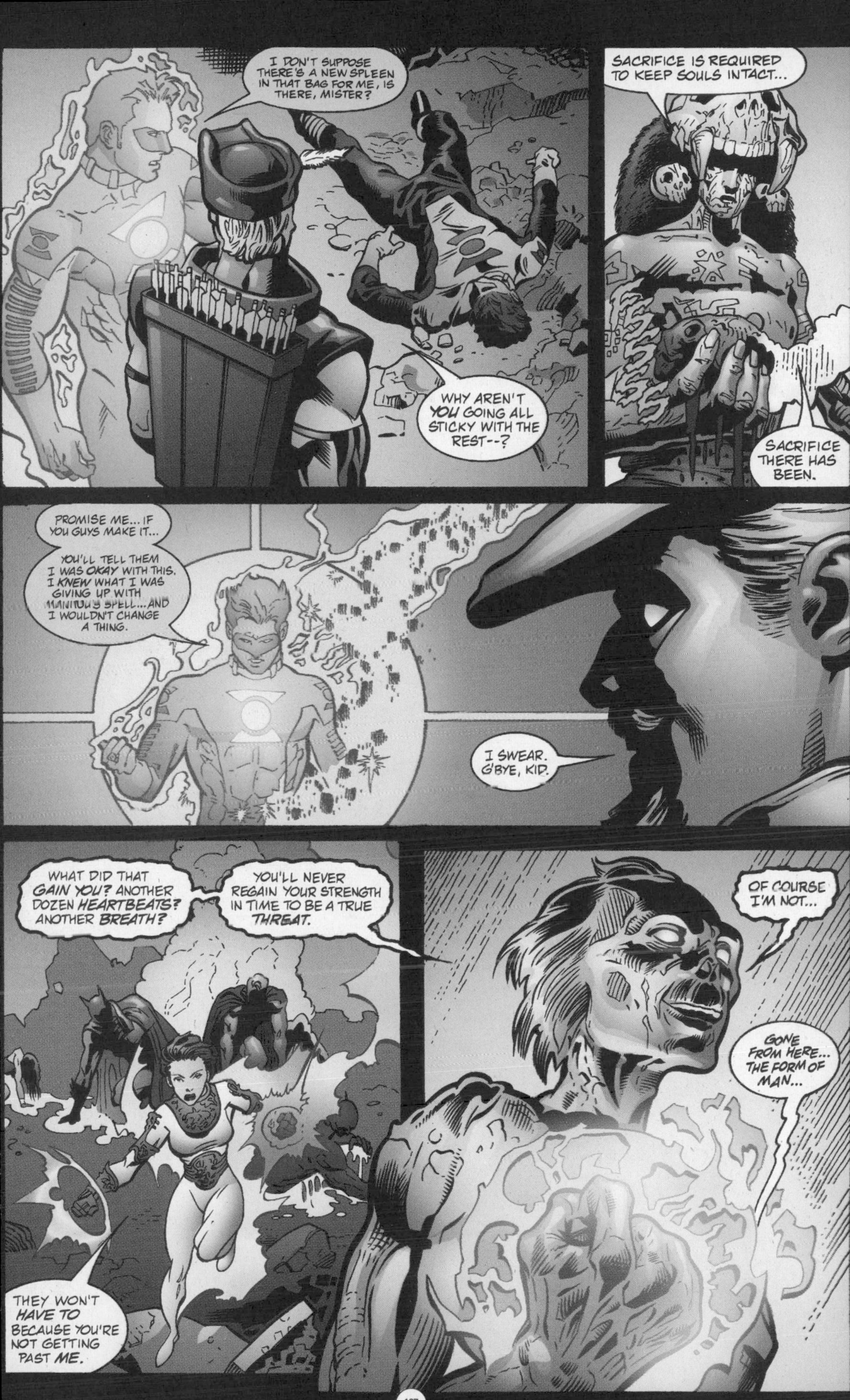

I DON'T SUPPOSE THERE'S A NEW SPLEEN IN THAT BAG FOR ME, IS THERE, MISTER?
WHY AREN'T *YOU* GOING ALL STICKY WITH THE REST--?
SACRIFICE IS REQUIRED TO KEEP SOULS INTACT...
SACRIFICE THERE HAS BEEN.
PROMISE ME... IF YOU GUYS MAKE IT...
YOU'LL TELL THEM I WAS *OKAY* WITH THIS. I *KNEW* WHAT I WAS GIVING UP WITH MANITOU'S SPELL... AND I WOULDN'T CHANGE A THING.
I SWEAR. G'BYE, KID.
WHAT DID THAT *GAIN YOU*? ANOTHER DOZEN *HEARTBEATS*? ANOTHER *BREATH*?
YOU'LL NEVER REGAIN YOUR STRENGTH IN TIME TO BE A TRUE *THREAT.*
THEY WON'T *HAVE TO* BECAUSE YOU'RE NOT GETTING PAST *ME*.
OF COURSE I'M NOT...
GONE FROM HERE... THE FORM OF MAN...

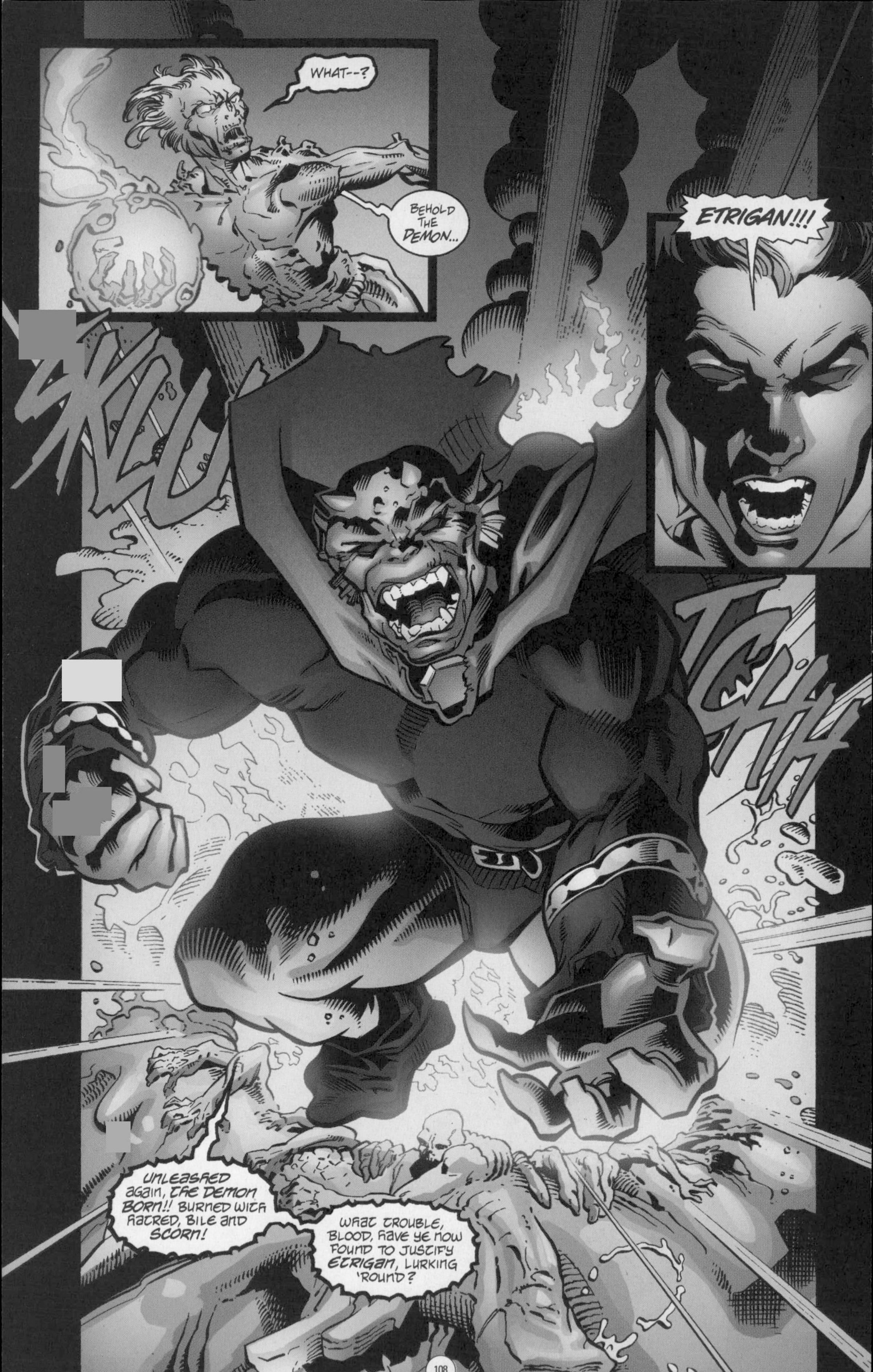
WHAT--?
BEHOLD THE DEMON...
ETRIGAN!!!
UNLEASHED AGAIN, THE DEMON BORN!! BURNED WITH HATRED, BILE AND SCORN!
WHAT TROUBLE, BLOOD, HAVE YE NOW FOUND TO JUSTIFY ETRIGAN, LURKING 'ROUND?

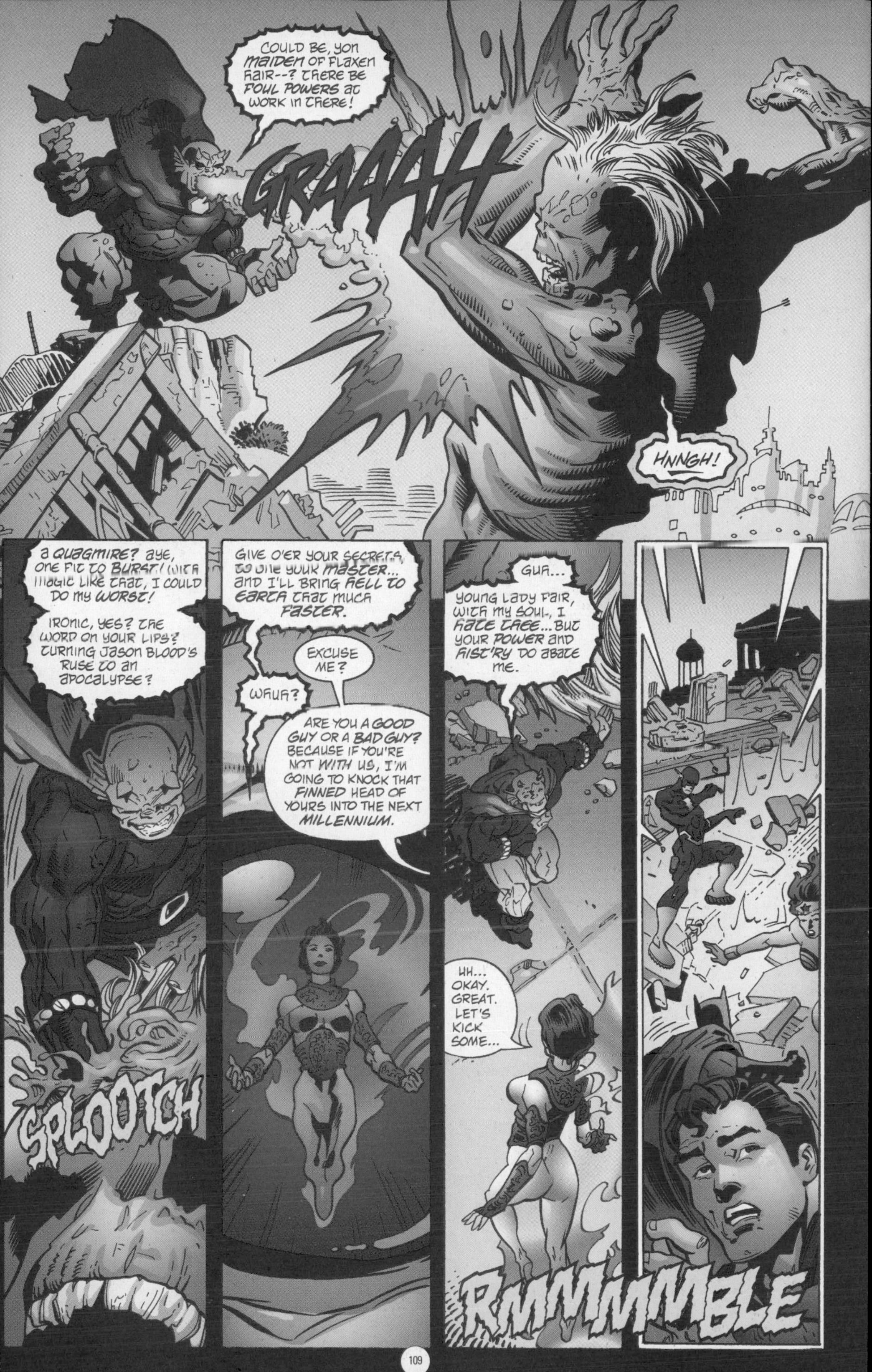
COULD BE, YON MAIDEN OF FLAXEN HAIR--? THERE BE FOUL POWERS AT WORK IN THERE!
GRAAAH
HNNGH!
A QUAGMIRE? AYE, ONE FIT TO BURST! WITH MAGIC LIKE THAT, I COULD DO MY WORST!
IRONIC, YES? THE WORD ON YOUR LIPS? TURNING JASON BLOOD'S RUSE TO AN APOCALYPSE?
SPLOOTCH
GIVE O'ER YOUR SECRETS, TO ONE YOUR MASTER... AND I'LL BRING HELL TO EARTH THAT MUCH FASTER.
EXCUSE ME?
WHAT?
ARE YOU A GOOD GUY OR A BAD GUY? BECAUSE IF YOU'RE NOT WITH US, I'M GOING TO KNOCK THAT FINNED HEAD OF YOURS INTO THE NEXT MILLENNIUM.
GUH...
YOUNG LADY FAIR, WITH MY SOUL, I HATE THEE... BUT YOUR POWER AND HIST'RY DO ABATE ME.
UH... OKAY. GREAT. LET'S KICK SOME...
RMMMMBLE

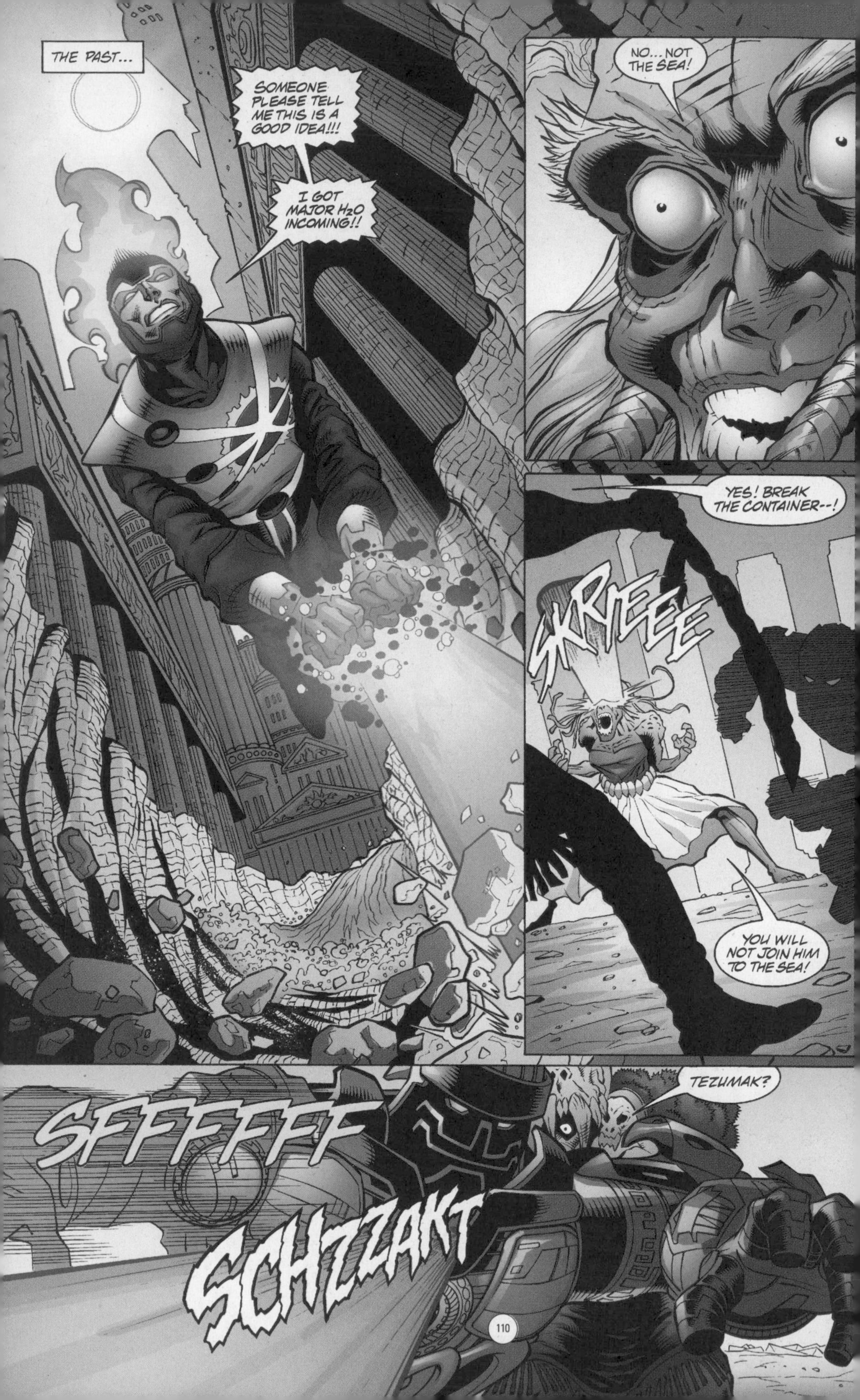
THE PAST...
SOMEONE PLEASE TELL ME THIS IS A GOOD IDEA!!!
I GOT MAJOR H2O INCOMING!!
NO... NOT THE SEA!
YES! BREAK THE CONTAINER--!
SKRYEEE
YOU WILL NOT JOIN HIM TO THE SEA!
SFFFFFF
TEZUMAK?
SCHZZAKT

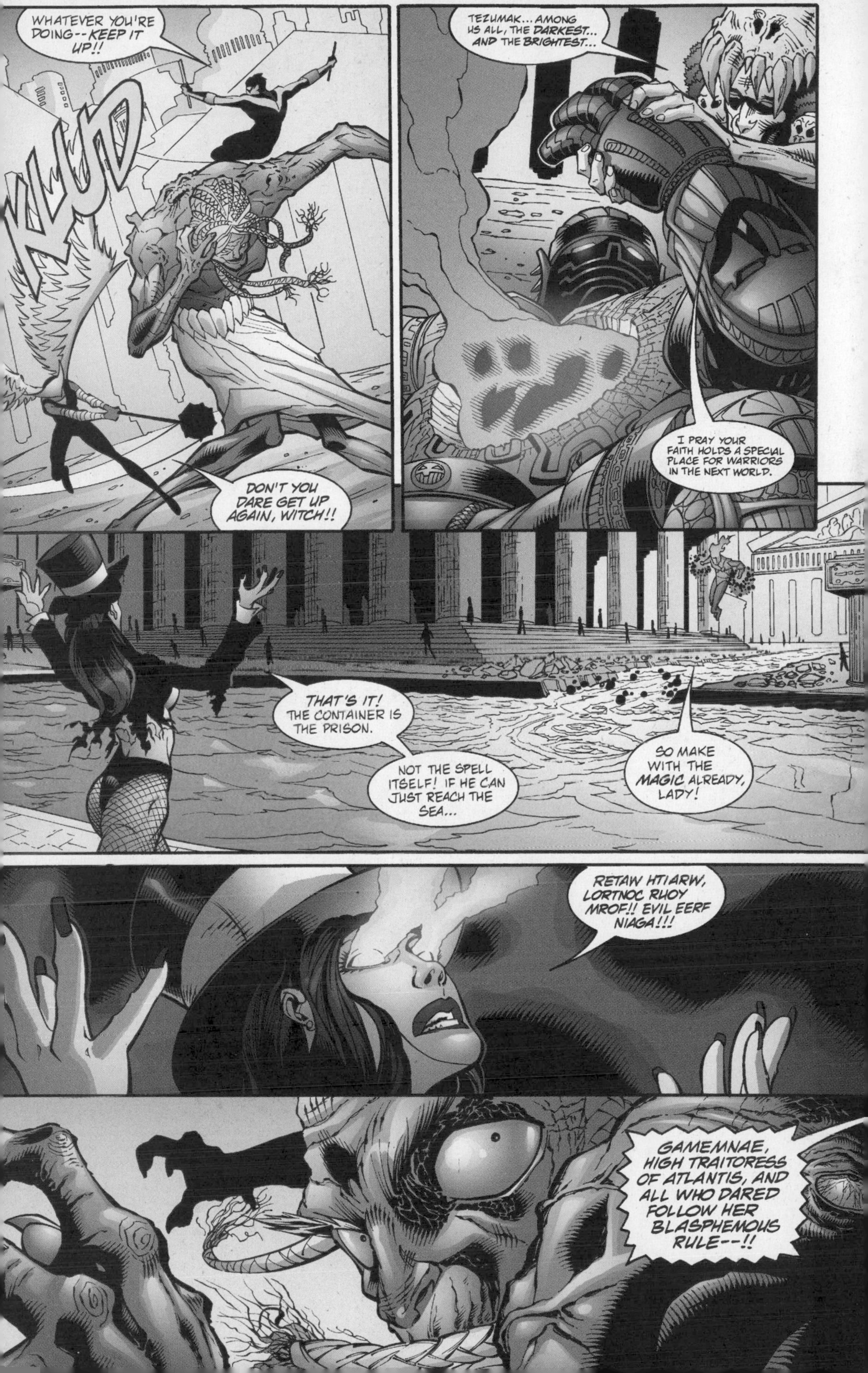
WHATEVER YOU'RE DOING--KEEP IT UP!!
KLUD
DON'T YOU DARE GET UP AGAIN, WITCH!!
TEZUMAK... AMONG US ALL, THE DARKEST... AND THE BRIGHTEST...
I PRAY YOUR FAITH HOLDS A SPECIAL PLACE FOR WARRIORS IN THE NEXT WORLD.
THAT'S IT! THE CONTAINER IS THE PRISON.
NOT THE SPELL ITSELF! IF HE CAN JUST REACH THE SEA...
SO MAKE WITH THE MAGIC ALREADY, LADY!
RETAW HTIARW, LORTNOC RUOY MROF!! EVIL EERF NIAGA!!!
GAMEMNAE, HIGH TRAITORESS OF ATLANTIS, AND ALL WHO DARED FOLLOW HER BLASPHEMOUS RULE--!!

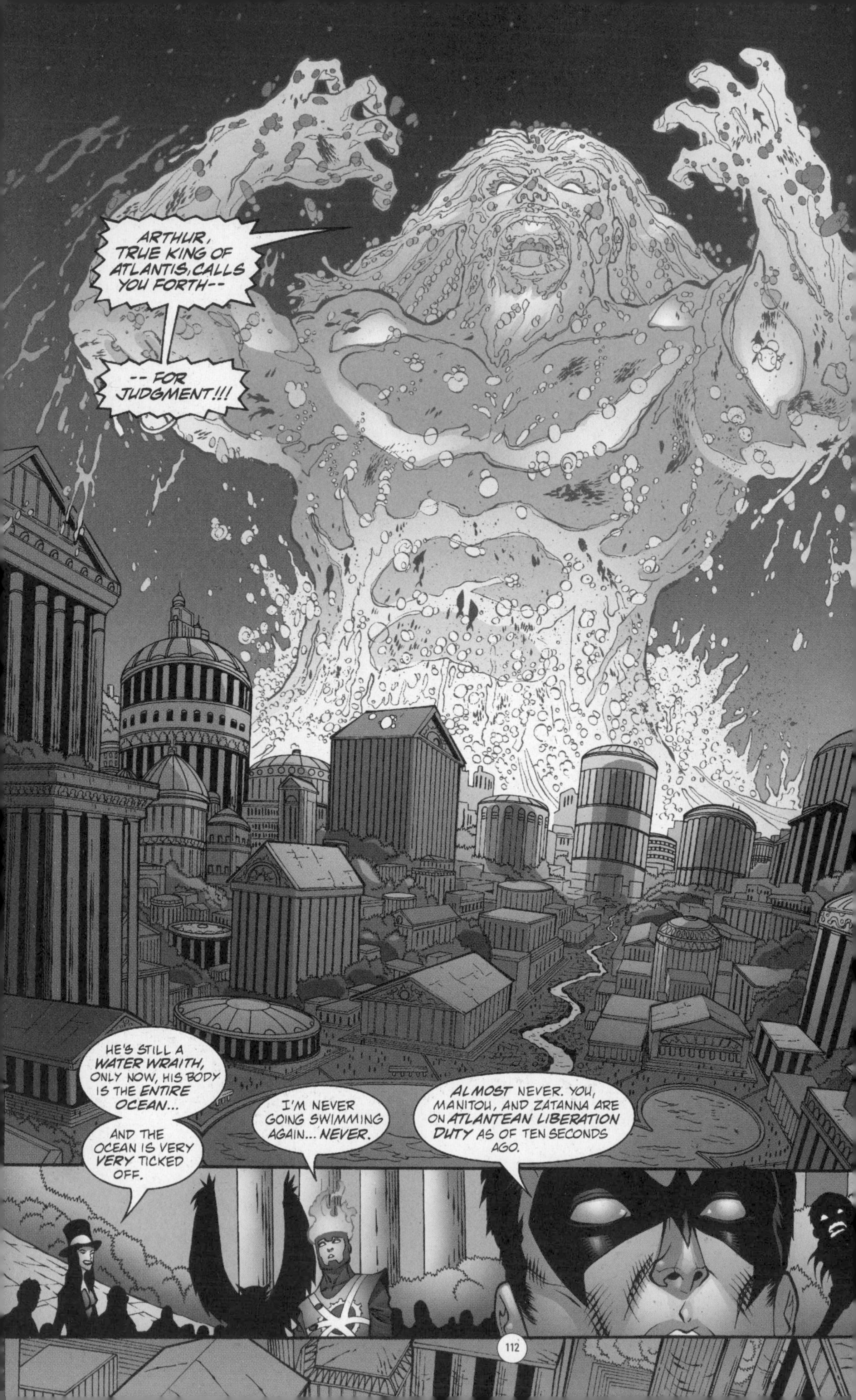
ARTHUR, TRUE KING OF ATLANTIS, CALLS YOU FORTH--
-- FOR JUDGMENT!!!
HE'S STILL A WATER WRAITH, ONLY NOW, HIS BODY IS THE ENTIRE OCEAN...
AND THE OCEAN IS VERY VERY TICKED OFF.
I'M NEVER GOING SWIMMING AGAIN... NEVER.
ALMOST NEVER. YOU, MANITOU, AND ZATANNA ARE ON ATLANTEAN LIBERATION DUTY AS OF TEN SECONDS AGO.

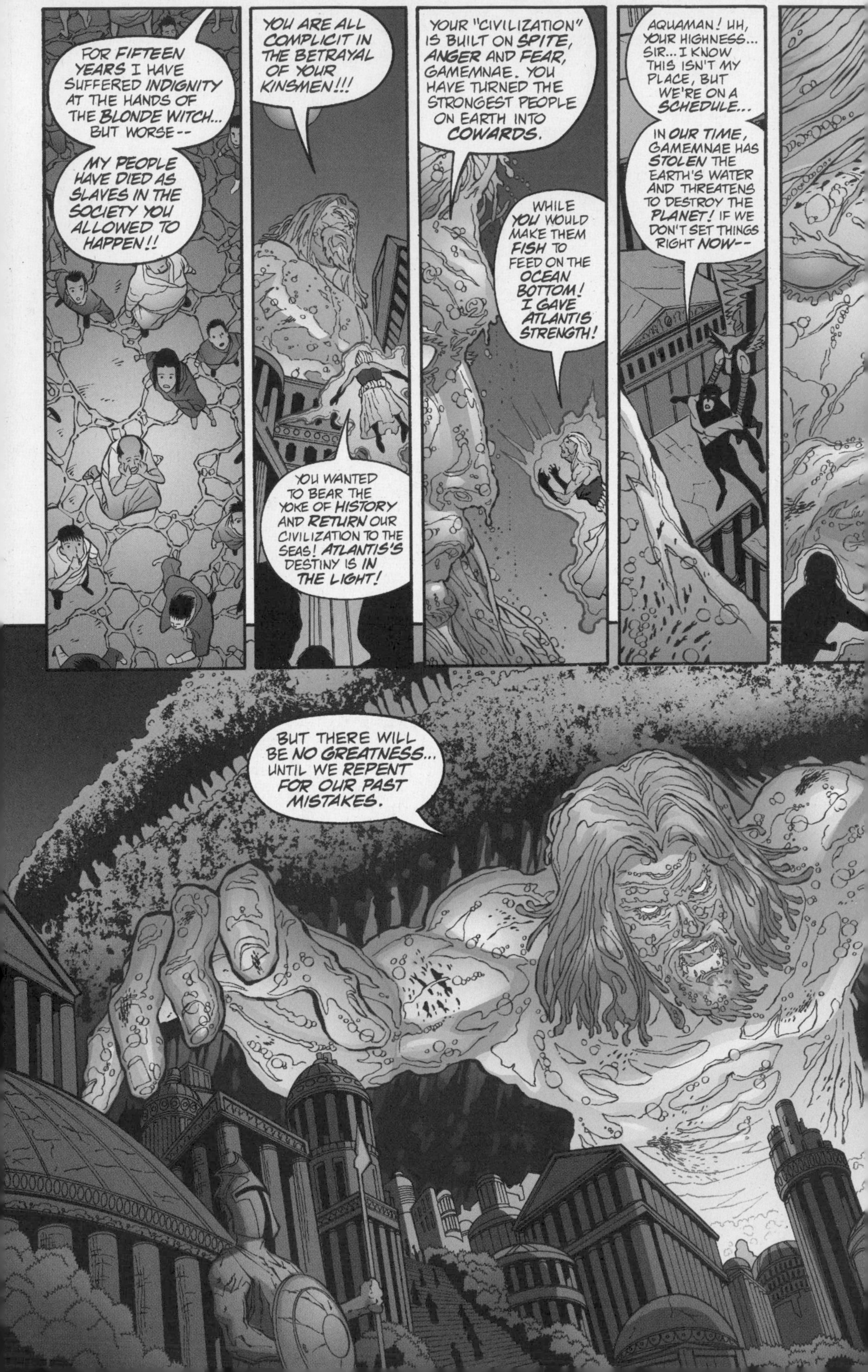
FOR FIFTEEN YEARS I HAVE SUFFERED INDIGNITY AT THE HANDS OF THE BLONDE WITCH... BUT WORSE--
MY PEOPLE HAVE DIED AS SLAVES IN THE SOCIETY YOU ALLOWED TO HAPPEN!!
YOU ARE ALL COMPLICIT IN THE BETRAYAL OF YOUR KINSMEN!!!
YOU WANTED TO BEAR THE YOKE OF HISTORY AND RETURN OUR CIVILIZATION TO THE SEAS! ATLANTIS'S DESTINY IS IN THE LIGHT!
YOUR "CIVILIZATION" IS BUILT ON SPITE, ANGER AND FEAR, GAMEMNAE. YOU HAVE TURNED THE STRONGEST PEOPLE ON EARTH INTO COWARDS.
WHILE YOU WOULD MAKE THEM FISH TO FEED ON THE OCEAN BOTTOM! I GAVE ATLANTIS STRENGTH!
AQUAMAN! UH, YOUR HIGHNESS... SIR... I KNOW THIS ISN'T MY PLACE, BUT WE'RE ON A SCHEDULE...
IN OUR TIME, GAMEMNAE HAS STOLEN THE EARTH'S WATER AND THREATENS TO DESTROY THE PLANET! IF WE DON'T SET THINGS RIGHT NOW--
BUT THERE WILL BE NO GREATNESS... UNTIL WE REPENT FOR OUR PAST MISTAKES.

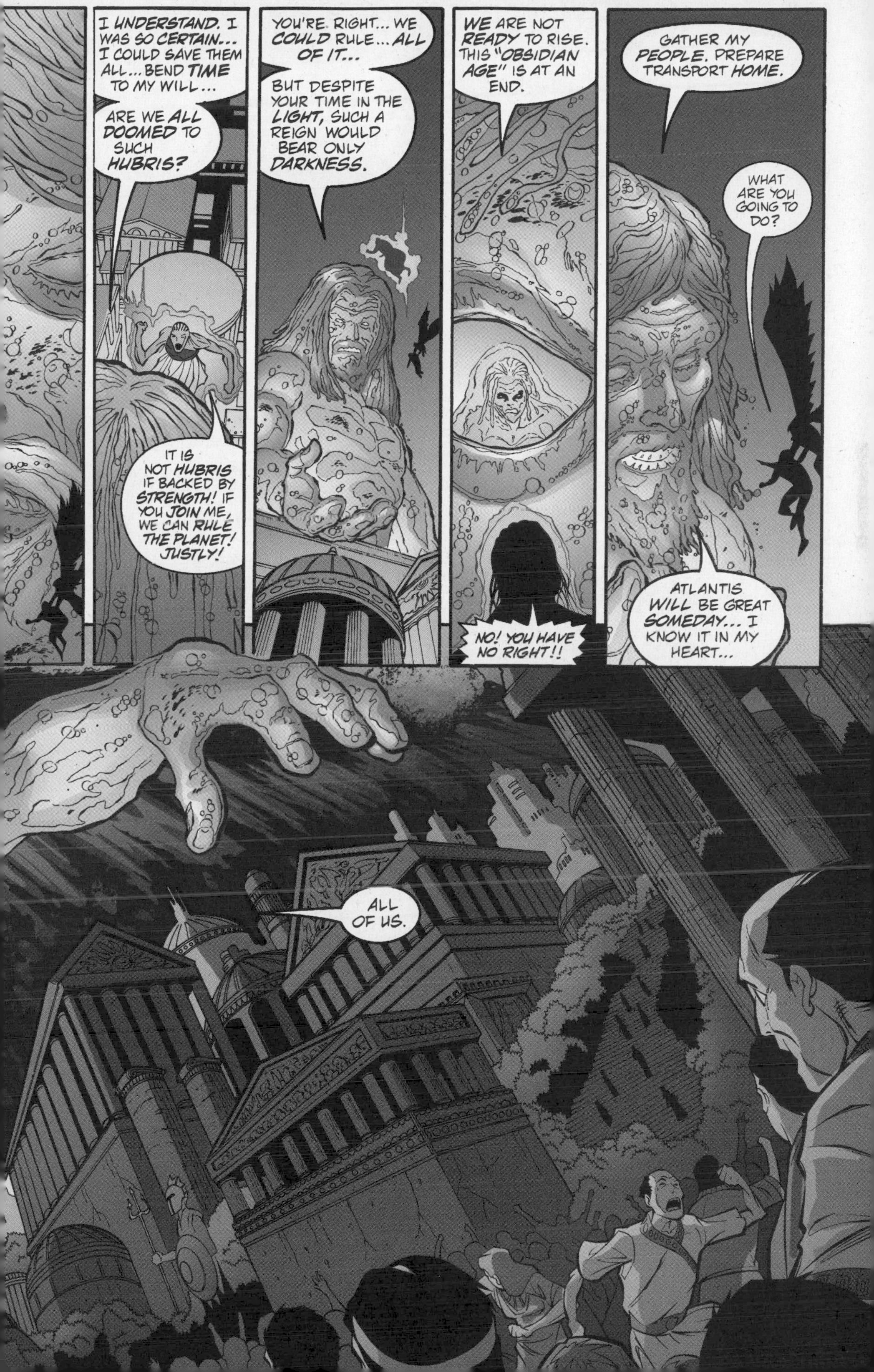
I UNDERSTAND. I WAS SO CERTAIN... I COULD SAVE THEM ALL... BEND TIME TO MY WILL...
ARE WE ALL DOOMED TO SUCH HUBRIS?
IT IS NOT HUBRIS IF BACKED BY STRENGTH! IF YOU JOIN ME, WE CAN RULE THE PLANET! JUSTLY!
YOU'RE RIGHT... WE COULD RULE... ALL OF IT...
BUT DESPITE YOUR TIME IN THE LIGHT, SUCH A REIGN WOULD BEAR ONLY DARKNESS.
WE ARE NOT READY TO RISE. THIS "OBSIDIAN AGE" IS AT AN END.
NO! YOU HAVE NO RIGHT!!
GATHER MY PEOPLE. PREPARE TRANSPORT HOME.
WHAT ARE YOU GOING TO DO?
ATLANTIS WILL BE GREAT SOMEDAY... I KNOW IT IN MY HEART...
ALL OF US.

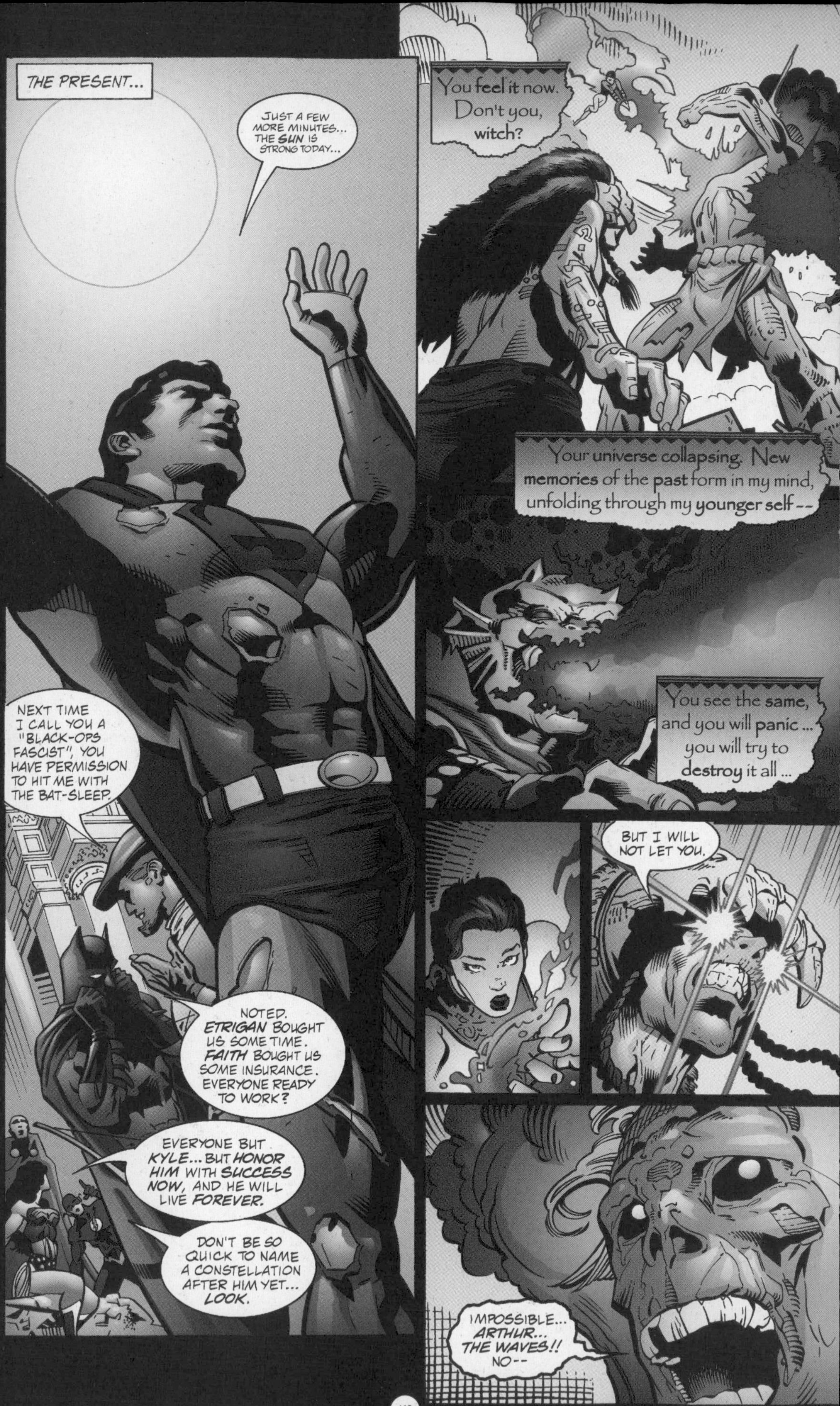
THE PRESENT...
JUST A FEW MORE MINUTES... THE SUN IS STRONG TODAY...
NEXT TIME I CALL YOU A "BLACK-OPS FASCIST", YOU HAVE PERMISSION TO HIT ME WITH THE BAT-SLEEP.
NOTED. ETRIGAN BOUGHT US SOME TIME. FAITH BOUGHT US SOME INSURANCE. EVERYONE READY TO WORK?
EVERYONE BUT KYLE... BUT HONOR HIM WITH SUCCESS NOW, AND HE WILL LIVE FOREVER.
DON'T BE SO QUICK TO NAME A CONSTELLATION AFTER HIM YET... LOOK.
You feel it now. Don't you, witch?
Your universe collapsing. New memories of the past form in my mind, unfolding through my younger self --
You see the same, and you will panic ... you will try to destroy it all ...
BUT I WILL NOT LET YOU.
IMPOSSIBLE... ARTHUR... THE WAVES!! NO--

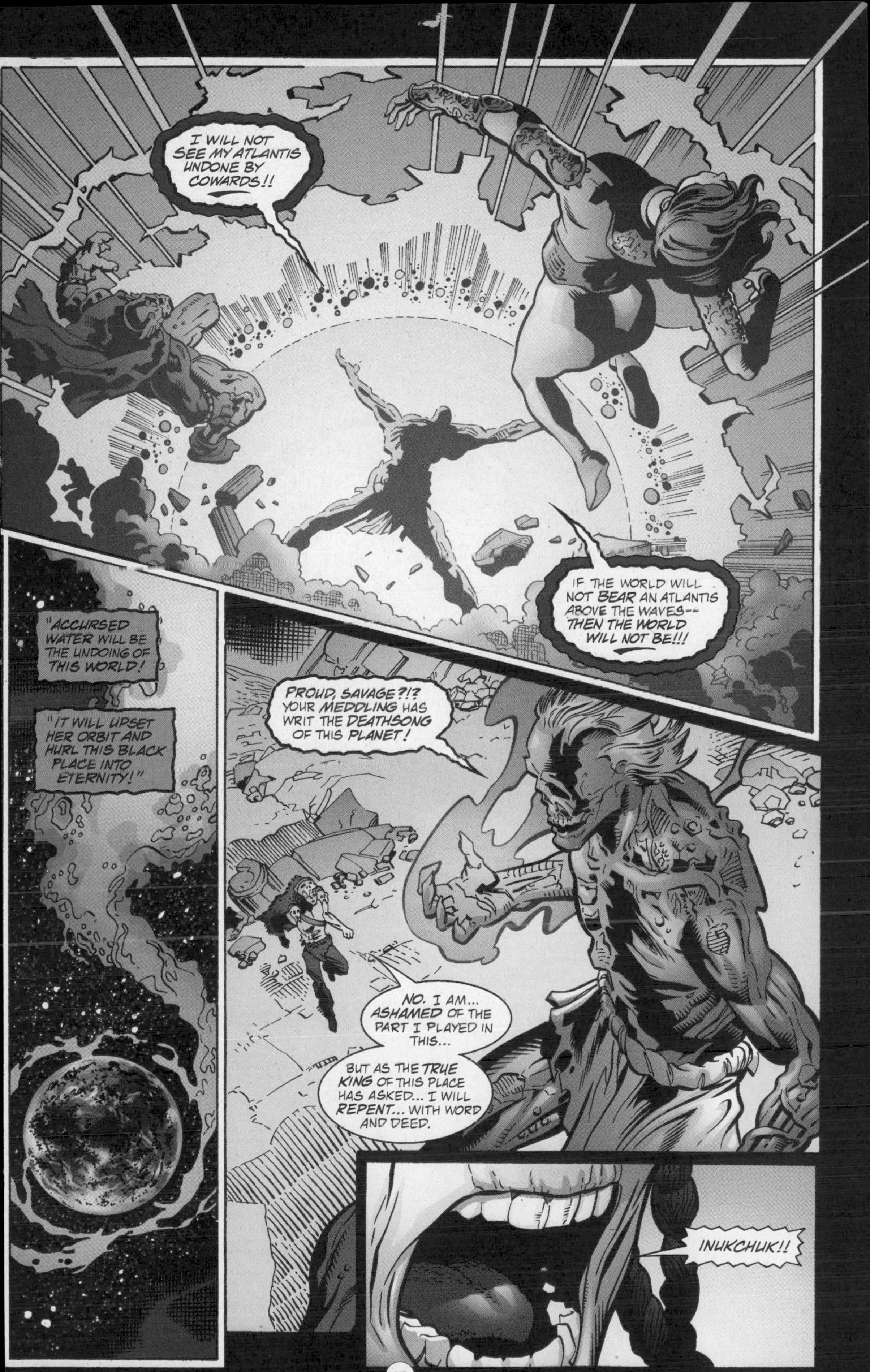
I WILL NOT SEE MY ATLANTIS UNDONE BY COWARDS!!
IF THE WORLD WILL NOT BEAR AN ATLANTIS ABOVE THE WAVES-- THEN THE WORLD WILL NOT BE!!!
"ACCURSED WATER WILL BE THE UNDOING OF THIS WORLD!
"IT WILL UPSET HER ORBIT AND HURL THIS BLACK PLACE INTO ETERNITY!"
PROUD, SAVAGE?!? YOUR MEDDLING HAS WRIT THE DEATHSONG OF THIS PLANET!
NO. I AM... ASHAMED OF THE PART I PLAYED IN THIS...
BUT AS THE TRUE KING OF THIS PLACE HAS ASKED... I WILL REPENT... WITH WORD AND DEED.
INUKCHUK!!

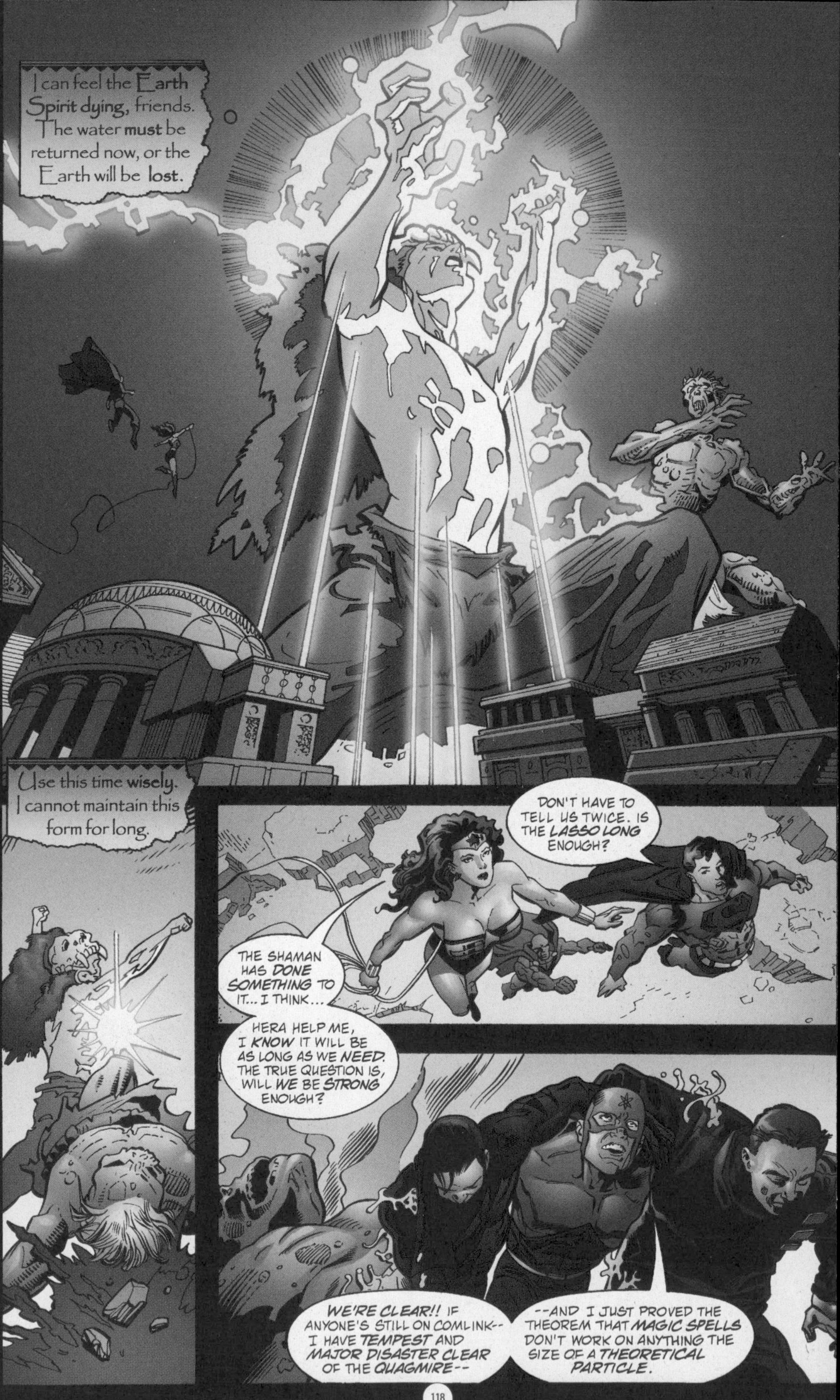
I can feel the Earth Spirit dying, friends. The water must be returned now, or the Earth will be lost.
Use this time wisely. I cannot maintain this form for long.
DON'T HAVE TO TELL US TWICE. IS THE LASSO LONG ENOUGH?
THE SHAMAN HAS DONE SOMETHING TO IT... I THINK...
HERA HELP ME, I KNOW IT WILL BE AS LONG AS WE NEED. THE TRUE QUESTION IS, WILL WE BE STRONG ENOUGH?
WE'RE CLEAR!! IF ANYONE'S STILL ON COMLINK-- I HAVE TEMPEST AND MAJOR DISASTER CLEAR OF THE QUAGMIRE--
--AND I JUST PROVED THE THEOREM THAT MAGIC SPELLS DON'T WORK ON ANYTHING THE SIZE OF A THEORETICAL PARTICLE.

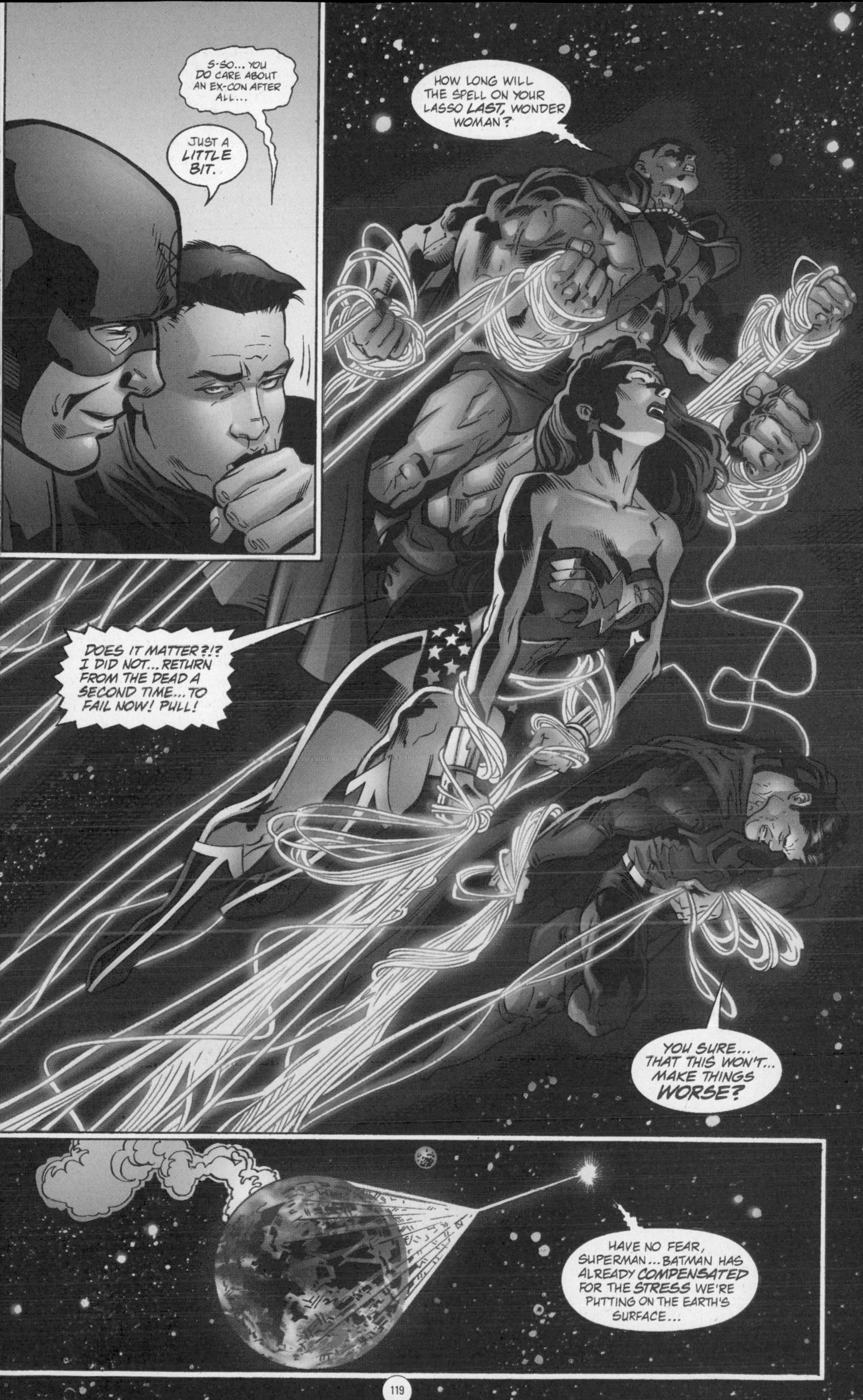
S-SO... YOU DO CARE ABOUT AN EX-CON AFTER ALL...
JUST A LITTLE BIT.
HOW LONG WILL THE SPELL ON YOUR LASSO LAST, WONDER WOMAN?
DOES IT MATTER?!? I DID NOT... RETURN FROM THE DEAD A SECOND TIME... TO FAIL NOW! PULL!
YOU SURE... THAT THIS WON'T... MAKE THINGS WORSE?
HAVE NO FEAR, SUPERMAN... BATMAN HAS ALREADY COMPENSATED FOR THE STRESS WE'RE PUTTING ON THE EARTH'S SURFACE...

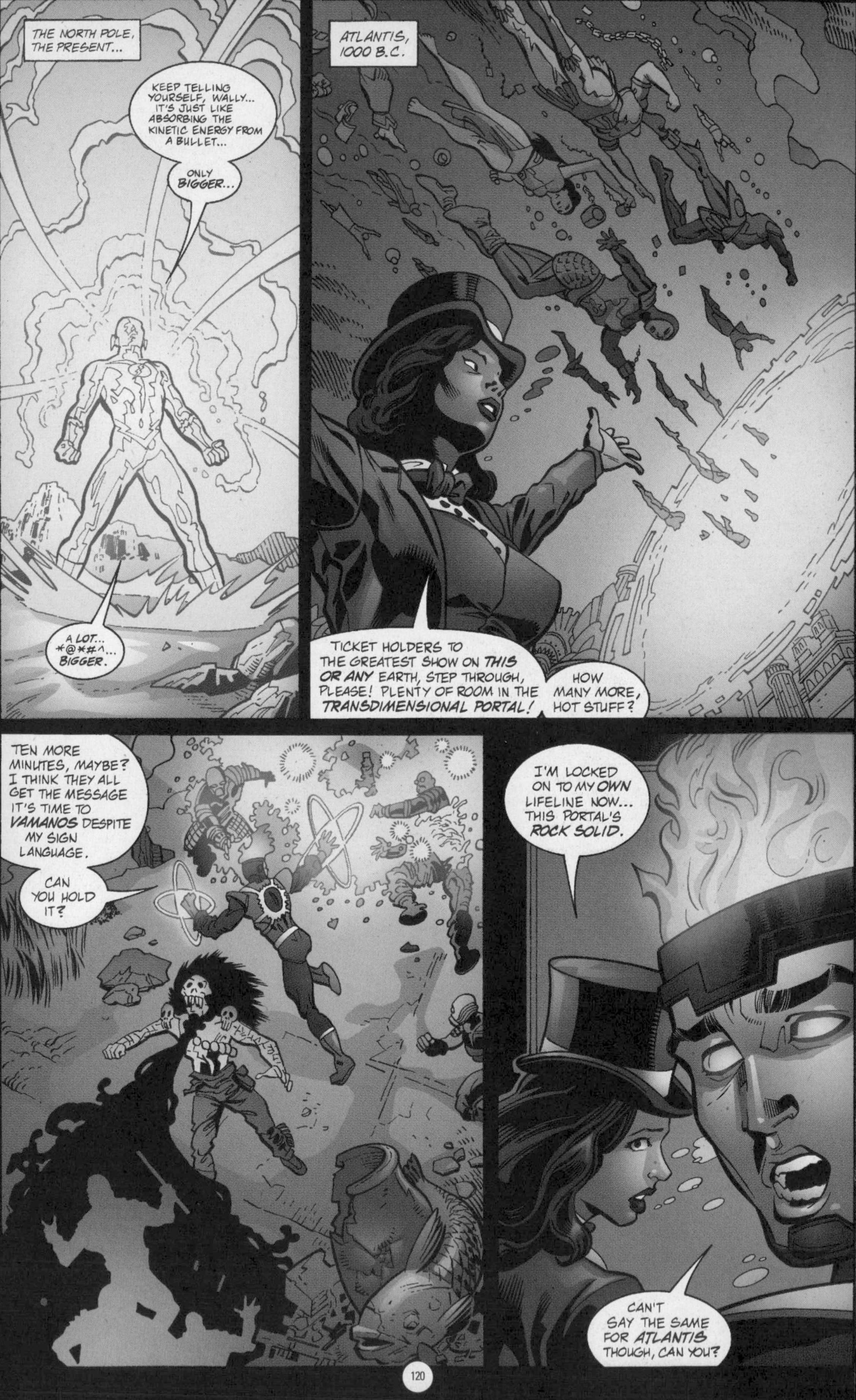
THE NORTH POLE, THE PRESENT...
KEEP TELLING YOURSELF, WALLY... IT'S JUST LIKE ABSORBING THE KINETIC ENERGY FROM A BULLET...
ONLY BIGGER...
A LOT... *@*#^... BIGGER.
ATLANTIS, 1000 B.C.
TICKET HOLDERS TO THE GREATEST SHOW ON THIS OR ANY EARTH, STEP THROUGH, PLEASE! PLENTY OF ROOM IN THE TRANSDIMENSIONAL PORTAL!
HOW MANY MORE, HOT STUFF?
TEN MORE MINUTES, MAYBE? I THINK THEY ALL GET THE MESSAGE IT'S TIME TO VAMANOS DESPITE MY SIGN LANGUAGE.
CAN YOU HOLD IT?
I'M LOCKED ON TO MY OWN LIFELINE NOW... THIS PORTAL'S ROCK SOLID.
CAN'T SAY THE SAME FOR ATLANTIS THOUGH, CAN YOU?

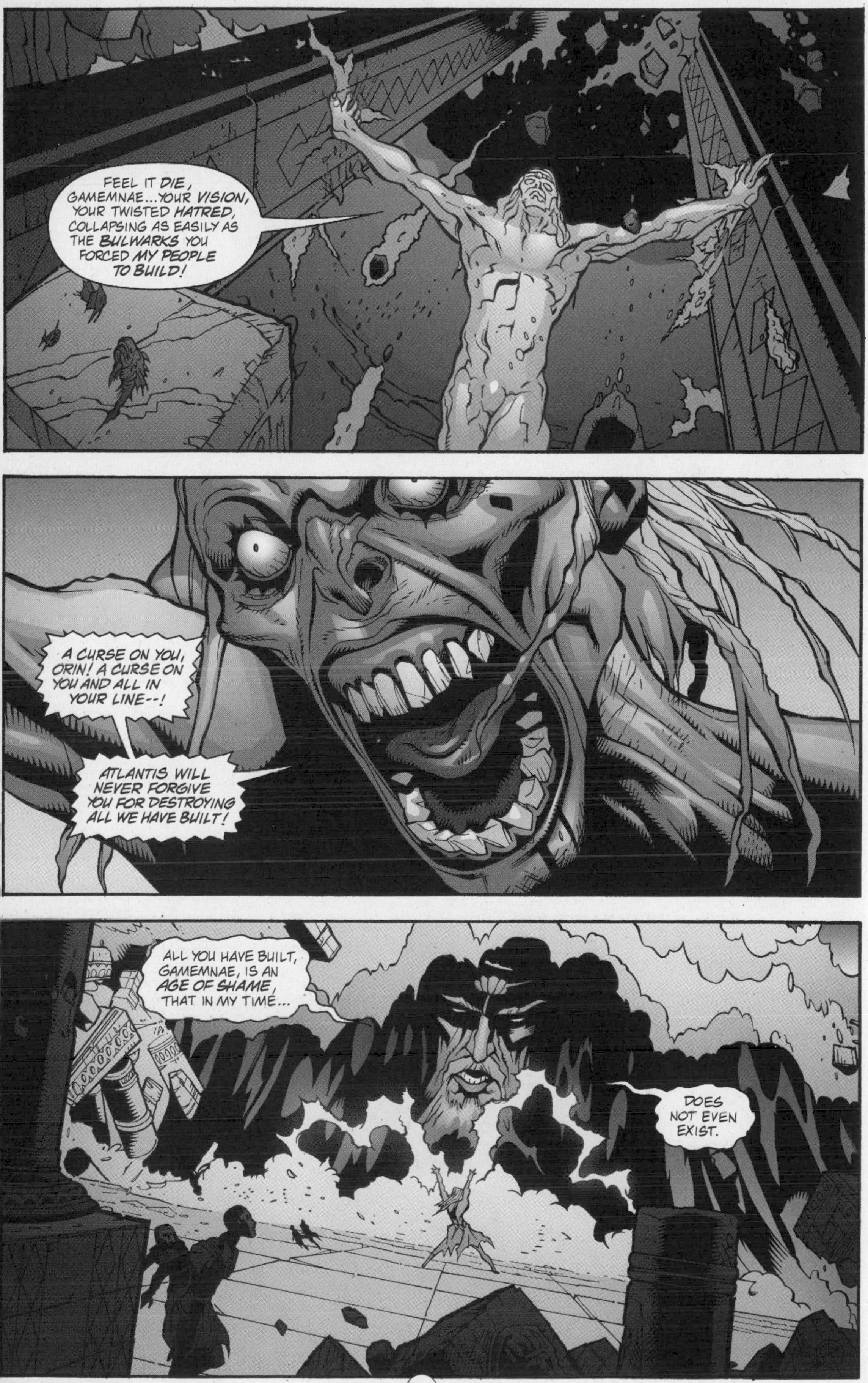
FEEL IT DIE, GAMEMNAE...YOUR VISION, YOUR TWISTED HATRED, COLLAPSING AS EASILY AS THE BULWARKS YOU FORCED MY PEOPLE TO BUILD!
A CURSE ON YOU, ORIN! A CURSE ON YOU AND ALL IN YOUR LINE--!
ATLANTIS WILL NEVER FORGIVE YOU FOR DESTROYING ALL WE HAVE BUILT!
ALL YOU HAVE BUILT, GAMEMNAE, IS AN AGE OF SHAME, THAT IN MY TIME...
DOES NOT EVEN EXIST.

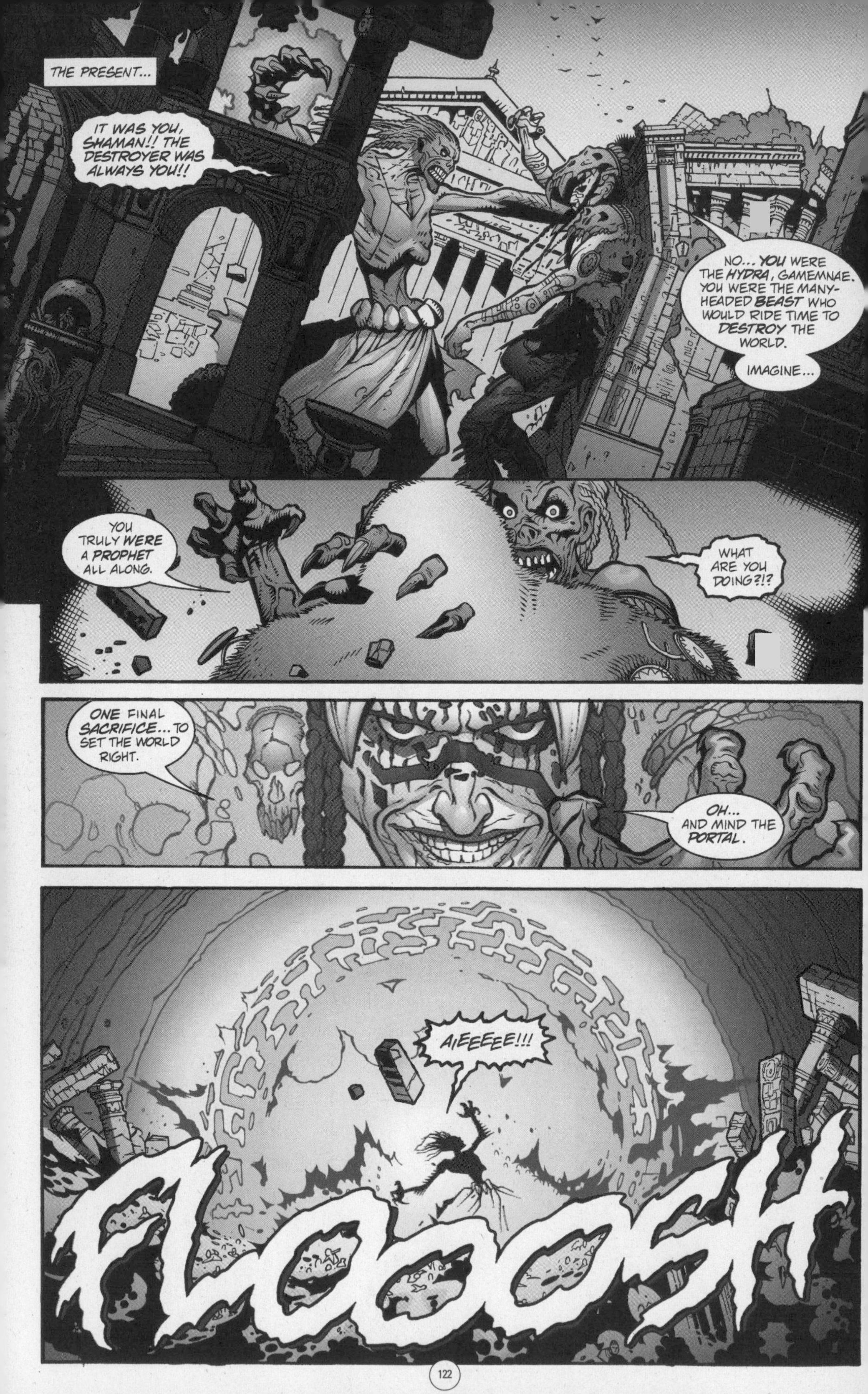
THE PRESENT...
IT WAS YOU, SHAMAN!! THE DESTROYER WAS ALWAYS YOU!!
NO... YOU WERE THE HYDRA, GAMEMNAE. YOU WERE THE MANY-HEADED BEAST WHO WOULD RIDE TIME TO DESTROY THE WORLD.
IMAGINE...
YOU TRULY WERE A PROPHET ALL ALONG.
WHAT ARE YOU DOING?!?
ONE FINAL SACRIFICE... TO SET THE WORLD RIGHT.
OH... AND MIND THE PORTAL.
AIEEEEE!!!
FLOOOSH

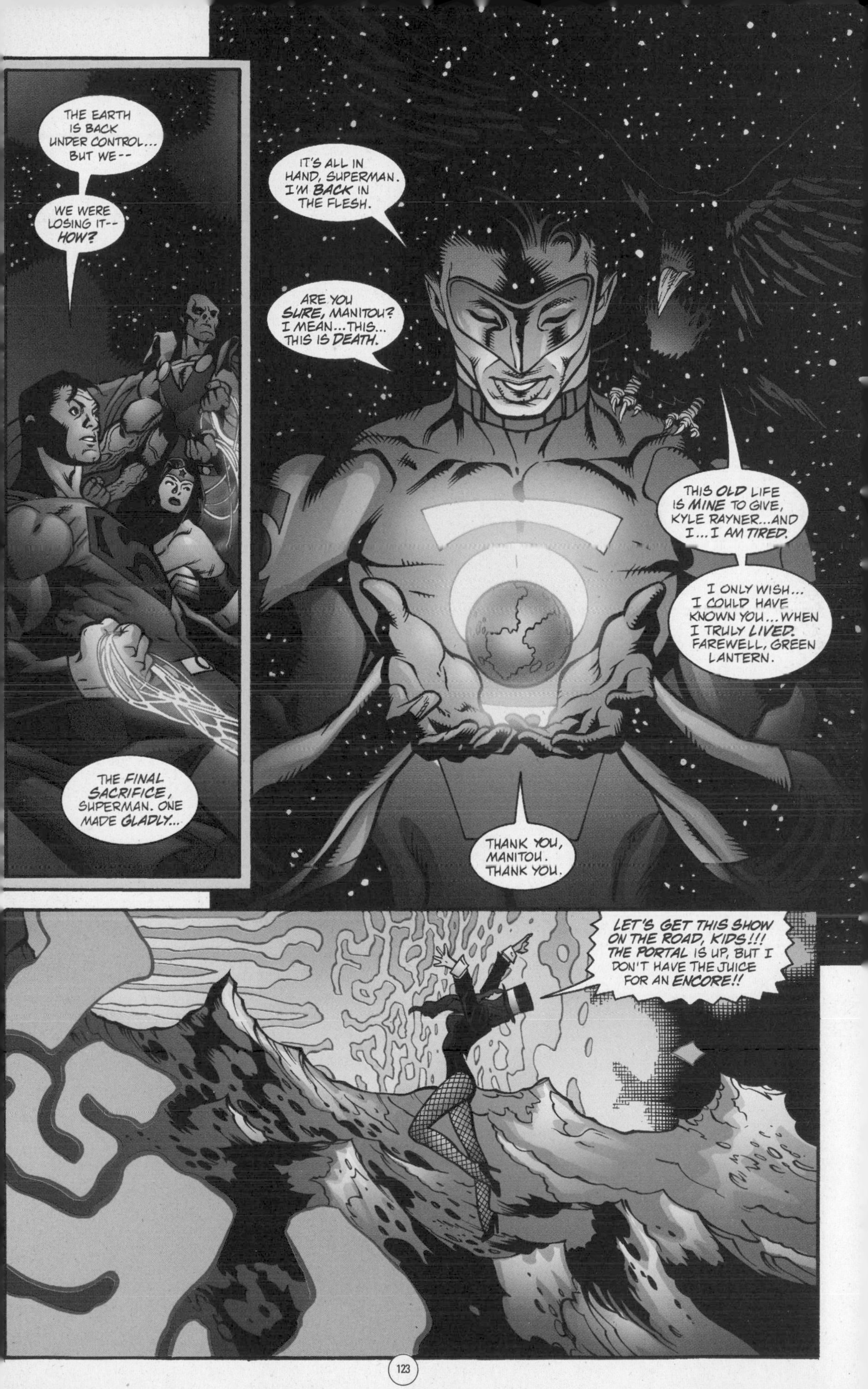
THE EARTH IS BACK UNDER CONTROL... BUT WE--
WE WERE LOSING IT-- HOW?
IT'S ALL IN HAND, SUPERMAN. I'M BACK IN THE FLESH.
ARE YOU SURE, MANITOU? I MEAN... THIS... THIS IS DEATH.
THIS OLD LIFE IS MINE TO GIVE, KYLE RAYNER... AND I... I AM TIRED.
I ONLY WISH... I COULD HAVE KNOWN YOU... WHEN I TRULY LIVED. FAREWELL, GREEN LANTERN.
THE FINAL SACRIFICE, SUPERMAN. ONE MADE GLADLY...
THANK YOU, MANITOU. THANK YOU.
LET'S GET THIS SHOW ON THE ROAD, KIDS!!! THE PORTAL IS UP, BUT I DON'T HAVE THE JUICE FOR AN ENCORE!!

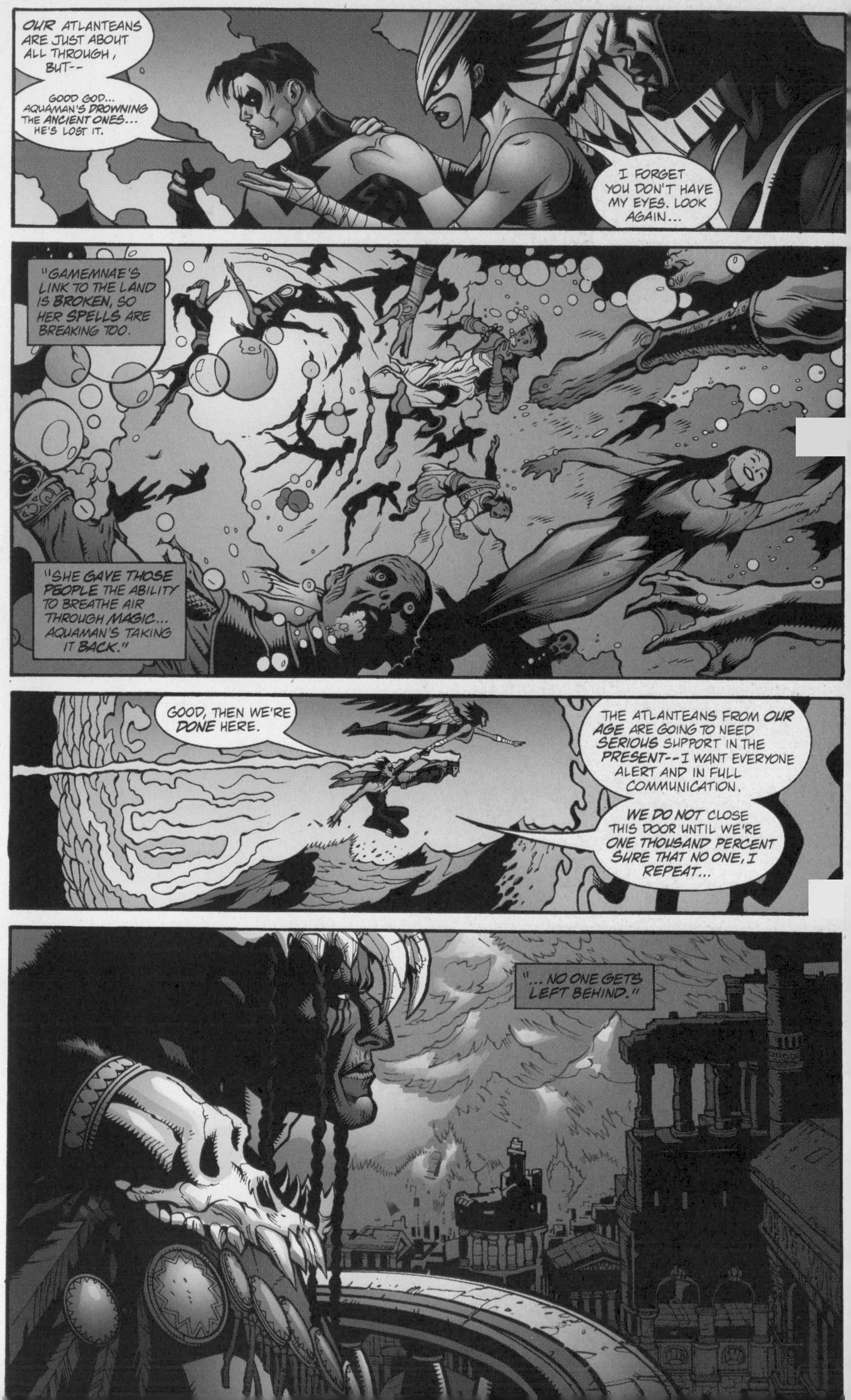
OUR ATLANTEANS ARE JUST ABOUT ALL THROUGH, BUT--
GOOD GOD... AQUAMAN'S DROWNING THE ANCIENT ONES... HE'S LOST IT.
I FORGET YOU DON'T HAVE MY EYES. LOOK AGAIN...
"GAMEMNAE'S LINK TO THE LAND IS BROKEN, SO HER SPELLS ARE BREAKING TOO.
"SHE GAVE THOSE PEOPLE THE ABILITY TO BREATHE AIR THROUGH MAGIC... AQUAMAN'S TAKING IT BACK."
GOOD, THEN WE'RE DONE HERE.
THE ATLANTEANS FROM OUR AGE ARE GOING TO NEED SERIOUS SUPPORT IN THE PRESENT--I WANT EVERYONE ALERT AND IN FULL COMMUNICATION.
WE DO NOT CLOSE THIS DOOR UNTIL WE'RE ONE THOUSAND PERCENT SURE THAT NO ONE, I REPEAT...
"...NO ONE GETS LEFT BEHIND."

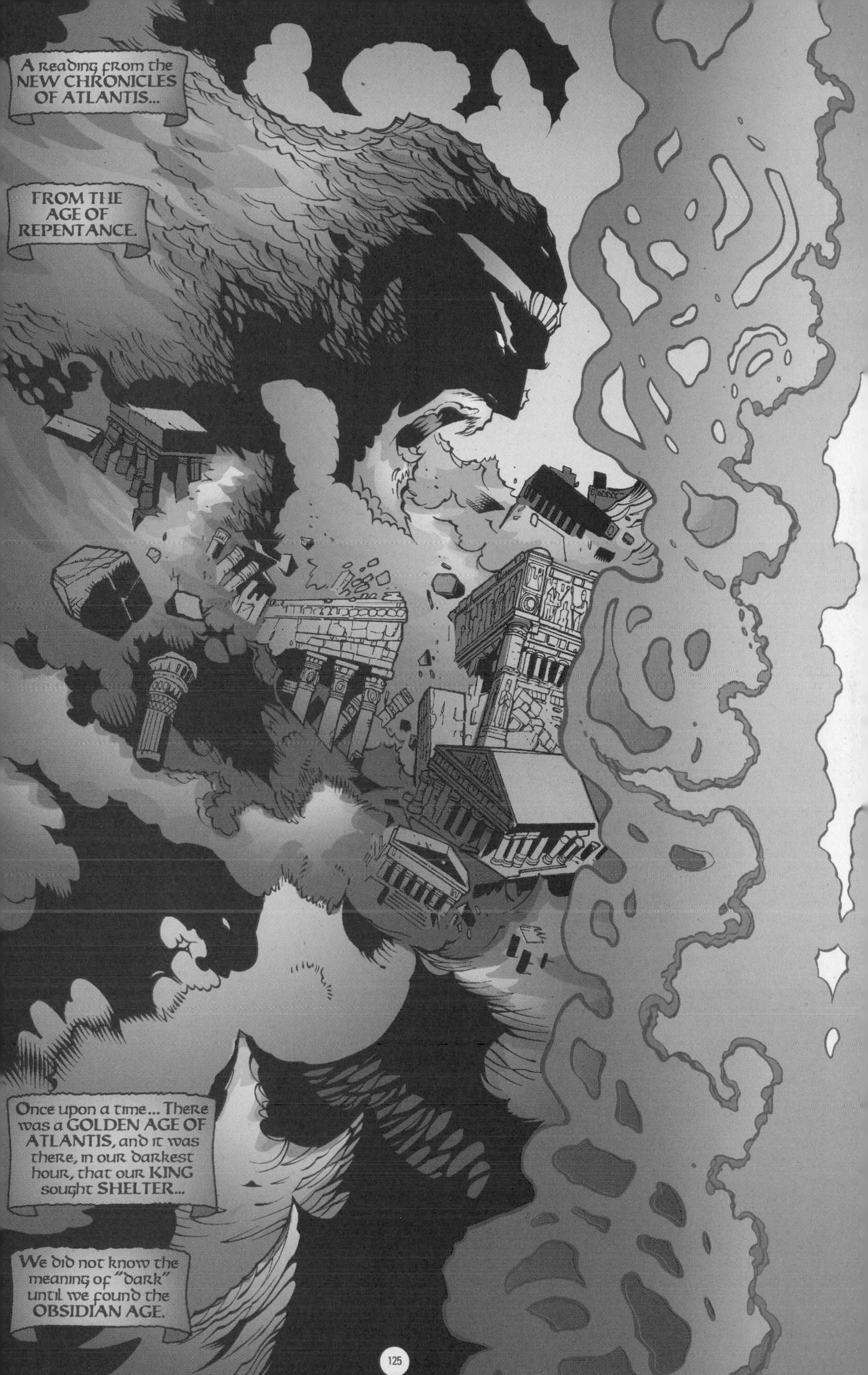
A reading from the NEW CHRONICLES OF ATLANTIS...
FROM THE AGE OF REPENTANCE.
Once upon a time... There was a GOLDEN AGE OF ATLANTIS, and it was there, in our darkest hour, that our KING sought SHELTER...
We did not know the meaning of "dark" until we found the OBSIDIAN AGE.

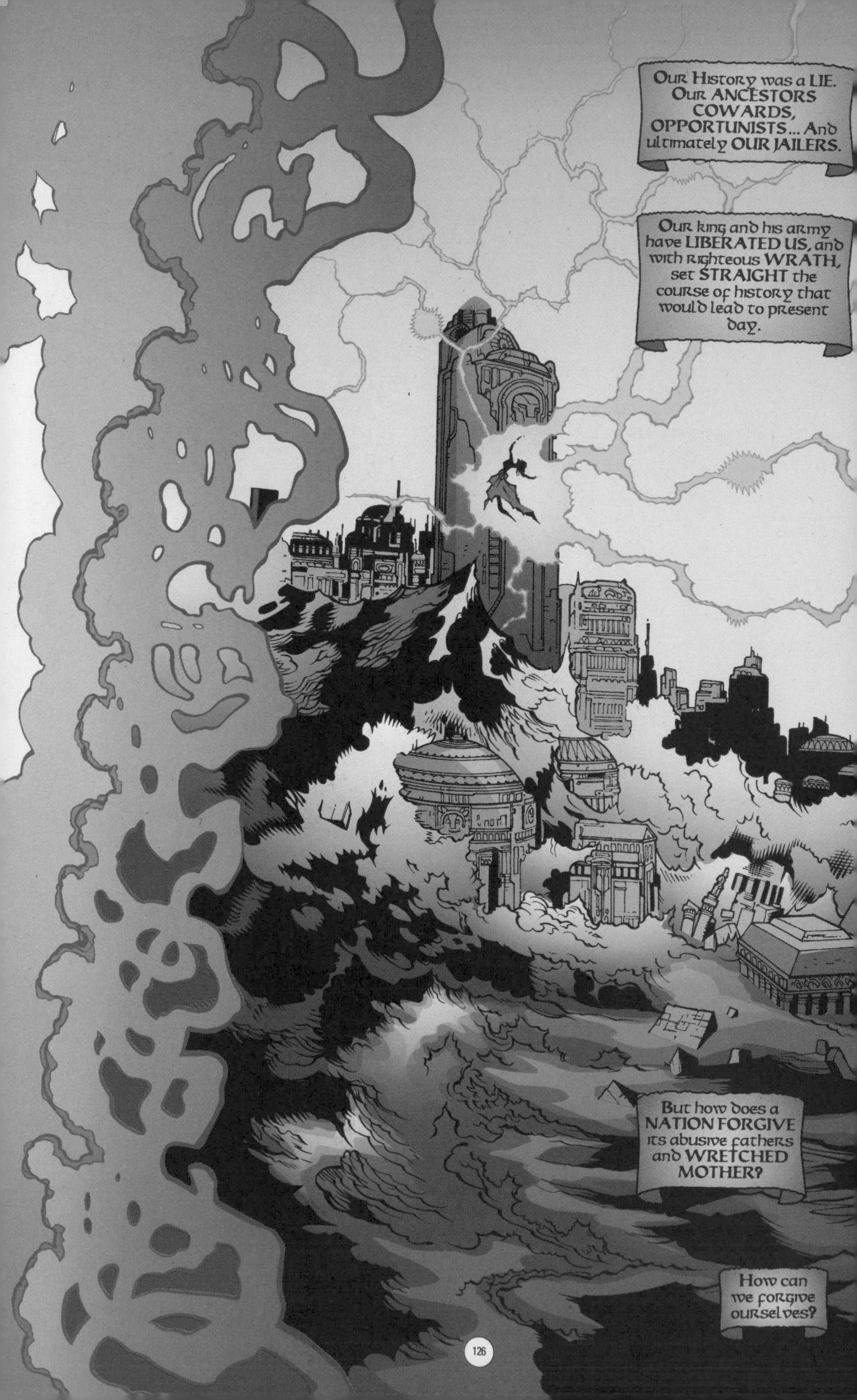
Our History was a LIE. Our ANCESTORS COWARDS, OPPORTUNISTS... And ultimately OUR JAILERS.
Our king and his army have LIBERATED US, and with righteous WRATH, set STRAIGHT the course of history that would lead to present day.
But how does a NATION FORGIVE its abusive fathers and WRETCHED MOTHER?
How can we forgive ourselves?

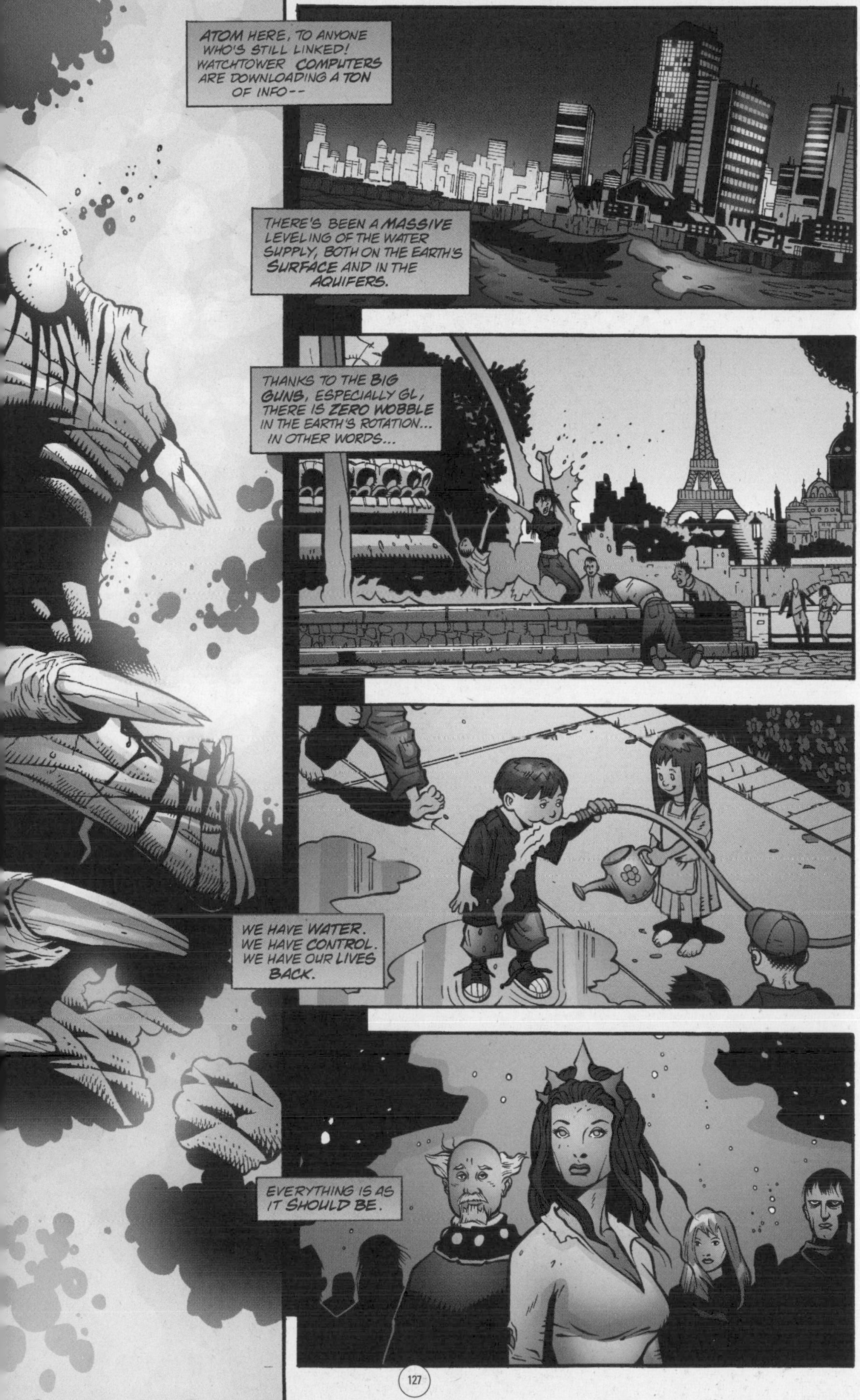
ATOM HERE, TO ANYONE WHO'S STILL LINKED! WATCHTOWER COMPUTERS ARE DOWNLOADING A TON OF INFO--
THERE'S BEEN A MASSIVE LEVELING OF THE WATER SUPPLY, BOTH ON THE EARTH'S SURFACE AND IN THE AQUIFERS.
THANKS TO THE BIG GUNS, ESPECIALLY GL, THERE IS ZERO WOBBLE IN THE EARTH'S ROTATION... IN OTHER WORDS...
WE HAVE WATER. WE HAVE CONTROL. WE HAVE OUR LIVES BACK.
EVERYTHING IS AS IT SHOULD BE.

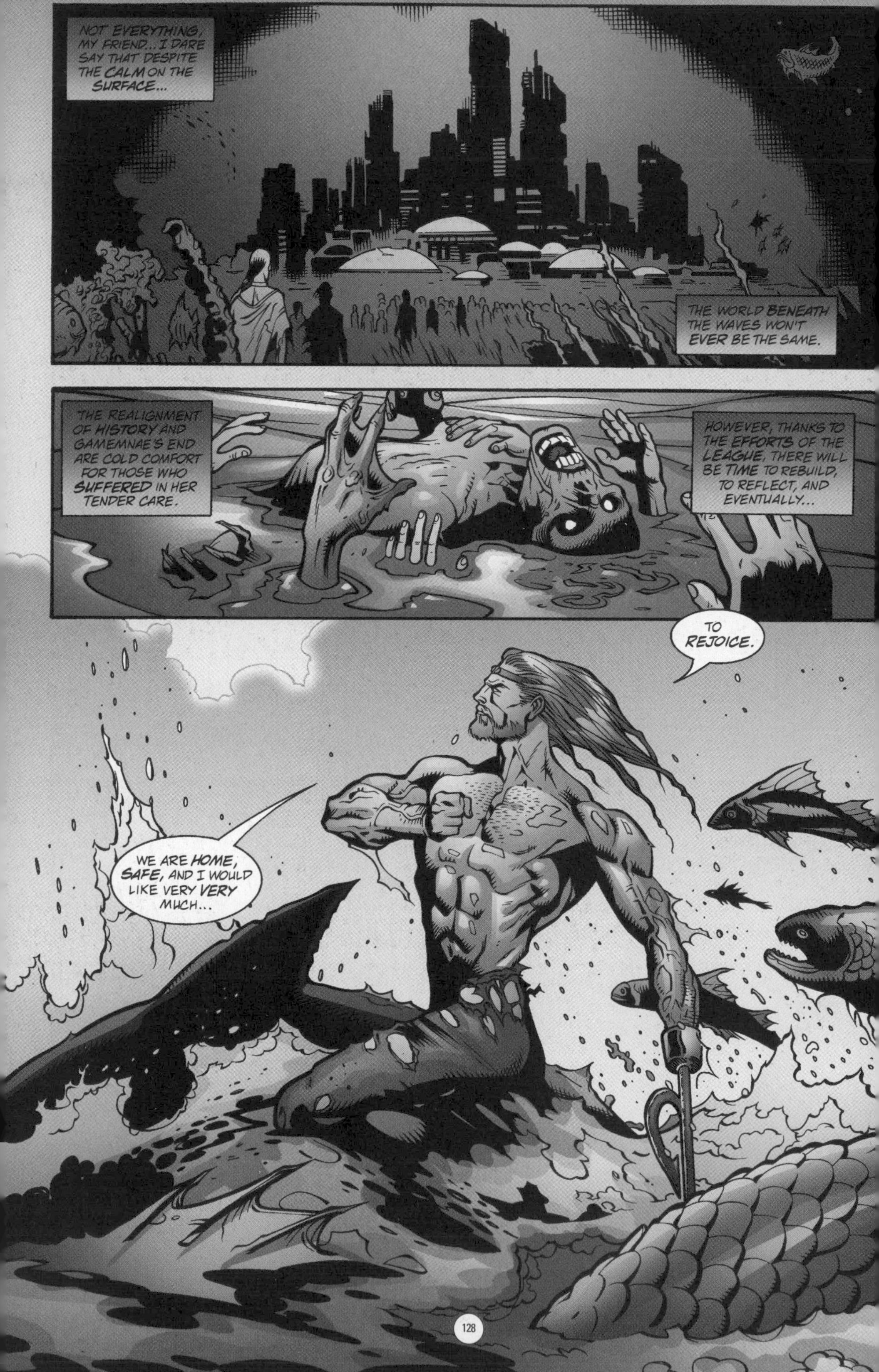
NOT EVERYTHING, MY FRIEND... I DARE SAY THAT DESPITE THE CALM ON THE SURFACE...
THE WORLD BENEATH THE WAVES WON'T EVER BE THE SAME.
THE REALIGNMENT OF HISTORY AND GAMEMNAE'S END ARE COLD COMFORT FOR THOSE WHO SUFFERED IN HER TENDER CARE.
HOWEVER, THANKS TO THE EFFORTS OF THE LEAGUE, THERE WILL BE TIME TO REBUILD, TO REFLECT, AND EVENTUALLY...
TO REJOICE.
WE ARE HOME, SAFE, AND I WOULD LIKE VERY VERY MUCH...

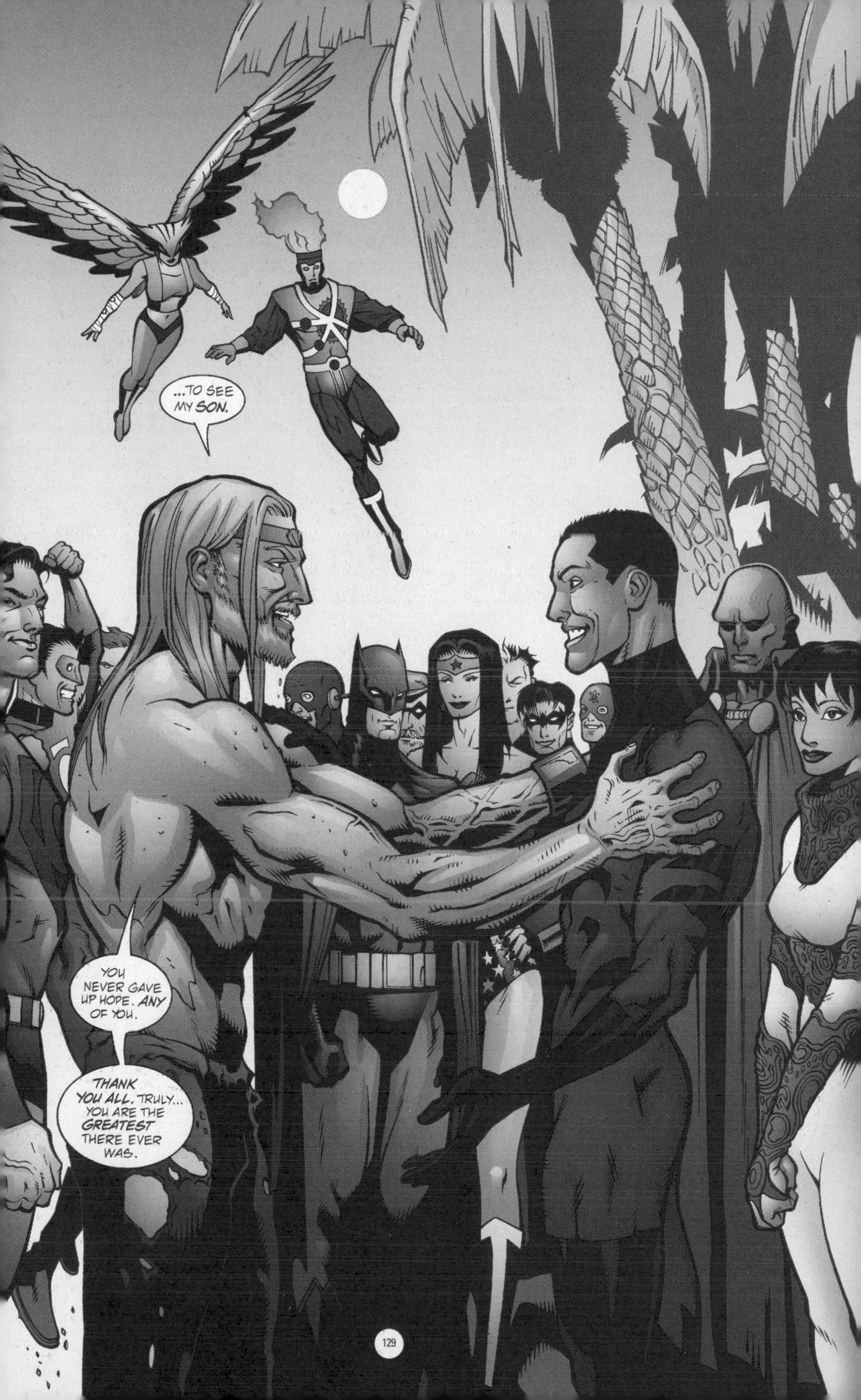
...TO SEE MY SON.
YOU NEVER GAVE UP HOPE. ANY OF YOU.
THANK YOU ALL. TRULY... YOU ARE THE GREATEST THERE EVER WAS.

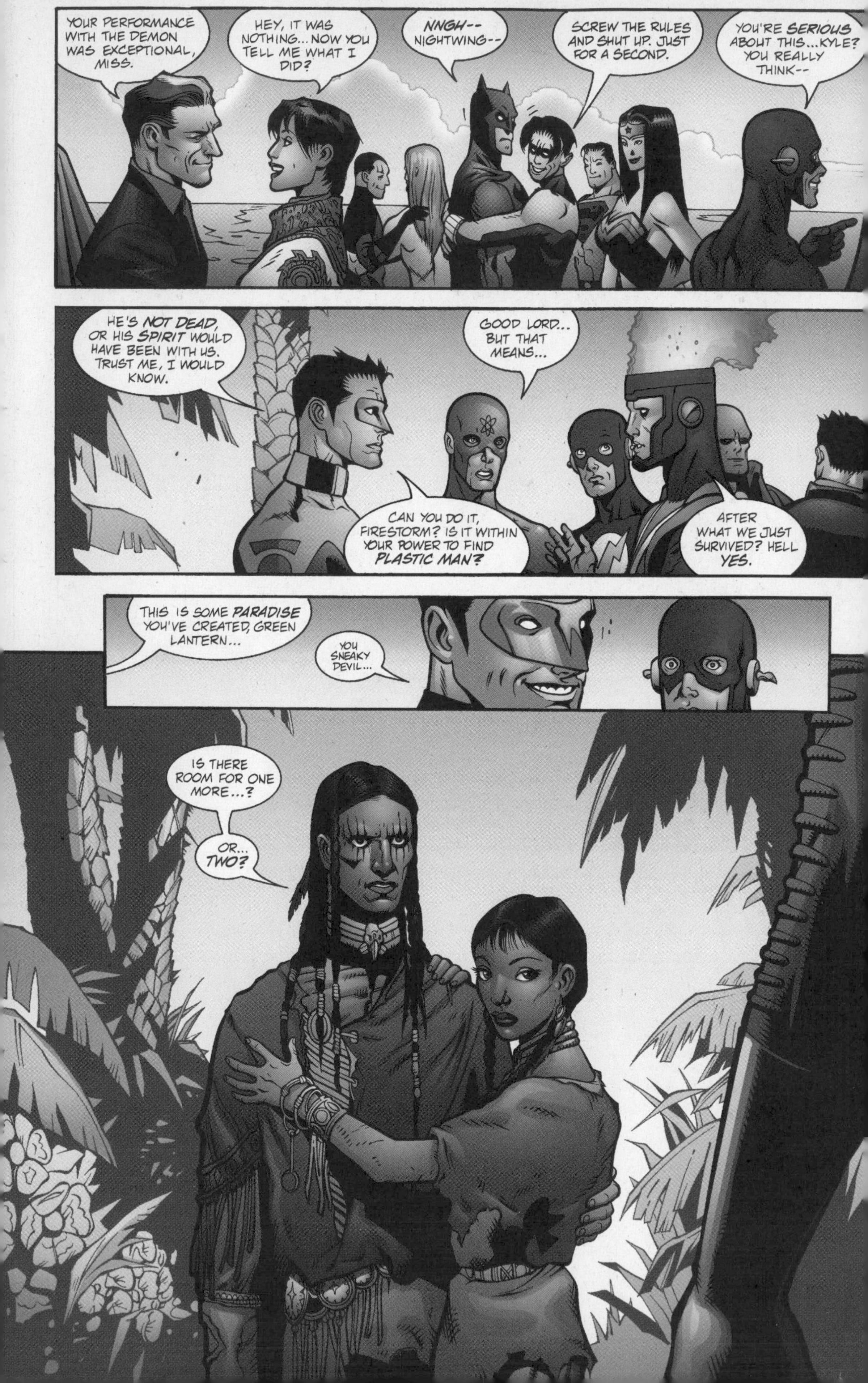

YOUR PERFORMANCE WITH THE DEMON WAS EXCEPTIONAL, MISS.
HEY, IT WAS NOTHING... NOW YOU TELL ME WHAT I DID?
NNGH-- NIGHTWING--
SCREW THE RULES AND SHUT UP. JUST FOR A SECOND.
YOU'RE SERIOUS ABOUT THIS... KYLE? YOU REALLY THINK--
HE'S NOT DEAD, OR HIS SPIRIT WOULD HAVE BEEN WITH US. TRUST ME, I WOULD KNOW.
GOOD LORD... BUT THAT MEANS...
CAN YOU DO IT, FIRESTORM? IS IT WITHIN YOUR POWER TO FIND PLASTIC MAN?
AFTER WHAT WE JUST SURVIVED? HELL YES.
THIS IS SOME PARADISE YOU'VE CREATED, GREEN LANTERN...
YOU SNEAKY DEVIL...
IS THERE ROOM FOR ONE MORE...?
OR... TWO?

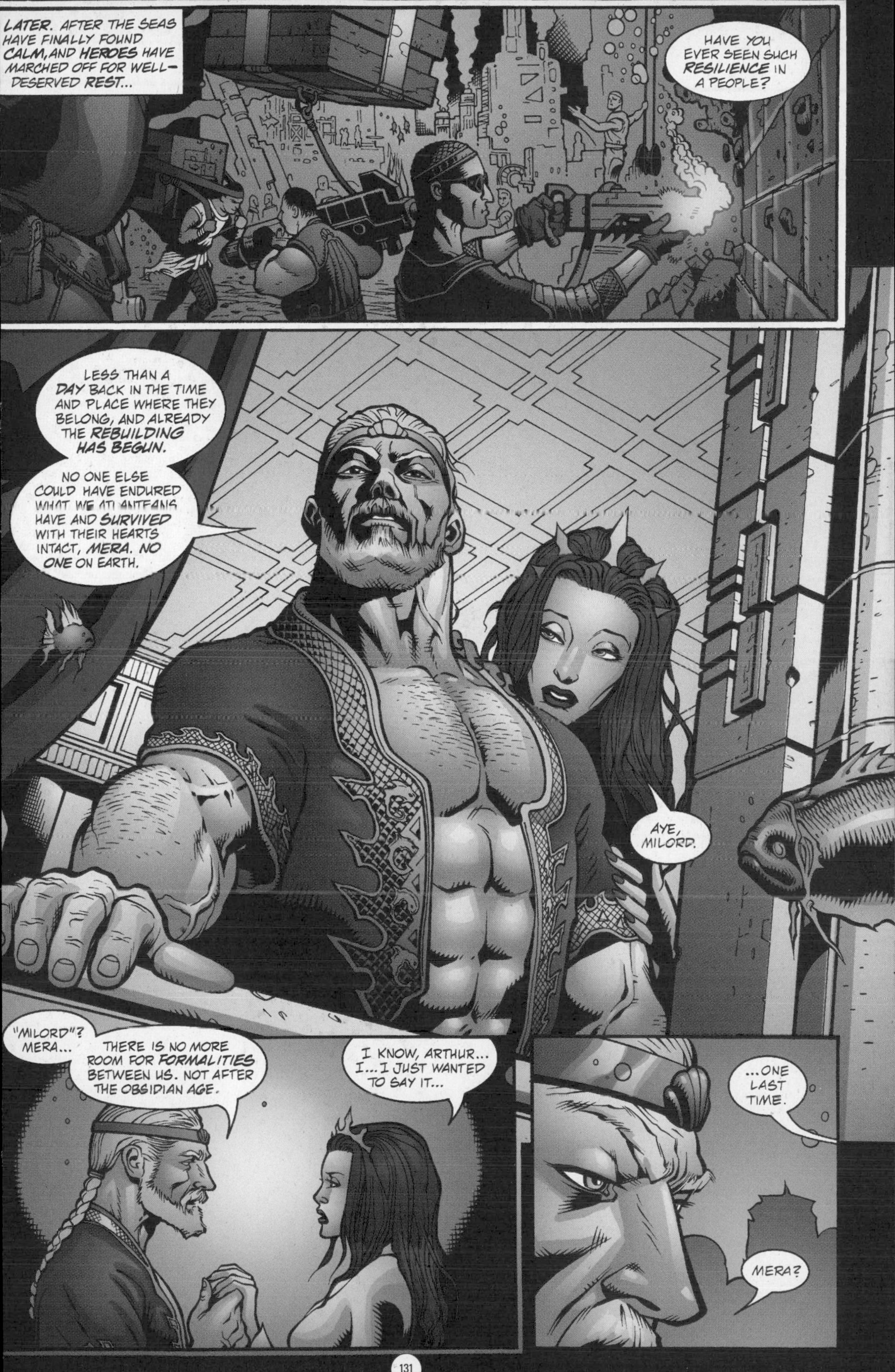
LATER. AFTER THE SEAS HAVE FINALLY FOUND CALM, AND HEROES HAVE MARCHED OFF FOR WELL-DESERVED REST...
HAVE YOU EVER SEEN SUCH RESILIENCE IN A PEOPLE?
LESS THAN A DAY BACK IN THE TIME AND PLACE WHERE THEY BELONG, AND ALREADY THE REBUILDING HAS BEGUN.
NO ONE ELSE COULD HAVE ENDURED WHAT WE ATLANTEANS HAVE AND SURVIVED WITH THEIR HEARTS INTACT, MERA. NO ONE ON EARTH.
AYE, MILORD.
"MILORD"? MERA...
THERE IS NO MORE ROOM FOR FORMALITIES BETWEEN US. NOT AFTER THE OBSIDIAN AGE.
I KNOW, ARTHUR... I... I JUST WANTED TO SAY IT...
...ONE LAST TIME.
MERA?

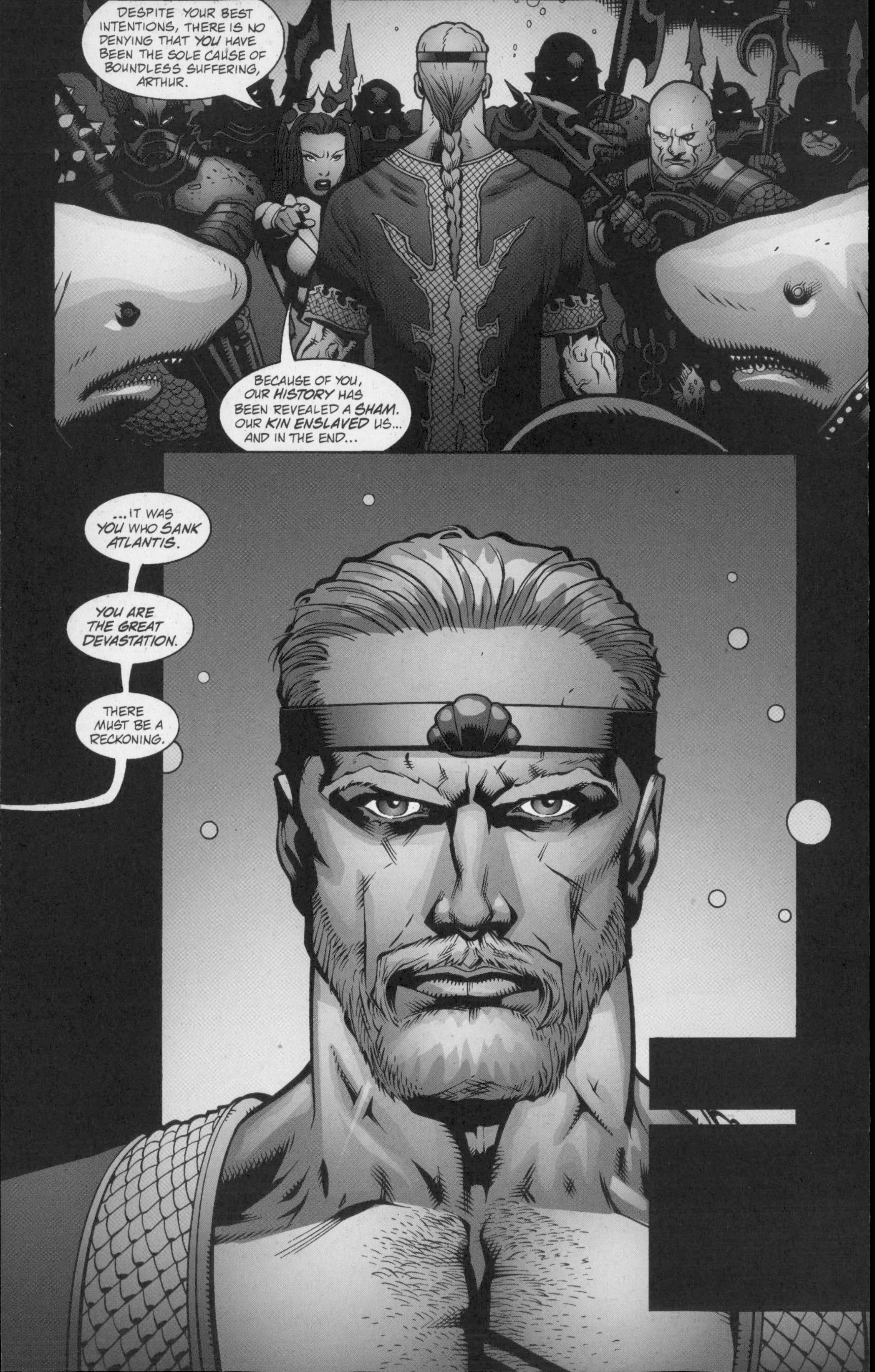
DESPITE YOUR BEST INTENTIONS, THERE IS NO DENYING THAT YOU HAVE BEEN THE SOLE CAUSE OF BOUNDLESS SUFFERING, ARTHUR.
BECAUSE OF YOU, OUR HISTORY HAS BEEN REVEALED A SHAM. OUR KIN ENSLAVED US... AND IN THE END...
...IT WAS YOU WHO SANK ATLANTIS.
YOU ARE THE GREAT DEVASTATION.
THERE MUST BE A RECKONING.

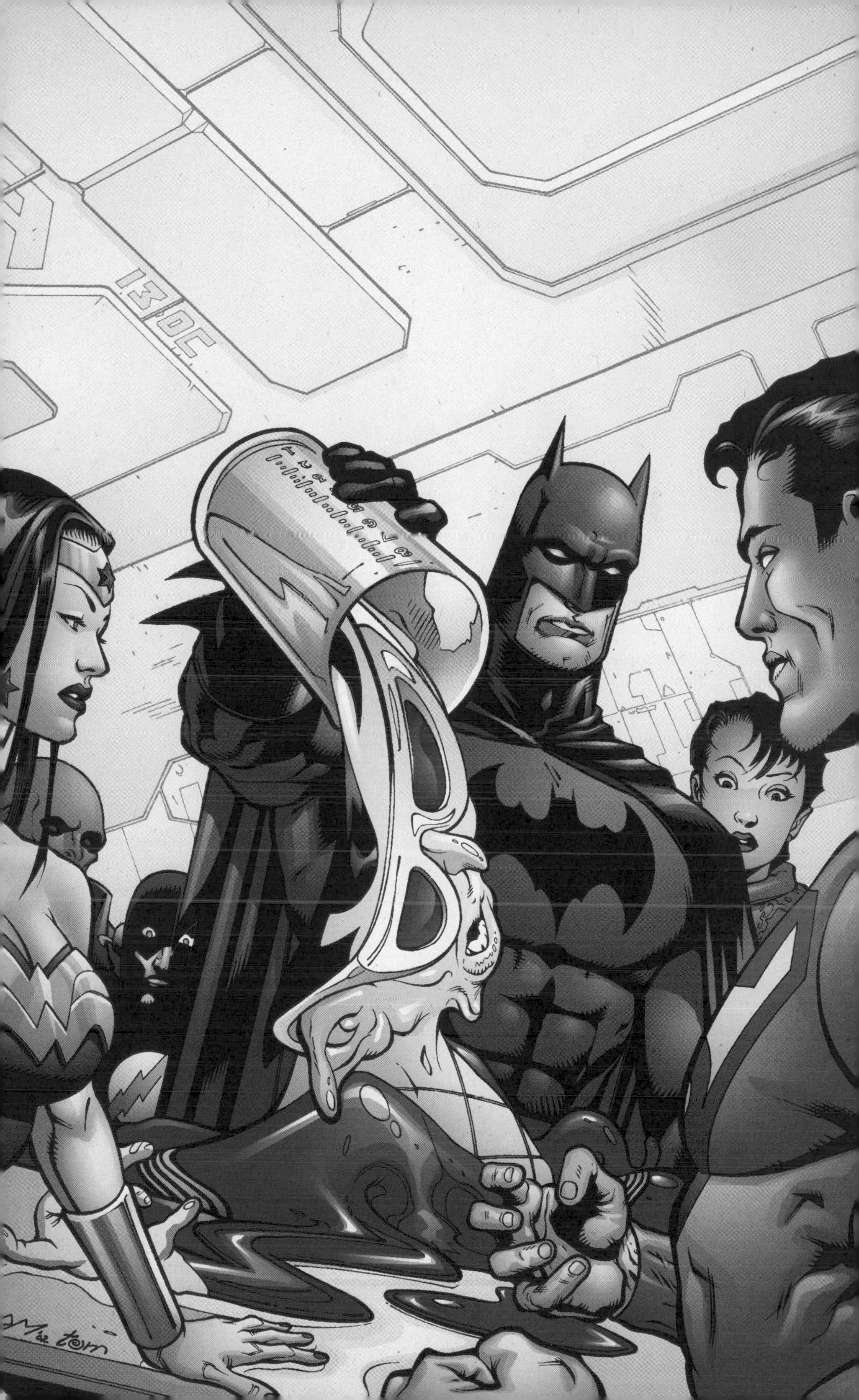

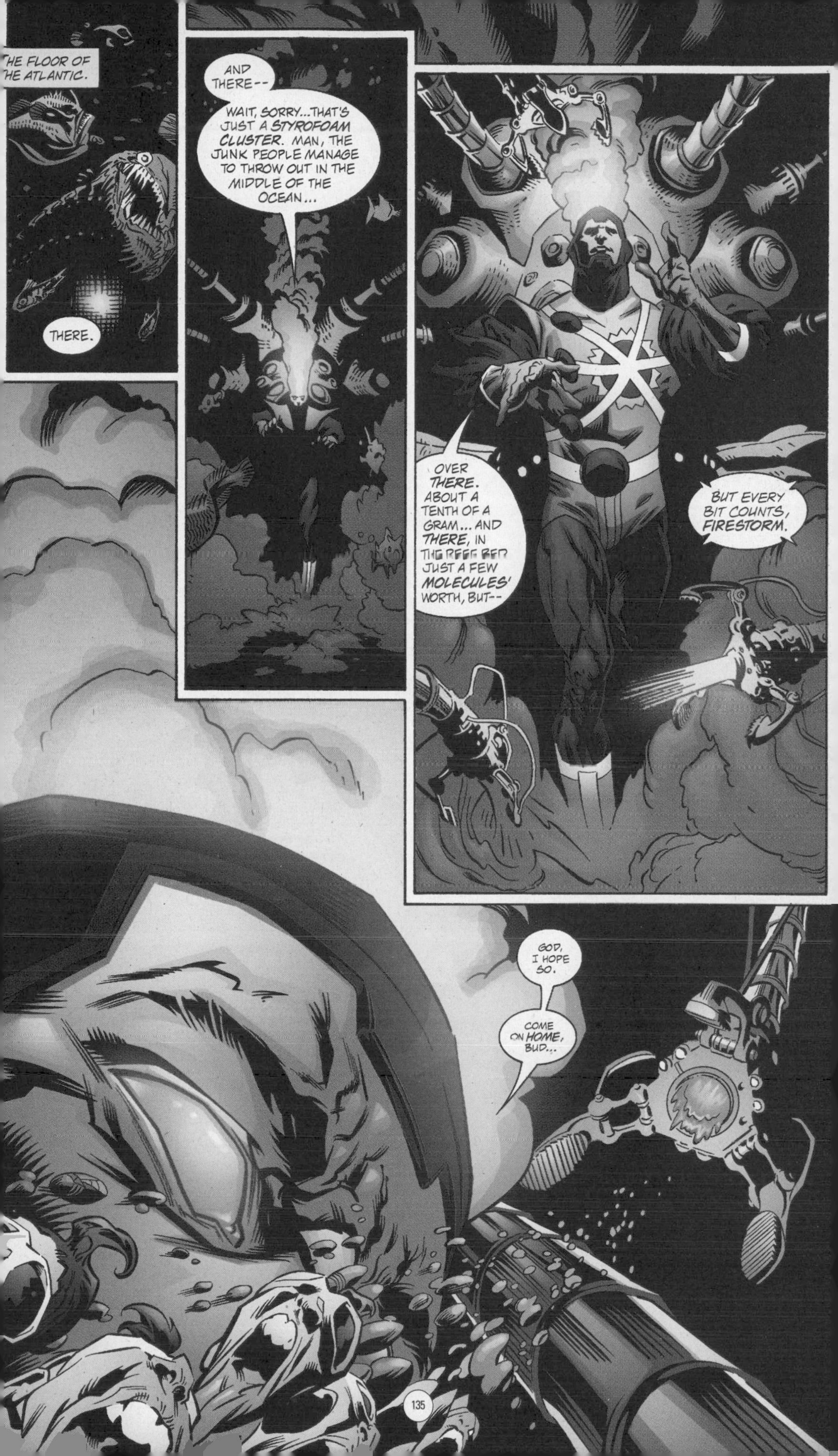
THE FLOOR OF THE ATLANTIC.
THERE.
AND THERE--
WAIT, SORRY...THAT'S JUST A STYROFOAM CLUSTER. MAN, THE JUNK PEOPLE MANAGE TO THROW OUT IN THE MIDDLE OF THE OCEAN...
OVER THERE. ABOUT A TENTH OF A GRAM... AND THERE, IN THE REEF BED JUST A FEW MOLECULES' WORTH, BUT--
BUT EVERY BIT COUNTS, FIRESTORM.
GOD, I HOPE SO.
COME ON HOME, BUD...

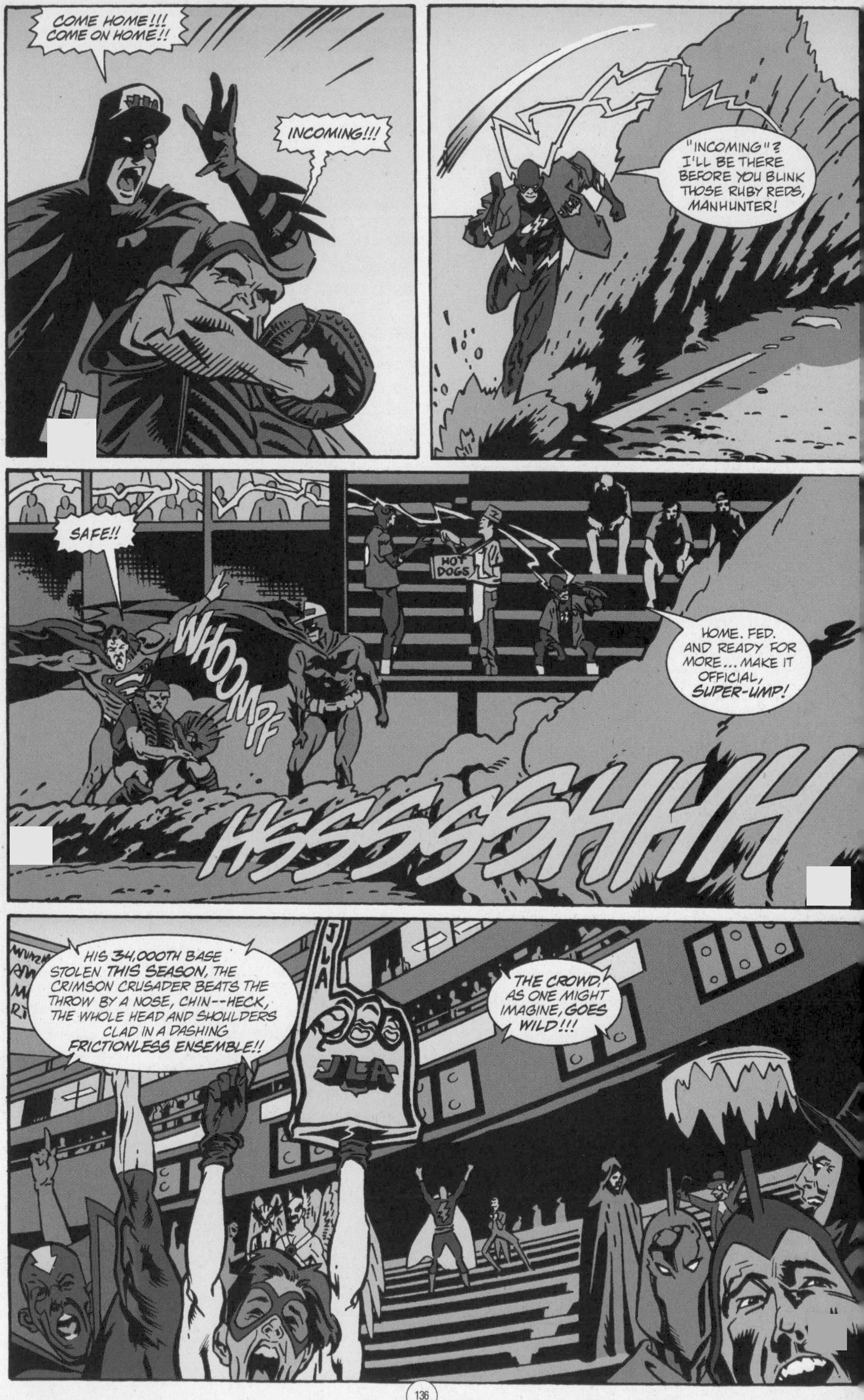
COME HOME!!! COME ON HOME!!
INCOMING!!!
"INCOMING"? I'LL BE THERE BEFORE YOU BLINK THOSE RUBY REDS, MANHUNTER!
SAFE!!
HOT DOGS
WHOOMPF
HOME. FED. AND READY FOR MORE... MAKE IT OFFICIAL, SUPER-UMP!
HSSSSSHHH
HIS 34,000TH BASE STOLEN THIS SEASON, THE CRIMSON CRUSADER BEATS THE THROW BY A NOSE, CHIN--HECK, THE WHOLE HEAD AND SHOULDERS CLAD IN A DASHING FRICTIONLESS ENSEMBLE!!
THE CROWD, AS ONE MIGHT IMAGINE, GOES WILD!!!
JLA
JLA

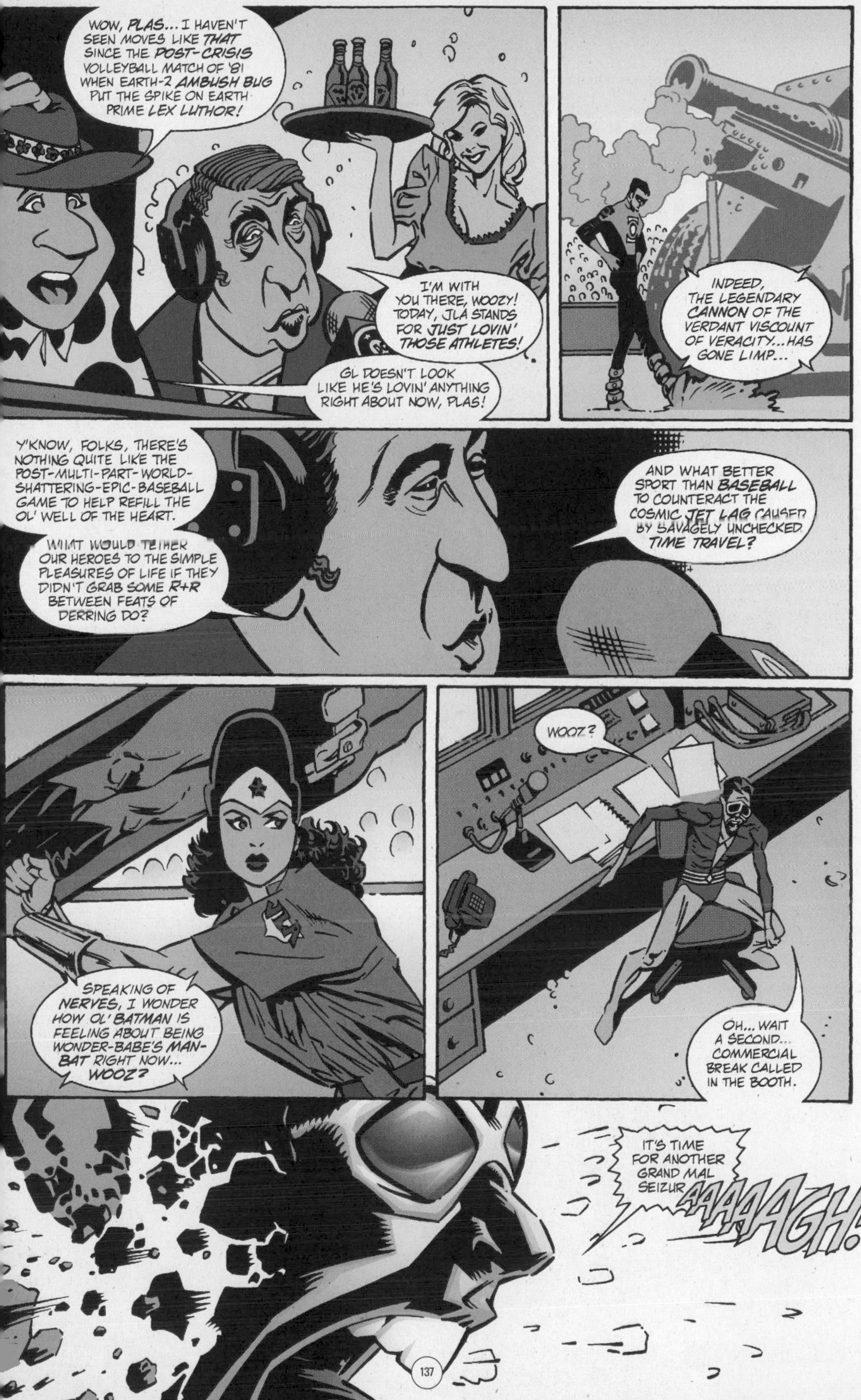
WOW, PLAS... I HAVEN'T SEEN MOVES LIKE THAT SINCE THE POST-CRISIS VOLLEYBALL MATCH OF '81 WHEN EARTH-2 AMBUSH BUG PUT THE SPIKE ON EARTH PRIME LEX LUTHOR!
I'M WITH YOU THERE, WOOZY! TODAY, JLA STANDS FOR JUST LOVIN' THOSE ATHLETES!
GL DOESN'T LOOK LIKE HE'S LOVIN' ANYTHING RIGHT ABOUT NOW, PLAS!
INDEED, THE LEGENDARY CANNON OF THE VERDANT VISCOUNT OF VERACITY... HAS GONE LIMP...
Y'KNOW, FOLKS, THERE'S NOTHING QUITE LIKE THE POST-MULTI-PART-WORLD-SHATTERING-EPIC-BASEBALL GAME TO HELP REFILL THE OL' WELL OF THE HEART.
WHAT WOULD TETHER OUR HEROES TO THE SIMPLE PLEASURES OF LIFE IF THEY DIDN'T GRAB SOME R+R BETWEEN FEATS OF DERRING DO?
AND WHAT BETTER SPORT THAN BASEBALL TO COUNTERACT THE COSMIC JET LAG CAUSED BY SAVAGELY UNCHECKED TIME TRAVEL?
SPEAKING OF NERVES, I WONDER HOW OL' BATMAN IS FEELING ABOUT BEING WONDER-BABE'S MAN-BAT RIGHT NOW... WOOZ?
WOOZ?
OH... WAIT A SECOND... COMMERCIAL BREAK CALLED IN THE BOOTH.
IT'S TIME FOR ANOTHER GRAND MAL SEIZUR
AAAAAGH!

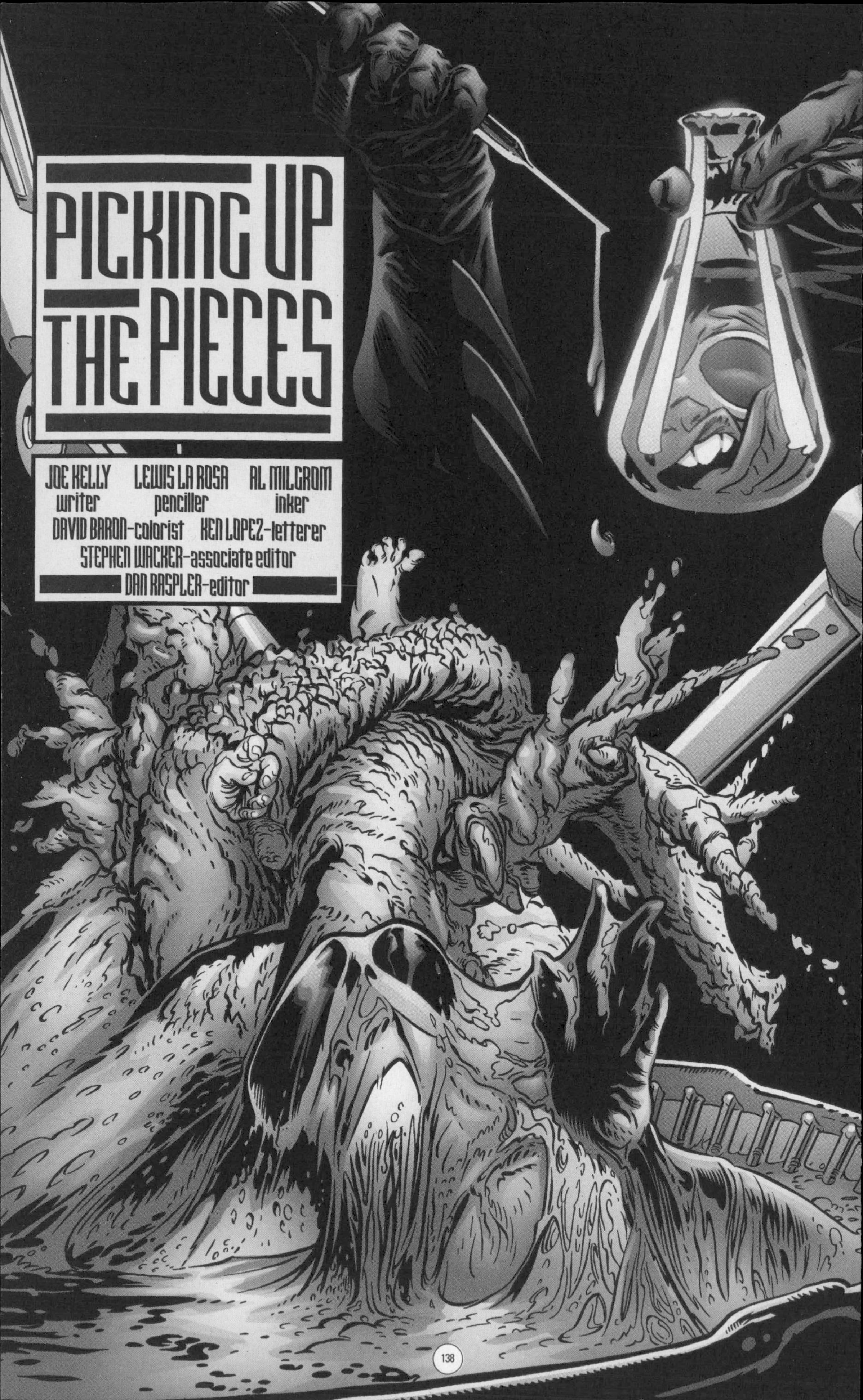
PICKING UP THE PIECES
JOE KELLY writer
LEWIS LA ROSA penciller
AL MILGROM inker
DAVID BARON-colorist
KEN LOPEZ-letterer
STEPHEN WACKER-associate editor
DAN RASPLER-editor

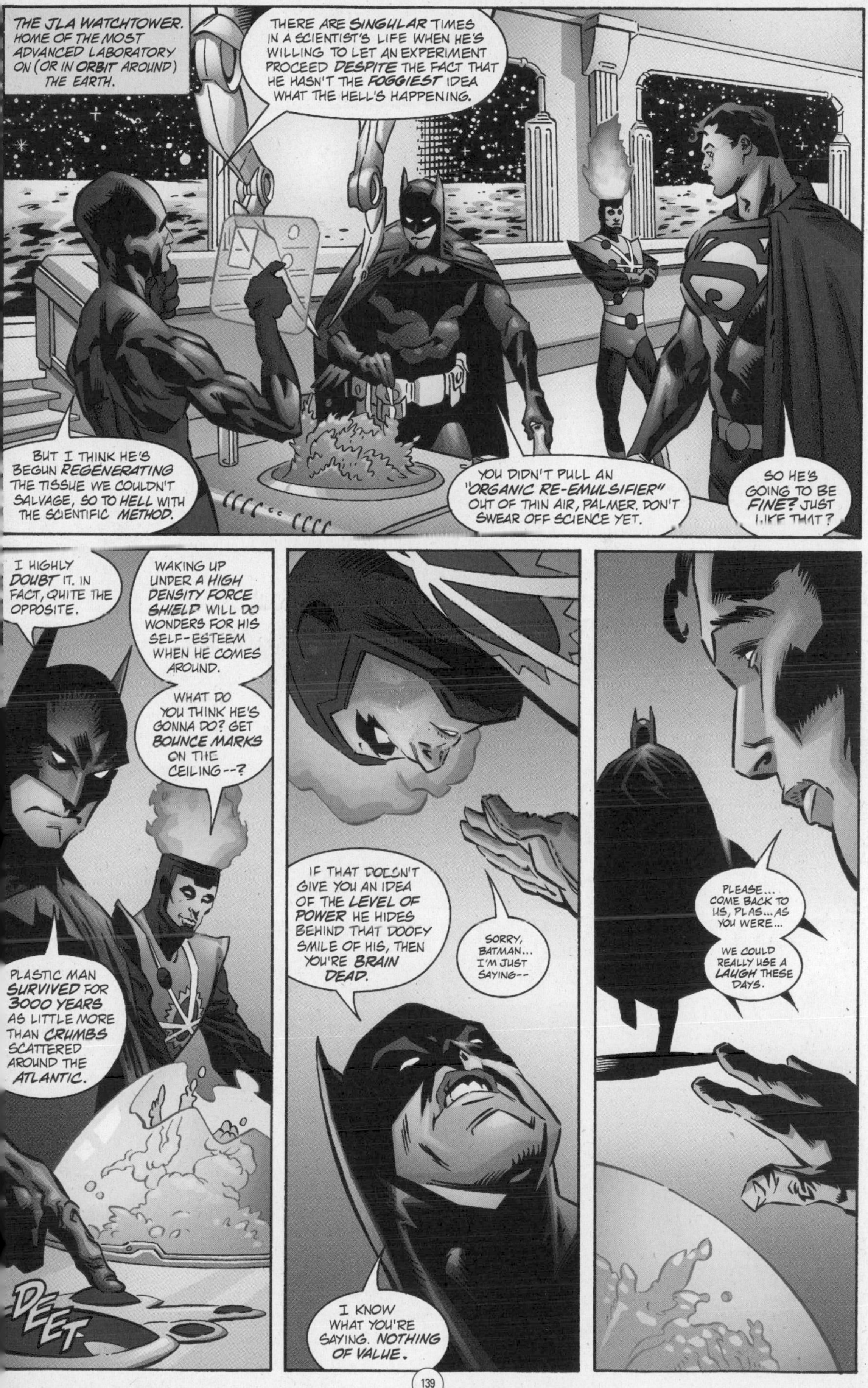
THE JLA WATCHTOWER. HOME OF THE MOST ADVANCED LABORATORY ON (OR IN ORBIT AROUND) THE EARTH.
THERE ARE SINGULAR TIMES IN A SCIENTIST'S LIFE WHEN HE'S WILLING TO LET AN EXPERIMENT PROCEED DESPITE THE FACT THAT HE HASN'T THE FOGGIEST IDEA WHAT THE HELL'S HAPPENING.
BUT I THINK HE'S BEGUN REGENERATING THE TISSUE WE COULDN'T SALVAGE, SO TO HELL WITH THE SCIENTIFIC METHOD.
YOU DIDN'T PULL AN "ORGANIC RE-EMULSIFIER" OUT OF THIN AIR, PALMER. DON'T SWEAR OFF SCIENCE YET.
SO HE'S GOING TO BE FINE? JUST LIKE THAT?
I HIGHLY DOUBT IT. IN FACT, QUITE THE OPPOSITE.
WAKING UP UNDER A HIGH DENSITY FORCE SHIELD WILL DO WONDERS FOR HIS SELF-ESTEEM WHEN HE COMES AROUND.
WHAT DO YOU THINK HE'S GONNA DO? GET BOUNCE MARKS ON THE CEILING--?
PLASTIC MAN SURVIVED FOR 3000 YEARS AS LITTLE MORE THAN CRUMBS SCATTERED AROUND THE ATLANTIC.
DEET
IF THAT DOESN'T GIVE YOU AN IDEA OF THE LEVEL OF POWER HE HIDES BEHIND THAT DOOFY SMILE OF HIS, THEN YOU'RE BRAIN DEAD.
SORRY, BATMAN... I'M JUST SAYING--
I KNOW WHAT YOU'RE SAYING. NOTHING OF VALUE.
PLEASE... COME BACK TO US, PLAS... AS YOU WERE...
WE COULD REALLY USE A LAUGH THESE DAYS.

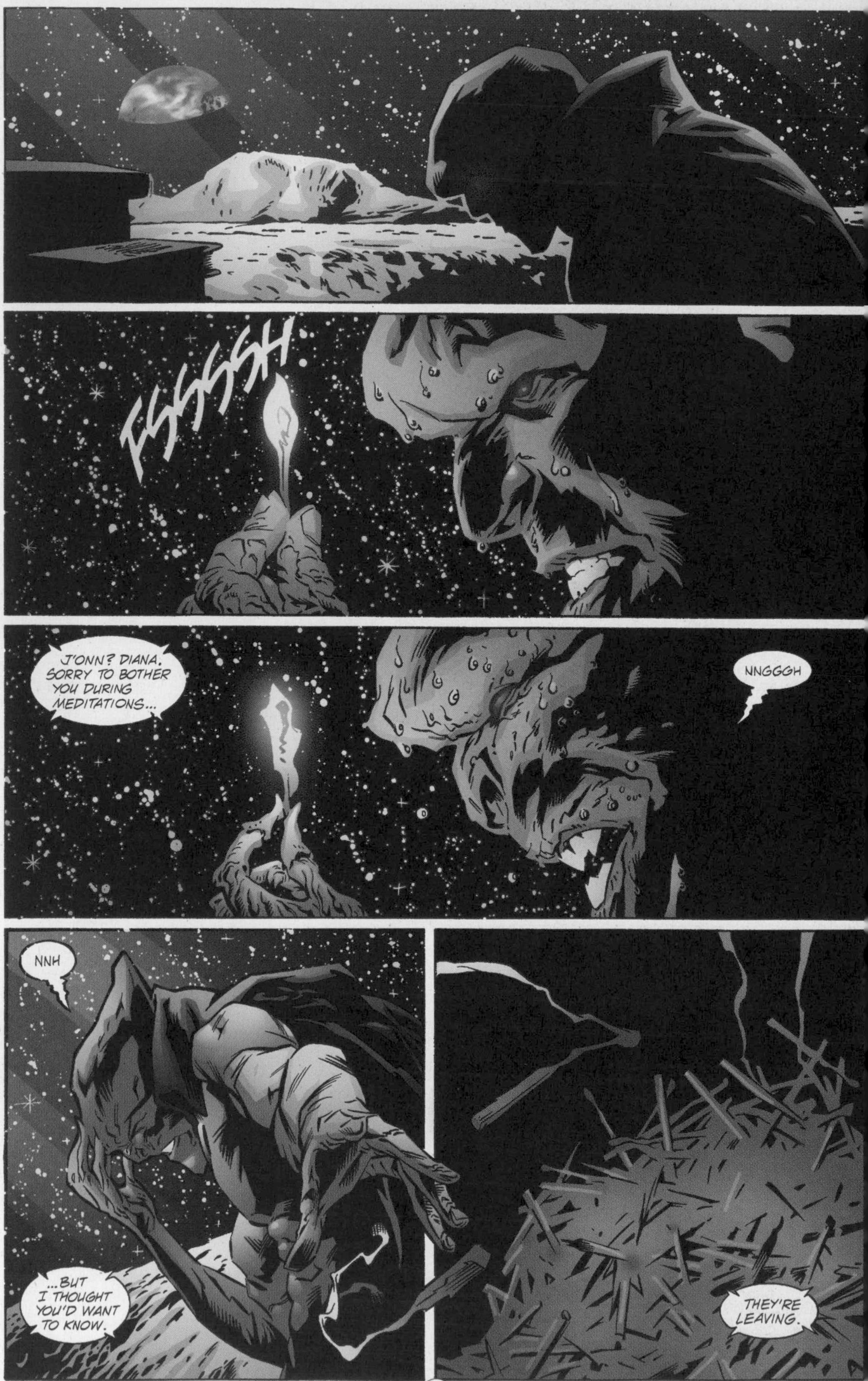
FSSSSH
J'ONN? DIANA. SORRY TO BOTHER YOU DURING MEDITATIONS...
NNGGGH
NNH
...BUT I THOUGHT YOU'D WANT TO KNOW.
THEY'RE LEAVING.

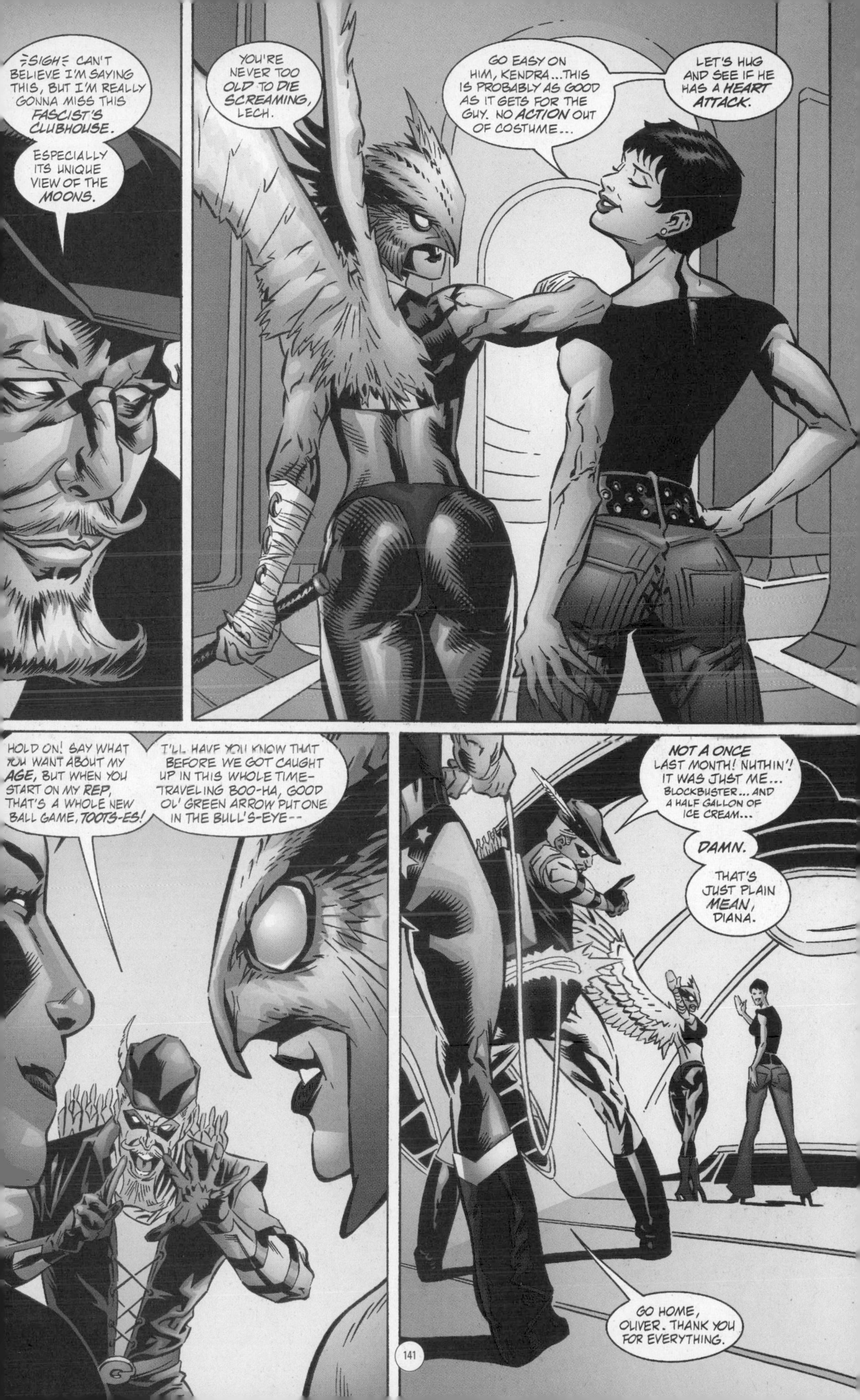

=SIGH= CAN'T BELIEVE I'M SAYING THIS, BUT I'M REALLY GONNA MISS THIS FASCIST'S CLUBHOUSE.
ESPECIALLY ITS UNIQUE VIEW OF THE MOONS.
YOU'RE NEVER TOO OLD TO DIE SCREAMING, LECH.
GO EASY ON HIM, KENDRA... THIS IS PROBABLY AS GOOD AS IT GETS FOR THE GUY. NO ACTION OUT OF COSTUME...
LET'S HUG AND SEE IF HE HAS A HEART ATTACK.
HOLD ON! SAY WHAT YOU WANT ABOUT MY AGE, BUT WHEN YOU START ON MY REP, THAT'S A WHOLE NEW BALL GAME, TOOTS-ES!
I'LL HAVE YOU KNOW THAT BEFORE WE GOT CAUGHT UP IN THIS WHOLE TIME-TRAVELING BOO-HA, GOOD OL' GREEN ARROW PUT ONE IN THE BULL'S-EYE--
NOT A ONCE LAST MONTH! NUTHIN'! IT WAS JUST ME... BLOCKBUSTER... AND A HALF GALLON OF ICE CREAM...
DAMN.
THAT'S JUST PLAIN MEAN, DIANA.
GO HOME, OLIVER. THANK YOU FOR EVERYTHING.

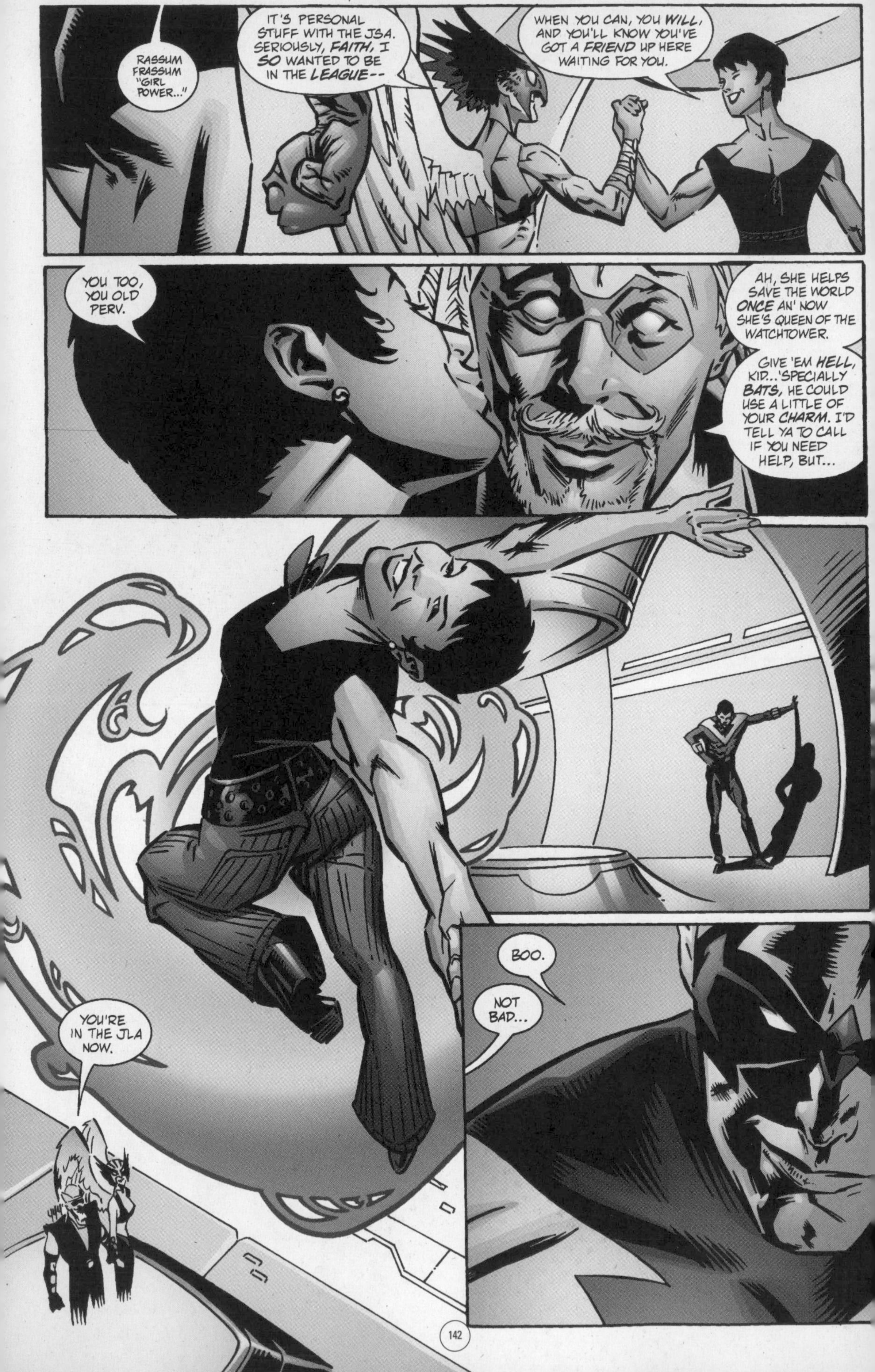
RASSUM FRASSUM "GIRL POWER..."
IT'S PERSONAL STUFF WITH THE JSA. SERIOUSLY, FAITH, I SO WANTED TO BE IN THE LEAGUE--
WHEN YOU CAN, YOU WILL, AND YOU'LL KNOW YOU'VE GOT A FRIEND UP HERE WAITING FOR YOU.
YOU TOO, YOU OLD PERV.
AH, SHE HELPS SAVE THE WORLD ONCE AN' NOW SHE'S QUEEN OF THE WATCHTOWER.
GIVE 'EM HELL, KID...'SPECIALLY BATS, HE COULD USE A LITTLE OF YOUR CHARM. I'D TELL YA TO CALL IF YOU NEED HELP, BUT...
YOU'RE IN THE JLA NOW.
BOO.
NOT BAD...

I BARELY GOT CLOSE ENOUGH TO KILL YOU.

THOUGHT YOU WEREN'T GONNA SAY GOODBYE.

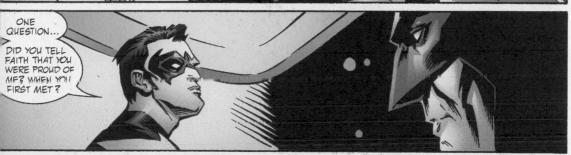

I'M NOT. I'M GOING TO GIVE YOU A BIT OF ADVICE.

YOU'RE READY TO *GRADUATE.* LEADING THE JLA PROVES IT. YOU CAN HANDLE *BIGGER* AND *BETTER* THAN YOU ARE NOW.

THANKS. I HAD A GOOD TEACHER, EXCEPT FOR THE *INTERPERSONAL SKILLS* AND ABILITY TO *WORK WITH OTHERS.* THAT WAS ME.

ONE QUESTION...

DID YOU TELL FAITH THAT YOU WERE PROUD OF ME? WHEN YOU FIRST MET?

ARE YOU GOING TO HUG ME AGAIN IF I SAY "YES"?

NO. I PUSHED IT ONCE IN ATLANTIS. YOU DIDN'T RAISE NO DUMMY.

IT WAS *BAD,* NOT HAVING YOU AROUND. THINKING YOU WERE *DEAD.*

I WAS DEAD.

I KNOW. SO SINCE I *GOT YOU* THIS SECOND CHANCE... HERE'S A LITTLE ADVICE.

USE IT TO SPEND TIME WITH THE *LIVING,* WOULD YOU?

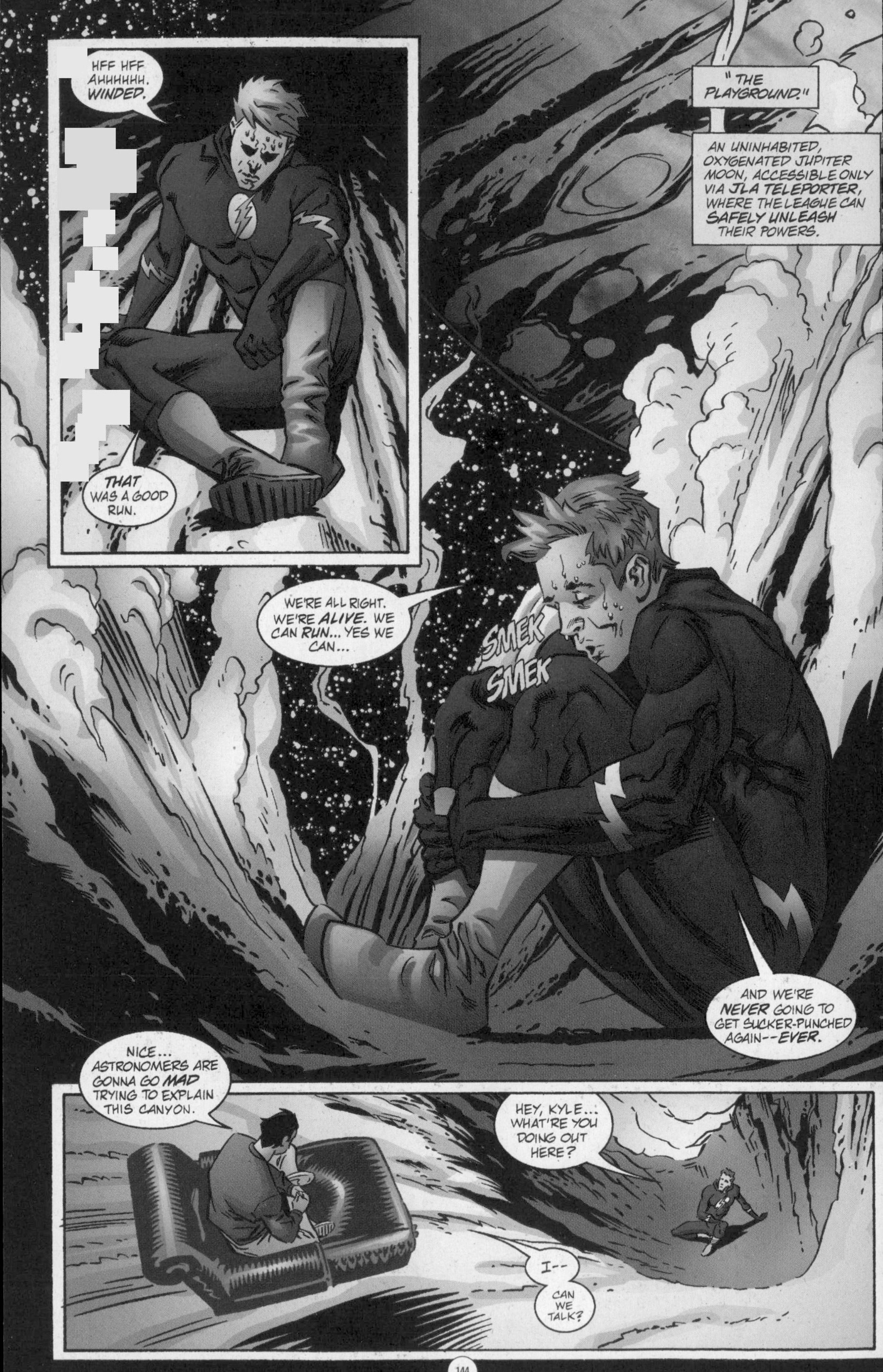
HFF HFF AHHHHHH. WINDED.
THAT WAS A GOOD RUN.
"THE PLAYGROUND."
AN UNINHABITED, OXYGENATED JUPITER MOON, ACCESSIBLE ONLY VIA JLA TELEPORTER, WHERE THE LEAGUE CAN SAFELY UNLEASH THEIR POWERS.
WE'RE ALL RIGHT. WE'RE ALIVE. WE CAN RUN... YES WE CAN...
SMEK
SMEK
AND WE'RE NEVER GOING TO GET SUCKER-PUNCHED AGAIN--EVER.
NICE... ASTRONOMERS ARE GONNA GO MAD TRYING TO EXPLAIN THIS CANYON.
HEY, KYLE... WHAT'RE YOU DOING OUT HERE?
I--
CAN WE TALK?

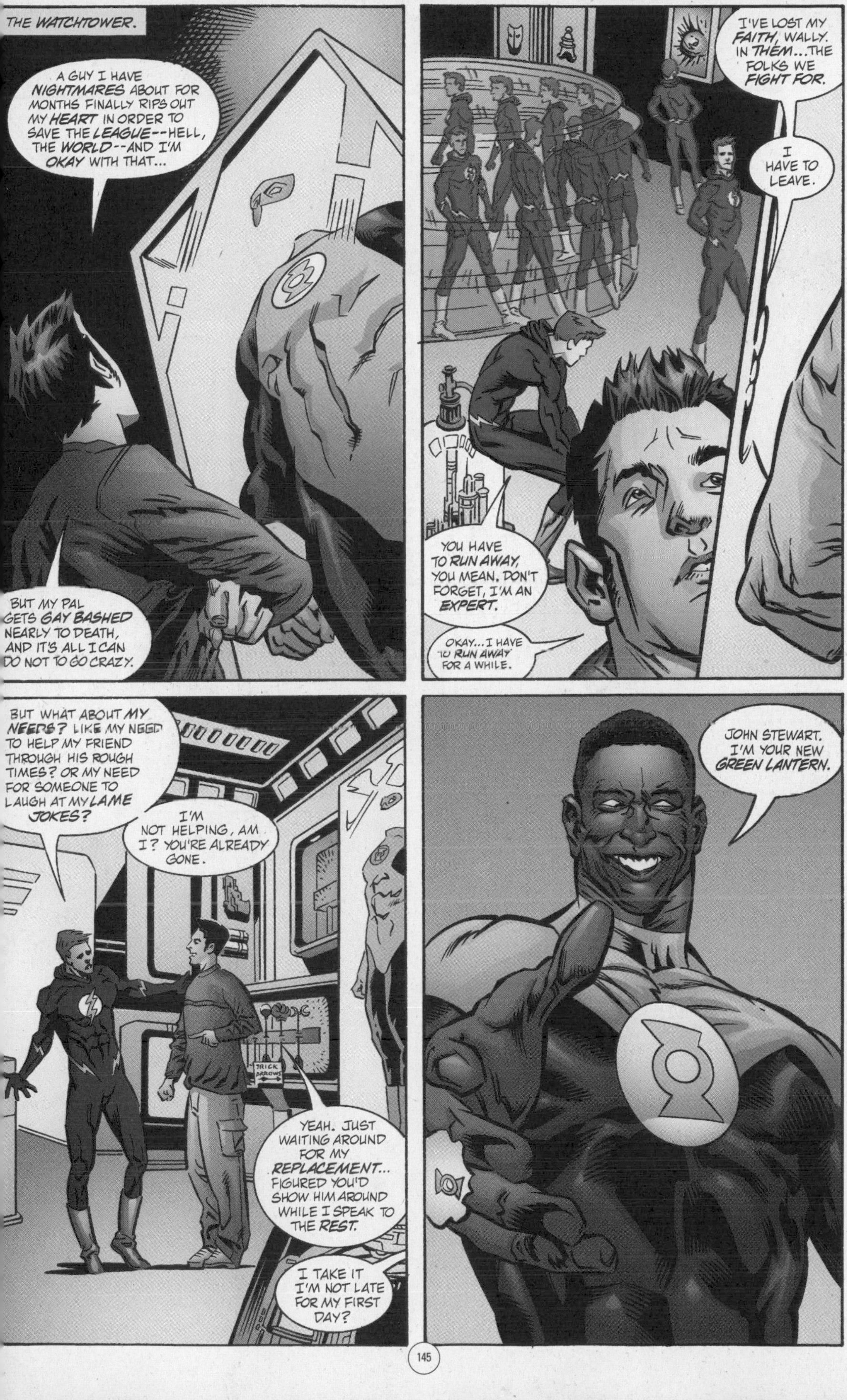
THE WATCHTOWER.
A GUY I HAVE NIGHTMARES ABOUT FOR MONTHS FINALLY RIPS OUT MY HEART IN ORDER TO SAVE THE LEAGUE--HELL, THE WORLD--AND I'M OKAY WITH THAT...
BUT MY PAL GETS GAY BASHED NEARLY TO DEATH, AND IT'S ALL I CAN DO NOT TO GO CRAZY.
I'VE LOST MY FAITH, WALLY. IN THEM...THE FOLKS WE FIGHT FOR.
I HAVE TO LEAVE.
YOU HAVE TO RUN AWAY, YOU MEAN. DON'T FORGET, I'M AN EXPERT.
OKAY...I HAVE TO RUN AWAY FOR A WHILE.
BUT WHAT ABOUT MY NEEDS? LIKE MY NEED TO HELP MY FRIEND THROUGH HIS ROUGH TIMES? OR MY NEED FOR SOMEONE TO LAUGH AT MY LAME JOKES?
I'M NOT HELPING, AM I? YOU'RE ALREADY GONE.
TRICK ARROWS
YEAH. JUST WAITING AROUND FOR MY REPLACEMENT... FIGURED YOU'D SHOW HIM AROUND WHILE I SPEAK TO THE REST.
I TAKE IT I'M NOT LATE FOR MY FIRST DAY?
JOHN STEWART. I'M YOUR NEW GREEN LANTERN.

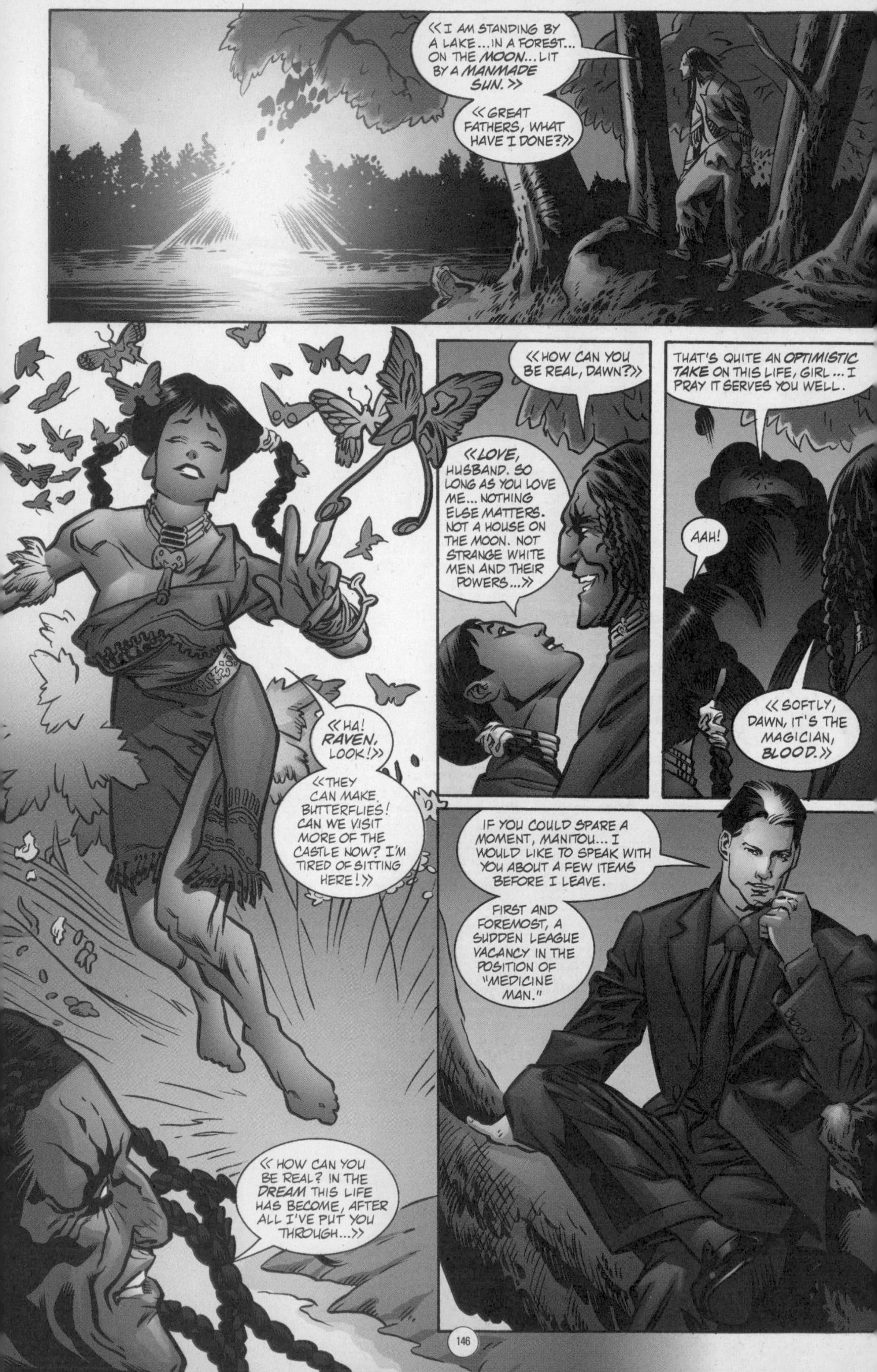

<<I AM STANDING BY A LAKE... IN A FOREST... ON THE MOON... LIT BY A MANMADE SUN.>>
<<GREAT FATHERS, WHAT HAVE I DONE?>>
<<HA! RAVEN, LOOK!>>
<<THEY CAN MAKE BUTTERFLIES! CAN WE VISIT MORE OF THE CASTLE NOW? I'M TIRED OF SITTING HERE!>>
<< HOW CAN YOU BE REAL? IN THE DREAM THIS LIFE HAS BECOME, AFTER ALL I'VE PUT YOU THROUGH...>>
<<HOW CAN YOU BE REAL, DAWN?>>
<<LOVE, HUSBAND. SO LONG AS YOU LOVE ME... NOTHING ELSE MATTERS. NOT A HOUSE ON THE MOON. NOT STRANGE WHITE MEN AND THEIR POWERS...>>
THAT'S QUITE AN OPTIMISTIC TAKE ON THIS LIFE, GIRL... I PRAY IT SERVES YOU WELL.
AAH!
<<SOFTLY, DAWN, IT'S THE MAGICIAN, BLOOD.>>
IF YOU COULD SPARE A MOMENT, MANITOU... I WOULD LIKE TO SPEAK WITH YOU ABOUT A FEW ITEMS BEFORE I LEAVE.
FIRST AND FOREMOST, A SUDDEN LEAGUE VACANCY IN THE POSITION OF "MEDICINE MAN."

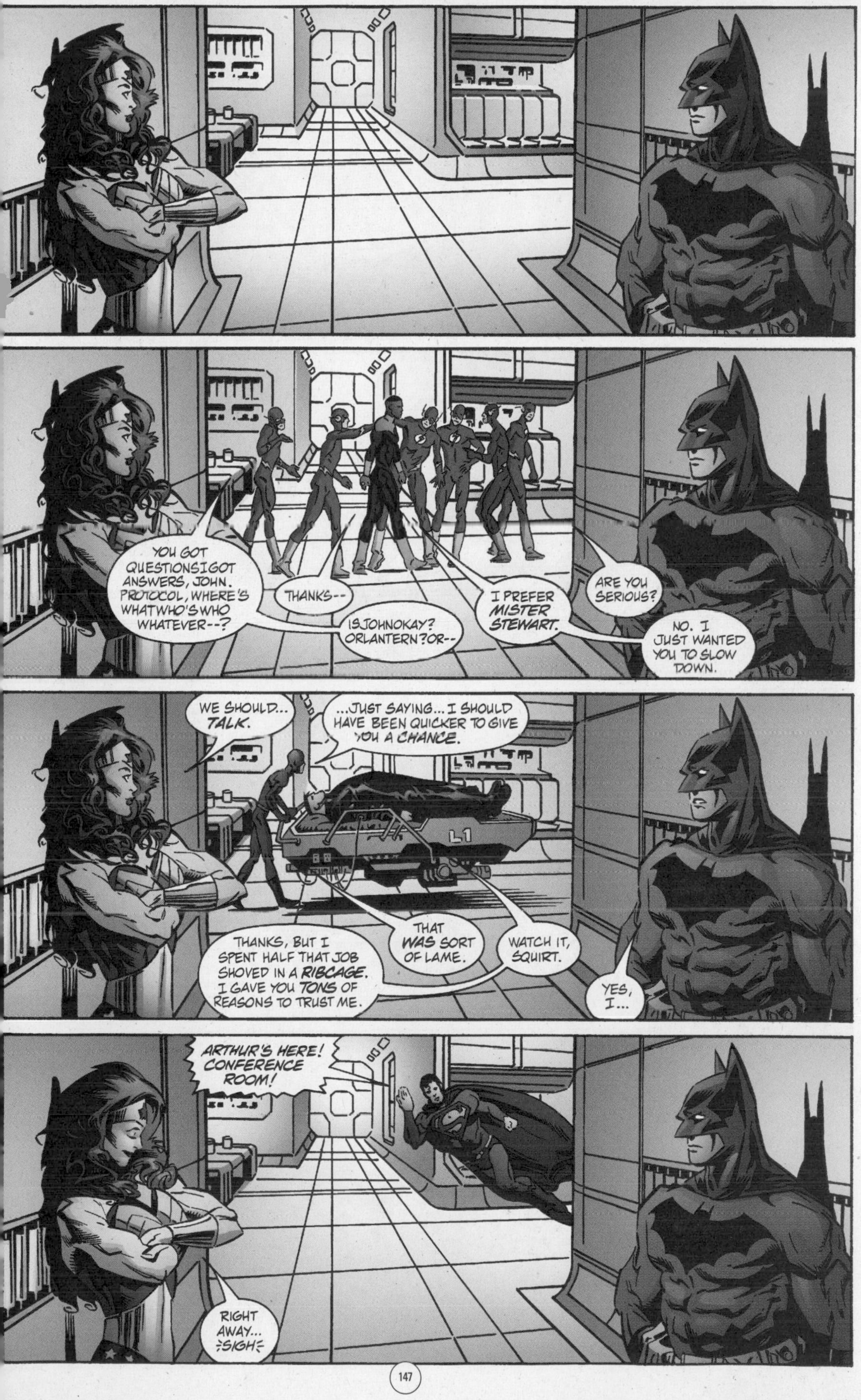
YOU GOT QUESTIONSIGOT ANSWERS, JOHN. PROTOCOL, WHERE'S WHATWHO'SWHO WHATEVER--?
THANKS--
ISJOHNOKAY? ORLANTERN?OR--
I PREFER *MISTER STEWART.*
ARE YOU SERIOUS?
NO. I JUST WANTED YOU TO SLOW DOWN.
WE SHOULD... *TALK.*
...JUST SAYING... I SHOULD HAVE BEEN QUICKER TO GIVE YOU A *CHANCE.*
THANKS, BUT I SPENT HALF THAT JOB SHOVED IN A *RIBCAGE.* I GAVE YOU *TONS* OF REASONS TO TRUST ME.
THAT *WAS* SORT OF LAME.
WATCH IT, SQUIRT.
YES, I...
ARTHUR'S HERE! CONFERENCE ROOM!
RIGHT AWAY... SIGH

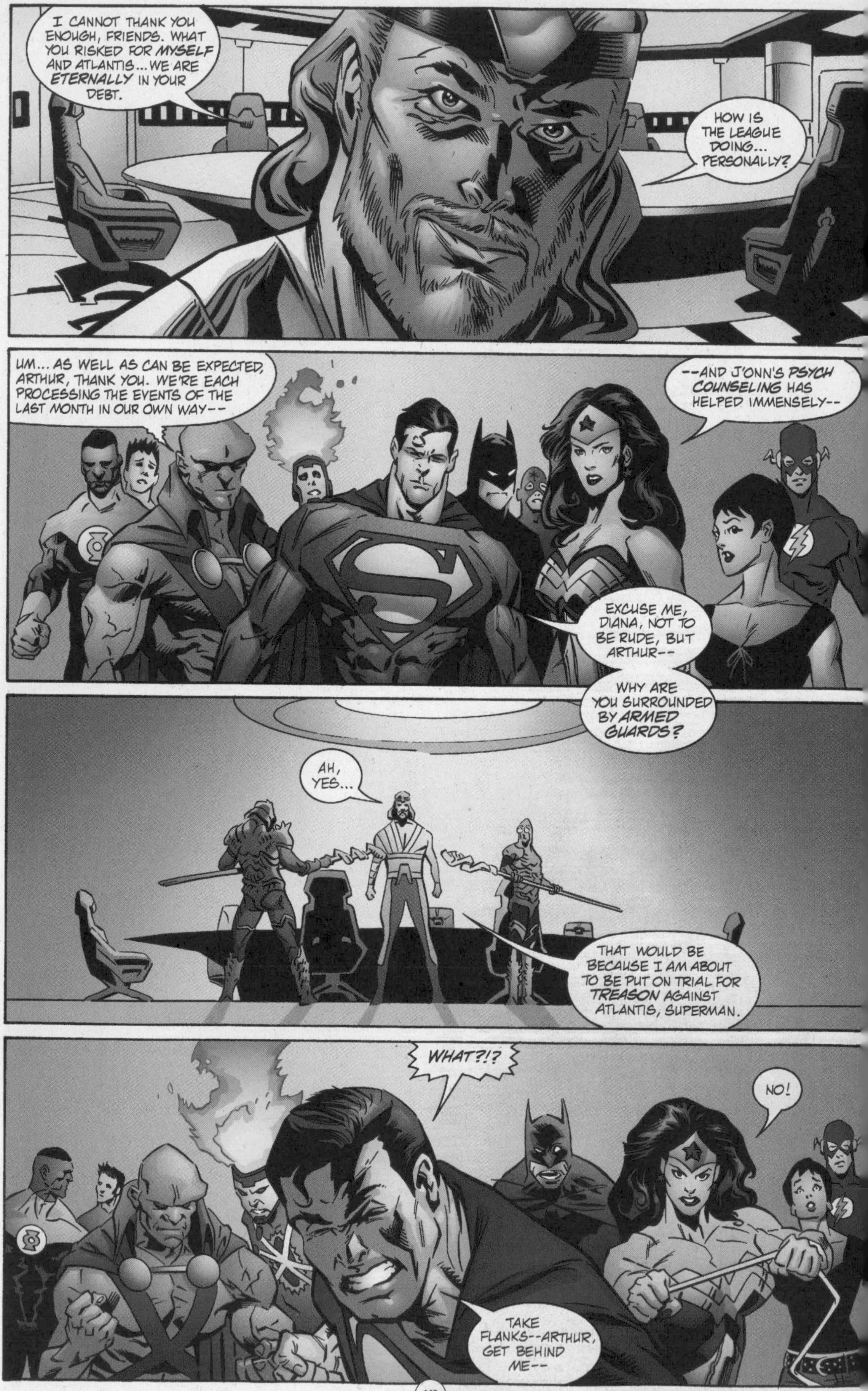
I CANNOT THANK YOU ENOUGH, FRIENDS. WHAT YOU RISKED FOR MYSELF AND ATLANTIS... WE ARE ETERNALLY IN YOUR DEBT.
HOW IS THE LEAGUE DOING... PERSONALLY?
UM... AS WELL AS CAN BE EXPECTED, ARTHUR, THANK YOU. WE'RE EACH PROCESSING THE EVENTS OF THE LAST MONTH IN OUR OWN WAY--
--AND J'ONN'S PSYCH COUNSELING HAS HELPED IMMENSELY--
EXCUSE ME, DIANA, NOT TO BE RUDE, BUT ARTHUR--
WHY ARE YOU SURROUNDED BY ARMED GUARDS?
AH, YES...
THAT WOULD BE BECAUSE I AM ABOUT TO BE PUT ON TRIAL FOR TREASON AGAINST ATLANTIS, SUPERMAN.
WHAT?!?
NO!
TAKE FLANKS--ARTHUR, GET BEHIND ME--

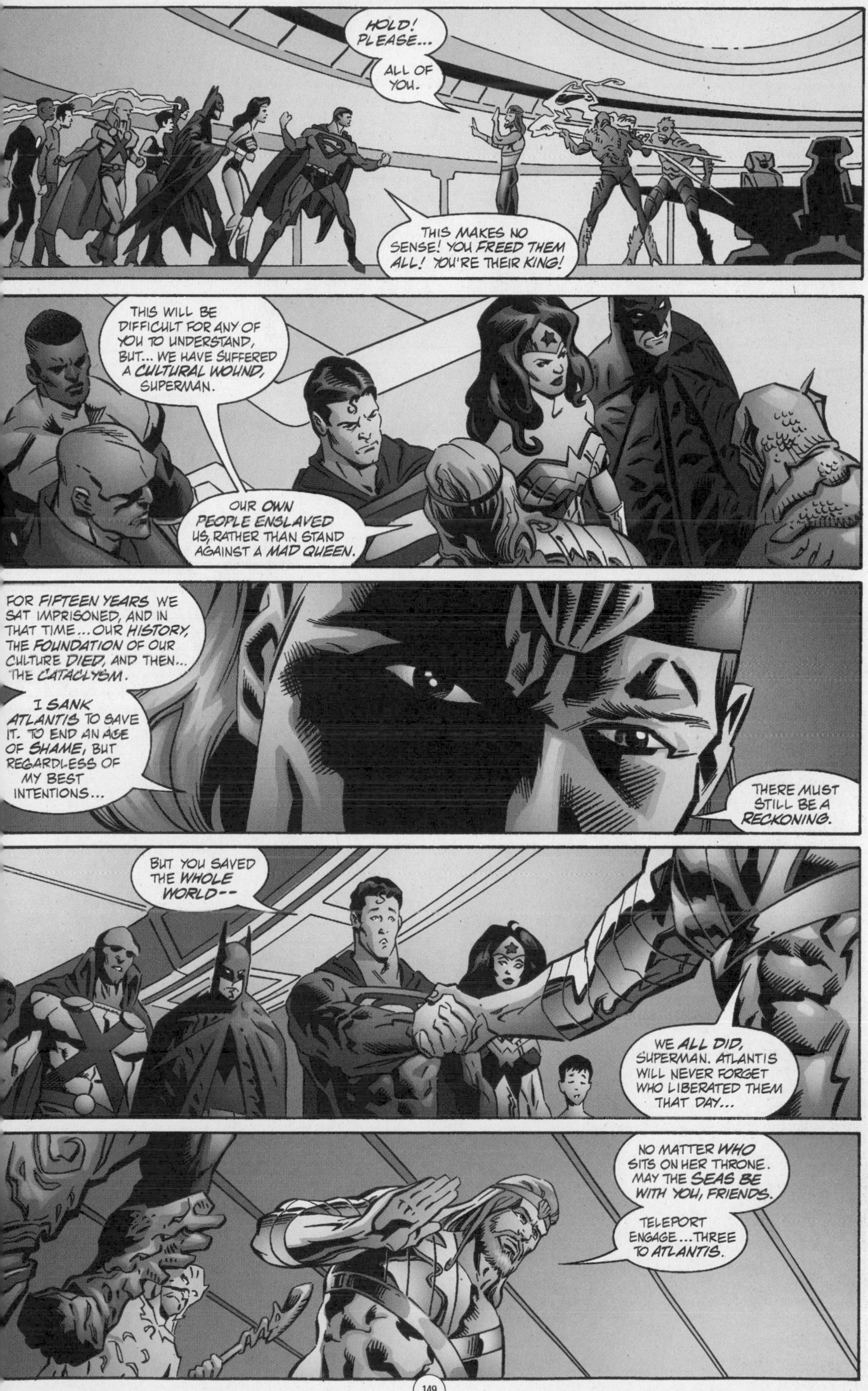
HOLD! PLEASE...
ALL OF YOU.
THIS MAKES NO SENSE! YOU FREED THEM ALL! YOU'RE THEIR KING!
THIS WILL BE DIFFICULT FOR ANY OF YOU TO UNDERSTAND, BUT... WE HAVE SUFFERED A CULTURAL WOUND, SUPERMAN.
OUR OWN PEOPLE ENSLAVED US, RATHER THAN STAND AGAINST A MAD QUEEN.
FOR FIFTEEN YEARS WE SAT IMPRISONED, AND IN THAT TIME... OUR HISTORY, THE FOUNDATION OF OUR CULTURE DIED, AND THEN... THE CATACLYSM.
I SANK ATLANTIS TO SAVE IT. TO END AN AGE OF SHAME, BUT REGARDLESS OF MY BEST INTENTIONS...
THERE MUST STILL BE A RECKONING.
BUT YOU SAVED THE WHOLE WORLD--
WE ALL DID, SUPERMAN. ATLANTIS WILL NEVER FORGET WHO LIBERATED THEM THAT DAY...
NO MATTER WHO SITS ON HER THRONE. MAY THE SEAS BE WITH YOU, FRIENDS.
TELEPORT ENGAGE... THREE TO ATLANTIS.

I DON'T GET IT... EVERYTHING YOU GUYS WENT THROUGH--YOU WON.

HE'LL BE ALL RIGHT, KAL. IT'S HIS *WAY* TO FACE THINGS ALONE. HE--

HE WON.

THERE ARE TIMES... WHEN *VICTORY* IS NOT ENOUGH.

PWHAMM

WHOOOP WHOOOOP WHOO-- WHOOOOP

SORRY.

THAT ALARM'S NOT FOR YOU.

IT'S THE *LAB.*

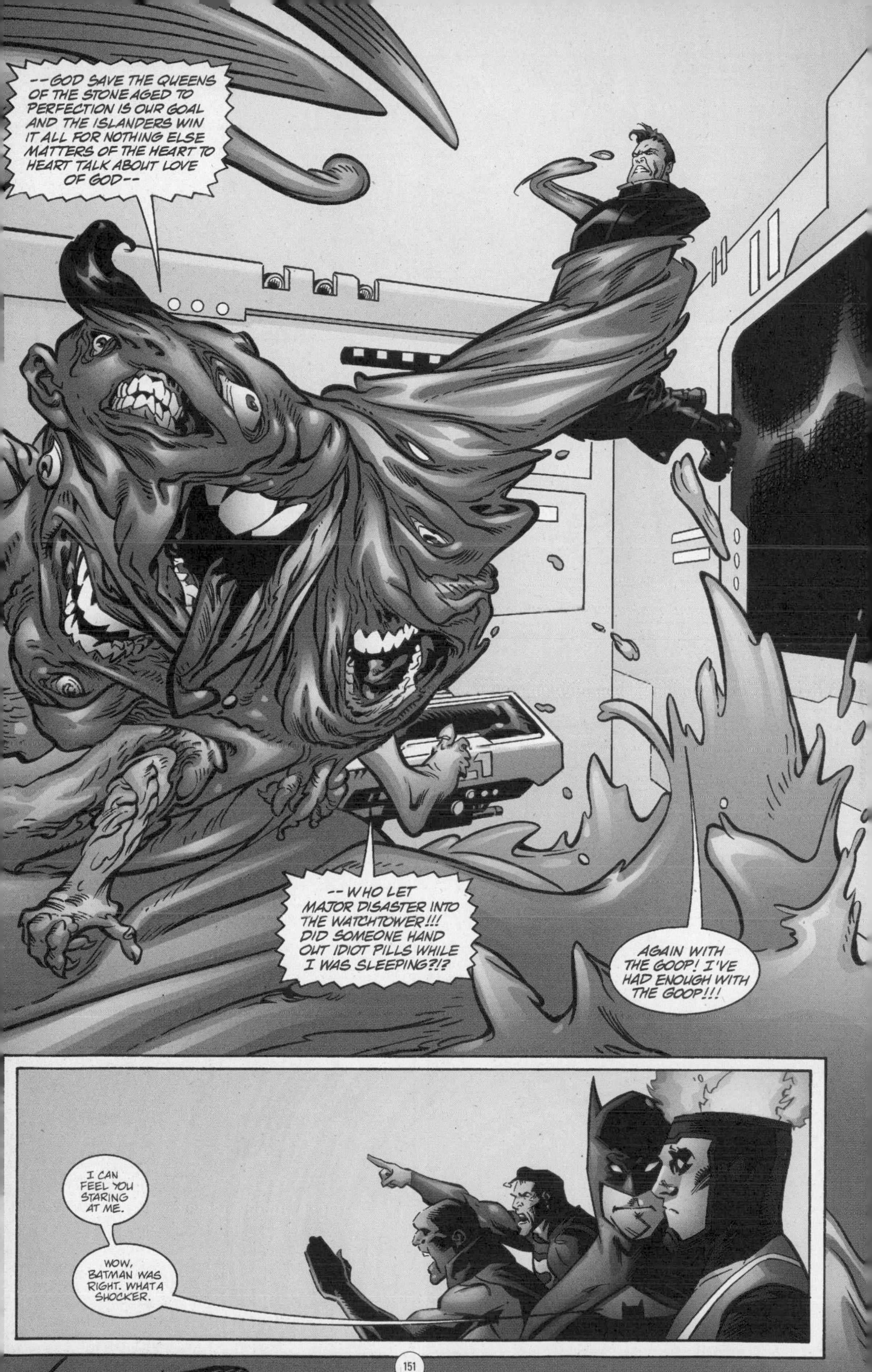
--GOD SAVE THE QUEENS OF THE STONE AGED TO PERFECTION IS OUR GOAL AND THE ISLANDERS WIN IT ALL FOR NOTHING ELSE MATTERS OF THE HEART TO HEART TALK ABOUT LOVE OF GOD--
--WHO LET MAJOR DISASTER INTO THE WATCHTOWER!!! DID SOMEONE HAND OUT IDIOT PILLS WHILE I WAS SLEEPING?!?
AGAIN WITH THE GOOP! I'VE HAD ENOUGH WITH THE GOOP!!!
I CAN FEEL YOU STARING AT ME.
WOW, BATMAN WAS RIGHT. WHAT A SHOCKER.

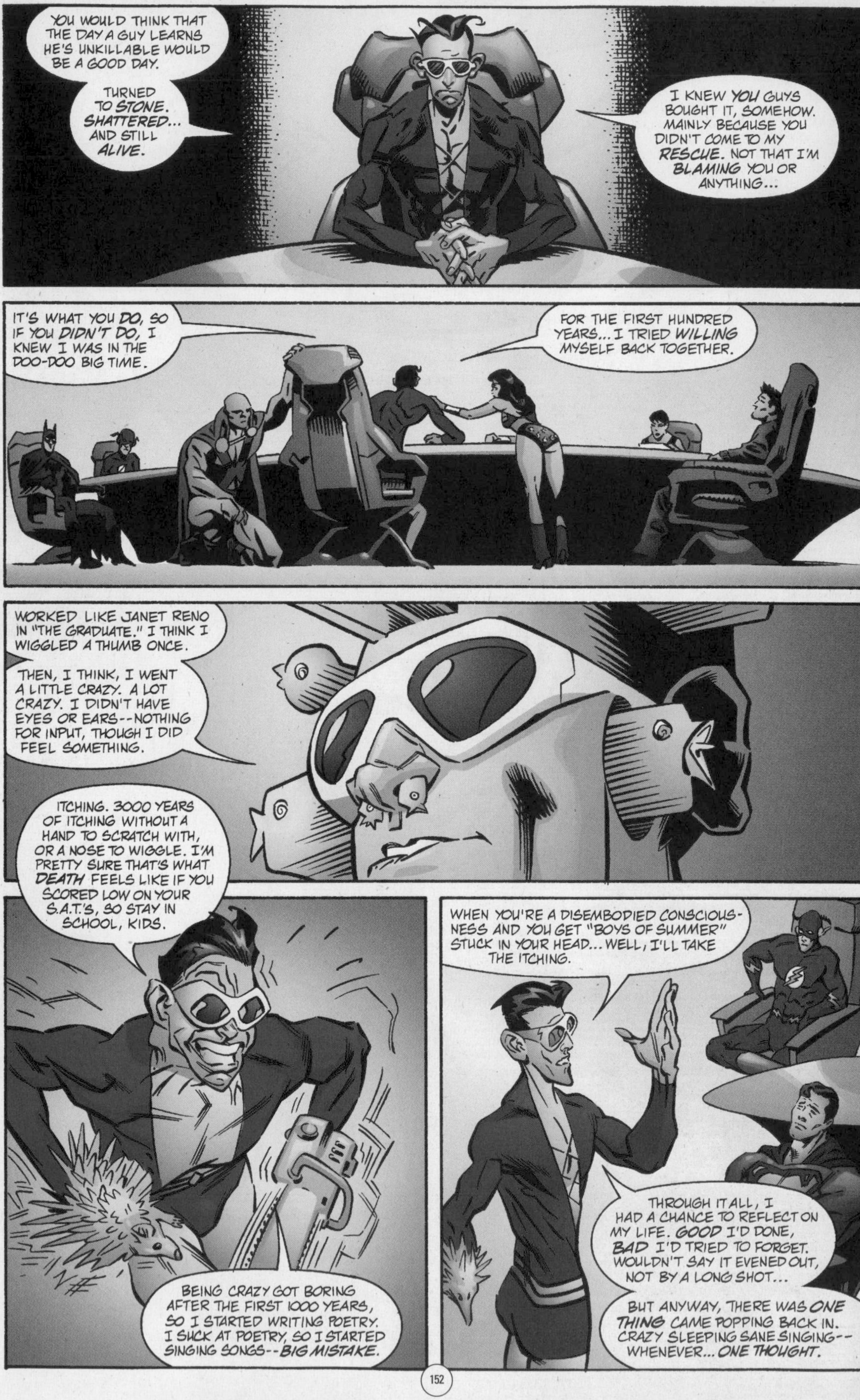

YOU WOULD THINK THAT THE DAY A GUY LEARNS HE'S UNKILLABLE WOULD BE A GOOD DAY.
TURNED TO STONE. SHATTERED... AND STILL ALIVE.
I KNEW YOU GUYS BOUGHT IT, SOMEHOW. MAINLY BECAUSE YOU DIDN'T COME TO MY RESCUE. NOT THAT I'M BLAMING YOU OR ANYTHING...
IT'S WHAT YOU DO, SO IF YOU DIDN'T DO, I KNEW I WAS IN THE DOO-DOO BIG TIME.
FOR THE FIRST HUNDRED YEARS... I TRIED WILLING MYSELF BACK TOGETHER.
WORKED LIKE JANET RENO IN "THE GRADUATE." I THINK I WIGGLED A THUMB ONCE.
THEN, I THINK, I WENT A LITTLE CRAZY. A LOT CRAZY. I DIDN'T HAVE EYES OR EARS--NOTHING FOR INPUT, THOUGH I DID FEEL SOMETHING.
ITCHING. 3000 YEARS OF ITCHING WITHOUT A HAND TO SCRATCH WITH, OR A NOSE TO WIGGLE. I'M PRETTY SURE THAT'S WHAT DEATH FEELS LIKE IF YOU SCORED LOW ON YOUR S.A.T.'S, SO STAY IN SCHOOL, KIDS.
BEING CRAZY GOT BORING AFTER THE FIRST 1000 YEARS, SO I STARTED WRITING POETRY. I SUCK AT POETRY, SO I STARTED SINGING SONGS--BIG MISTAKE.
WHEN YOU'RE A DISEMBODIED CONSCIOUS-NESS AND YOU GET "BOYS OF SUMMER" STUCK IN YOUR HEAD... WELL, I'LL TAKE THE ITCHING.
THROUGH IT ALL, I HAD A CHANCE TO REFLECT ON MY LIFE. GOOD I'D DONE, BAD I'D TRIED TO FORGET. WOULDN'T SAY IT EVENED OUT, NOT BY A LONG SHOT...
BUT ANYWAY, THERE WAS ONE THING CAME POPPING BACK IN. CRAZY SLEEPING SANE SINGING--WHENEVER... ONE THOUGHT.

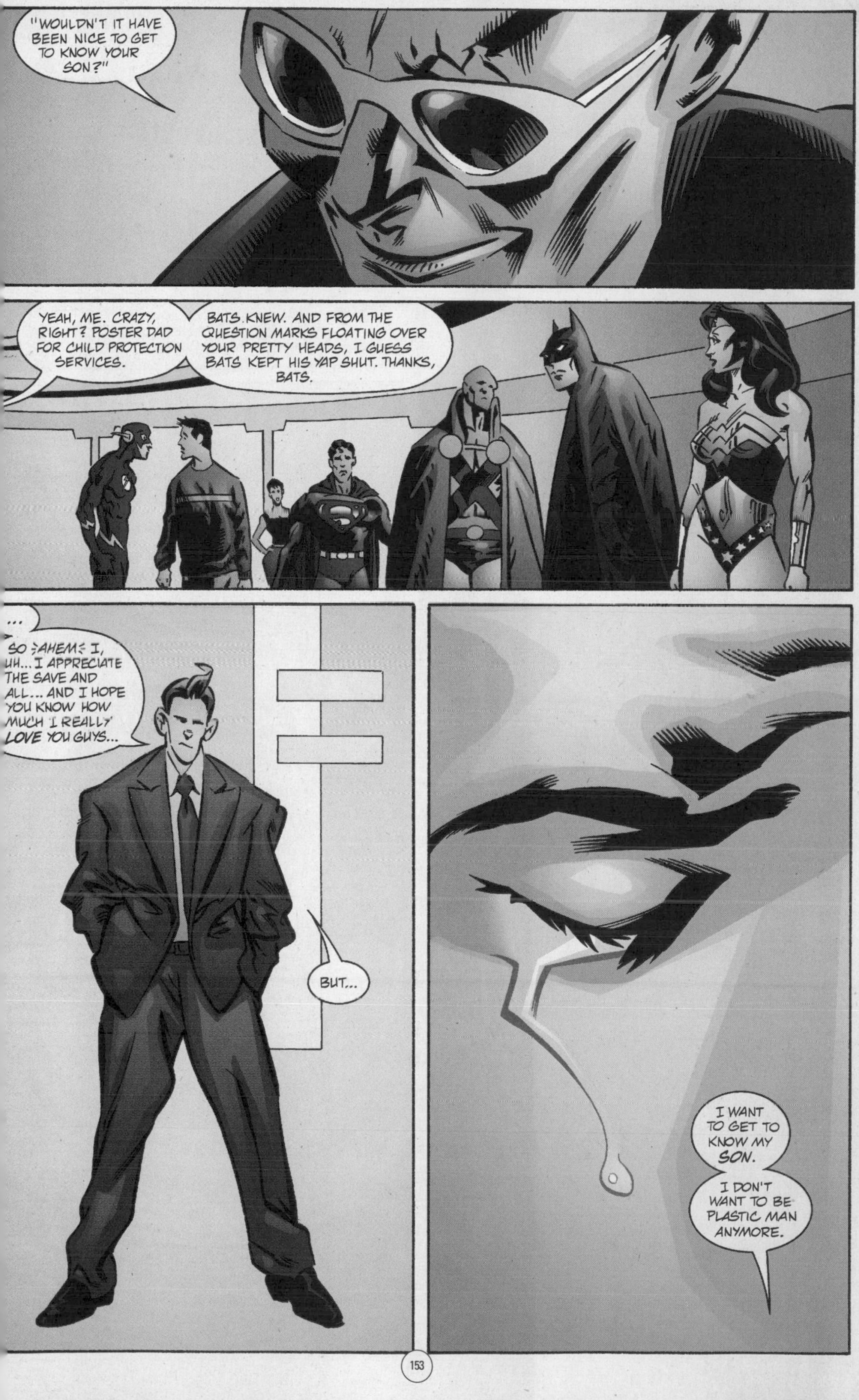
"WOULDN'T IT HAVE BEEN NICE TO GET TO KNOW YOUR SON?"
YEAH, ME. CRAZY, RIGHT? POSTER DAD FOR CHILD PROTECTION SERVICES.
BATS KNEW. AND FROM THE QUESTION MARKS FLOATING OVER YOUR PRETTY HEADS, I GUESS BATS KEPT HIS YAP SHUT. THANKS, BATS.
...
SO ⋞AHEM⋟ I, UH... I APPRECIATE THE SAVE AND ALL... AND I HOPE YOU KNOW HOW MUCH I REALLY LOVE YOU GUYS...
BUT...
I WANT TO GET TO KNOW MY SON.
I DON'T WANT TO BE PLASTIC MAN ANYMORE.

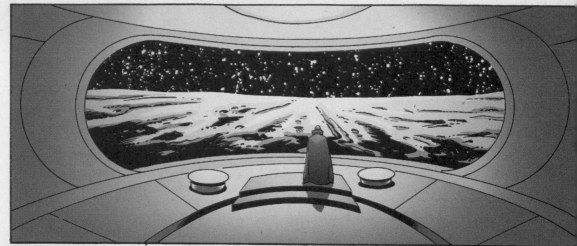

I WAS COMING TO SEE IF YOU WANTED TO DO SOMETHING TO CHEER US UP...

WHY DO I THINK THAT'S NOT GOING TO HAPPEN?

...

YOU'RE LEAVING TOO... AREN'T YOU?

YES.

FOR GOOD?

NO. THINK OF IT AS A WORKING VACATION.

YOUR FIRST SINCE THE LEAGUE BEGAN? COME ON, J'ONN--

CLARK... EVERYONE SUFFERED IN THE OBSIDIAN AGE. I KNOW THAT...

BUT NOT EVERYONE WATCHED THEIR BEST FRIENDS DIE, JUST BECAUSE SOMEONE SET A FIRE.

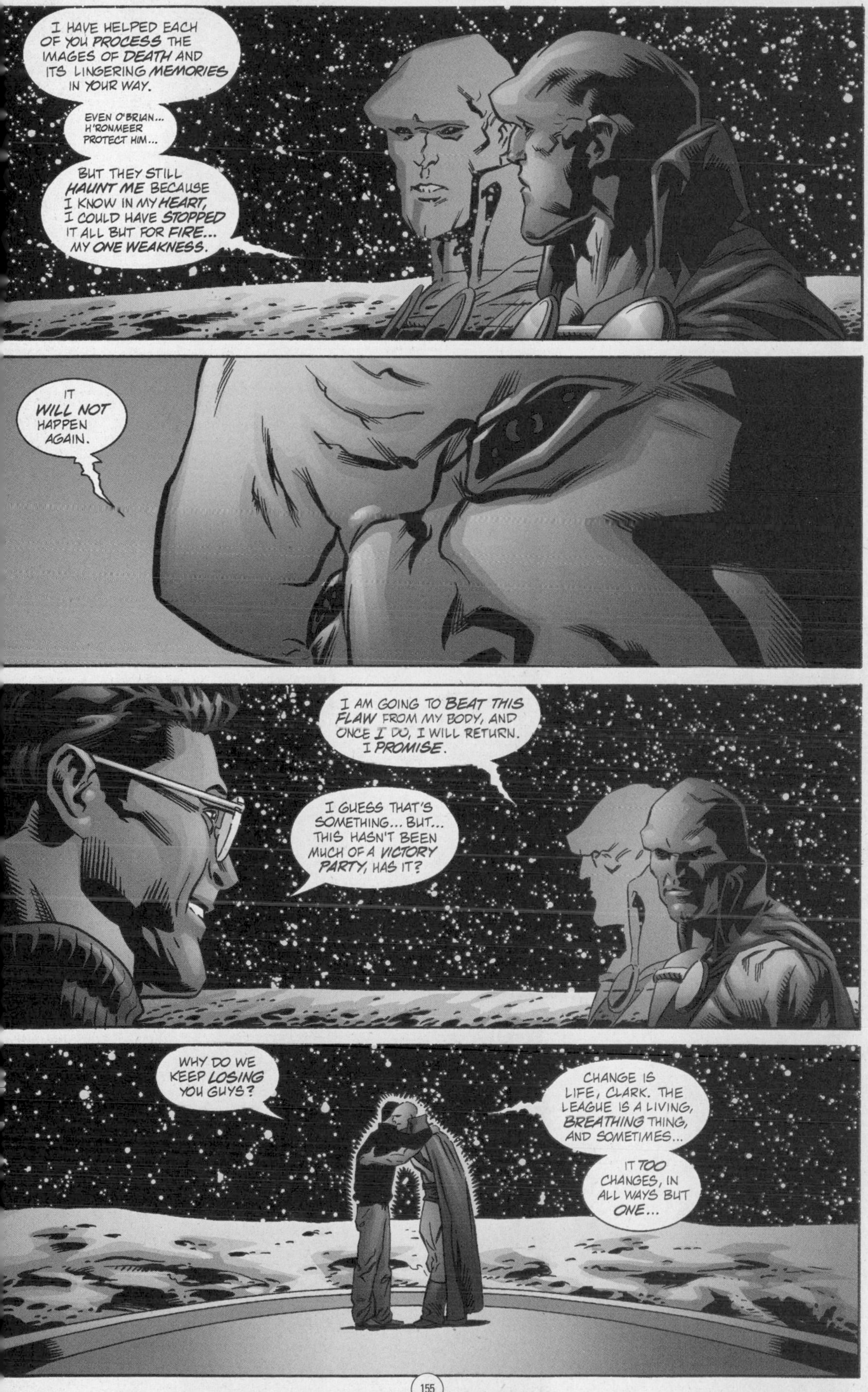

I HAVE HELPED EACH OF YOU PROCESS THE IMAGES OF DEATH AND ITS LINGERING MEMORIES IN YOUR WAY.
EVEN O'BRIAN... H'RONMEER PROTECT HIM...
BUT THEY STILL HAUNT ME BECAUSE I KNOW IN MY HEART, I COULD HAVE STOPPED IT ALL BUT FOR FIRE... MY ONE WEAKNESS.
IT WILL NOT HAPPEN AGAIN.
I AM GOING TO BEAT THIS FLAW FROM MY BODY, AND ONCE I DO, I WILL RETURN. I PROMISE.
I GUESS THAT'S SOMETHING... BUT... THIS HASN'T BEEN MUCH OF A VICTORY PARTY, HAS IT?
WHY DO WE KEEP LOSING YOU GUYS?
CHANGE IS LIFE, CLARK. THE LEAGUE IS A LIVING, BREATHING THING, AND SOMETIMES...
IT TOO CHANGES, IN ALL WAYS BUT ONE...

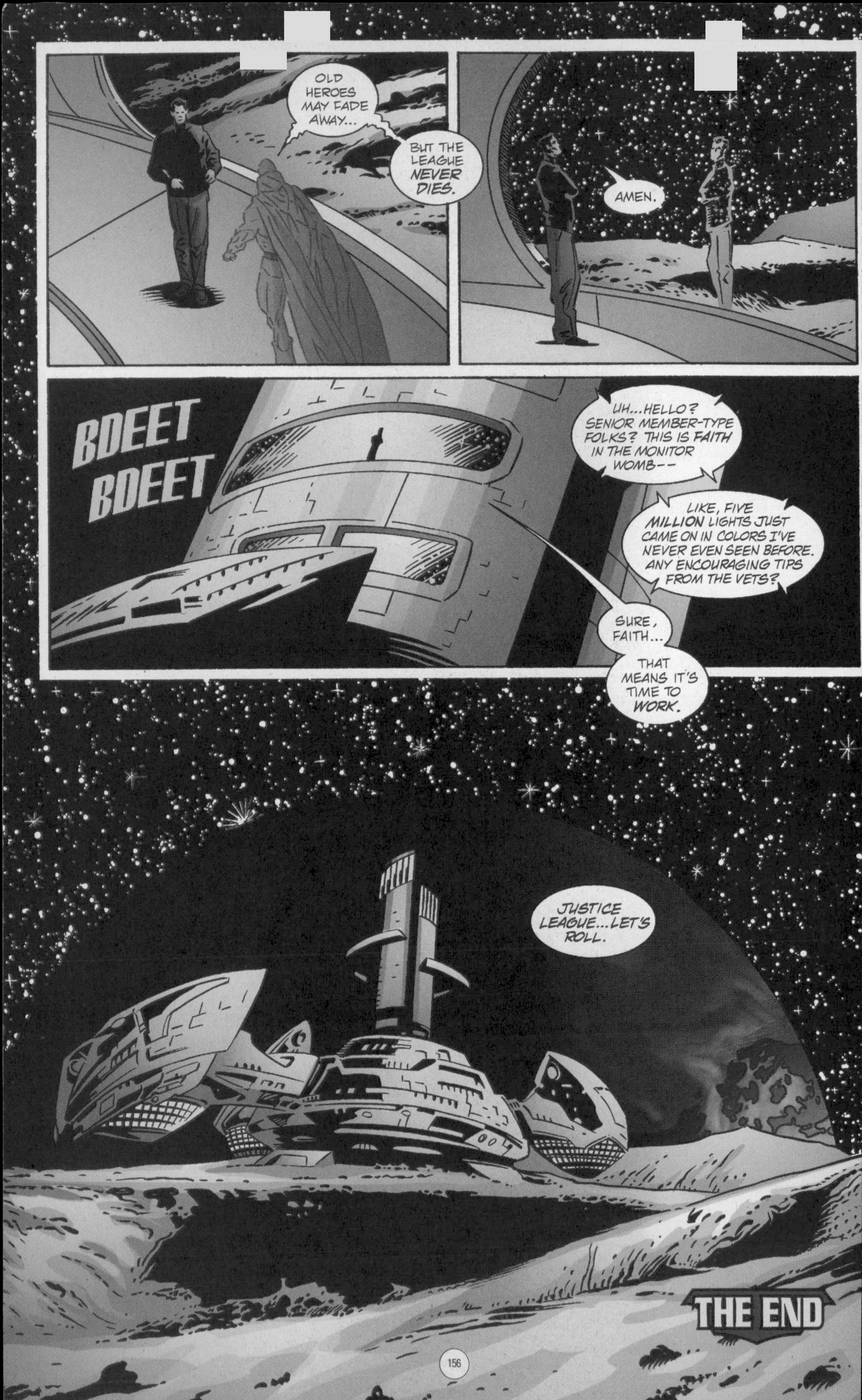
OLD HEROES MAY FADE AWAY...
BUT THE LEAGUE NEVER DIES.
AMEN.
BDEET BDEET
UH...HELLO? SENIOR MEMBER-TYPE FOLKS? THIS IS FAITH IN THE MONITOR WOMB--
LIKE, FIVE MILLION LIGHTS JUST CAME ON IN COLORS I'VE NEVER EVEN SEEN BEFORE. ANY ENCOURAGING TIPS FROM THE VETS?
SURE, FAITH...
THAT MEANS IT'S TIME TO WORK.
JUSTICE LEAGUE...LET'S ROLL.
THE END

AFTERWORD

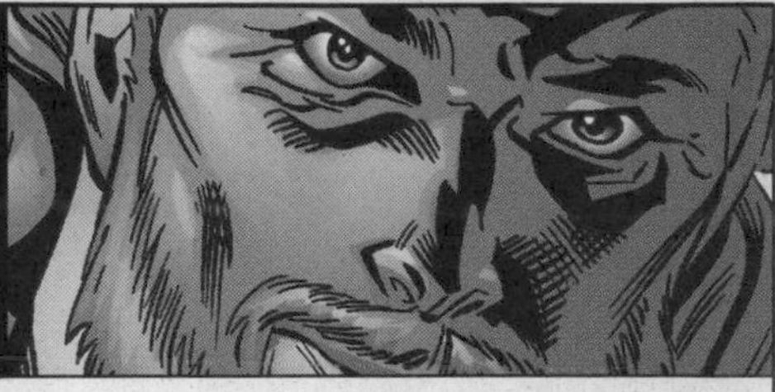

Pwhew.

That was a lot of comic.

And now you have to plod through my prattling on about it. All the thrills of a "second audio track" only without the hassle of trying to jam this beast into your DVD player. Up front, let me just say that *all* of the actors in the project were a pleasure to work with, despite what the media have reported. We had a great time shooting, and aside from that unfortunate "Beer slide" incident between Green Lantern and Steve Wacker, no laws were seriously broken...

Can you tell I'm stalling?

I've never written an "afterword" before, nor do I tend to write about my own work — I hardly ever *read* it once it's done due to a crippling lack of ego — so bear with me as I delay the inevitable for as long as possible...

And discuss the *Super Friends*.

The *Super Friends*, for those of you who might remember the dimensions of the womb, was a Hanna-Barbera cartoon, featuring DC's top heroes, that ran from about 1973 to 1986 under a variety of titles. While the membership rosters of the *Super Friends* shifted almost yearly, the program essentially stuck to a tried and true formula. Earth's greatest heroes worked together with one mission: "To fight injustice. To right that which is wrong. And to serve all mankind!" All this achieved weekly in something like eight frames of hand-drawn glory per second.

A look back at the episodes as an adult reveals the series' shortcomings: limited animation, flat characterization, silly plots... but adventure is not for cynics. As a kid, I *loved* the *Super Friends*. I *lived* for it. Batman and Superman and Green Lantern and Wonder Woman and everyone else getting together in the Hall of Justice (the most profound architectural achievement of all time!) and taking on the Legion of Doom, who lived in the swamp in a fortress that looked like a tripped-out skull (second most profound!). It was brilliant Nirvana on a Saturday Morning, Amen.

And you're asking... "What *exactly* does this have to do with the Obsidian Age?"

The Obsidian Age came to be as the result of three questions posited from three different sources.

The Fans: "So... we liked OUR WORLDS AT WAR and all, but seriously... When is Aquaman coming back?"

Dan Raspler, JLA Editor: "We've seen a version of the League from a million years into the future. What about one from the ancient past? Would that be cool?"

Me: "I know the League has magicians... but do you think we could get away with one more if I built him up slowly in a really *epic* story... And he's actually Apache Chief?"

Apache Chief. *Super Friends* shaman introduced in 1978 (*Challenge of the Super Friends*) with the power to grow into a giant by calling out the word "Inukchuk!" Yes, he had a feather in his head-

band and a leather vest. He was a new character introduced to the Super Friends along with other paragons of justice such as Samurai, Black Vulcan, and El Dorado. Notice a trend? Having had our collective consciousness forever altered (for good or bad?) by the mantle of "Political Correctness," it's easy to dismiss these new characters as simply a rounding out of the ethnic structure of the *Super Friends*. In my innocent (for good or bad?) childhood days of the late seventies, however, I had no such filter through which to view these characters. If they were good enough to fight alongside Superman and Flash, they *must* have been good! And they *were*, because of the enthusiasm, mystery, and energy I would bring to them. There was fertile ground to explore with the new characters that the ol' favorites simply didn't have (especially not after one learned that Robin was also Shaggy who was also Casey Casem... Talk about "Ignore the man behind the curtain!"). Apache Chief, as far as I was concerned, was *cool*, and he stuck in my mind long after the Super Friends disappeared into the hallowed halls of TV land....

And the next thing you know, I'm writing JLA. I've only been on the book for a few months, and I've already been asked to construct a story big enough to justify the return of Aquaman (and Atlantis, for that matter!) in a blockbuster "event." Dan's thrown me a juicy bone with the idea of an "Ancient League." I'm chewing on some new character ideas, and this seems like the right time to introduce them... Hell, why not introduce a whole *new* league, just to get everyone's hearts started. See what sticks. Just so long as it's *big*. *Huge* enough to justify not one but *two* JLA's. MAMMOTH.

Hence the sometimes twisted homunculus of a tale now called the Obsidian Age was born. It is by far the most complicated story I've ever pulled off in mainstream comics. (If we ever get a chance to finish STEAMPUNK, I'll be able to retract that statement — plug plug, write your letters and tell your friends you're dying to see Abe Lincoln kick Victorian hoo-ha!) And overall, I'm proud of it. There are always things one could have done better, but issue to issue, I dig the characters, the twists, and the surprises, and I hope you do too. The art teams did a herculean job of pulling together past and present, old and new, life and death into a visual feast worthy of the nine-plus issues of material you've just read. To the particulars...

"Batman's B-League," in my humble opinion, was *fun.* The League reimagined by the MOST cynical, most paranoid, most pragmatic member of the team to be unleashed against the one thing that could *kill* him. Does the team make sense? Are they the natural choices? Check the Internet, and you'll get a resounding *maybe* when you average the folks who went along for the ride with me and the ones who hit the brakes. Here's the quick take on why we chose this roster: HAWKGIRL — Yes, I put her in to reflect the television show, *but*, I also think she's a fantastic character with a savage side. JASON BLOOD — I *love* Zatanna, but if I'm Batman and I need a *soldier*, I'll take the guy who's been keeping dark forces at bay for a millennium. NIGHTWING — His ultimate graduation. I think everyone liked him. GREEN ARROW — Horny old socialist with an axe to grind? I cannot resist! Plus, he was instrumental for Batman in DARK KNIGHT, so I figured Bats trusted him. FIRESTORM — One of *the* most powerful characters in the DCU, and he's a juvenile to boot. FAITH — She's new. She's got mystery. It's time for fresh blood. ATOM — Not really "new" per se. But we needed a science guy, and I like that he's a "grown-up." MAJOR DISASTER — again, Dark Knight picks dark anti-hero who can call *asteroids* out of the sky. He wins a spot on sheer power.

"The Ancients." There was a ton of research that went into these characters that simply did not fit on the page. Each one has a pretty well imagined backstory, but I just couldn't work them into the

Obsidian Age. That's a real regret. Dan and Steve chimed in more than a little with research into ancient cultures, Hebrew Mysticism, and world history that never saw the light of day. Eventually, I'd like to revisit these goliaths in their own special project… But that's up to you folks, as usual.

But there's still a "why?" left to answer.

At the close of the Obsidian Age arc, someone in the comics press asked me if there wasn't a bit of "vanity" involved in introducing new characters to the League, specifically Manitou Raven and Faith. "You're assuming that people know who Apache Chief was, even though a lot of your readers have probably never even seen the *Super Friends* cartoon… And every time a writer brings new characters into the League, it's just to kill them, so why bother?" I got a bit snitty in my response, to be honest. "It's the same 'vanity' that makes you think you can write a good JLA story," I choked out, not really sure how to respond. Then I thought about it a bit… Why *would* a writer bother to bring new characters into the "Big 7" mix when it clearly works?

"Inukchuk."

When I sit down to tell a story, it doesn't matter what angle or narrative style or dramatic trickery I decide to experiment with; it all springs from one source. I try to tell a story that captures the elements I enjoy when I'm plopped in the seat and flipping through the pages of my favorite work. I like a dense plot. I like character conflict. I like comedy. I like smart-talking heroes who sometimes fight among themselves but are still noble in their own way. I like clever bits of time travel and magic. I *love* shamans. I love the mythology, the magic, and the culture they embody. I love Spirit Guides and Dream Walking. I like seeing my favorite heroes reduced to ash and thrill in watching them find a way to triumph all the same.

For me, the only vanity in throwing out a brand-new character like Manitou or Faith is a belief that the readers might enjoy the sort of things that I do. The Obsidian Age was a transitional story for me—taking the "Big 7" that have run the League for the last few years and shaking them up a bit in the biggest centrifuge I could find. It's the bridge from the stories I think people expect to the ones I'd like to try to tell. The ones I think you'll enjoy.

If you've made it this far, thanks for your indulgence, and apologies for devouring the last ten minutes of your life. Next time I'll tell you about all of the hidden "Easter eggs" in the Obsidian Age, and how to unlock the blooper reel… You haven't lived until you see Batman pants Dan Raspler… heh…

Until then, I hope you'll come across the bridge with me that leads out of the Obsidian Age into the unknown, where we'll both be guided along by my childish fantasies and various "vanities." And if it turns out that I'm wrong, and I've horribly misjudged your tastes…you can always send Aquaman back in time to turn off the *Super Friends* and teach me to play water polo.

Thanks for reading.

— Joe Kelly